2018 MINUTES OF THE GENERAL ASSEMBLY CUMBERLAND PRESBYTERIAN CHURCH

Office of the General Assembly

Cumberland Presbyterian Church

August 2018

8207 Traditional Place
Cordova (Memphis), Tennessee 38016

©2018 Office of the General Assembly, CPC

All Rights Reserved. No part of this book may be reproduced or transmitted in any form or by any means, electronic or mechanical, including photocopying, recording, or by any information storage or retrieval system, without permission in writing from the publisher. For information address Office of the General Assembly, Cumberland Presbyterian Center, 8207 Traditional Place, Cordova (Memphis), Tennessee, 38016-7414.

Published and distributed by The Discipleship Ministry Team, CPC
Memphis, Tennessee

The Discipleship Ministry Team of the Ministry Council of the Cumberland Presbyterian Church is the successor organization to the Board of Christian Education of the Cumberland Presbyterian Church.

Funded, in part, by your contributions to Our United Outreach.

First Edition 2018

ISBN-13: 978-1-945929-18-2
ISBN-10: 1-945929-18-9

OUR UNITED OUTREACH
Made Possible In Part By Your Tithe To Our United Outreach

Vision of Ministry

Biblically-based and Christ-centered
    born out of a specific sense of mission,
    the Cumberland Presbyterian Church strives to be true to its heritage:
    to be open to God's reforming spirit,
    to work cooperatively with the larger Body of Christ,
    and to nurture the connectional bonds that make us one.
The Cumberland Presbyterian Church seeks—to be the hands and feet of Christ in witness and service to the world and, above all, the Cumberland Presbyterian Church lives out the love of God to the glory of Jesus Christ.

TABLE OF CONTENTS

Vision of Ministry 1
Program 3
Commissioners 5
Youth Advisory Delegates 6
Committees and Abbreviations 6
Committee Meeting Rooms 6
Committee Assignments 7
Referrals to Committees 8
Recommendations at a Glance 9
Assembly Meetings and Officers 10
By Laws of General Assembly Corporation 13
Memorial Roll of Ministers 23
Living General Assembly Moderators 24
Membership of Boards and Agencies 25

Reports
    Moderator 33
    Stated Clerk 34
    Ministry Council 40
    Board of Stewardship, Foundation and Benefits 53
    Board of the Historical Foundation 63
    Board of Trustees of Memphis Theological Seminary 72
    OUO Committee 86
    Commission on Chaplains and Military Personnel 88
    Permanent Judiciary Committee 90
    Nominating Committee 93
    Place of Meeting Committee 96
    Unified Committee on Theology and Social Concerns 98
    Unification Task Force 100
    Board of Trustees of Bethel University 106
    Board of Trustees of the Cumberland Presbyterian Children's Home 108
    Joint Committee on Amendments 111

Resolution 112

Agency Budgets 114

General Assembly Minutes 123

Audits 131

Appendices 273

Church Calendar 297

2018 THE CUMBERLAND PRESBYTERIAN CHURCH

PROGRAM SCHEDULE

Assembly Meetings:	Embassy Suites Hotel & Convention Center
General Assembly Office:	North Park
Women's Ministry Office:	Event Concierge
Retiring Moderator:	The Reverend David Lancaster, West Tennessee Presbytery
Co-Hosts:	Choctaw Presbytery, Oklahoma Churches of Red River Presbytery (CPC) & Brazos River Presbytery (CPCA)
Co-Pastor Hosts:	The Reverend Leslie Johnson and The Reverend Marian Sontowski, Red River Presbytery
Worship Director:	The Reverend Melissa Malinoski, West Tennessee Presbytery

SUNDAY, JUNE 17, 2018

Location	Time	Event	Location
Hotel Lobby	1:00 p.m.	Welcome Table	
Convention Center	3:00 p.m.	GA Office open	North Park
		Registration for Women's Ministry Convention	Event Concierge
Convention Center		Setup displays	Convention Center Hallways

EVENING PROGRAM

Location	Time	Event	Location
Convention Center	7:00 p.m.	Joint Opening GA Worship/Communion Service	Ballroom E & F

FIRST DAY - MONDAY, JUNE 18, 2018

Location	Time	Event	Location
Convention Center	8:00 a.m.	Women's Ministry Registration (open until noon)	Event Concierge
Convention Center	8:30 a.m.	Orientation for Commissioners and Youth Advisory Delegates	Ballroom G & H
		Orientation for Committee Chairs and Co-Chairs	

(Commissioner/YAD packets may be picked up before or after the orientation session.)

Location	Time	Event	Location
Convention Center	10:30 a.m.	Opening GA Business Session	Ballroom E & F
		Constitution of the CPC General Assembly	
		Adoption of the Agenda	
		Report of the Credentials Committee	
		Election of Moderator	
		Election of Vice-Moderator	
		Presentation by the Stated Clerk, Mike Sharpe	
		Communications	
		Corrections to Preliminary Minutes	
		Committee Appointments and Referrals to Committees	
		Welcome, Pastor Host, Local Officials	
		Introduction of Board and Agency Representatives	
Convention Center	10:30 a.m.	CP Women's Ministry Regional Council Meeting (for Regional Delegates only)	Boomer A & B
	12:00 p.m.	CP Women's Ministry Regional Council Luncheon	Boomer A & B
	2:00 p.m.	Joint Choctaw Anniversary Celebration	Ballroom E & F
	4:30 p.m.	Joint Moderator & Anniversary Reception	Ballroom E & F
	5:00 p.m.	Dinner Break	
	5:30 p.m.	Fellowship Dinner (reservations required) (sponsored by Discipleship Ministry Team)	Eastlake CP Church

EVENING PROGRAM

Location	Time	Event	Location
Convention Center	7:00 p.m.	GA Committees meet	Various Locations (see bottom of page 6)
		CP Women's Ministry & National Missonary Society Gathering	Ballroom G & H

SECOND DAY - TUESDAY, JUNE 19, 2018

Location	Time	Event	Location
Legacy Park	7:00 - 9:00am	Joint Devotions / FUN RUN & WALK	Legacy Park
Convention Center	8:00 a.m.	Convention Registration	Event Concierge
	10:00 a.m.	GA Committee meetings (until 5pm)	Various Locations
	10:00 a.m.	Gathering of CP Women's Ministry	Ballroom G & H
	12:00 p.m.	CPCA National Missionary Society Luncheon	Ballroom E
	2:00 p.m.	Off-site Field Trip (must be Pre-Registered)	Conference Center Southeast Door
	.	On-site Bible Study	Ballroom G & H
	5:30 p.m.	Bethel University Dinner	Ballroom E

EVENING PROGRAM

	7:00 p.m.	GA Committees Meet	Various Locations
	8:30 p.m.	Joint Reception Honoring Women in Ministry	Ballroom G & H

THIRD DAY - WEDNESDAY, JUNE 20, 2018

Location	Time	Event	Location
Convention Center	8:30 a.m.	Joint Devotions/Presentations	Ballroom F
	9:30 a.m.	GA Committees Meet (until 5 pm)	Various Locations
	9:30 a.m.	Women's Ministry Convention	Ballroom G & H
	12:00 p.m.	MTS/PAS Luncheon	Ballroom E
	2:00 p.m.	Women's Ministry Convention	Ballroom G & H
	5:00 p.m.	Conclusion of Committee Meetings	Various Locations
	5:30 p.m.	CP Children's Home Dinner	Ballroom E

EVENING PROGRAM

Convention Center	7:00 p.m.	Evening Worship/Progam led by Young Adults	Ballroom F

FOURTH DAY - THURSDAY, JUNE 21, 2018

Location	Time	Event	Location
Convention Center	8:30 a.m.	Devotional led by Yahaira Patricio, Youth Advisory Delegate, Tennessee-Georgia Presbytery	Ballroom F
	9:00 a.m.	Break	
	9:30 a.m.	General Assembly Business	Ballroom F
	9:30 a.m.	Women's Ministry Convention Reconvenes	Ballroom G & H
	12:00 noon	Lunch Break	
	12:00 p.m.	Cumberland Presbyterian Women's Luncheon	Ballroom E
	2:00 p.m.	General Assembly Business	Ballroom F
	5:00 p.m.	Dinner Break Take Down Displays	

EVENING PROGRAM

Convention Center	7:00 p.m.	General Assembly Business Closing Devotion led by Reverend Melissa Malinoski, West Tennessee Presbytery	Ballroom F

(In the event that business is not concluded on Thursday,
the closing worship will be at the conclusion
of business on Friday morning.)

COMMISSIONERS
to the
ONE HUNDRED EIGHTY-EIGHTH GENERAL ASSEMBLY

PRESBYTERY	MINISTER	COMMITTEE	ELDER	COMMITTEE
Andes (2)	Juan Castano	MC		
Arkansas (2)	Victor Jones	S/E	B.A. DeWoody	HE/CPCH
	Rian Puckett	HE/CPCH	Janis Wilson	S/E
Cauca Valley (3)			Agustin Garcia Salazar	MC
Choctaw (1)	Hannah Bryan	S/E	Ron Lewis	TSC/UTF
Columbia (2)	Sherry Ladd	C/HF	Brenda Howell	TSC/UTF
	Charles (Buddy) Pope	J	George Ladd	J
Covenant (3)	James Fulton	MC	Rudy Fowler	S/E
	Robert Goodman	HE/CPCH	Katie Heim	MC
	Drew Gray	C/HF	Brenda Shoulta	HE/CPCH
Cumberland (3)	Kevin Brantley	J	Diann Phelps	C/HF
	John Butler	HE/CPCH	Kathy Allen	MC
Cumberland East Coast (1) (NONE)				
Del Cristo (1)	Jerry Smyrl	HE/CPCH	Tom McWilliams	TSC/UTF
East Tennessee (3)	David Koopman	J	Mary Kay Buckner	HE/CPCH
	Randall Mayfield	TSC/UTF	Larry White	S/E
	Milton Ortiz	C/HF	Richard Snowden	J
Emaus (1)			Cecilia Taborda	MC
Grace (3)	Timothy Lee	S/E	Pat Crouse	TSC/UTF
	Sherrad Hayes	J	Delores Moore	C/HF
			Grady Prevost	J
Hong Kong (2)	Ha Ting Bong	HE/CPCH		
	Jackson Tsui	HE/CPCH		
Hope (1)	Jimmy Cox	C/HF	James Letsinger	C/HF
Japan (1)	(NONE)			
Missouri (1)	Michael Reno	S/E	Mary Lyn Hunter	HE/CPCH
Murfreesboro (4)	Ronnie Pittenger	S/E	Cathy Hiveley	HE/CPCH
	Barry Boggs	J	Brenda Johnson	TSC/UTF
	Chris Warren	C/HF	Billy Goodman	S/E
	Blake Stephens	MC	Brenda Tate	HE/CPCH
Nashville (3)	Jay Earheart-Brown	J	Lisa Collins	J
	Jesse Freeman	S/E	Ben Lindamood	HE/CPCH
	Sandra Shepherd	TSC/UTF		
North Central (2)	Ralph Blevins	TSC/UTF	Victory Moore	C/HF
	Lisa Scott	J	Roy Shanks	J
Red River (3)	Kevin Henson	TSC/UTF	Ben Brown	HE/CPCH
	Randy Hardisty	S/E	Bill Clure	S/E
	Terra Sisco	MC	Vicki Goodwin	MC
Robert Donnell (1)	Micaiah Tanck	HE/CPCH	Frances Dawson	J
Tenn./Georgia (3)	Jimmy Byrd	TSC/UTF	James Condra	C/HF
	Courtney Krueger	S/E	Sylvia Hall	S/E
	Perry Whitaker	MC	Christy Cooper	MC
Trinity (2)	Gloria Villa Diaz	C/HF	James Webb	TSC/UTF
	Jack Holt	J		
West Tennessee (5)	David Lancaster	MC	Patricia Coleman	TSC/UTF
	Melissa Malinoski	TSC/UTF	Gwen Holland	HE/CPCH
	Debbie Marshall	C/HF	Kyong Hwan Im	MC
	Ron McMillan	HE/CPCH	Gary Page	S/E
	Andy McClung	S/E	Linda Drylie	C/HF

YOUTH ADVISORY DELEGATES
to the
ONE HUNDRED EIGHTY-SIXTH GENERAL ASSEMBLY
(Each Presbytery is eligible to send two Youth Advisory Delegates)

PRESBYTERY	DELEGATE	COMMITTEE
Arkansas	(no youth)	
Choctaw	(no youth)	
Columbia	(no youth)	
Covenant	Dyllan Simmons	MC
Cumberland	Eden Sheftall	HE/CPCH
del Cristo	(no youth)	
East Tennessee	Kennedy Holloway	C/HF
Grace	Isaac Barkley	HE/CPCH
	Callie Swindle	C/HF
Hope	Sydney Holder	J
Japan	(no youth)	
Missouri	Nathaniel Woods	HE/CPCH
Murfreesboro	Abigail Mathis	J
	Leigh Ann Morgan	S/E
Nashville	Jenna Snipes	MC
	Kailey Sundstrom	S/E
North Central	Colten Lash	J
Red River	Elena Riedel	S/E
Robert Donnell	Katy Barnes	TSC/UTF
	Lacey Young	MC
Tennessee Georgia	Yahaira Patricio	TSC/UTF
Trinity	Chloe Martin	S/E
	Natalia Rodriguez	TSC/UTF
West Tennessee	Emily Jerrolds	TSC/UTF
	Joseph Keenan	J

COMMITTEES ABBREVIATIONS AND MEETING ROOMS

ABBREV.	COMMITTEE	MEETING ROOMS
C/HF	Chaplains/Historical Foundation	Boomer A
HE/CPCH	Higher Education/Children's Home	Oklahoma D
J	Judiciary	Oklahoma C
MC	Ministry Council	University C
S/E	Stewardship/Elected Officers	Oklahoma B
TSC/UTF	Theology & Social Concerns/Unification Task Force	Oklahoma A

COMMITTEE ASSIGNMENTS

1. **CHAPLAINS/HISTORICAL FOUNDATION** *(Boomer A)*
   Chair: Reverend Sherry Ladd   **Co-Chair:** Reverend Chris Warren
   Ministers: Jimmy Cox, Gloria Diaz, Drew Gray, Sherry Ladd, Debbie Marshall, Milton Ortiz, Chris Warren
   Elders: James Condra, Linda Drylie, James Letsinger, Delores Moore, Victory Moore, Dianne Phelps
   Youth Advisory Delegates: Kennedy Holloway, Callie Swindle

2. **HIGHER EDUCATION/CHILDREN'S HOME** *(Oklahoma D)*
   Chair: Reverend Ron McMillan   **Co-Chair:** Elder Mary Lyn Hunter
   Ministers: Ha Ting Bong, John Butler, Robert Goodman, Ron McMillan, Rian Puckett, Jerry Smyrl, Micaiah Tanck, Jackson Tsui
   Elders: Ben Brown, Mary Kay Buckner, B.A. DeWoody, Cathy Hiveley, Gwen Holland, Mary Lyn Hunter, Ben Lindamood, Brenda Shoulta, Brenda Tate
   Youth Advisory Delegates: Isaac Barkley, Eden Sheftall, Nathaniel Woods

3. **JUDICIARY** *(Oklahoma C)*
   Chair: Reverend Buddy Pope   **Co-Chair:** Elder Frances Dawson
   Ministers: Barry Boggs, Kevin Brantley, Jay Earheart-Brown, Sherrad Hayes, Jack Holt, David Koopman, Buddy Pope, Lisa Scott
   Elders: Lisa Collins, Frances Dawson, George Ladd, Grady Prevost, Roy Shanks, Richard Snowden
   Youth Advisory Delegates: Sydney Holder, Joseph Keenan, Colten Lash, Abigail Mathis

4. **MINISTRY COUNCIL** *(University C)*
   Chair: Reverend David Lancaster   **Co-Chair:** Reverend Terra Sisco
   Ministers: Juan Castano, James Fulton, David Lancaster, Terra Sisco, Blake Stephens, Perry Whitaker
   Elders: Kathy Allen, Christy Cooper, Vicki Goodwin, Katie Heim, Kyong Hwan Im, Agustin Garcia Salazar, Cecilia Taborda
   Youth Advisory Delegates: Dyllan Simmons, Jenna Snipes, Lacey Young

5. **STEWARDSHIP/ELECTED OFFICERS** *(Oklahoma B)*
   Chair: Reverend Andy McClung   **Co-Chair:** Elder Sylvia Hall
   Ministers: Hannah Bryan, Jesse Freeman, Randy Hardisty, Victor Jones, Courtney Kruger, Timothy Lee, Andy McClung, Ronnie Pittenger, Michael Reno
   Elders: Rudy Fowler, Billy Goodman, Sylvia Hall, Bill Clure, Gary Page, Larry White, Janis Wilson
   Youth Advisory Delegates: Chloe Martin, Leigh Ann Morgan, Elena Riedel, Kailey Sundstrom

6. **THEOLOGY & SOCIAL CONCERNS/UNIFICATION TASK FORCE** *(Oklahoma A)*
   Chair: Reverend Randall Mayfield   **Co-Chair:** Reverend Sandra Shepherd
   Ministers: Ralph Blevins, Jimmy Byrd, Kevin Henson, Melissa Malinoski, Randall Mayfield, Sandra Shepherd
   Elders: Patricia Coleman, Pat Crouse, Brenda Howell, Brenda Johnson, Ron Lewis, Tom McWilliams, James Webb
   Youth Advisory Delegates: Katy Barnes, Emily Jerrods, Yahaira Patricio, Natalia Rodriquez

7. **CREDENTIALS:**
   Chair: Reverend Gloria Diaz
   Co-Chair: Elder Richard Snowden
   Member: Elder Diann Phelps
   Youth Advisory Delegate: Isaac Barkley

REFERRALS TO COMMITTEES

Referrals to the Committee on Chaplains/Historical Foundation
Page Report
- 63 The Report of the Board of Trustees of the Historical Foundation
- 88 The Report of the Commission on Military Chaplains and Personnel

Referrals to the Committee on Children's Home/Higher Education
Page Report
- 72 The Report of the Board of Trustees of Memphis Theological Seminary
- 106 The Report of the Board of Trustees of Bethel University
- 108 The Report of the Board of Trustees of the Cumberland Presbyterian Children's Home

Referrals to the Committee on Judiciary
Page Report
- 90 The Report of the Permanent Committee on Judiciary
- 111 The Report of the Joint Committee on Amendments

Referrals to the Committee on Ministry Council
Page Report
- 40 The Report of the Ministry Council, except item I.B.6 and Appendix A Questions for the Unification Task Force, which are referred to the Committee on Theology & Social Concerns/Unification Task Force
- 112 Resolution from Arkansas Presbytery Regarding the Mission and Purpose of the Encounter Publication

Referrals to the Committee on Stewardship/Elected Officers
Page Report
- 33 The Report of the Moderator
- 34 The Report of the Stated Clerk
- 53 The Report of the Board of Stewardship, Foundation and Benefits
- 86 The Report of the Our United Outreach Committee
- 96 The Report of the Place of Meeting Committee
- 114 Line Item Budgets Submitted by General Assembly Agencies

Referrals to the Committee on Theology and Social Concerns/Unification Task Force
Page Report
- 42 The Report of the Ministry Council, item I.B.6
- 46 The Report of the Ministry Council, Appendix A Questions for the Unification Task Force
- 98 The Report of the Unified Committee on Theology and Social Concerns
- 100 The Report of the Unification Task Force

RECOMMENDATIONS AT A GLANCE

Report of the Moderator
(No Recommendations)

Report of the Stated Clerk
Page 35   Recommendation 1
        36   Recommendation 2

Report of the Ministry Council
Page 44   Recommendation 1

Report of the Board of Stewardship, Foundation and Benefits
Page 58   Recommendation 1

Report of the Board of Trustees of the Historical Foundation
Page 64   Recommendations 1 - 2
        65   Recommendation 3

Report of the Board of Trustees of Memphis Theological Seminary
Page 73   Recommendation 1
        77   Recommendation 2
        80   Recommendation 3

Report of the Our United Outreach Committee
Page 86   Recommendation 1
        87   Recommendations 2-3

Report of the Commission on Chaplains and Military Personnel
Page 88   Recommendations 1-3

Report of the Permanent Judiciary Committee
Page 90   Recommendation 1
        91   Recommendations 2-6
        92   Recommendations 7-9

Report of the Place of Meeting Committee
(No Recommendations)

Report of the Unified Committee on Theology and Social Concerns
(No Recommendations)

Report of the Unification Task Force
Page 100   Recommendation 1
Page 105   Recommendations 2-3

Report of the Board of Trustees of Bethel University
Page 107   Recommendation 1

Report of the Board of Trustees of the CP Children's Home
(No Recommendations)

Report of the Joint Committee on Amendments
(No Recommendations)

Resolution from Arkansas Presbytery
(Page 112-113)

Budgets of General Assembly Board/Agencies
(Pages 114-122)

ASSEMBLY MEETINGS AND OFFICERS

Historical Review of the Stated Meetings and Officers of:

THE CUMBERLAND PRESBYTERY, 1810-1813

Date	Place	Moderator	Clerk	Members
1810, February	Sam McAdow's House, Dickson Co., TN	Samuel McAdow	Young Ewing	3
1810, March 20	Ridge Meeting-House, Sumner Co., TN.	Samuel McAdow	Young Ewing	14
1810, October 23	Lebanon Meeting-House	Finis Ewing	Young Ewing	16
1811, March 19	Big Spring, Wilson Co., TN	Robert Bell	Young Ewing	19
1811, October 9	Ridge Meeting-House	Thomas Calhoun	David Foster	23
1812, April 7	Suggs Creek Meeting-House	Hugh Kirkpatrick	James B. Porter	28
1812, November 3	Lebanon, KY	Finis Ewing	Hugh Kirkpatrick	22
1813, April 6	Beech Meeting-House, Sumner Co. TN	Robert Bell	James B. Porter	34

THE CUMBERLAND SYNOD, 1813-1828

Date	Place	Moderator	Clerk	Members
1813, October 5	Beech Meeting-House	William McGee	Finis Ewing	13
1814, April 5	Suggs Creek	David Foster	James B. Porter	27
1815, October 17	Beech Meeting-House	William Barnett	David Foster	15
1816, October 15	Free Meeting-House, TN	Thomas Calhoun	David Foster	22
1817, October 21	Mt. Moriah, KY	Robert Donnell	Hugh Kirkpatrick	27
1818, October 20	Big Spring, TN	Finis Ewing	Robert Bell	27
1819, October 19	Suggs Creek, TN	Samuel King	William Barnett	24
1820, October 17	Russellville, KY	Thomas Calhoun	William Moore	30
1821, Third Tues. in Oct.	Russellville, KY	Minutes not recorded		
1822, October 15	Beech Meeting-House	James B. Porter	David Foster	47
1823, October 21	Russellville, KY	John Barnett	Aaron Alexander	48
1824, October 19	Cane Creek, TN	Samuel King	William Moore	68
1825, October 18	Princeton, KY	William Barnett	Hiram McDaniel	76
1826, Third Tues. in Oct.	Russellville, KY	Minutes not recorded		
1827, November 20	Russellville, KY	James S. Guthrie	Laban Jones	63
1828, October 21	Franklin, TN	Hiram A. Hunter	Richard Beard	94

THE GENERAL ASSEMBLY, 1829-

Date	Place	Moderator	Clerk	Members
1829, May 19	Princeton, KY	Thomas Calhoun	F. R. Cossitt	26
1830, May 18	Princeton, KY	James B. Porter	F. R. Cossitt	36
1831, May 17	Princeton, KY	Alex Chapman	F. R. Cossitt	34
1832, May 15	Nashville, TN	F. R. Cossitt	F. R. Cossitt	36
1833, May 21	Nashville, TN	Samuel King	F. R. Cossitt	35
1834, May 20	Nashville, TN	Thomas Calhoun	James Smith	48
1835, May 19	Princeton, KY	Sam King	James Smith	42
1836, May 17	Nashville, TN	Reuben Burrow	James Smith	43
1837, May 16	Lebanon, TN	Robert Donnell	James Smith	49
1838, May 15	Princeton, KY	Hiram A. Hunter	James Smith	47
1840, May 19	Elkton, KY	Reuben Burrow	James Smith	55
1841, May 18	Owensboro, KY	William Ralston	C. G. McPherson	56
1842, May 17	Owensboro, KY	Milton Bird	C. G. McPherson	57
1843, May 16	Owensboro, KY	A. M. Bryan	C. G. McPherson	68
1845, May 20	Lebanon, TN	Richard Beard	C. G. McPherson	95
1846, May 19	Owensboro, KY	M. H. Bone	C. G. McPherson	86
1847, May 18	Lebanon, Ohio	Hiram A. Hunter	C. G. McPherson	71
1848, May 16	Memphis, TN	Milton Bird	C. G. McPherson	100
1849, May 16	Princeton, KY	John L. Smith	C. G. McPherson	75
1850, May 21	Clarksville, TN	Reuben Burrow	Milton Bird	102
1851, May 20	Pittsburgh, PA	Milton Bird	Milton Bird	71
1852, May 18	Nashville, TN	David Lowry	Milton Bird	107
1853, May 17	Princeton, KY	H. S. Porter	Milton Bird	108
1854, May 16	Memphis, TN	Isaac Shook	Milton Bird	112
1855, May 15	Lebanon, TN	M. H. Bone	Milton Bird	101
1856, May 15	Louisville, KY	Milton Bird	Milton Bird	99
1857, May 21	Lexington, MO	Carson P. Reed	Milton Bird	106
1858, May 20	Huntsville, AL	Felix Johnson	Milton Bird	124
1859, May 19	Evansville, IN	T. B. Wilson	Milton Bird	131
1860, May 17	Nashville, TN	S. G. Burney	Milton Bird	168
1861, May 16	St. Louis, MO	A. E. Cooper	Milton Bird	51
1862, May 15	Owensboro, KY	P. G. Rea	Milton Bird	58
1863, May 21	Alton, IL	Milton Bird	Milton Bird	73
1864, May 19	Lebanon, OH	Jesse Anderson	Milton Bird	65
1865, May 18	Evansville, IN	Hiram Douglas	Milton Bird	78
1866, May 17	Owensboro, KY	Richard Beard	Milton Bird	155
1867, May 16	Memphis, TN	J. B. Mitchell	Milton Bird	176
1868, May 21	Lincoln, IL	G. W. Mitchell	Milton Bird	184
1869, May 20	Murfreesboro, TN	S. T. Anderson	Milton Bird	173
1870, May 19	Warrensburg, MO	J. C. Provine	Milton Bird	167

Date	Place	Moderator	Clerk	Members
1871, May 18	Nashville, TN	J. B. Logan	Milton Bird	173
1872, May 16	Evansville, IN	C. H. Bell	Milton Bird	182
1873, May 15	Huntsville, AL	J. W. Poindexter	John Frizzell	165
1874, May 21	Springfield, MO	T. C. Blake	John Frizzell	185
1875, May 20	Jefferson, TX	W. S. Campbell	John Frizzell	169
1876, May 18	Bowling Green, KY	J. M. Gill	John Frizzell	184
1877, May 17	Lincoln, IL	A. B. Miller	John Frizzell	171
1878, May 16	Lebanon, TN	D. E. Bushnell	John Frizzell	205
1879, May 15	Memphis, TN	J. S. Grider	John Frizzell	143
1880, May 20	Evansville, IN	A. Templeton	John Frizzell	194
1881, May 19	Austin, TX	W. J. Darby	John Frizzell	187
1882, May 18	Huntsville, AL	S. H. Buchanan	John Frizzell	188
1883, May 17	Nashville, TN	A. J. McGlumphey	T. C. Blake	204
1884, May 15	McKeesport, PA	John Frizzell	T. C. Blake	148
1885, May 21	Bentonville, AR	G. T. Stainback	T. C. Blake	185
1886, May 20	Sedalia, MO	E. B. Crisman	T. C. Blake	193
1887, May 19	Covington, OH	Nathan Green	T. C. Blake	187
1888, May 17	Waco, TX	W. H. Black	T. C. Blake	217
1889, May 16	Kansas City, MO	J. M. Hubbert	T. C. Blake	217
1890, May 15	Union City, TN	E. G. McLean	T. C. Blake	220
1891, May 21	Owensboro, KY	E. F. Beard	T. C. Blake	213
1892, May 19	Memphis, TN	W. T. Danley	T. C. Blake	229
1893, May 18	Little Rock, AR	W. S. Ferguson	T. C. Blake	226
1894, May 17	Eugene, OR	F. R. Earle	T. C. Blake	167
1895, May 16	Meridian, MS	M. B. DeWitt	T. C. Blake	208
1896, May 21	Birmingham, AL	A. W. Hawkins	J. M. Hubbert	200
1897, May 20	Chicago, IL	H. S. Williams	J. M. Hubbert	224
1898, May 19	Marshall, MO	H. H. Norman	J. M. Hubbert	221
1899, May 18	Denver, CO	J. M. Halsell	J. M. Hubbert	181
1900, May 17	Chattanooga, TN	H. C. Bird	J. M. Hubbert	230
1901, May 16	West Point, MS	E. E. Morris	J. M. Hubbert	226
1902, May 15	Springfield, MO	S. M. Templeton	J. M. Hubbert	255
1903, May 21	Nashville, TN	R. M. Tinnon	J. M. Hubbert	247
1904, May 19	Dallas, TX	W. E. Settle	J. M. Hubbert	251
1905, May 18	Fresno, CA	J. B. Hail	J. M. Hubbert	249
1906, May 17	Decatur, IL	Ira Landrith	J. M. Hubbert	279
1906, May 24	Decatur, IL	J. L. Hudgins	T. H. Padgett	106
1907, May 17	Dickson, TN	A. N. Eshman	J. L. Goodknight	140
1908, May 21	Corsicana, TX	F. H. Prendergast	J. L. Goodknight	136
1909, May 20	Bentonville, AR	J. T. Barbee	J. L. Goodknight	142
1910, May 19	Dickson, TN	J. H. Fussell	J. L. Goodknight	144
1911, May 18	Evansville, IN	J. W. Duvall	J. L. Goodknight	109
1912, May 16	Warrensburg, MO	J. D. Lewis	J. L. Goodknight	119
1913, May 15	Bowling Green, KY	J. H. Milholland	J. L. Goodknight	112
1914, May 21	Wagoner, OK	F. A. Brown	J. L. Goodknight	105
1915, May 20	Memphis, TN	William Clark	D. W. Fooks	116
1916, May 18	Birmingham, AL	J. L. Price	D. W. Fooks	125
1917, May 17	Lincoln, IL	F. A. Seagle	D. W. Fooks	102
1918, May 16	Dallas, TX	C. H. Walton	D. W. Fooks	117
1919, May 15	Fayetteville, AR	J. H. Zwingle	D. W. Fooks	101
1920, May 15	McKenzie, TN	J. E. Cortner	D. W. Fooks	123
1921, May 19	Greenfield, MO	Judge John B. Tally	D. W. Fooks	108
1922, May 18	Greeneville, TN	Hugh S. McCord	D. W. Fooks	102
1923, May 17	Fairfield, IL	P. F. Johnson, D. D.	D. W. Fooks	105
1924, May 15	Austin, TX	D. M. McAnulty	D. W. Fooks	93
1925, May 21	Nashville, TN	W. E. Morrow	D. W. Fooks	114
1926, May 20	Columbus, MS	I. K. Floyd	D. W. Fooks	111
1927, May 19	Lakeland, FL	T. A. DeVore	D. W. Fooks	97
1928, May 21	Jackson, TN	J. L. Hudgins	D. W. Fooks	97
1929, May 16	Princeton, KY	H. C. Walton	D. W. Fooks	98
1930, May 15	Olney, TX	O. A. Barbee	D. W. Fooks	92
1931, May 21	Evansville, IN	J. L. Elliot	D. W. Fooks	98
1932, May 19	Chattanooga, TN	G. G. Halliburton	D. W. Fooks	104
1933, June 14	Memphis, TN	W. B. Cunningham	D. W. Fooks	94
1934, June 14	Springfield, MO	A. C. DeForest	D. W. Fooks	103
1935, June 13	McKenzie, TN	C. A. Davis	D. W. Fooks	104
1936, June 18	San Antonio, TX	E. K. Reagin	D. W. Fooks	100
1937, June 16	Knoxville, TN	George E. Coleman	D. W. Fooks	109
1938, June 16	Russellville, AR	D. D. Dowell	D. W. Fooks	117
1939, June 15	Marshall, MO	E. R. Ramer	D. W. Fooks	126
1940, June 13	Cookeville, TN	Keith T. Postlethwaite	D. W. Fooks	116
1941, June 19	Denton, TX	L. L. Thomas	D. W. Fooks	120
1942, June 18	McKenzie, TN	George W. Burroughs	D. W. Fooks	108
1943, June 17	Paducah, KY	A. A. Collins	D. W. Fooks	94
1944, June 15	Bowling Green, KY	I. M. Vaughn	D. W. Fooks	94
1945, May 31	Lewisburg, TN	S. T. Byars	Wayne Wiman	103
1946, June 13	Birmingham, AL	C. R. Matlock	Wayne Wiman	105
1947, June 12	Knoxville, TN	Morris Pepper	Wayne Wiman	108

Date	Place	Moderator	Clerk	Members
1948, June 17	Nashville, TN	Paul F. Brown	Wayne Wiman	105
1949, June 16	Muskogee, OK	Blake Warren	Wayne Wiman	109
1950, June 15	Los Angeles, CA	L. P. Turnbow	Wayne Wiman	98
1951, June 14	Longview, TX	John E. Gardner	Wayne Wiman	105
1952, June 12	Memphis, TN	Emery A. Newman	Wayne Wiman	120
1953, June 18	Gadsden, AL	Charles L. Lehning, Jr.	Wayne Wiman	107
1954, June 17	Dyersburg, TN	John S. Smith	Wayne Wiman	124
1955, June 16	Lubbock, TX	Ernest C. Cross	Shaw Scates	118
1956, June 21	Cookeville, TN	Hubert Morrow	Shaw Scates	118
1957, June 21	Evansville, IN	William T. Ingram, Jr.	Shaw Scates	119
1958, June 18	Birmingham, AL	Wayne Wiman	Shaw Scates	116
1959, June 17	Springfield, MO	Virgil T. Weeks	Shaw Scates	120
1960, June 15	Nashville, TN	Arleigh G. Matlock	Shaw Scates	130
1961, June 21	Florence, AL	Ollie W. McClung	Shaw Scates	126
1962, June 20	Little Rock, AR	Eugene L. Warren	Shaw Scates	126
1963, June 19	Austin, TX	Franklin Chesnut	Shaw Scates	117
1964, June 17	Chattanooga, TN	Vaughn Fults	Shaw Scates	123
1965, June 16	San Francisco, CA	Thomas Forester	Shaw Scates	114
1966, June 15	Memphis, TN	John W. Sparks	Shaw Scates	124
1967, June 21	Paducah, KY	Raymon Burroughs	Shaw Scates	123
1968, June 19	Oklahoma City, OK	Loyce S. Estes	Shaw Scates	115
1969, June 18	San Antonio, TX	J. David Hester	Shaw Scates	116
1970, June 17	Knoxville, TN	L. C. Waddle	Shaw Scates	116
1971, June 16	Jackson, TN	E. Thach Shauf	Shaw Scates	116
1972, June 19	Kansas City, MO	Claude D. Gilbert	Shaw Scates	110
1973, June 18	Ft. Worth, TX	Thomas H. Campbell	Shaw Scates	101
1974, June 17	Bowling Green, KY	David A. Brown	Shaw Scates	116
1975, June 16	McKenzie, TN	Roy E. Blakeburn	Shaw Scates	120
1976, June 21	Tulsa, OK	Hubert W. Covington	T. V. Warnick	115
1977, June 30	Tampa, FL	Fred W. Bryson	T. V. Warnick	122
1978, June 19	McKenzie, TN	Jose Fajardo	T. V. Warnick	120
1979, June 18	Albuquerque, NM	James C. Gilbert	T. V. Warnick	126
1980, June 16	Evansville, IN	Robert L. Hull	T. V. Warnick	126
1981, June 15	Denton, TX	W. Jean Richardson	T. V. Warnick	126
1982, June 21	Owensboro, KY	W. A. Rawlins	T. V. Warnick	124
1983, June 20	Birmingham, AL	Robert G. Forester	T. V. Warnick	127
1984, June 11	Chattanooga, TN	C. Ray Dobbins	T. V. Warnick	125
1985, June 17	Lexington, KY	Virgil H. Todd	Roy E. Blakeburn	125
1986, June 23	Odessa, TX	James W. Knight	Roy E. Blakeburn	125
1987, June 15	Louisville, KY	Wilbur S. Wood	Roy E. Blakeburn	125
1988, June 6	Tulsa, OK	Beverly St. John	Robert Prosser	119
1989, June 12	Knoxville, TN	William Rustenhaven, Jr.	Robert Prosser	96
1990, June 25	Ft. Worth, TX	Thomas D. Campbell	Robert Prosser	88
1991, June 24	Paducah, KY	Floyd T. Hensley, Jr.	Robert Prosser	106
1992, June 22	Jackson, TN	John David Hall	Robert Prosser	102
1993, June 21	Little Rock, AR	Robert M. Shelton	Robert Prosser	100
1994, June 20	Albuquerque, NM	Donald C. Alexander	Robert Prosser	100
1995, June 19	Nashville, TN	Clinton O. Buck	Robert Prosser	102
1996, June 17	Huntsville, AL	Merlyn A. Alexander	Robert Prosser	95
1997, April 11	Nashville, TN	Merlyn A. Alexander	Robert Prosser	80
1997, June 16	Louisville, KY	W. Lewis Wynn	Robert Prosser	95
1998, June 15	Chattanooga, TN	Masaharu Asayama	Robert Prosser	97
1999, June 21	Memphis, TN	Gwendolyn Roddye	Marjorie Shannon	96
2000, June 19	Bowling Green, KY	Bob G. Roberts	Robert D. Rush	96
2001, June 18	Odessa, TX	Randolph Jacob	Robert D. Rush	88
2002, June 17	Paducah, KY	Bert L. Owen	Robert D. Rush	95
2003, June 23	Knoxville, TN	Charles McCaskey	Robert D. Rush	96
2004, June 21	Irving, TX	Edward G. Sims	Robert D. Rush	87
2005, June 27	Franklin, TN	Linda H. Glenn	Robert D. Rush	91
2006, June 18	Birmingham, AL	Donald Hubbard	Robert D. Rush	87
2007, June 18	Hot Springs, AR	Frank Ward	Robert D. Rush	84
2007, December 7	Nashville, TN	Frank Ward	Robert D. Rush	62
2008, June 7	Japan	Jonathan Clark	Robert D. Rush	82
2009, June 15	Memphis, TN	Sam Suddarth	Robert D. Rush	86
2010, June 13	Dickson, TN	Boyce Wallace	Robert D. Rush	88
2011, June 20	Springfield, MO	Don M. Tabor	Michael Sharpe	82
2012, June 18	Florence, AL	Robert D. Rush	Michael Sharpe	90
2013, June 17	Murfreesboro, TN	Forest Prosser	Michael Sharpe	93
2014, June 16	Chattanooga, TN	Lisa Anderson	Michael Sharpe	86
2015, June 20	Colombia, South America	Michele Gentry	Michael Sharpe	91
2016, June 20	Nashville, Tennessee	Dwayne Tyus	Michael Sharpe	84
2017, June 19	Palm Harbor, Florida	David Lancaster	Michael Sharpe	77
2018, June 17	Norman, Oklahoma	Jay Earheart-Brown	Michael Sharpe	86

BYLAWS

Bylaws of the Cumberland Presbyterian Church General Assembly Corporation
A Non-profit Religious Corporation Organized and Existing
Under the Laws of the State of Tennessee

ARTICLE 1-RELIGIOUS CORPORATION

1.01 Purpose. The Cumberland Presbyterian Church is a spiritual body comprised of a portion of the universal body of believers confessing Jesus Christ as Lord and Savior. As an ecclesiastical body, the Cumberland Presbyterian Church is a connectional Church which includes all of the judicatories of the Church. The highest judicatory of this ecclesiastical body is the General Assembly of the Cumberland Presbyterian Church (referred to in these Bylaws as "the Church"). This corporation has been formed to serve and support the Church by holding real and personal property of the Church, employing staff to serve the Church, and performing other secular and legal functions.

1.02 Ecclesiastical Authority Not Limited by Corporate Powers. The enumeration in state statutes or these Bylaws of specific powers which may be exercised by the Commissioners, Board of Directors, or the officers of the corporation when acting in their corporate capacity shall not limit their authority when acting in their ecclesiastical capacity for the Church.

1.03 Church Authorities. The doctrine of the Cumberland Presbyterian Church, expressed in the Confession of Faith, Constitution, Rules of Discipline, and Rules of Order of the Cumberland Presbyterian Church, shall have precedence over any inconsistent provision of these Bylaws.

ARTICLE 2-TERMINOLOGY

2.01 Delegates. The corporation's delegates shall be called "Commissioners."
2.02 General Assembly. A meeting of the Commissioners shall be called a "General Assembly."
2.03 President. The corporation's president shall be called the "Stated Clerk."
2.04 Ecumenical Representative. A person who is not a member of a Cumberland Presbyterian Chuch or presbytery but who supports the mission of a denominational entity and is elected to a term of service on that entity shall be called an "Ecumenical Representative."

ARTICLE 3-OFFICES

3.01 Location. The principal office of the corporation in the State of Tennessee shall be located in Shelby County, Tennessee. The corporation may have such other offices, either within or outside the State of Tennessee, as the General Assembly or the Board of Directors may direct from time to time.

ARTICLE 4–COMMISSIONERS

4.01 Commissioners. The Commissioners shall have the powers and authority described in the corporation's charter and these Bylaws. Included among them are the power to:

   a. Elect the elected members of the Board of Directors.
   b. Approve any amendment to the corporation's charter except an amendment to delete the names of the original directors; to change the name of the registered agent, or to change the address of the registered office;
   c. Elect and remove the Moderator, Stated Clerk, and the Engrossing Clerk.
   d. Fill vacancies on the corporation's various boards, agencies and committees, and on the boards of any subsidiaries;
   e. Approve the merger or dissolution of the corporation, or the sale of substantially all of the corporation's assets; and
   f. Transact such other business of the corporation as may properly come before any meeting of the Commissioners.

4.02 Selection of Commissioners: Number and Qualifications. Commissioners shall be selected by the presbyteries. A presbytery shall be entitled to send one minister and one elder for each 1,000, or fraction thereof, active members (including ordained clergy) in the presbytery. Each elder selected as a Commissioner must be serving as a member of a session at the time of the General Assembly at which he or she will serve. A Commissioner shall continue to serve until no longer qualified or until his or her successor is selected and qualified. The clerk of each presbytery shall certify the presbytery's duly elected commissioners, youth advisory delegates, and alternates to the Stated Clerk in a manner provided by the Stated Clerk.

4.03 Youth Advisory Delegates. Each presbytery may select not more than two youth advisory delegates who should be from 15 through 19 years of age. Advisory delegates may serve as members with full rights on General Assembly committees, but shall not vote as Commissioners.

4.04 Annual Meeting and Notice. The Commissioners shall meet annually at a date and time established by the General Assembly. The meeting shall be continued from day to day until adjournment. Written notice of the meeting shall be mailed to the stated clerks of all presbyteries and published in the Cumberland Presbyterian at least sixty (60) days prior to the proposed meeting.

4.05 Special Meetings and Notice. The Moderator, or in case of the Moderator's absence, death, or inability to act, the Stated Clerk, may with the written concurrence or at the written request of twenty Commissioners, ten of whom shall be ministers and ten elders, representing at least five presbyteries, call a special meeting of the Commissioners. If warranted by a change of circumstances, a called special meeting may be cancelled by the Moderator, or in case of the Moderator's absence, death, or inability to act, the Stated Clerk, with the written concurrence of at least ten of the Commissioners who requested or concurred in the call of the special meeting. Written notice of any special meeting shall be mailed to the stated clerks of all presbyteries, to all Commissioners, and to their alternates at least sixty (60) days prior to the meeting. The notice shall specify the particular business of the special meeting, and no other business shall be transacted.

4.06 Place of Meeting. The General Assembly may designate any place within or outside the state of Tennessee as the place for an annual meeting. If the Commissioners fail to designate a place for an annual meeting, or if an emergency requires the place to be changed, the Board of Directors may designate a place for the annual meeting. The Moderator or the Stated Clerk, as the case may be, when calling a special meeting shall designate the time and place of the meeting in the notice of the meeting.

4.07 Quorum. Any twenty or more Commissioners, of whom at least ten are ministers and ten elders, entitled to vote shall constitute a quorum at any General Assembly. When a quorum is once present to organize a meeting, business may continue to be conducted and votes taken despite the subsequent withdrawal of any Commissioner. A meeting may be adjourned despite the absence of a quorum.

4.08 Voting. Every Commissioner shall be entitled to one vote, which must be cast by the Commissioner in person; no proxies are permitted. All corporate actions shall be taken by majority vote except as otherwise provided by the corporation's parliamentary authority. Voting for members of the Board of Directors shall be non-cumulative.

ARTICLE 5-BOARD OF DIRECTORS

5.01 Authority. The Board of Directors shall manage the business and affairs of the corporation except for any power or authority which is reserved to the Commissioners or delegated to any other agency of the corporation. The Board of Directors is authorized to amend the corporation's charter only to delete the names of the original directors; to change the name of the registered agent; or to change the address of the registered office.

5.02 Composition of the Board of Directors. The Board of Directors shall consist of seven (7) members, who shall be the directors of the corporation. Six (6) members shall be elected by the Commissioners and the Stated Clerk shall serve by virtue of office. All members, whether elected or ex officio, shall have all of the privileges of office.

5.03 Qualification for Election. Each person elected to the Board of Directors shall be a natural person who is a person in good standing of a presbytery or local Cumberland Presbyterian Church. No two directors shall be from the same presbytery, provided, however, that a director who moves from one presbytery to another may continue to serve until the expiration of his or her term of office.

5.04 Election and Tenure. The elected members of the Board of Directors shall serve terms of three (3) years each. The terms shall be staggered so that two (2) directors shall be elected each year. Each person elected shall serve until his or her successor has been elected and qualified.

5.05 Action of Board in Emergency or By Default. If, for any reason, the General Assembly fails to fill a vacancy on the Board of Directors at the next General Assembly, then the Board of Directors may fill the vacancy by majority vote of the members then in office.

5.06 Meetings. The Board of Directors shall meet annually or more often at such time and place as it may set. Special meetings may be called by or at the request of the Stated Clerk or any three directors at any place, either within or outside the state of Tennessee.

5.07 Notice. Notice of any meeting shall be given at least five (5) days before the date of the meeting, except that notice by mail shall be given at least ten (10) days before the date of the meeting. Notice may be communicated in person; by telephone, fax, or electronic mail; or by first class mail or courier. Except as specifically provided by these Bylaws, neither the business to be transacted at nor the purpose of any special or regular meeting of the Board of Directors need be specified in the notice of the meeting.

5.08 Notice of Special Actions. Any meeting of the Board of Directors at which one or more of the following actions shall be considered must be preceded by seven (7) days written notice to each member that the matter will be voted upon, unless notice has been waived. Actions requiring such notice are: amendment or restatement of the corporate charter; approval of a plan of merger for the corporation; sale of all or substantially all of the corporation's assets; and dissolution of the corporation.

5.09 Officers of the Board of Directors. The Board of Directors may have such officers of the board as it may deem appropriate.

5.10 Quorum and Voting. A majority of the members shall constitute a quorum for the transaction of business at any meeting of the Board of Directors. When a quorum is once present to organize a meeting, it is not broken by the subsequent withdrawal of any of those present. A meeting may be adjourned despite the lack of a quorum. The vote of a majority of the members present at a meeting at which a quorum is present shall be the act of the Board of Directors unless a greater vote is specifically required by the Charter or the Bylaws.

5.11 Conference Meetings. Any or all the members of the Board of Directors or any committee designated by it may meet by means of conference telephone or similar communications equipment which permits all persons participating in the meeting to hear each other simultaneously. A member who participates in a meeting by such means is deemed to be present in person at the meeting.

5.12 Action by Written Consent. Whenever the members of the Board of Directors are required or permitted to take any action by vote, such action may be taken without a meeting on written consent, setting forth the action so taken and signed by all of the members entitled to vote,

5.13 Emergency Actions. If the Board of Directors determines by a vote of three-fourths of all its members that an emergency exists of such magnitude as to threaten the work of the whole Church, or of all boards and other agencies of the Church, and that the emergency requires action before the next meeting of the General Assembly, then the Board of Directors shall exercise the powers of the Commissioners in such emergency.

5.14 Compensation. Members of the Board of Directors shall receive no compensation in their capacity as members of the Board of Directors. Members may be paid their expenses, if any, of attendance at each meeting of the Board of Directors.

5.15 Removal of Directors. An elected member of the Board of Directors may be removed by the Commissioners for misfeasance or if he or she is no longer qualified to be elected to the Board of Directors.

ARTICLE 6-WAIVER OF NOTICE

6.01 Written Waiver. Any notice required to be given to any member of the Board of Directors or a Commissioner under these Bylaws, the Charter, or the laws of Tennessee may be waived. The waiver shall be in writing, signed (either before or after the event requiring notice) by the person entitled to the notice, and delivered to the corporation.

6.02 Waiver by Attendance. The attendance of a member of the Board of Directors or a Commissioner at any meeting shall constitute a waiver of notice of the meeting, unless the person attends a meeting for the express purpose of objecting to the transaction of any business because the meeting was not properly called or convened.

ARTICLE 7-MODERATOR AND VICE-MODERATOR

7.01 Nomination and Election. At the beginning of each annual meeting the General Assembly shall elect a Commissioner to serve as Moderator until the next annual meeting. Nominations for Moderator shall come from the floor. One nominating speech, not to exceed ten minutes, shall be permitted on behalf of each nominee. If there is more than one nominee, the election shall be conducted by written ballot. A committee appointed and supervised by the Stated Clerk shall receive the ballots, count them, and certify the election. If no nominee receives a majority of the votes cast, a run-off election shall be conducted. Only those leading nominees who together received a majority of the votes cast on the preceding ballot shall be included in the run-off election.

7.02 Nature of Office. The Moderator of the General Assembly is the ecclesiastical head of the Cumberland Presbyterian Church during the tenure of the office and a spiritual representative of the Cumberland Presbyterian Church wherever God leads. The Moderator receives a precious gift and great opportunity for service in the Church: the freedom to go anywhere and to listen to the mind, heart and spirit of the denomination and to speak with and to the Church. The office of Moderator has great honor and respect, and the person elected to the Office is a priest, prophet, and pastor of the Church at large. The Moderator prays with and for the work of the Spirit of God in the life of the denomination at every opportunity. The Moderator participates in the life and work of the Church as far as possible, and pays particular attention to ecumenical relations, especially with the Cumberland Presbyterian Church in America. Judicatories, congregations, and others are urged to invite the Moderator, and the Moderator is encouraged to attend meetings of Church entities and judicatories to observe the life and work of the Church at every level.

7.03 Duties and Privileges of Office.
  a. The Moderator shall preside at all meetings of the General Assembly.
  b. The Moderator shall appoint, with the consent of the General Assembly, such special committees as are needed;
  c. The Moderator shall serve as chairperson of the General Assembly Program Committee and as a member of the Place of Meeting Committee;
  d. The Moderator shall perform such other duties as may be assigned by the General Assembly.
  e. The Moderator shall serve as an advisory member of the Ministry Council during tenure in office.
  f. The Moderator shall observe the places and times God is calling the Church to service, assess the need for a Denominational response to God's call, and report items that concern the General Assembly.
  g. The Moderator shall wear the official cross and stoles of office during the term of office.

7.04 Expenses of Office. Any allowance budgeted by the General Assembly to offset the expenses of the Moderator shall be administered by the Stated Clerk. Persons issuing an invitation to the Moderator are encouraged to agree in advance on arrangements for the payment of travel expenses. Upon the Moderator's retirement from office, a gavel and a replica of the Moderator's cross shall be presented to the Moderator.

7.05 Vice-Moderator. The General Assembly shall elect a Vice-Moderator in like manner. The Vice-Moderator shall perform such duties as may be assigned by the Moderator of the General Assembly and perform the duties of the Moderator in the event of the Moderator's disability or absence from office for any reason.

7.06 Removal. The Moderator or Vice-Moderator may be removed by the General Assembly whenever in its judgment the removal would serve the best interests of the corporation.

ARTICLE 8-STATED CLERK

8.01 President. The Stated Clerk is the principal executive officer of the corporation and shall also have the titles of "president" and "treasurer".

8.02 Nomination and Election. The Nominating Committee may nominate the serving Stated Clerk for re-election. If the Nominating Committee declines to nominate the serving Stated Clerk for re-election, or if the Stated Clerk has vacated the office, resigned, or declined to be re-nominated, then the Corporate Board shall conduct a search for and nominate a candidate to the General Assembly. In either event, further nominations may be made by the Commissioners. The Commissioners shall elect the Stated Clerk by majority vote.

8.03 Term of Office. The Stated Clerk shall be elected to a term of four (4) years. The regular term of office begins on January 1 and ends on December 31. There is no limit on the number of terms which may be served by an individual Stated Clerk.

8.04 Duties. The Stated Clerk shall be concerned with the spiritual life of the Church and with maintaining and strengthening a united witness for the Church. The Stated Clerk shall also generally supervise and control the business affairs of the corporation and see that all orders and resolutions of the General Assembly are carried into effect. In fulfillment of these duties, the Stated Clerk shall:
  01. Have responsibility to provide for the orderly governance of the Church in accordance with the Constitution, Rules of Order and Rules of Discipline.
  02. Maintain records of the corporation and respond to requests for official records of General Assembly actions and interpretations of its actions.
  03. Represent the Church when an official of the General Assembly is needed.
  04. Represent the Cumberland Presbyterian Church in establishing and maintaining relations with other Churches, particulary those of the Presbyterian and Reformed tradition, and in addressing common concerns.
  05. Sign all documents on behalf of the corporation or the Cumberland Presbyterian Church.
  06. Represent the corporation or the Church in litigation or other legal matters affecting the Cumberland Presbyterian Church, including the selection and employment of legal counsel.
  07. Make suitable arrangements for General Assembly meetings, including researching possible meeting sites, contracting for facilities, and arranging space for committee meetings and sessions of the General Assembly;
  08. Provide for printing and other communication needs of the General Assembly while in session.
  09. Call meetings of the Place of Meeting Committee and the Program Committee.

10. Prepare and distribute an information form to be completed by Commissioners for the Moderator's use in making committee appointments.
11. Advise the Moderator in the appointment of committees.
12. In consultation with the Moderator, refer all matters to come before the next General Assembly; and provide copies of all such referrals to the Commissioners and advisory delegates before the General Assembly convenes.
13. Prepare and distribute preliminary minutes and an agenda for General Assembly meetings which shall provide time for the consideration of any appropriate business, including memorials from a judicatory or denominational entity delivered to the Stated Clerk in writing by April 30.
14. Supervise the recording and publication of minutes and a summary of actions taken by each General Assembly.
15. Make copies of General Assembly minutes available to ordained ministers, licentiates, candidates, commissioners, clerks of sessions, members of denominational entities, schools of the Church, synod, and presbytery clerks, to the Stated Clerk's exchanges and other interested persons in order to encourage lower judicatories and persons in the Church to implement the actions of the General Assembly.
16. File the minutes of each General Assembly with the Historical Foundation as a permanent record.
17. Maintain and update annually the Digest of the General Assembly actions.
18. Represent the Church at large on the Ministry Council.
19. Provide support services for the Moderator and all denominational entities.
20. Receive and make any appropriate response to communications to the Cumberland Presbyterian Church or General Assembly.
21. Maintain a name and address file on congregations, session clerks, pastors, and other leadership of congregations with statistical information about congregations, presbyteries, and synods.
22. Solicit, receive, publish, and disseminate annual reports from churches.
23. Review reports by denominational entities and assist them in complying with correct reporting and budgeting procedures and in avoiding duplication of work.
24. Hold, report annually, and distribute as authorized by the General Assembly or the Ministry Council the Contingency Fund and all other General Assembly Funds not entrusted to the care of a denominational entity.
25. Call the Judiciary Committee into session or by other means secure the advice of the committee on appropriate matters.
26. Communicate with presbyteries and synods on behalf of the General Assembly and attend their meetings from time to time.
27. Provide training for presbytery and synod clerks and orientations for General Assembly commissioners.
28. Generally perform duties as are prescribed in the Constitution or directed by the General Assembly.

8.05 Removal. The Stated Clerk may be removed by the General Assembly whenever in its judgment the removal would serve the best interests of the corporation.

ARTICLE 9-OTHER OFFICERS

9.01 Secretary. The chief executive officer of the Ministry Council shall, by virtue of office, be the secretary of the corporation, and shall in general perform all duties incident to the office of secretary.

9.02 Engrossing Clerk. The Engrossing Clerk shall be elected by the General Assembly to a term of four (4) years. The regular term of office begins on January 1 and ends on December 31. There is no limit on the number of terms which may be served by an individual Engrossing Clerk. The Engrossing Clerk shall serve as Stated Clerk pro tempore during the meeting of the General Assembly in the event the Stated Clerk is absent or unable to serve. The Engrossing Clerk shall perform such other duties as may from time to time be prescribed by the Board of Directors or the General Assembly.

9.03 Additional Officers. The corporation may have such additional officers as it may from time to time find necessary or appropriate.

ARTICLE 10-ORGANIZATION AND RELATIONSHIPS

10.01 Generally. The following are denominational entities related to the Cumberland Presbyterian Church:

01. Subsidiary corporations: Board of Stewardship, Foundation and Benefits of the

Cumberland Presbyterian Church; Memphis Theological Seminary of the Cumberland Presbyterian Church; Ministry Council of the Cumberland Presbyterian Church.
02. Related corporations: Bethel University; Cumberland Presbyterian Children's Home; Historical Foundation of the Cumberland Presbyterian Church and the Cumberland Presbyterian Church in America.
03. Commissions: Chaplains and Military Personnel.
04. Committees: Committee on Nominations; Joint Committee on Amendments; Judiciary, Our United Outreach; Place of Meeting Committee; Program Committee; Unified Committee on Theology and Social Concerns.

10.02 Election and Tenure. The following qualifications and rules relate to service on any denominational entity.
01. Unless elected as an Ecumenical Representative, no person shall be qualified to serve except a member in good standing in a presbytery or local congregation of the Cumberland Presbyterian Church.
02. No person who is employed in an executive capacity including Chief Executive, Vice-President, Team Leader, Director, or equivalent in the Cumberland Presbyterian Church is eligible to serve on a denominational entity. No employee of a denominational entity is eligible for service on the same denominational entity.
03. Each person shall be elected for a term of three years unless elected to fill the remainder of an unexpired term. However, if a person elected to serve on a denominational entity where residence in a particular synod is a qualification for election shall move to another synod while in office, the term to which he or she was elected shall terminate at the close of the next meeting of the General Assembly. When nominating persons to boards and agencies, priority consideration be given to persons whose individual life and/or church involvement demonstrates a commitment to support Our United Outreach.
04. Members of the Committee on Nominations may not be elected to a consecutive term. All other persons may serve up to three consecutive terms for a total not to exceed nine years in office.
05. A Cumberland Presbyterian who has served on any entity is not eligible to serve on the same entity (except for an authorized consecutive term) until at least two (2) years have elapsed since the conclusion of the previous service.
06. A Cumberland Presbyterian who is serving on any entity is not eligible to serve on another entity until at least one (1) year has elapsed since the conclusion of the previous service.
07. An Ecumenical Representative who is serving or has served on any entity is not eligible to serve on any other entity (except for an authorized consecutive term on the same entity) until at least one (1) year has elapsed since the conclusion of the previous service.

10.03 Resignation or Removal.
01. Any person serving on a denominational entity who is no longer qualified or eligible to serve shall be deemed to have resigned.
02. Any person serving on an incorporated denominational entity may resign by delivering written notice of resignation to the secretary or an executive officer of the denominational entity, who shall promptly report the resignation to the Stated Clerk. Any person serving on an unincorporated denominational entity may resign by delivering written notice of resignation to the Stated Clerk. A resignation is effective when delivered unless some other effective date is specified in the written resignation.
03. No member who continues to meet the standard requirements for election or appointment to any denominational entity shall be removed from office except for misfeasance. Removal of a person elected by the General Assembly shall be by vote of the General Assembly.

10.04 Board of Stewardship, Foundation and Benefits. The corporation shall elect the eleven (11) directors of the Board of Stewardship as provided in its charter.

10.05 Historical Foundation. The corporation shall elect six (6) of the twelve (12) directors of the Historical Foundation as provided in its charter. The corporation shall elect the directors of the Historical Foundation in such a manner that, immediately following any election, there shall be at least one (1) member from each synod and no person shall be elected if the election would cause two directors from the same presbytery to be serving simultaneously. The remaining six (6) directors shall be elected by the Cumberland Presbyterian Church in America.

10.06 Memphis Theological Seminary. The corporation shall elect the twenty-four (24) directors of Memphis Theological Seminary as provided in its charter. The corporation shall elect the directors in such a manner that, immediately following any election, there shall be eleven (11) directors who are members of of denominations other than the Cumberland Presbyterian Church.

10.07 Ministry Council.
01. The corporation shall elect the fifteen (15) directors of the Ministry Council as provided in its charter.
02. The corporation shall elect the directors of the Ministry Council in such a manner that immediately following any election, there shall be three (3) directors from each synod; at least six (6) but no more than nine (9) directors who are ordained clergy; and no more than nine (9) directors of the same gender.
03. The Stated Clerk and Moderator shall be designated as Advisory Members to the board of directors of the Ministry Council. In addition, the corporation shall elect three (3) Youth Advisory Members who shall be between the ages of 15 - 17 be elected for 1-year terms, with eligibility for re-election for one additional term.

10.08 Commission on Chaplains and Military Personnel. The commission shall consist of three (3) members elected by the corporation.

ARTICLE 11-COMMITTEES

11.01 General. The corporation shall have the committees provided for in these Bylaws and such other standing or special committees as the General Assembly may create from time to time. Except as otherwise provided in these Bylaws, the Moderator, in consultation with the Stated Clerk, shall appoint all committees.

11.02 Committees of Commissioners and Youth Advisory Delegates. Prior to each General Assembly, the Moderator, in consultation with the Stated Clerk, shall organize the Commissioners and Youth Advisory Delegates into the following committees: Chaplains/Missions/Pastoral Development, Children's Home/Historical Foundation, Higher Education, Judiciary, Ministry Council/Communications/Discipleship, Stewardship/Elected Officers, and Theology and Social Concerns. Each committee shall consider such matters expected to come before the General Assembly as are referred to it by the Stated Clerk. Any denominational organization, the work of which is affected by a matter before a committee, shall be entitled to address the committee.

11.03 Committee on Nominations.
01. The committee shall consist of ten (10) persons elected by the corporation in such a manner that, immediately following any election, the committee shall have at least one minister and one lay person from each synod. It is preferred but not required that no two members shall be from the same presbytery.
02. Approximately one third of the members of the committee shall be elected each year by the General Assembly and shall serve one term not to exceed three years.
03. The committee shall meet not earlier than February 15 each year and shall nominate to the General Assembly qualified persons to fill all vacancies to be filled by vote of the General Assembly, including vacancies on the Committee on Nominations, unless another method of nomination is provided in these Bylaws. The report of the committee shall list the names of nominees, the presbytery if a minister, and the presbytery and the local congregation if a lay person. The Committee on Nominations shall be intentional in nominating persons who represent the global nature of the Church.
04. Presbyteries and synods and their moderators and stated clerks are requested to assist the Committee on Nominations by recommending persons for any position by providing the name and qualifications of the potential nominees to the Stated Clerk no later than February 1 on a form to be provided by the Stated Clerk. Nominations from the floor shall also be in order.
05. No person shall be nominated for election by the General Assembly unless the nominee has within the past year given his or her consent to the nomination.

11.04 Joint Committee on Amendments. The Judiciary Committee shall appoint as many as five of its members to act in committee with an equal number of members of the Judiciary Committee of the Cumberland Presbyterian Church in America. Upon the request of the General Assembly of the Cumberland Presbyterian Church or the General Assembly of the Cumberland Presbyterian Church in America, this Joint Committee shall prepare for the consideration of both general assemblies proposed amendments to the Confession of Faith, Catechism, Constitution, Rules of Discipline, Directory for Worship, and Rules of Order.

11.05 Judiciary Committee.
01. The committee shall consist of nine (9) persons elected by the corporation in such a manner that, immediately following any election, the committee shall have at least four members (4) who are ordained ministers and at least three (3) members who are licensed attorneys-at-law. The Stated Clerk shall be staff liaison to the committee,

attending its meetings and providing resources and counsel.
02. The committee shall meet at least annually upon the call of its chairperson or the Stated Clerk.
03. The committee shall provide advice and counsel to the Stated Clerk. Upon the written request of any judicatory or denominational entity made to the chairperson or Stated Clerk, the committee shall render an advisory opinion on matters of church law or procedure. The chairperson shall secure the views of all members of the committee and write the advisory opinion based on the majority view of the members. The committee shall not render legal opinions on matters of civil law nor otherwise engage in the practice of law.
04. At least one member of the committee shall attend each meeting of the General Assembly to advise with its officers and Commissioners on matters of church law or procedure. At the Moderator's request a member of the committee shall be available to advise the Moderator during the business sessions of the General Assembly.
05. The committee shall be a commission within the meaning of section 2.5 of the Rules of Discipline to hear and determine appeals from synods.
06. The committee shall have oversight of and responsibility for ecclesiastical decisions made by a body acting in the place of a presbytery with respect to mission work and mission fields. The oversight and responsibility exercised by 4 the committee shall be the same as that exercised by a synod with respect to a presbytery under its care, specifically Constitution 8.5, a, b and c.

11.06 Our United Outreach Committee.
01. The committee shall consist of five (5) persons elected by the corporation in such a manner that, immediately following any election, the committee shall have one person from each synod. Seven (7) additional members will include a member of the Ministry Council, a member of the Corporate Board, a member of the Board of Stewardship, Foundation and Benefits, a member of the Board of Trustees of the Historical Foundation, and a Cumberland Presbyterian member of the Boards of Trustees of Bethel University, the Cumberland Presbyterian Children's Home, and Memphis Theological Seminary. The executives of the above named denominational entities shall serve as non-voting, Resource/Advocacy members. In addition, the corporation shall elect three (3) Youth Advisory members who shall be between the ages of 15-17 and be elected for one (1) year terms, with eligibility for re-election for one additional term.
02. The Office of the General Assembly will be responsible for the expenses of the representative of each synod. The represented denominational entities will be responsible for the expenses of their representatives and executives.

11.07 Place of Meeting. The committee shall consist of the Moderator, the Stated Clerk and a representative of the Cumberland Presbyterian Women's Ministries.

11.08 Program Committee. The committee shall consist of the Moderator, Stated Clerk, Director of Ministries, Assistant to the Stated Clerk who serves as secretary, the pastor of the host church, four elected representatives designated by the Ministry Council from among its ministry teams, and one representative designated by each of the following: Bethel University, Board of Stewardship, Foundation, and Benefits, Cumberland Presbyterian Children's Home, Historical Foundation, Memphis Theological Seminary, and the Cumberland Presbyterian Women's Ministry. The committee will begin planning for two years prior to the meeting of a particular General Assembly.

11.09 Unified Committee on Theology and Social Concerns. The committee shall consist of eight (8) members elected by the corporation, the Stated Clerk, and the President of Memphis Theological Seminary. At least one member of the committee other than the Seminary's president shall be a Cumberland Presbyterian member of the faculty of Memphis Theological Seminary.

ARTICLE 12-INDEMNIFICATION

12.01 Indemnification. The corporation shall indemnify any director, officer or employee who is, or is threatened to be, made a party to a completed, pending, or threatened action or proceeding from any liability arising from the director's, officer's or employee's official capacity with the corporation. This indemnification shall extend to the personal representation of a deceased person if the person would be entitled to indemnification under these Bylaws if living.

12.02 Costs and Expenses Covered by Indemnification. Indemnification provided under these Bylaws shall extend to the payment of a judgment, settlement, penalty, or fine, as well as attorney's fees, court costs, and other reasonable and necessary expenses incurred by the director or officer with respect to the action or proceeding.

12.03 Limitation on Indemnification. No indemnification shall be made to or on behalf of any

person if a judgment or other final adjudication adverse to that person establishes his or her liability:
> 01. for any breach of the duty of loyalty to the corporation;
> 02. for acts or omissions not in good faith or which involve intentional misconduct or a knowing violation of law; or
> 03. for any distribution of the assets of the corporation which is unlawful under Tennessee law.

ARTICLE 13-TRUSTEE FOR THE CORPORATION

13.01 Trustee. The Board of Stewardship, Foundation and Benefits of the Cumberland Presbyterian Church, a nonprofit corporation existing under the laws of the state of Tennessee, holds certain real property and other assets of the Church as trustee for the use and benefit of the Church. The Board of Stewardship may continue to hold such real property and other assets, but after the adoption of these Bylaws, it shall hold those assets as trustee for the use and benefit of the Cumberland Presbyterian Church General Assembly Corporation.

13.02 Other Assets. Other, additional property may from time to time be conveyed to the Board of Stewardship to be held by it as trustee for the corporation. All assets held by the Board of Stewardship as trustee for the corporation shall be held at the pleasure and direction of the General Assembly.

ARTICLE 14-PARLIAMENTARY AUTHORITY

14.01 Designation. The parliamentary authority of the corporation in all meetings shall be the latest revised edition of the Rules of Order as set out in the Confession of Faith and Government of the Cumberland Presbyterian Church. In matters not provided for in the Rules of Order, the parliamentary authority shall be Robert's Rules of Order, latest revised edition.

14.02 Standing Rules. The following shall be Standing Rules for meetings of the General Assembly and may be suspended as provided in the parlimentary authority. (see Rules of Order 8.34c)

Standing Rules

1. Unless otherwise determined by the General Assembly or by the Stated Clerk in the event of an emergency, the annual General Assembly shall meet on the third or fourth Monday of June at two o'clock in the afternoon to organize, elect a moderator and transact business, and shall close on Thursday or Friday of the same week.

2. Reports of all standing and special committees shall be considered in the order established by the Moderator in consultation with the Stated Clerk. Committee reports may be presented orally or in writing provided to all Commissioners and youth advisory delegates. Those presenting committee reports shall have the opportunity to make remarks and give explanation, such presentations not to exceed ten minutes unless time is extended by two-thirds vote taken without debate. All committee recommendations shall be submitted in writing.

3. All materials from denominational entities for consideration or action by a General Assembly shall be submitted to the Stated Clerk at least thirty (30) days before the meeting of General Assembly.

4. Resolutions and memorials proposed for adoption by individual commissioners rather than denominational entities or judicatories of the Cumberland Presbyterian Church shall be introduced no later than the close of business on the second day of a meeting of General Assembly, and, when introduced, shall be referred by the Moderator, in counsel with the Stated Clerk, to the appropriate committee or committees for report and recommendations to the Assembly.

ARTICLE 15-REPORTS AND AUDITS

15.01 Congregational Reports. Annually by December 1, the Stated Clerk shall send to session clerks statistical forms for reporting congregational data. Session clerks shall mail the completed forms to presbytery clerks by February 1. The presbytery clerk shall mail the composite statistical report for all congregations of a presbytery to the Stated Clerk by February 10.

15.02 Institutional Reports. In order to be considered for inclusion in the General Assembly budget, all denominational entities shall deliver to the Stated Clerk an annual report including a concise description of the organization's work during the previous year and a line item budget for the forthcoming year. Financial reports should be condensed as much as possible while conveying all essential information on the organization's operations. All denominational entities except academic institutions on a fiscal year are requested to maintain their books on a calendar year.

15.03 Reporting Schedule. An electronic copy and two written copies of the annual report signed by two officers of the organization shall be delivered to the Stated Clerk by March 15 each year. Organizations requesting funds from Our United Outreach shall submit multi-year program budgets to the Our United Outreach Committee.

15.04 Audits. Organizations and operations included in the General Assembly budget shall be audited annually by a certified public accountant. Copies of the auditor's report, including any recommendations for changes in the procedures relating to internal financial controls, shall be delivered to the Stated Clerk. Organizations with total receipts of $100,000 or less are not required to have an audit but shall submit their books and financial statements to the Stated Clerk annually.

15.05 Bonds. Each organization or person whose financial records are required to be audited shall have a fidelity bond in an amount adequate to protect all funds held by the organization or person.

ARTICLE 16-AMENDMENTS

16.01 Manner of Amendment. Except as provided below, these Bylaws may be amended or repealed only by the affirmative vote of two-thirds of the votes cast in a duly constituted meeting of the General Assembly. No portion of the Bylaws may be amended or repealed by the Board of Directors. Fair and reasonable notice of any proposed amendment shall be provided as required by state law.

16.02 Extraordinary Actions. In order to be effective the following actions must be approved by (1) the affirmative vote of two consecutive General Assemblies, or (2) a ninety percent (90%) vote of a single General Assembly.

01. Terminating the existence of a denominational entity named in Bylaw 10.01
02. Creating a new denominational entity other than a temporary committee or task force.
03. Decreasing the Our United Outreach budget allocation to a denominational entity by more than 40% of the amount distributed to it during the previous calendar year; or
04. Taking any other actions which would cause a drastic change in the mission or structure of the Cumberland Presbyterian Church.

MEMORIAL ROLL OF MINISTERS

IN MEMORY OF
MINISTERS LOST BY DEATH

NAME	PRESBYTERY	AGE	DATE
Bagby, Larry	West TN	76	08/12/17
Bynum, Ronald	Robert Donnell	87	04/28/18
Clark, Jonathan	Murfreesboro	69	03/02/18
Coleman, Don	West TN	81	04/30/18
Eatherly, John	Columbia	77	10/14/17
English, Don	Grace	90	06/22/17
Gross, Ronald	North Central	86	01/15/17
Hom, Paul	del Cristo	85	03/14/17
Jacob, Randy	Choctaw	80	01/29/17
Jones, Joseph	Cumberland	88	12/15/17
Kelley, Lawrence	Columbia	102	12/04/17
Lunn, Calvin	Columbia	70	06/06/17
Maynard, Terrell	Grace	72	03/14/17
Moore, Hillman C	Covenant	84	03/13/18
Mosley, Karen	West TN	60	04/14/18
Murrie, Willard	Covenant	97	04/20/17
Parish, Johnny	Nashville	59	01/26/18
Parsons, Hugh	Trinity	83	04/17/18
Perkins, William	Cumberland	85	01/08/18
Ranson, Doris	Cumberland	86	05/12/18
Shelton, Robert M	Red River	83	03/04/18
Shirey, John	Covenant	92	07/02/17
Smith, Albert J	North Central	87	02/10/17
Stone, Paul	Covenant	67	12/08/17
Vasseur, Terry	Covenant	78	02/05/17
Wallace, Boyce	Cauca Valley	87	01/04/17
Westfall, Charles	Covenant	89	03/12/17
Yaple, George	Hope	90	04/24/17

LIVING GENERAL ASSEMBLY MODERATORS

2018—REV. JAY EARHEART-BROWN, 475 N Highland Street, Apt 9L, Memphis, TN 38122
2017—REV. DAVID LANCASTER, 426 Fuqua Road, Martin, TN 38237
2016—REV. DWAYNE TYUS, 426 Old Hickory Boulevard, Madison, TN 37115
2015—REV. MICHELE GENTRY, Urb San Jorge casa 28, Km 8 via a La Tebaida
    Armenia, Quindio, COLOMBIA, SA
2014—REV. LISA HALL ANDERSON, 1790 Faxon Avenue, Memphis, TN 38112
2013—REV. FOREST PROSSER, 1157 Mountain Creek Road, Chattanooga, TN 37405
2012—REV. ROBERT D. RUSH, 12935 Quail Park Drive, Cypress, TX 77429
2011—REV. DON M. TABOR, 9611 Mitchell Place, Brentwood, TN 37027
2009—ELDER SAM SUDDARTH, 206 Ha Le Koa Court, Smyrna, TN 37167
2007—REV. FRANK WARD, 8207 Traditional Place, Cordova, TN 38016
2006—REV. DONALD HUBBARD, 2128 Campbell Station Road, Knoxville, TN 37932
2005—REV. LINDA H. GLENN, 49 Mason Road, Threeway, TN 38343
2004—REV. EDWARD G. SIMS, 2161 N. Meadows Drive, Clarksville, TN 37043
2003—REV. CHARLES MCCASKEY, 679 Canter Lane, Cookeville, TN 38501
1999—ELDER GWENDOLYN G. RODDYE, 3728 Wittenham Drive, Knoxville, TN 37921
1998—REV. MASAHARU ASAYAMA, 3-15-9 Higashi, Kunitachi-shi, Tokyo, JAPAN
1996—REV. MERLYN A. ALEXANDER, 80 N. Hampton Lane, Jackson, TN 38305
1995—REV. CLINTON O. BUCK, PO Box 770068, Memphis, TN 38117
1992—REV. JOHN DAVID HALL, 109 Oddo Lane SE, Huntsville, AL 35802
1990—REV. THOMAS D. CAMPBELL, PO Box 315, Calico Rock, AR 72519
1989—REV. WILLIAM RUSTENHAVEN, Jr., 703 W. Burleson, Marshall, TX 75670
1981—REV. W. JEAN RICHARDSON, 7533 Lancashire, Powell, TN 37849

IN MEMORY OF:

Moderator of the 178th General Assembly
REV. JONATHAN CLARK
Died March 2, 2018

Moderator of the 163rd General Assembly
REV. ROBERT M. SHELTON
Died March 4, 2018

GENERAL ASSEMBLY OFFICERS

MODERATOR
THE REVEREND DANIEL J. EARHEART-BROWN
475 N Highland Street, Apt 9L
Memphis, TN 38122
jayearheartbrown@gmail.com
(901)463-0007

VICE MODERATOR
THE REVEREND BUDDY POPE
2391 Fairfield Pike
Shelbyville, TN 37160
pope6897@yahoo.com
(931)205-6897

STATED CLERK AND TREASURER
THE REVEREND MICHAEL SHARPE
8207 Traditional Place
Cordova, TN 38016
(901)276-4572
FAX (901)272-3913
msharpe@cumberland.org

ENGROSSING CLERK
THE REVEREND VERNON SANSOM
7810 Shiloh Road
Midlothian, TX 76065
(972)825-6887
vernon@sansom.us

THE BOARD OF DIRECTORS OF THE GENERAL ASSEMBLY CORPORATION

(Members whose terms expire in 2019)
(2)MR. TIM GARRETT, 150 Third Avenue South, Suite 2800, Nashville, TN 37201
  tgarrett@bassberry.com
(2)REV. BOBBY COLEMAN, 704 E Webb Street, Mountain View, AR 72560
  bobby.coleman@gmail.com

(Members whose terms expire in 2020)
(2)REV. JOHN BUTLER, 501 Cherokee Drive, Campbellsville, KY 42718
  rev.butlerj8134@gmail.com
(2)MS. BETTY JACOB, PO Box 158, Broken Bow, OK 74728
  chocpres@pine-net.com

(Members whose terms expire in 2021)
(2)MS. CALOTTA EDSELL, 7044 Woodsong Cove, Germantown, TN 38138
  cedsell@hotmail.com
(2)REV. NORLAN SCRUDDER, 29688 S 534 Road, Park Hill, OK 74451
  ndscrudder@gmail.com

*Ecumenical Partners   +Cumberland Presbyterian Church in America

MINISTRY COUNCIL

(Members whose terms expire in 2019)
(1)MS. KAREN AVERY, 9420 Layton Court NE, Albuquerque, NM 87111
(1)MS. CARLA BELLIS, 19264 Law 2170, Aurora, MO 65605
(3)REV. TROY GREEN, 105 Cobb Hollow Lane, Petersburg, TN 37144
(1)MS. TSURUKO SATOH, 8710 Hickory Falls Lane, Pewee Valley, KY 40056
(1)REV. MIKE WILKINSON, 1504 Clear Brook Drive, Knoxville, TN 37922

(Members whose terms expire in 2020)
(3)REV. DONNY ACTON, 1413 Oakridge Drive, Birmingham, AL 35242
(1)MR. DAVID CORREA, Calle 76 #87-14, Medellin, COLOMBIA, SOUTH AMERICA
(1)MS. SAMANTHA HASSELL, 510 N Main Street, Sturgis, KY 42459
(3)REV. LANNY JOHNSON, 120 S Mill Street, Morrison, TN 37357
(1)MS. CHARELLE WEBB, 3507 Pickering Lane, Pearland, TX 77584

(Members whose terms expire in 2021)
(3)MR. KENNETH BEAN, 1035 Stonewall Street N, McKenzie, TN 38201
(2)REV. KENNY BUTCHER, 4608 Cather Court, Nashville, TN 37214
(2)REV. PHILLIP LAYNE, 10699 Griffith Highway, Whitwell, TN 37397
(2)MS. VICTORY MOORE, 17388 Chandlerville Road, Virginia, IL 62691
(1)MS. MELINDA REAMS, 10 W Azalea Lane, Russellville, AR 72802

YOUTH ADVISORY MEMBERS
(1)MS. SYDNEY HOLDER, 6589 County Road 747, Cullman, AL 35055
(1)MS. MADISON HOLLAND, 565 County Road 17, Scottsboro, AL 35768
(2)MS. LEIGHANN MORGAN, 1468 Williams Cove Road, Winchester, TN 37398

ADVISORY MEMBERS
REV. DANIEL J. EARHEART-BROWN, 475 N Highland Street, Apt 9L, Memphis, TN 38122
REV. MICHAEL SHARPE, 8207 Traditional Place, Cordova, TN 38016

COMMUNICATIONS MINISTRY TEAM

(Members whose terms expire in 2020)
(1)MS. FREDERICKA JOHNS, PO Box 234, Calico Rock, AR 72519
(2)MS. DUSTY LUTHY, 2026 Washington Street, Paducah, KY 42003

(Members whose terms expire in 2021)
(1)REV. NATHANIEL MATHEWS, 1006 Woodland Drive, New Johnsonville, TN 37134

DISCIPLESHIP MINISTRY TEAM

(Members whose terms expire in 2019)
(2)REV. NANCY MCSPADDEN, 120 Roberta Drive, Memphis, TN 38112
(2)REV. JOSEFINA SANCHEZ, 7 Hancock Street, Melrose, MA 02176
(1)REV. JESSE THORNTON, 2518 IL Highway 15, Fairfield, IL 62837
(Members whose terms expire in 2020)
(2)MS. LE ILA DIXON, 4406 John Reagan Street, Marshall, TX 75672
(2)REV. DREW GRAY, 12304 Wickliffe Road, Kevil, KY 42053
(1)REV. BILLY PRICE, 12510 Buttermilk Road, Knoxville, TN 37932
(Members whose terms expire in 2021)
(1)MS. CANDY BARR, 3291 McLean Drive, Rogersville, AL 35652
(3)MS. RACHEL COOK, 210 Bynum Street, Scottsboro, AL 35768
(1)MR. EAN TAYLOR, 437 Peach Creek Crescent, Nashville, TN 37214

MISSIONS MINISTRY TEAM

(Members whose terms expire in 2019)
(2)REV. VICTOR HASSELL, 510 N Main Street, Sturgis, KY 42459
(2)MR. DOMINIC LAU, 3820 Anza Street, San Francisco, CA
(2)REV. BRITTANY MEEKS, 710 N Avalon Street, Memphis, TN 38107
(2)REV. CHRIS WARREN, 906 Prince Lane, Murfreesboro, TN 37129
(Members whose terms expire in 2020)
(1)MS. DONNA CHRISTIE, 3221 Whitehall Road, Birmingham, AL 35209
(Members whose terms expire in 2021)
(3)REV. CARDELIA HOWELL-DIAMOND, 1580 Jeff Road NW, Huntsville, AL 35806
(1)MR. OLLIE MCCLUNG, 2912 Riverwood Lane, Birmingham, AL 35243
(3)MS. MELINDA REAMS, 10 W Azalea Lane, Russellville, AR 72802 (resigned)
(1)MS. MARGIE SHANNON, 2307 Littlemore Drive, Cordova, TN 38016

PASTORAL DEVELOPMENT MINISTRY TEAM

(Members whose terms expire in 2019)
(2)REV. SANDRA SHEPHERD, 1432 Wexford Downs Lane, Nashville, TN 37211
(Members whose terms expire in 2020)
(2)REV. AMBER CLARK, 2353 Blue Springs Road, Decherd, TN 37324
(1)REV. PAUL EARHEART-BROWN, 866 N McLean Boulevard, Memphis, TN 38107
(Members whose terms expire in 2021)
(3)REV. DUAWN MEARNS, 15347 County Road 3537, Ada, OK 74820
(1)REV. LISA ANDERSON, 1790 Faxon Avenue, Memphis, TN 38112

GENERAL ASSEMBLY BOARD OF:

I. TRUSTEES OF BETHEL UNIVERSITY

(Members whose terms expire in 2018)
(3)MR. CHARLIE GARRETT, 107 Willow Green Drive, Jackson, TN 38305
(2)+REV. ELTON C. HALL, SR., 305 Tiffton Circle, Hewitt, TX 76643
(2)MS. DEWANNA LATIMER, 193 Moses Drive, Jackson, TN 38305
(1)*DR. E. RAY MORRIS, PO Box 924628, Norcross, GA 30010
(1)MR. STEVE PERRYMAN, 535 Ranch Road, Rogersville, MO 65742
(Members whose terms expire in 2019)
(2)MR. JEFF AMREIN, 11711 Paramont Way, Prospect, KY 40059
(3)*JUDGE BEN CANTRELL, 1485A Woodmont Boulevard, Nashville, TN 37215
(1)*MR. SCOTT CONGER, 143 Fawn Ridge Drive, Jackson, TN 38305
(3)+DR. ARMY DANIEL, 3125 Searcy Drive, Huntsville, AL 35810
(2)MR. BILL DOBBINS 5716 Quest Ridge Road, Franklin, TN 37064
(3)DR. ROBERT LOW, c/o New Prime, Inc., 2740 W Mayfair Avenue, Springfield, MO 65803
(1)*DR. BROCK MARTIN, 419 Browning Avenue, Huntingdon, TN 38344
(Members whose terms expire in 2020)
(1)DR. NANCY BEAN, PO Box 205, McKenzie, TN 38201
(3)*MS. LISA COLE, PO Box 198615, Nashville, TN 37219
(3)MR. CHESTER (CHET) DICKSON, 24 W Rivercrest Drive, Houston, TX 77042
(2)REV. NANCY MCSPADDEN, 120 Roberta Drive, Memphis, TN 38112
(3)DR. ED PERKINS, 721 Paris Street, McKenzie, TN 38201
(2)MR. KENNETH (KEN) D. QUINTON, 2912 Waller Omer Road, Sturgis, KY 42459
(1)MR. TOMMY SURBER, 825 Hico Road, McKenzie, TN 38201
(2)REV. ROBERT (BOB) WATKINS, 10950 West Union Hills Drive #1356, Sun City, AZ 85373

Trustee Emeritus – Dr. Vera Low, 3653 Prestwick Court, Springfield, MO 65809 (deceased)

II. TRUSTEES OF CUMBERLAND PRESBYTERIAN CHILDREN'S HOME

(Members whose terms expire in 2019)
(3)MR. RICHARD DEAN, 2140 Cove Circle North, Gadsden, AL 35903
(3)*MS. PATRICIA LONG, 525 E Oak Street, Aledo, TX 76008
(1)REV. JOYCE MERRITT, 3929 Snail Shell Cove, Rockvale, TN 37153
(1)MR JAY THOMAS, 3301 Cooperbranch E, Denton, TX 76209
(1)*MR. CAMERON MARONE, 3933 Park Haven Drive, Denton, TX 76210
(Members whose terms expire in 2020)
(1)MR. PETE CARTER, 306 Jackson Hills Drive, Maryville, TN 37804
(2)*MR. CHARLES W. HARRIS, 3293 Birch Avenue, Grapevine, TX 76051
(1)MR. BRIAN MARTIN, 614 County Road 4608, Troup, TX 75789
(2)MR. KNIGHT MILLER, 509 Brixham Park Drive, Franklin, TN 37069
(1)+REV. PERRYN RICE, 8525 Audelia Road, Dallas, TX 75238
(1)MRS. GUIN TYUS, 903 W Hickory Boulevard, Madison, TN 37115
(Members whose terms expire in 2021)
(2)REV. DUANE DOUGHERTY, 212 County Road 4705, Troup, TX 75789
(2)MRS. CAROLYN HARMON, 4435 Newport Highway, Greeneville, TN 37743

*Ecumenical Partners +Cumberland Presbyterian Church in America

III. TRUSTEES OF HISTORICAL FOUNDATION

(Members whose terms expire in 2019)
(1)MS. ROBIN MCCASKEY HUGHES, 1205 Olde Bridge Road, Edmond, OK 73034
(3)REV. MARY KATHRYN KIRKPATRICK, 401 1/2 Henley-Perry Drive, Marshall, TX 75670
(1)MS. ASHLEY LINDSEY, 2090 Claypool Boyce Road, Alvaton, KY 42122

(Members whose terms expire in 2020)
(1)+MS. JACKIE COOPER, 4705 Inidan Summer Drive, Nashville, TN 37207
(3)MR. MICHAEL FARE, 401 E Deanna Lane, Nixa, MO 65714
(3)*MS. DOROTHY M. HAYDEN, 3103 Carolina Avenue, Bessemer, AL 35020
(1)+REV. JOE HOWARD, III, 2903 Al Lipscomb Way, Dallas, TX 75215
(2)+MS. PAT WARD, 2620 Rabbit Lane, Madison, AL 35756

(Members whose terms expire in 2021)
(2)REV. LISA OLIVER, 110 Allen Drive, Hendersonville, TN 37075
(1)MS. KELLY SHANTON, 3932 W Beaver Creek Drive, Powell, TN 37849

IV. TRUSTEES OF MEMPHIS THEOLOGICAL SEMINARY OF THE CUMBERLAND PRESBYTERIAN CHURCH

(Members whose terms expire in 2019)
(3)MR. MICHAEL R. ALLEN, 149 Windwood Circle, Alabaster, AL 35007
(3)MS. DIANE DICKSON, 24 West Rivercrest, Houston, TX 77042
(1)*MS. JANE ASHLEY FOLK, 4405 Dunwick Lane, Fort Worth, TX 76109
(1)*MR. HARRY HILLIARD, 206 E Bankhead Street, New Albany, MS 38652
(2)*DR. RICK KIRCHOFF, 2044 Thorncroft Drive, Germantown, TN 38138
(3)*DR. INETTA RODGERS, 1824 S Parkway E, Memphis, TN 38114
(1)*DR. DEBORAH SMITH, 584 E McLemore Avenue, Memphis, TN 38106
(1)MS. MARIANNA (MOLLY) WILLIAMS, 947 Troy Avenue, Dyersburg, TN 28024

(Members whose terms expire in 2020)
(2)*REV. NANCY COLE, 3346 Arcadia Drive, Tuscaloosa, AL 35404
(2)REV. ANNE HAMES, 118 Paris Street, McKenzie, TN 38201
(1)+MS. VANESSA K. MIDGETT, 118 Thunderbird Drive, Huntsville, AL 35749
(1)REV. JASON MIKEL, 410 Ramblewood Lane, Nolensville, TN 37135
(1)*REV. JIMMY JOHNATHAN MOSBY, PO Box 45843, Little Rock, AR 72214
(2)REV. SUSAN PARKER, 655 York Drive, Rogersville, AR 35652 (resigned)
(1)*MR. REGINALD PORTER, JR., 4458 Whitephine Cove, Memphis, TN 38109
(1)REV. KIP RUSH, 516 Franklin Road, Breentwood, TN 37027

(Members whose terms expire in 2021)
(1)REV. DANIEL BARKLEY, 2732 Rexford Street, Hokes Bluff, AL 35903
(1)REV. RON FELL, 212 Ouachita 54, Camden, AR 71701
(2)REV. LINDA HOWELL, PO Box 80050, Keller, TX 76244 (resigned)
(1)DR. YOONG KIM, 225 Bayswater Drive, Suwanee, GA 30024
(1)REV. RIAN PUCKETT, 55 Ham Street, Batesville, AR 72501
(3)MS. SONDRA RODDY, 2583 Hedgerow Lane, Clarksville, TN 37043
(3)+REV. MELVIN CHARLES SMITH, 1263 Haynes Street, Memphis, TN 38114
(3)+MS. LATISHA TOWNS, The Med, 877 Jefferson Avenue, Memphis, TN 38103

V. STEWARDSHIP, FOUNDATION AND BENEFITS

(Members whose terms expire in 2019)
(1)REV. KEN BYFORD, 23716 Highway 9 N, Piedmont, AL 36272
(2)REV. CHARLES (BUDDY) POPE, 2391 Fairfield Pike, Shelbyville, TN 37160
(3)MS. DEBBIE SHELTON, 1255 MG England Road, Manchester, TN 37355
(1)MS. ANDREA SMITH, 1715 Water Cure Road, Winchester, TN 37398

---

*Ecumenical Partners   +Cumberland Presbyterian Church in America

(Members whose terms expire in 2020)
(2)MR. RANDY DAVIDSON, PO Box 880, Ada, OK 74821
(1)REV. MARK HESTER, 763 Finn Long Road, Friendsville, TN 37737
(1)REV. GARY TUBB, 103 Forest Drive, Mountain Home, AR 72653
(1)REV. DWAYNE TYUS, 426 W Old Hickory Boulevard, Madison, TN 37115
(Members whose terms expire in 2021)
(1)MS. DEBBIE SHANKS, 3997 N 100th Street, Casey, IL 62420
(2)MR. JAMES SHANNON, 2307 Littlemore Drive, Cordova, TN 38016
(3)MR. MICHAEL ST. JOHN, 324 Carriage Place, Lebanon, MO 65536

GENERAL ASSEMBLY COMMISSIONS:

I. MILITARY CHAPLAINS AND PERSONNEL

(2) Term Expires in 2019–REV. CASSANDRA THOMAS, 1920 Dancy Street, Fayetteville, NC 28301
(1) Term Expires in 2020–REV. CHARLES MCCASKEY, 679 Canter Lane, Cookeville, TN 38501
(2) Term Expires in 2021–REV. TONY JANNER, 104 Northwood Drive, McKenzie TN 38201

These three persons and the Stated Clerk represent the denomination as members of the Presbyterian Council for Chaplains and Military Personnel, 4125 Nebraska Avenue NW, Washington, DC 20016

GENERAL ASSEMBLY COMMITTEES

I. JUDICIARY

(Members whose terms expire in 2019)
(3)REV. ANDY MCCLUNG, 919 Dickinson Street, Memphis, TN 38107
    scubarev@att.net
(1)MS. RACHEL MOSES, 1138 Blaine Avenue, Cookeville, TN 38501
    coachrach@aol.com
(1)REV. JAN OVERTON, 3320 Pipe Line Road, Birmingham, AL 35243
    jan@crestlinechurch.org
(Members whose terms expire in 2020)
(1)MS. PAMELA BROWN, 6400 North Grove Avenue, Warr Acres, OK 73012
    pambrownlaw@cox.net
(2)REV. HARRY CHAPMAN, 4908 El Picador Court SE, Rio Rancho, NM 87124
    wrightrev2gmail.com
(1)REV. GEOFFREY KNIGHT, 2119 Avalon Place, Houston, TX 77019
    geoff@cphouston.org
(Members whose terms expire in 2021)
(3)REV. ANNETTA CAMP, 2303 Mill Creek Road, Halls, TN 38040
    anetta@cumberlandchurch.com
(1)REV. JIM RATLIFF, 13 Hernando Drive, Cherokee Village, AR 72529
    pastorjimfcpc@yahoo.com
(2)MR. BILL TALLY, 907 Tipperary Drive, Scottsboro, AL 35768
    wtally@scottsboro.org

*Ecumenical Partners   +Cumberland Presbyterian Church in America

II. JOINT COMMITTEE ON AMENDMENTS

The committee consists of five members of the Judiciary Committee of the Cumberland Presbyterian Church in America and the Cumberland Presbyterian Church.

III. NOMINATING

(Members whose terms expire in 2019)
(1)MS. FAYE DELASHMIT, 2705 Garrett Drive, Bowling Green, KY 42104
   steve.delashmit@twc.com
(1)REV. DEREK JACKS, 341 Shadeswood Drive, Hoover, AL 35226
   pastorderek@homewoodcpc.com
(1)REV. STEPHEN LOUDER, 98 Gallant Court, Clarksville, TN 37043
   pastorsteve@clarksvillecpc.com
(1)MS. JANIE STAMPS, 4008 Logan Lane, Fort Smith, AR 72903
   bjstamps@msn.com

(Members whose terms expire in 2020)
(1)REV. BRIAN HAYES, 69 Cactus Drive, Benton, KY 42025
   cprevbhayes@gmail.com
(1)MR. LEE HOLDER, 6589 County Road 747, Cullman, AL 35055
   holder4bama@yahoo.com
(1)REV. TOM SPENCE, PO Box 802, Burns Flat, OK 73624
   tomspence0302@gmail.com
(1)MS. JENANN LESLIE, 300 Henley Perry Drive, Marshall, TX 75670
   jenann.leslie@gmail.com

(Members whose terms expire in 2021)
(1)MR. ETHAN MORGAN, 119 Mountain Top Lane, Cookeville, TN 38506
   remorgan8@gmail.com
(1)REV. RANDY SHANNON, 30282 Highway H, Marshall, MO 65340
   pastor_randy_shannon@yahoo.com

IV. OUR UNITED OUTREACH COMMITTEE

(Members whose terms expire in 2019)
(1)REV. BRUCE HAMILTON, 1037 Binns Drive, Monticello, AR 71655

(Members whose terms expire in 2020)
(1)MS. MARY ANN COLE, 1726 Karen Circle, Bowling Green, KY 42104
(1)MR. MIKEL DAVIS, 102 Willow Wood Lane, Ovilla, TX 75154

(Members whose terms expire in 2018)
(1)MS. GWEN RODDYE, 3728 Wittenham Drive, Knoxville, TN 37921
(3)MS. ROBIN WILLS, 4607 E Richmond Shop Road, Lebanon, TN 37090

V. PLACE OF MEETING

THE STATED CLERK OF THE GENERAL ASSEMBLY
THE MODERATOR OF THE GENERAL ASSEMBLY
A REPRESENTATIVE OF WOMEN'S MINISTRIES OF THE MISSIONS MINISTRY TEAM

VI. UNIFIED COMMITTEE ON THEOLOGY AND SOCIAL CONCERNS

(Members whose terms expire in 2019)

(3)+MRS. JIMMIE DODD, c/o Hopewell CPCA, 4100 Millsfield Highway, Dyersburg, TN 38024
 dodd125@gmail.com
(3)REV. BYRON FORESTER, 2376 Eastwood Place, Memphis, TN 38112
 bforester@bellsouth.net; (901)246-1242
(1)REV. MARCUS HAYES, 3225 McCart Avenue, Fort Worth, TX 76110
 marcus.hayes@att.net
(2)REV. JOHN A. SMITH, 916 Allen Road, Nashville, TN 37214
 john.a.smith.81@gmail.com; (615)545-6486
(3)+ELDER JOY WALLACE, 6940 Marvin D Love Freeway, Dallas, TX 75237
 jwallace1951@gmail.com

(Members whose terms expire in 2020)

(1)+MS. SHARON COMBS, PO Box 122, Sturgis, KY 42459
 (270)860-4175
(1)+REV. EDMUND COX, 249 Mimosa Circle, Maryville, TN 37801
 edmundcox765@gmail.com
(2)+DR. NANCY FUQUA, 1963 County Road 406, Towncreek, AL 35672
 fuq23@bellsouth.net; (256)566-1226
(1)REV. RICHARD MORGAN, 1468 Williams Cove Road, Winchester, TN 37398
 icthuse3@gmail.com
(1)REV. LISA SCOTT, (address on file in GA office)
 lascott1979@att.net
(1)+REV. ROBERT E THOMAS, 1017 N Englewood, Tyler, TX 75702
 (903)592-0238

(Members whose terms expire in 2021)

(1)REV. MITCH BOULTON, 80 Topsy Lane, Savannah, TN 38372
 steelermitch@gmail.com
(1)REV. MICHAEL QUALLS, 5355 June Cove, Horn Lake, MS 38637
 mqualls1@yahoo.com
(1)MS. MELISSA WILSON, 107 Hillwood Drive, Dickson, TN 37055
 milzwilz@yahoo.com
President of Memphis Theological Seminary - Ex-officio Member

OTHER DENOMINATIONAL PERSONNEL

REPRESENTATIVES TO:

Caribbean and North American Area Council, World Communion of Reformed Churches:
STATED CLERK MICHAEL SHARPE, 8207 Traditional Place, Cordova, TN 38016

(Member whose terms expire in 2020)

(1)MS. SHERRY POTEET, PO box 313, Gilmer, TX 75644
 spoteet1@aol.com

*Ecumenical Partners +Cumberland Presbyterian Church in America

THE REPORT OF THE MODERATOR

With only a few weeks left in this term as the Moderator of the 187th General Assembly, it is with a profound sense of gratitude and humble awareness of the privilege and honor of serving in this office for the past year that I submit this report. The kindness and graciousness which greeted me at each visit will remain a cherished memory and magnificent reminder of "a people called Cumberland Presbyterians." I can only pray that in some effective manner that my gratefulness was amply demonstrated during my visits, and that your compassion more than compensated for the wear and tear of travel and time away from home.

The assistance, kindness and wisdom of General Assembly Stated Clerk, Reverend Michael Sharpe, and his administrative assistant, Mrs. Elizabeth Vaughn, provided constant encouragement and support, and, no doubt, helped me avoid countless faux pas I could have easily committed.

In addition, Vice-Moderator Reverend Lisa Scott, ably and gladly traveled to presbyteries which I was unable to reach, guaranteeing that appreciation and gratitude was conveyed to all of our brothers and sisters in the states. Her kind and cheerful cooperation during the Assembly meeting last summer and these visits demonstrated the great leadership which she offers our beloved community.

It was an honor to participate in the meeting of the Ministry Council and as a guest of the Board of Trustees of our Memphis Theological Seminary. As with the various presbyteries, the welcome was always kind and gracious. An opportunity to speak at the greater Huntsville, Alabama area Denomination Day celebration was also a highlight, as it likewise afforded me an opportunity to speak at the historic Church Street CPCA congregation, pastored by my dear friend and college classmate, the Reverend Doctor Mitchell Walker and his wife, Elaine.

In my visits and preaching opportunities, one theme was sounded repeatedly with as much enthusiasm and determination as I could muster: the Biblical mandate to share the Gospel in our communities and across the world. As a means of providing a touchstone, I encouraged all of us to review regularly our annual yearbook, paying special attention to column 5 in the reports of our congregations. No better sign of health and wellness of churches can be employed than by the number of persons coming to know the Lord through our ministries.

In addition, the Sharon, Tennessee congregation which I have served for almost ten years has provided an incredible amount of prayer and support during this year. They have provided me with an immeasurable dose of encouragement repeatedly, and demonstrated their concern for my wellbeing.

Finally, whether leaving home or returning, the love and godly influence of my late wife, Barb, accompanied me every mile of the way. The manner in which she enriched our lives empowered me to serve in this capacity in a manner which cannot be adequately explained but neither can in the least bit be doubted. Our four children and their families are also testimonies to her faith and love.

Thanks be to God and to my dear church family for the privilege of serving you as your moderator this past year.

Respectfully submitted,

R. David Lancaster
Moderator of the 187th General Assembly

THE REPORT OF THE STATED CLERK

I. THE OFFICE OF THE STATED CLERK

The Constitution, the Rules of Discipline, the Rules of Order, and the General Assembly Bylaws (found in the front of the General Assembly Minutes) list the many responsibilities for the person who holds the position of Stated Clerk, the primary task is to maintain and strengthen a united witness for the Church. The Stated Clerk shall also generally supervise and control the business affairs of the Corporation, and see that all directives of the General Assembly are implemented.

The Office of the General Assembly also provides budgeting, accounting, and support services for commissions, committees, agencies and task forces without executive assistance.

Additional services and activities provided through the office of the Stated Clerk this past year include:
- Providing assistance to the Unification Task Force
- Developing and maintaining a web presence for the following General Assembly Committees/Commissions without staff: Nominating Committee, Unified Committee on Theology and Social Concerns, Commission on Military Chaplains and Personnel, Our United Outreach Committee and the Unification Task Force.
- Creation of spring and fall Denominational News Updates, a compilation of talking points obtained from each board and agency that may be shared by visiting denominational staff and the moderator when making visits to presbyteries and in other settings. The updates are also shared with presbytery clerks.
- Development of a Travel Chart, to assist with the coordination of travel plans by denominational staff to meetings of presbyteries. The travel chart is also shared with presbytery clerks.
- Hosted the annual conference for Presbytery and Synod Clerks.

A significant portion of the Stated Clerk's time has been spent responding to various judicial and legal questions affecting local churches and presbyteries. The Clerk is appreciative for advice provided to this office from both the Permanent Judiciary Committee and from Mr. Jamie Jordan who serves as legal counsel for the Office of the General Assembly.

The Stated Clerk is grateful to the Church for calling him to serve in this position and appreciates the support of the Church for the Office and for the person who holds this position.

II. STAFF

Ms. Elizabeth Vaughn serves as the Assistant to the Stated Clerk, a position that requires her to maintain accurate records of ministers, probationers, congregations, record income and expenses and to authorize payment of all items in the Office of the General Assembly budget. The Church is fortunate to have a person with such knowledge, efficiency and dedication to work. The Stated Clerk and the Assistant to the Stated Clerk are currently the only employees of the Office of the General Assembly.

Reverend Vernon Sansom continues to serves as Engrossing Clerk and is to be commended for the accuracy in recording the minutes of the General Assembly. Vernon also leads the orientation session for those who serve as chairperson and co-chairperson for each General Assembly appointed Committee and provides valuable assistance in the preparation of committee reports at each meeting of the General Assembly.

III. ECUMENICAL RELATIONSHIPS

The Cumberland Presbyterian Church has historically been involved in ecumenical relationships. Through co-operative ministries, chaplains for the military and veteran's hospitals are endorsed, migrant workers and persons in Appalachia are served, and missionaries are sent into a variety of countries. Through ecumenical partnerships disaster relief funds are distributed. Through working co-operatively church school and camping materials are developed. The Cumberland Presbyterian witness is more effective through participation with other Christians in these and various other ministries.

A. CUMBERLAND PRESBYTERIAN CHURCH IN AMERICA

The Cumberland Presbyterian Church in America and the Cumberland Presbyterian Church have one heritage, one Confession of Faith and share in several co-operative relationships and ministries such as the Historical Foundation, the United Board of Christian Discipleship, youth ministry, and the Unified Committee on Theology and Social Concerns. The Cumberland Presbyterian Church in America and the Cumberland Presbyterian Church also participate with other Reformed bodies in ministry. Although working through partnerships, the witness of the Cumberland Presbyterian Church in America and the Cumberland Presbyterian Church would be greatly enhanced through a union of the two denominations.

B. WORLD COMMUNION OF REFORMED CHURCHES

Both the Cumberland Presbyterian Church and the Cumberland Presbyterian Church in a America are members of World Communion of Reformed Churches (WCRC). The WCRC was formed in 2010 by a merger of the World Alliance of Reformed Churches and the Reformed Ecumenical Council. The WCRC represents approximately eighty million members of two hundred thirty denominations from one hundred seven countries, including Reformed, Congregationalists, Presbyterian and United Churches. Resources and updates from the World Communion of Reformed Churches are available on their website: (www.wcrc.ch).

Reverend Christopher Ferguson serves as general secretary of the WCRC and offices in Hanover, Germany where the headquarters for WCRC is located.

IV. CONSTITUTIONAL AMENDMENTS

The 187th General Assembly submitted to the presbyteries the following Constitutional Amendment:

Constitution 9.5 be renumbered as 9.6 and a new 9.5 be inserted, reading as follows:

9.5 The General Assembly, in order to promote the mission work of the Church and the development of new churches outside the United States, may authorize a synod or its missions entity (utilizing ordained personnel) to act in place of a presbytery with respect to persons, ministers, and churches outside the United States and outside the bounds of any existing presbytery. The missions entity or synod may attach mission work to an existing presbytery, with the presbytery's approval.

The following presbyteries voted in the affirmative: Arkansas, Columbia, Covenant, Cumberland, del Cristo, East Tennessee, Grace, Hong Kong, Japan, Missouri, Murfreesboro, Nashville, North Central, Red River, Robert Donnell, Tennessee-Georgia, Trinity, and West Tennessee.
The following presbytery voted in the negative: Hope.
The following presbytery did not report: Andes, Cauca Valley, Choctaw, East Coast and Emaus.

RECOMMENDATION 1: That the 188th General Assembly declare that the Constitutional Amendment has been approved.

V. THE CORPORATE BOARD

In the called meeting in December 2007, the General Assembly elected a new board of directors for the General Assembly Incorporation, thus the Corporate Board was formed. The responsibilities for the Corporate Board are listed in the General Assembly Bylaws, Article 5.

The Corporate Board met once this past year.

The Center Interagency Team (CIT) comprised of the Center's Principle Executive Officers, continues to be responsible for oversight of the day-to-day maintenance and property needs at the Denominational Center. Current CIT members include: Mike Sharpe (Office of the General Assembly), Robert Heflin (Board of Stewardship, Foundation and Benefits), Susan Gore (Historical Foundation), and Edith Old (Ministry Council). The Shared Services budget covers the cost for maintaining the Center offices and property (see page 122).

VI. ENDORSEMENTS FOR MODERATOR

The Reverend Jay Earheart-Brown, Nashville Presbytery and the Reverend Lisa Scott, North Central Presbytery have been endorsed as Moderator of the 188th General Assembly.

VII. MINUTES OF THE GENERAL ASSEMBLY

The Office of the General Assembly continues to make the minutes of the General Assembly available on a CD, and mailing them to persons requesting them. The resource center also prints and sells a few printed copies of the General Assembly Minutes each year. For information contact Matthew Gore, mhg@cumberland.org. It is permissible to download and print a copy of the minutes from the website (www.cumberland.org/gao).

VIII. STATISTICAL INFORMATION

The annual congregational report forms are sent to the session clerk on December 1, and due in the office of the Stated Clerk of the Presbytery on February 1, and all reports are to be in the Office of the General Assembly by February 10.

In 2017 a hundred and eighty-one congregations failed to report, thus statistics are not accurate. The statistics for a non-reporting congregation may be several years old, but it is the latest information available. The General Assembly Office continues to shorten and simplify the reporting process. Efforts also continue to further simplify online reporting for those able to utilize the technology. Hard copies of the report forms will still be made available for those congregations who do not have access to the internet.

The 178th and 179th General Assembly directed "that each presbytery request that its Board of Missions or similar agency, as they minister to the needs of the churches within their presbyteries, remind the churches that it is important that they submit annual reports which are part of our history and offer assistance when needed in preparation of these reports." If a congregation fails to receive a report, a duplicate form can be requested from the Office of the General Assembly or one may be printed from the web site (www.cumberland.org/gao), and going to the section on congregational reports.

Compiled statistical information is available in the annual Yearbook available online (www.cumberland.org/gao) or in print format, available through Cumberland Resource Distribution – resources@cumberland.org (901-276-4581)

VIII. CHURCH CALENDAR 2018-2019

The 182nd General Assembly, directed the Office of the General Assembly to be responsible for reporting the "Church Calendar" to the General Assembly for adoption. Listed below are the dates received from the Boards and Agencies of the denomination.

RECOMMENDATION 2: That the 188th General Assembly approve the following dates for the 2018-2019 Church Calendar:

CHURCH CALENDAR 2018-2019

July-2018
7	Program of Alternate Studies Graduation
7-21	PAS Summer Extension School, Bethel, McKenzie, Tennessee
14	Children's Fest
14	Middle Schooler's Event
21	Children's Fest East

August-2018
4	Bethel University Commencement
5-Sept 30	Christian Education Season
19	Seminary/PAS Sunday
20	Bethel University Fall Semester Begins

25	MTS Fall Semester Begins *(tentative)*
28	MTS Opening convocation *(tentative)*
30	Bethel University Spring Convocation

September-2018
9	Family Sunday
9	Senior Adult Sunday
16	Christian Service Recognition Sunday
16	International Day of Prayer and Action for Human Habitat

October-2018
	Clergy Appreciation Month
7	Worldwide Communion Sunday
7	Pastor Appreciation Sunday
21	Native American Sunday

November-2018
	Any Sunday Loaves and Fishes Program
1	All Saints Day
2	World Community Day (Church Women United)
4	Bethel University Sunday
4	Stewardship Sunday
11	Day of Prayer for People with Aids and Other Life-Threatening Illnesses
18	Bible Sunday
25	Christ the King Sunday

December-2018
	Any Sunday Gift to the King Offering
2-24	Advent in Church and Home
8	Bethel University Commencement
24	Christmas Eve
25	Christmas Day

January-2019
6	Epiphany
7	BU Spring Semester Begins
7	Human Trafficking Awareness Day
7-8	Stated Clerks' Conference
15	Deadline for receipt of 2018 Our United Outreach Contributions

February-2019
	Black History Month
1	Annual congregational reports due in General Assembly office
3	Denomination Day
3	Historical Foundation Offering
3	Souper Bowl Sunday
10	Our United Outreach Sunday
17	Youth Sunday

March-2019
	Women's History Month (USA)
6	Ash Wednesday, the beginning of Lent
6–April 21	Lent to Easter
14	Palm/Passion Sunday
17	Children's Home Sunday
24-30	National Farm Workers Awareness Week

April-2019
18   Maundy Thursday
19   Good Friday
21   Easter

May-2019
3   Friendship Day (Church Women United)
5   Bethel University Commencement
12   MTS Closing Convocation & Graduation
27   Memorial Day Offering for Military Chaplains & Personnel for USA churches

June-2019
9   Stott-Wallace Missionary Fund Offering/World penMission Sunday
9   Pentecost
16   CPC Ministries Sunday
10-14 General Assembly, Huntsville, Alabama
11-13 CPWM Convention, Huntsville, Alabama
23   Unification Sunday
23-28 Cumberland Presbyterian Youth Conference, Bethel University, McKenzie, Tennessee

July-2019
6   Children's Fest
6   Middle Schooler's Event
7   Outdoor Ministries Sunday
13   Program of Alternate Studies Graduation
13-27 PAS Summer Extension School, Bethel, McKenzie, Tennessee
16-20 Presbyterian Youth Triennium

August-2019
4   Bethel University Commencement
4-Sept 30 Christian Education Sunday & Season
18   MTS Fall Semester Begins *(tentative)*
22   Seminary/PAS Sunday
22   Bethel University Fall Semester Begins
25   MTS Fall Semester Begins *(tentative)*
28   MTS Opening convocation *(tentative)*
30   Bethel University Spring Convocation

September-2019
4   MTS Opening convocation *(tentative)*
8   Family Sunday
8   Senior Adult Sunday
15   Christian Service Recognition Sunday
15   International Day of Prayer and Action for Human Habitat

October-2019
      Clergy Appreciation Month
6   Worldwide Communion Sunday
6   Pastor Appreciation Sunday
20   Native American Sunday

November-2019
      Any Sunday Loaves and Fishes Program
1   All Saints Day
1   World Community Day (Church Women United)
3   Bethel University Sunday
3   Stewardship Sunday
10   Day of Prayer for People with Aids and Other Life-Threatening Illnesses
17   Bible Sunday
24   Christ the King Sunday

December-2019

	Any Sunday Gift to the King Offering
2	PAS Advisory Council
2-24	Advent in Church and Home
8	Bethel University Commencement
24	Christmas Eve
25	Christmas Day

XI. CONTINGENCY FUND

The Stated Clerk is to hold, distribute and report annually the General Assembly Contingency Fund (see Bylaws 8.04, #24). Below is a summary Contingency Fund Activity for the 2017 Calendar Year.

Summary of 2017 Activity

Balance Forward 1/1/2017 $ 50,453.06

Income in 2017:
    Our United Outreach/Contributions $ 10,990.00
    Interest   1,423.79
    Total Income: **$ 12,413.79**

Expenditures in 2017:
    Bethel University Covenant Review Committee $ 201.45
    Children's Home Covenant Review Committee $ 879.71
    Total Expenses: **$ 1,051.16**

Total Fund Balance as of 12/31/17 $ 61,815.69

*Restricted Funds:

     $ 4,100.00   The current balance designated by the 178th General Assembly to print the Catechism in the various languages represented in the church.

     1,011.51   Pastoral Development Ministry Team/General Assembly Ordination Task Force

Total Amount of *Restricted Funds: $ 5,111.51 (12/31/17)

Total Amount of Unrestricted Amount: $ 56,704.18 (12/31/17)

Total Fund Balance: $ 61,815.69 (12/31/17)

Respectfully submitted,
Michael Sharpe, Stated Clerk

THE REPORT OF THE MINISTRY COUNCIL

To the 188th General Assembly of the Cumberland Presbyterian Church meeting in session at the Embassy Suites and Conference Center, in Norman, Oklahoma on June 17-21, 2018.

I. MINISTRY COUNCIL

A. INTRODUCTION

The Ministry Council (MC) serves as the primary long- and short-range program planning agency of the Church, striving to ensure that all segments work on a unified mission and human and material resources are utilized to carry out ministries of the Church in an effective manner. The Ministry Council is accountable to the General Assembly (GA).

Due to the scope of the work related to denominational ministries under the MC, our report has historically been quite lengthy, necessitating the division of the report to multiple GA committees. At the urging of the Stated Clerk, and with the intention of providing crucial information in a concise manner, we made significant changes to our report format last year. This condensed report focuses on recommendations to the GA. A more detailed annual report of the work of the MC and Ministry Teams is available to commissioners and guests at this GA and on our web page *https://cpcmc.org/mc/ga18-supplement/*. We encourage commissioners and others to visit the Ministry Council booth to meet elected members and staff and to share ideas for enhancing ministries.

1. Ministry Council (MC) Elected Membership and Terms

MC elected members are subject to GA requirements of endorsement by presbytery (clergy) or church (laity), as well as geographical (synodic) and gender representation. It is our belief that God calls people from across the denomination to serve in leadership roles, and that the limited number of Personal Data Forms and related endorsements on file in the Office of General Assembly does not reflect the abundance of qualified leaders within the Church. The Ministry Council respectfully reminds all Commissioners of an action of the 186th General Assembly that urged each presbytery ***"to proactively recruit and encourage qualified leaders to prayerfully consider opportunities to serve as elected board members at the denominational level, to include the Ministry Council and all other denominational entities."***

The terms of Ken Bean, Reverend Kenny Butcher, Reverend Phillip Layne, Reverend Ron McMillan and Victory Moore expire in 2018. All are eligible for an additional term of service. The one-year term of Youth Advisory Member, LeighAnne Morgan, concludes with this General Assembly. She is eligible for a second one-year term. The terms of Youth Advisory Members, Mr. Cameron Alderson and Ms. Charli Uhlrich, conclude with this General Assembly. Having served two one-year terms, Alderson and Uhlrich are ineligible for an additional one-year term. We express appreciation to Mr. Alderson and Ms. Ulrich for their service. The Ministry Council is the only denominational entity board with Youth Advisory Members.

2. Ministry Teams plan and implement the program ministries of the Church and are made up of both Staff and Elected Team Members. Ministry Teams report to the Ministry Council. **Elected Team Members** are elected by the MC and reflect the GA model to ensure representation among gender, laity and clergy.

Communications Ministry Team (CMT) elected member Reverend Jim McGuire and Reverend Dr. Michael Clark have both completed three terms of service. The CMT and Ministry Council are grateful for their wisdom and institutional knowledge which will be sorely missed. At its February 2018 meeting, the Ministry Council elected Reverend Nathaniel Mathews to replace Reverend Michael Clark. It is hoped that prior to General Assembly another individual will be elected to fill the position vacated by Reverend Jim McGuire.

Discipleship Ministry Team (DMT) elected member, Joanna Wilkinson, completed three terms. DMT and the Ministry Council are grateful for her creativity and generous spirit. The term of Reverend Christian Smith is complete and he has asked not to be re-elected due to work demands. We thank Christian for his thoughtful insights and wonderful team attitude. At its February 2018 meeting, the Ministry Council re-elected Rachel Cook who has completed two terms. The Council also elected Ean Taylor to replace Joanna Wilkinson and Candy Barr to replace Reverend Christian Smith.

Missions Ministry Team (MMT) elected member Sherry Poteet completed three terms. MMT and the Council appreciates the energy and enthusiasm she imbued into the work of the MMT. At its February

2018 meeting, the Council elected Margie Shannon to replace Sherry Poteet, and re-elected Reverend Cardelia Howell-Diamond and Melinda Reams who both completed two terms. The Council also elected Ollie McClung to serve on the MMT.

The Council re-elected Reverend Duawn Mearns who completed two terms on the **Pastoral Development Ministry Team (PDMT)**. Reverend Linda Snelling completed three terms on PDMT. The Council is grateful for her wisdom and vision for the work of PDMT. The Council elected Reverend Lisa Anderson to replace Reverend Linda Snelling and Paul Earheart-Brown to replace Reverend Drew Hayes who resigned due to work demands.

The Ministry Council elects Ministry Team members in accordance with General Assembly requirements that individuals have current personal data forms and recommendations from their presbytery (clergy) or pastor (laity) on file with the Stated Clerk prior to General Assembly. A complete list of Ministry Team members appears at *https://cpcmc.org/mc/*.

Staff Team Members are employees of the Ministry Council:
- **CMT**: Senior Art Director Sowgand Sheikholeslami and CMT Leader Mark J. Davis.
- **DMT**: Coordinator of Resource Development and Distribution Matt Gore; Coordinator of Adult Ministry Cindy Martin; Coordinator of Children and Family Ministry Jodi Hearn Rush (Nashville, Tennessee office); Coordinator of Youth and Young Adult Ministry Reverend Nathan Wheeler; and DMT Leader Reverend Elinor S. Brown. The Ministry Council, DMT staff and elected members mourned the loss of Shipping Clerk Greg Miller who died in December 2017. Greg was a familiar affable face at the CP Center, having worked here for longer than any other employee. Hired by Pat Owen when she was bookstore manager, Greg worked for Pat Owen, Pat White, Brenda Hooks, Frank Ward, and Elinor Brown, much of that time under the supervision of Matthew Gore. Greg will certainly be missed by the Center family as well as his many devoted friends.
- **MMT**: Coordinator for Women's Ministry and Congregational Ministry Reverend Pam Phillips-Burk; Cross-Culture Immigrant USA Ministry Reverend Johan Daza; Manager, Finance and Administration Jinger Ellis; Evangelism and New Church Development Reverend T. J. Malinoski; Bilingual English/Korean Administrative Assistant Julie Min; Director Global Missions Reverend Lynn Thomas (Birmingham, AL office); and MMT Leader Reverend Dr. Milton Ortiz.
- **PDMT**: PDMT Leader Reverend Charles R. "Chuck" Brown resigned in April 2017 for health reasons. The Ministry Council appreciates Chuck's passion for nurturing clergypersons and those considering their call to varied forms of ministry.

3. The **Global Ministries Leadership Team (GMLT)** is made up of the four Ministry Team Leaders and Director of Ministries. This body works together to apply the vision/mission of the MC to the many varied programs and resource materials planned and produced by the Ministry Teams, coordinating ministries in a unified, collaborative manner. GMLT meets monthly and minutes are disseminated to all members of the MC and Ministry Teams.

4. **Administration:** Director of Ministries Edith Busbee Old gives executive leadership to the MC in accomplishing duties defined by its Bylaws and supervises the GMLT. The Director of Ministries is under direct employment of and is responsible to the Ministry Council. The Council is grateful that Edith is globally minded without neglecting the stateside church and for her creative and consistent approach to inviting cooperation instead of conflict. Due to budget constraints, the Assistant to the Executive Director position remains vacant.

B. GENERAL INFORMATION
   1. Meetings: The MC met twice in regular session since the 187th General Assembly. A Summary of Action for meetings appears at *https://cpcmc.org/mc/soa/*.
   2. Future Meeting Dates: August 16, 2018 (Thursday) – Orientation for newly elected MC and newly elected Ministry Team Members at the Denominational Center, Cordova, Tennessee.
August 17–18, 2018 (Friday and Saturday) – MC and Teams meet concurrently at Faith Cumberland Presbyterian Church, Bartlett, TN (10 minutes from the Denominational Center).
February 16–17, 2019 (Saturday and Sunday) – MC Corporation Annual Meeting of the Board of Directors with Team Leaders and Director of Ministries at the Denominational Center.

3. Elected member accountability and training: Elected MC members and Ministry Team members receive orientation prior to their first MC/MT meeting. In 2016, we introduced a mentoring approach, partnering current MC members with newly elected members. Each year, all elected members sign a Covenant reinforcing their commitment to answering the call to serve God through service to the Church. Elected members set individual annual goals and complete annual self-evaluations reflecting on their service. These tools serve as metrics to help guide the MC and Ministry Teams. The MC Covenant may be seen at *https://cpcmc.org/mc/covenant/*.

4. Human Resources: When a staff position becomes vacant, the MC invests time in a thorough revision of that job description. Input is gathered from elected members, GMLT and relevant staff. Since the 187th General Assembly, the Council has prayerfully considered current and future ministries for all of its four ministry teams. Two of its teams, Communications and Pastoral Development, experienced staff changes resulting in the need for the Council to painstakingly review and revise job descriptions. The PDMT Leader position was vacant following the aforementioned resignation in April 2017. The Council worked with PDMT elected members and surveyed pastors at the 187th General Assembly to gather ideas for PDMT future ministry. At the February 2018 meeting the MC approved a revised job description and authorized the position to be advertised. It is hoped that the PDMT position will be filled prior to this General Assembly. At that same Ministry Council meeting, CMT Leader Mark J. Davis announced his plans to retire effective June 1, 2018. The Council incorporated ideas from the CMT elected members and revised the CMT Leader job description to focus on technology and also created a new CMT position, that of Publications Manager/Editor. As of this writing, applications are being accepted and it is hoped that both CMT positions will be filled prior to the 188th General Assembly.

5. The Ministry Council expresses its gratitude to Mark J. Davis for the leadership he provided in establishing the Ministry Council website, and its ongoing enhancements. Mark is to be commended for his constant efforts to ensure CPs around the world had access to current information relate to the Ministry Council and its many programs, resources and events. The Ministry Council and its staff wish blessings to Mark and his family as he begins writing this new chapter and he explores retirement.

6. Unification: The 187th General Assembly instructed boards and agencies listed in the Unification Task Force's revised plan to provide a report to the next General Assembly (188th) asking these boards and agencies to provide: 1.) Their ideas with respect to the best ways to implement unification within their board or agency, 2.) Their assessment explaining if their board or agency needs structural changes as part of unification and what those changes should be, and 3.) What the board or agency anticipates will be the approximate costs implementing unification and or restructure of their board or agency.

In mid-September 2017, the Ministry Council sent a communication to the Unification Task Force with questions regarding the proposed Revised Plan for the Union of the Cumberland Presbyterian Church and the Cumberland Presbyterian Church in America. Unfortunately, when the Ministry Council met in mid-February 2018, the UTF had not yet met and thus, hadn't responded to the Council's questions which are included as **Appendix A**.

7. The 187th General Assembly submitted the following questions to the Ministry Council to address, sample the local congregations, and report the results to the Ministry Council Committee of the 188th General Assembly and publish for the denomination to view for visioning on all church levels: 1) Where are the greatest opportunities for our congregations to thrive in the future that you see? 2) What do you see as the greatest threat(s) to continued, effective ministry in and through our congregations? 3) What can we do individually, collectively and institutionally to overcome these dangers?

The Ministry Council decided to collect the data through an online survey to increase responses and aid in data collection. We believe, for the most part, it was a good choice. We did however encounter some unexpected problems: there were a handful of people who apparently completed the survey more than once (duplicates were removed), the answer options had to be complex to allow for a variety of perspectives, but this also made analyzing the results complicated. The biggest problem was that the data between the various languages was not easy for us to combine and for that reason our report gives percentages for the English version and highlights the findings for Spanish, Korean and Japanese translations. A total of 366 responses were received: 286 English language responses, 76 Spanish and 4 Japanese. Two English language churches assisted individuals in their congregations to complete the survey on paper, sent those paper responses in and they were included in the 286 received. **The complete English language survey and results appear as Appendix B**.

The survey was translated into Japanese, Korean and Spanish and along with the English version made available on the MC website. Four individuals completed the Japanese translation, 76 individuals completed the Spanish translation and likely due to errors on our part, we did not collect data for the Korean translation. We noticed some statistical differences between respondents of the Spanish translation survey compared to those of the English translation.

1) According to respondents of the Spanish translation, the greatest opportunity that Cumberland Presbyterians currently see before them is small groups/Bible studies/Sunday school with more than 81% of respondents seeing an opportunity there. Three other items that were recognized as opportunities were leadership development, worship services, and personal evangelism which all with each receiving more than 71%. What this reveals is that discipleship and spiritual maturity are seen as essential elements to growing the church. As leaders develop more leaders the hope is more and more people can be reached. The most significant difference between the Spanish language respondents to English respondents is the opportunity of leadership development. English translation respondents did not identify it as being as great an opportunity. Japanese language survey respondents saw the greatest opportunities in small groups, Sunday worship and special services, 75% of respondents identifying these as opportunities. This indicates a belief that consistent discipleship with the right mix of special events will be beneficial to the local church.

2) Do you believe that the churches in your area are effective ministerially? This is essentially an approval rating of how churches in a particular area are doing when it comes to their effectiveness in ministry. When asked if they believe the churches in their area are ministerially effective, 81% felt like the churches in their area were at least somewhat effective. This is very encouraging news and means that there is a high degree of confidence and potential for these churches in the view of congregational leadership and membership. One concern is that only 14% of people felt like they congregations were absolutely effective with 43 % feeling they were mostly effective. These results should give us hope and also reveal a need for growth. The Japanese language survey respondents also believed the churches in their area were at least somewhat effective with 100% of respondents believing this. But only 25% felt like the churches in their area were absolutely effective. Going forward, these results should increase as we encourage churches to make use of the opportunities around them. It would be wise for all church leaders to ask their congregations specifically about ministerial effectiveness in order to better understand the feelings of their church. If people do not believe their church is ministerial effective they will most likely not be energized for evangelism and will eventually leave. If on the other hand, they believe their church is effective they cannot help but invite others to come and take part in its ministries!

3) What do you think are the greatest threats to achieve effective ministry in your area? (Respondents could select up to seven) By far the biggest threat identified by respondents in the Spanish language survey was the resource limitations of time with 75% of respondents seeing this as a threat. The next closest threats were the resource of limitations of money with 67% of respondents seeing this as a problem and spiritual development with 63% feeling this is a threat. When you have money and time concerns it becomes difficult to develop people spiritually because you end up having to focus on other things. It is worth noting that the English language respondents' major concern of an aging congregation was not much of a concern for the Spanish language survey respondents. The concern over resources discussed above was not seen as a significant threat for the English language respondents. This indicates that the threats identified are unique to the locations of participants and this should be acknowledged as solutions are developed. But we should remember that where challenges arise so does the opportunity for a daring faith which relies on God as we minister in these times.

4) What can we do as individuals, congregations and a denomination to address the threats we face? The three main solutions that were offered to help address the threats that we face were pray, develop leaders, and engage members in ministry. Of these three prayer and engaging members in ministry both scored high with 88% respondents identifying prayer and 79% identifying developing leaders as potential solutions. Another 72% believed involving more members was a solution. These results are very similar to the English and Japanese language surveys. The only difference is the continued identification of the need for leadership development. This reveals a desire for congregations to seek God's aid in ministry and to develop stronger leaders capable of doing this. There were also many other options chosen and they have been listed above and would benefit from closer examination. These results speak to the strain respondents feel as they serve and have an ever increasing number of responsibilities coming their way. These results should cause every church to consider how they best might provide help to their leaders and members who are giving so much of their time and talents to the kingdom of God.

Although we completed it imperfectly we believe making the survey available in the four most common languages of Cumberland Presbyterians was the best choice and would encourage the denomination to do the same for any future surveys. Having the survey online also allowed a large variety of people to respond and effectively eliminated expenses.

Ministry Council elected members Reverend Kenny Butcher (pastorkenny@brushhillchurch.org) and Reverend Troy Green (petersburgpreacher@att.net) were survey managers and are glad to discuss the survey and its results with anyone might want to look at the original data or have questions.

II. MINISTRIES

A. PARAMETERS

The MC created "**Parameters to Guide the Work of Our Ministry Teams**" as a standard for all work done by the Ministry Teams. Parameters appear on the MC website *https://cpcmc.org/mc/mt-work-params/*.

B. CMT

The Communications Ministry Team continues to explore ways to use technology not only as a means to support our denomination's connectional nature, but in an effort to ensure that we are being the best stewards of our resources that we can be. Working in partnership with the other ministry teams, CMT provides support for website management, audio/visual services, social networking platforms, and web-based application support and consulting. In addition to its responsibilities around editing and publishing THE CUMBERLAND PRESBYTERIAN magazine and the annual Program Planning Calendar, the team also manages the dissemination of time-sensitive news and information via News of the Church. The team's Senior Art Director, Sowgand Sheikholeslami, provides layout and design support for numerous projects and programs related to the ministries of the church.

C. DMT

The Cumberland Presbyterian Constitution recognizes that "God has given different gifts to ministers of the word and sacrament and the Church recognizes various types of ministry … not only as pastors of particular churches but as teachers of religion in various kinds of schools, editors of religious publications, chaplains to the military forces and to various types of institutions, missionaries, evangelists, counselors, administrators of church programs and institutions, directors of Christian education in particular churches and as leaders in other fields of service directly related to the church." (2.64 Constitution, *Confession of Faith*)

The Cumberland Presbyterian Church has a long-standing history of helping people to discern their calls. There is a need to recognize that "pulpit ministry," or "lead pastor in charge," are not the only calls to Christian ministry. Calls to ministries with youth, calls to Christian Educators, calls to serve as Associate Pastors, calls to serve in urban ministries or to social justice, calls to serve as missionaries are all unique and valid calls and within those calls there are times when these ministers are called to serve the sacraments and to have a voice in the Church's judicatories.

The Constitution 6.34 gives presbyteries a means to allow individuals to serve the Church more effectively and with excellence. It also provides individuals who feel called to receive biblical and theological training, knowledge of Cumberland Presbyterian structure and resources, skill development, support, and accountability.

The Constitution 6.34 can help the CPC better recognize that an individual who has a particular call, is willing to serve Christ's Church and has made a commitment to fulfill the required standards for academic training, experience, and continuing study needed to serve with excellence in a particular area of ministry is also a minister of Word and Sacrament.

The late Phyllis Tickle asserted that every 500 years or so the Church has a "rummage sale." Historically, every 500 years there is a critical change or shift in history that necessitates the Church "going through its 'stuff'" and reevaluating what it keeps and what it lets go. The Church is shifting. The need for pulpit ministers is still very real; but as the Church shifts so too must we see the ministry of Word and Sacrament in a broader way than when the Digest interpreted Constitution 6.34 more narrowly. The Cumberland Presbyterian Church offers two routes to ordination: a Master's of Divinity and a certificate from the Program of Alternate Studies. Interpreting the Constitution to include this third route to ordination would encourage persons called to ministry outside of the pulpit and would enrich the Church by equipping persons in various specialized areas of ministry to serve. It would also recognize the shift of paradigm in the Church and our desire to shift with it.

RECOMMENDATION 1: That the 188th General Assembly interpret the phrase "a degree in a graduate school of theology" Constitution 6.34 to be inclusive of Master's degrees in other forms of Christian ministry (for example MA Youth Ministry, MA Christian Ministry) and not restricted to Master of Divinity.

D. MISSIONS

The purpose of the Missions Ministry Team is to serve and equip Cumberland Presbyterian congregations and judicatories in pursuing God's mission of redemption and reconciliation. Specifically, MMT facilitates those phases of the Church's mission that are concerned with outreach in terms of evangelism and the establishing of congregations, and other means of Christian witness in the US and around the world.

MMT focuses on five areas: Women's Ministries, Evangelism and New Church Development, Cross-Culture Immigrant Ministries, Global Missions, and Compassion and Advocacy Ministries.

Last year a modification of MMT's meeting was made to provide the necessary time for elected members and staff to work in two areas: Global Missions and Church Development Innovation (US). MMT is one team, but its meetings are divided into two groups/sections.

Global Missions consists of four "ordained" people (there must be at least one ordained elder and pastor in the global group) elected by the Ministry Council (nominated by staff) and assigned by MMT to global missions. They function as the mission committee (presbytery judicatory) and as a brainstorming and discussion group. Its members are expected to be knowledgeable about missiological concepts. They gather to learn missiological concepts, hear reports, discuss concerns, act on judicatory needs, provide counsel and insights, hear about missionary needs and challenges, brain-storm, discuss fund raising for missions, etc. MMT invites liaisons and other people from outside the US to attend the Global Missions group meeting to provide information.

Church Development and Innovation (US) consists of four people elected by the Ministry Council (nominated by MMT staff) and assigned by MMT to Church Development and Innovation (US). They function as a brainstorming and discussion group. Its members are expected to be knowledgeable about church development and innovation concepts. They gather to learn about successful development of new and existing churches, hear reports, discuss concerns, provide counsel and insights, hear about needs and challenges, brain-storm, discuss fund raising for church development, etc. MMT invites church planters, liaisons, and other people to attend the Church Development and Innovation (US) group meeting to provide additional information.

Both groups/sections have joint MMT meetings where all present hear reports on different MMT programs, staff reports, or shared event planning meetings. However the two groups spend most of their time in their separate meetings. MMT retreats and workshops will use the two group format. Obviously there should be flexibility and the two groups can spend more time in joint meetings as needs dictate. Communications about global issues and judicatory actions is only with the global mission group, not the entire MMT. The global group can have global group meetings when necessary at a time and place determined by the MMT Leader, including video conferencing.

III. FUNDING

Since the inception of the "new structure" in 2007, the Ministry Council and its Ministry Teams have shared in planning new and ongoing ministries. Each year the collegial environment has grown stronger, enabling the reality of a truly comprehensive budget. Funding sources include Our United Outreach, donations, grants, Investment Loan Program (ILP) and endowments (listed within Board of Stewardship section of the preliminary minutes). The endowment program is an important part of our funding, though endowments do not generate usable funds until they reach sufficient size to generate interest payments that can be used.

Ministry Council and Ministry Teams hope donors will contribute directly to programs of the Church, thus providing much needed funds to meet immediate programming needs.

IV. MINISTRY COUNCIL CONCLUSION

The 52 MC/Ministry Team elected and advisory members and 17 staff members are committed to serving as conduits of information to and from the Council. We remain committed to serving God through the CPC and ask that the Church remain in prayer for our collaborative work.

We are thankful for the sustaining guidance of the Holy Spirit as we work to enhance and implement ministries that draw people to Christ. We encourage 188th General Assembly Commissioners and guests to visit the MC booth. We encourage you to pick up materials to share with your congregation, groups and presbytery. MC/Ministry Team staff and elected members serve as booth hosts and are eager to listen to your ideas and answer questions.

Not unlike other denominations, ours is an aging denomination. We yearn to see Cumberland Presbyterians of all generations serving in leadership roles throughout the Church. We yearn for Cumberland Presbyterians everywhere to commit to actively sharing in the work of the Church, for leaders to rise up from across the globe to further the work of the Church around the world as we say together, Send Me.

Respectfully Submitted,

The Ministry Council of the Cumberland Presbyterian Church
Reverend Mike Wilkinson, President
Reverend Donny Acton, First Vice President
Ken Bean, Second Vice President
Victory Davidsmeier Moore, Secretary
Edith B. Old, Director of Ministries/Treasurer

MINISTRY COUNCIL APPENDICES

(Appendix A)

Questions for the Unification Task Force from the Ministry Council of the Cumberland Presbyterian Church regarding the proposed Revised Plan for the Union of the Cumberland Presbyterian Church and the Cumberland Presbyterian Church in America

Names:
If the current Plan for Union is enacted, the Ministry Council of the Cumberland Presbyterian Church (hereafter referred to as simply the Ministry Council) is uncertain if we will be legally dissolved or if the chartered and legal name of the Ministry Council will merely be changed to the Mission Program Agency of the Cumberland Presbyterian Church United.

The same uncertainty exists about the current Ministry Teams of the Ministry Council; will each team be legally dissolved or merely have their names legally changed (Discipleship Ministry Team to Christian Education and Nurture; Missions Ministry Team to Missions; Pastoral Development Ministry Team to Clergy Care and Development; and, Communications Ministry Team to Communications)?

Question #1: Can the Unification Task Force clarify the two-abovementioned issues before submitting a final Plan for Union? Their resolution is not merely a preference of name, but could require a new charter from the State of Tennessee and possibly an additional charter from the State of Alabama and other states given the creation of three to five new regional office sites instead of a singular denominational center.

The Ministry Council is concerned that by calling all the work of the new Church missions — as implied by the name Mission Programing Agency—that the distinctive and traditional emphasis on missions, outreach, cross-culture ministries, church growth, and church planting will be gradually diluted. Our concern is that when all things become "missions", nothing becomes missions.

Question #2: Before submitting a final Plan for Union, will the Unification Task Force consider changing the name of the new programing/ministry agency to Ministry Program Agency thus giving distinction of purpose to the newly created Missions entity?

Board Makeup:
The Ministry Council currently has fifteen (15) elected/voting members—three (3) from each of the five (5) Synods of the Cumberland Presbyterian Church elected by General Assembly—and five (5) advisory members—the sitting Moderator of the General Assembly, the Stated Clerk of the General Assembly, and three (3) Youth Advisory Members elected by General Assembly. If the current Plan for Union is enacted, it calls for sixteen (16) members (one staff employee from each ministry entity (i.e., Missions); one elected member from each ministry entity—assumed by the Ministry Council to mean from the elected Ministry Team members of each ministry entity, though these positions are not mentioned specifically anywhere in the current Plan for Union; and one elected member from each of the eight Synods of the Cumberland Presbyterian Church United—assumed to mean elected by General Assembly; to serve as its governing board. (Ministry Council members are elected by General Assembly; Ministry Team members are elected by the Ministry Council.)

The Ministry Council is concerned about the proposed new structure because it would mean that staff would be serving on the governing board that has oversight of the work of the staff and is responsible for the hiring of staff. This is one of the reasons behind dissolving the General Assembly Council of the Cumberland Presbyterian Church and establishing the current Ministry Council back in 2007.

Question #3: Before submitting a final Plan for Union, will the Unification Task Force consider changing the membership makeup of the governing board of the Mission (preferred Ministry) Program Agency to reflect that no staff member/employee of the new united denomination be allowed to serve as an elected/voting member on its governing board while they are employed by the new denomination?

Question #4: Before submitting a final Plan for Union, will the Unification Task Force consider changing the membership makeup of the governing board of the Mission (preferred Ministry) Program Agency so that is consists of sixteen (16) elected members —two (2) from each of the eight newly created Synods—and six (6) Advisory Members—the sitting Moderator of the new General Assembly, the Stated Clerk of the new General Assembly, the Associate Stated Clerk of the new General Assembly, and three (3) Youth Advisory Members elected by General Assembly?

Question #5: Before submitting a final Plan for Union, can the Unification Task Force clarify as to whether or not the new programing/ministry entities will continue to have elected Ministry Team members. If the answer to this question is "yes", then the Ministry Council requests that before submitting a final Plan for Union, the Unification Task Force clarify the new role of these elected Ministry Team members. If the answer to this question is that there will be no more elected Ministry Team members, then in order to increase representation of the Church-at-large in the programing/ministry of the new denomination, that our previous question be amended to read: Before submitting a final Plan for Union, will the Unification Task Force consider changing the membership makeup of the governing board of the Mission (preferred Ministry) Program Agency so that is consists of twenty-four (24) elected members—three (3) from each of the eight newly created Synods—and six (6) Advisory Members—the sitting Moderator of the new General Assembly, the Stated Clerk of the new General Assembly, the Associate Stated Clerk of the new General Assembly, and three (3) Youth Advisory Members elected by General Assembly?

Denominational Staff and Personnel:

The current Plan for Union both calls for the elimination of the position of Director of Ministries and for the creation of the new position of Ministry Coordinator. The Ministry Council assumes that this is a name change only and that the Ministry Coordinator will be an employee of the Mission (preferred Ministry) Program Agency. The current Plan for Union states that duties and parameters of the Ministry Coordinator "and the corresponding selection process will be determined during the Implementation Phase and detailed in the Standing Rules." If the new Mission (preferred Ministry) Program Agency is to be legally chartered in the either of the State of Tennessee and/or the State of Alabama, the executive head of the Mission (prefer Ministry) Program Agency must be hired by its governing board and not elected/selected by the new General Assembly. At least, that was the legal advice given at the time of the formation of the current Ministry Council.

Question #6: Before submitting a final Plan for Union, will the Unification Task Force consider including language that clearly states that the Ministry Coordinator is hired by and reports to the Mission (preferred Ministry) Program Agency of the Cumberland Presbyterian Church United?

Cumberland Presbyterian Digest:

The "Cumberland Presbyterian Digest" and "Summary of Actions" consist of General Assembly advisories and interpretations containing to the *Constitution*, *Rules of Discipline*, and *Rules of Order* for both the Cumberland Presbyterian Church and the Cumberland Presbyterian Church in America. The current Plan for Union states that both of these compilations will continue serve as "resource tools" for the new united denomination and that "A new *Digest* will begin with the formation of the Cumberland Presbyterian Church United." With due respect to the Unification Task Force, the Ministry Council would prefer stronger wording regarding previous General Assembly rulings and interpretations.

Question #7: Before submitting a final Plan for Union, will the Unification Task Force consider including a statement that says that all previous General Assembly ruling and interpretations currently contained in the "Cumberland Presbyterian Digest" will remain valid for the new united denomination until and unless a future General Assembly of the Cumberland Presbyterian Church United renders a new ruling and/or interpretation on a previous ruling and/or interpretation?

Question #8: Before submitting a final Plan for Union, will the Unification Task Force consider including language that says that all previous theological statements/opinions issued by General Assembly of either denomination will remain valid for the new united denomination until and unless a future General Assembly of the Cumberland Presbyterian Church United issues a different theological statement/ opinion?

Funding:
The current Plan of Union does not address the funding of the new Missions (preferred Ministry) Program Agency of the newly created Cumberland Presbyterian Church United. With the addition of a staff position within the Office of General Assembly, how might *Our United Outreach* percentages for all remaining denominational entities be affected?

Question #9: Before submitting a final Plan for Union, will the Unification Task Force include details regarding the method of funding for the work of the newly created Mission (preferred Ministry) Program Agency of the Cumberland Presbyterian Church United.

Respectfully submitted,
Reverend Mike Wilkinson
President of the Ministry Council of the Cumberland Presbyterian Church

After the Ministry Council approved the above questions, they were submitted to our Ministry Teams Leaders and the Director of Global Cross-Culture Missions Program Lynn Thomas to obtain insight from those "on the front line" of ministry. Their comments/questions may be helpful to the Unification Task Force; hence, their inclusion in this document.

Comment #1: A Board of 30 people is BIG. Too Big?
This comment relates to above listed Question #5 under Board Makeup. The Ministry Council's preference is for structure of the elected Ministry Teams to remain intact and the makeup of the new board be the one listed in Question #4 (16 elected members and 6 advisory members) under Board Makeup.

Comment #2: The ministry agency would initially be chartered where? As new offices are opened in other states, would those offices be chartered in those states? Typically, such charters require boards within those specific states - multiple boards?
These questions relate to above listed Question #1 under Names.

Comment #3: The ministry agency board would need representation from the mission field under the care of the MMT -- whose synod is the Permanent Judiciary Committee.
This question is not covered in the above listed questions, but relates to the proposed Constitutional Amendment being recommended by the Permanent Judiciary Committee.

Comment #4: The ministry agency will need a director as well as the ability to establish the teams it determines are needed to conduct the ministry of the church. These teams will have team leaders. Teams will need to be formed and dissolved as needed.
This question relates to Question #6 under Denominational Staff and Personnel

**SURVEY OF OPPORTUNITIES AND THREATS BEFORE
THE CUMBERLAND PRESBYTERIAN CHURCH**

(Appendix B)

A. What are the great opportunities for growth or success that you see in the churches in your area?

Ministry for special needs groups (children, the elderly, people with disabilities)	162	43.8%
Leadership development	115	31.1%
Ministry with communities in need	213	57.6%
Personal evangelism	137	37.0%

Small groups/Bible studies/Sunday school	182	49.2%
Worship services/preaching	168	45.4%
Special events	135	36.5%
Revival services or evangelism	57	15.4%

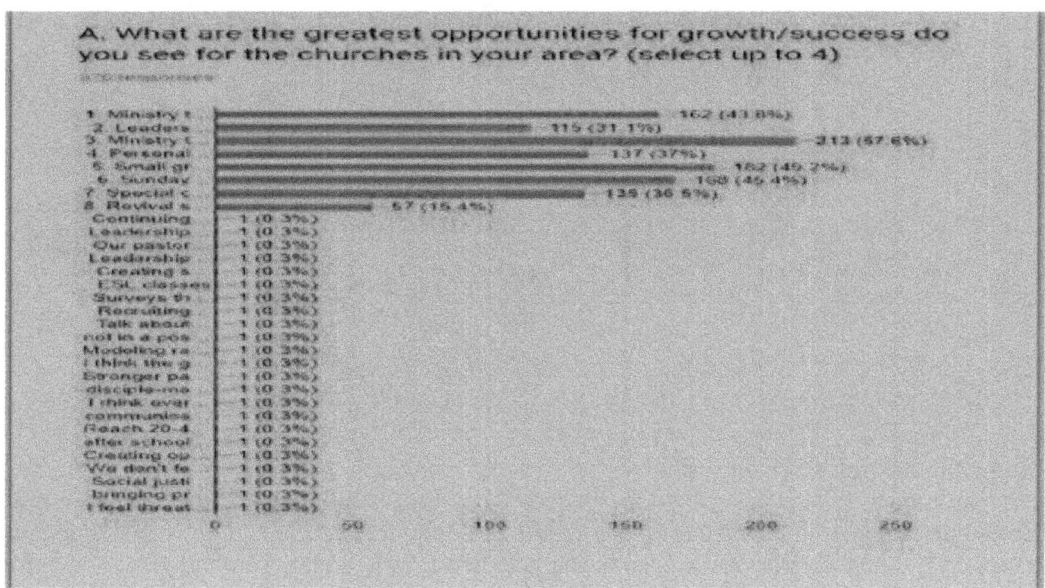

(Respondents could select up to four) The greatest opportunity that Cumberland Presbyterians who completed the English version currently see before them is Ministry to community needs with more than 57% of respondents choosing it. The second greatest opportunity identified was small groups/Bible Studies/Sunday school with almost 50% of respondents seeing an opportunity there. Two other items that were recognized as opportunities were ministry to special needs groups and Sunday worship services/preaching with each receiving more than 43%. What this reveals is that the majority of people see value in ongoing ministry that meet real life needs, grows disciples, and brings people to Christ. Revivals, special church events, leadership development, and personal evangelism all had a significant showing as well but when taken together it is clear that intentional discipleship within the church and on-going ministry to the community is where most people see the largest opportunities going forward.

B. Do you believe that the churches in your area are effective ministerially?	Of a total of 366 total respondents
No	8.6%
A little	11.1%
Most, yes	28.4%
Some	45.1%
Absolutely	6.8%

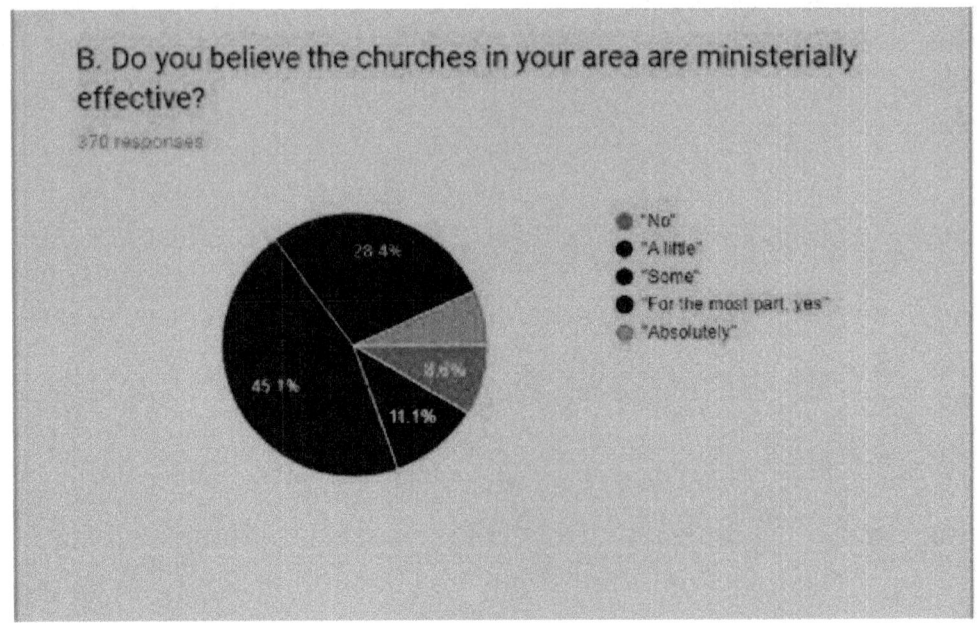

This is essentially an approval rating of how churches in a particular area are doing when it comes to their effectiveness in ministry. When asked if they believe the churches in your area are ministerially effective, 80.3% felt like the churches in their area were at least somewhat effective. This is very encouraging news and means that there is a high degree of confidence and potential for these church in the view of congregational leadership and membership. One concern is that the largest number of people felt like their congregations were only somewhat effective with 45.1% feeling this way. Only 6.8% felt like the congregations near them were absolutely effective and 28.4% felt they were effective for the most part. This means that of the 366 respondents, only 35% believe the congregations near them are for the most part effective. These results should concern us but also give us hope. As we encourage churches to make use of the opportunities around them going forward these results should increase. It would be wise for all church leaders to ask their congregations specifically about ministerially effectiveness in order to better understand the feelings of their church. If people do not believe their church is ministerial effective they will most likely not be energized for evangelism and will eventually leave. If on the other hand, they believe their church is effective they cannot help but invite others to come and take part in its ministries!

C. What do you think are the greatest threats to achieve effective ministries in your area?

	Results	
Demographic problems limited or descending population	69	18.6%
Demographic problems of economic disruption	35	9.5%
Demographic geographical location problems	36	9.7%
Demographics: contrast between the membership and the surrounding community	101	27.3%
Resources: limited money	116	31.4%
Resources: few facilities	37	10.0%
Resources: people have no time	125	33.8%
Membership: aging membership	254	68.6%
Membership: disinterest towards ministry outside the church	118	31.9%
Membership: poor spiritual development or Christian maturity	68	18.4%

Membership does not use the spiritual gifts	90	24.3%
Membership not involved in the ministry	148	40.0%
Leadership: inadequate vision of the ministry	60	16.2%
Leadership without passion or motivation	68	18.4%
Leadership without planning or organization	40	10.8%
Leadership involved in ethical problems	21	5.7%
Leadership: insufficient leadership for the tasks of the churches	83	22.4%
Leadership changed or burned out	98	26.5%
Cultural disinterest in God or faith	97	26.2%
Cultural moral relativism, points of view that resist the belief in absolute truths	59	15.9%
Cultural materialism, yearning for prosperity	55	14.9%
Cultural government restrictions	4	1.1%
Cultural negative vision of the concept of church	95	25.7%

(Respondents could select up to seven) By far the biggest threat identified by respondents in this survey was membership issue of an aging membership with more than 68.6% of respondents seeing this as a threat. The next closest threat was members not being engaged in ministry with 40% of respondents seeing this as a problem. It seems that these two issues are connected because aging congregations lead to less member engaging in ministry because of natural limitations that come with age. This is a very troubling trend that and one that if left unaddressed will have a major negative impact on the denomination as a whole. There were a number of other threats that compile these problems such as resource limitations (33.8%) which come from shrinking congregations and demographic contrast (27%) between membership and the community. All of these lead to the same results of an aging and shrinking congregation. This also has led to another threat of members becoming less interested in people outside of the church which 32% of respondents reported. This has also led to another danger that has been reported which is burnout. These taken together with the cultural threats of a culture less interested in God/faith and a negative view of the church could discourage even the most optimistic person, but where challenges arise so does the opportunity for a daring faith which relies on God and ourselves as we minister in these times.

D. What can we do as individuals, congregations, and a denomination to address the threats we face?

	Results	
Pray	286	77.0%
Develop Leaders	215	58.1%
Involve more members in the ministry	264	71.4%

The three main solutions that were offered to help address the threats that we face were pray, develop leaders, and engage members in ministry. Of these three prayer and engaging members in ministry both scored high with more than 71% of respondents identifying these as potential solutions. Another 58% believed developing leaders was a solution. This reveals a desire for congregations to seek God's aid in ministry and to seek the aid of their fellow church members. Both of these speak to the strain respondents feel as they serve and have an ever increasing number of responsibilities coming their way. These results should cause every church to consider how they best might provide help to their leaders and members who are giving so much of their time and talents to the kingdom of God.

THE REPORT OF THE BOARD OF STEWARDSHIP, FOUNDATION, AND BENEFITS

I. GENERAL INFORMATION

A. BOARD MEETINGS AND ORGANIZATION

The Board of Stewardship, Foundation and Benefits under the direction of its officers, President Randy Davidson, Vice-president Mike St. John, Secretary Debbie Shelton, and Treasurer Robert Heflin, met two times in regular session.

B. BOARD MEMBERS WHOSE TERMS EXPIRE

Members whose terms expire at the 2018 General Assembly, with their years of service, are as follows: Jim Shannon, three years and Mike St. John, six years. Board member Andy Frazier passed away in October 2017, and board member Sue Rice, decided to resign. Jim Shannon and Mike St. John are eligible for another term and have agreed to serve. We want to thank them for their service and dedication to the Board of Stewardship, Foundation and Benefits. We would also like to thank Andy Frazier for his service and remember his family.

C. BOARD REPRESENTATIVE TO THE 187TH GENERAL ASSEMBLY

The board's representative to the 187th General Assembly is Randy Davidson.

D. STAFF

Kathryn Gilbert Craig serves as Administrative Assistant, Mark Duck serves as Coordinator of Benefits and Robert Heflin serves as Executive Secretary.

E. 2019 BUDGET

The 2019 line-item budget has been filed with the Office of the General Assembly. (see page 118)

F. 2017 AUDIT

Certified copies of the 2017 audit reports from Fouts and Morgan will be filed with the Office of the General Assembly in compliance with General Regulations E.5. and E.6. The 2017 audit will be printed in the audit section of the 2018 minutes.

II. FINANCIAL FOUNDATION DEVELOPMENT AND MANAGEMENT

A. PURPOSE

One area of work of the board is in financial foundation development and management. The purpose of this program is as follows:
To secure a firm financial undergirding for the ongoing ministry of congregations and the agencies of presbyteries, synods, and the General Assembly as they bear witness to the saving love of God, the grace of our Lord Jesus Christ, and the fellowship and communion of the Holy Spirit.

B. 2017 IN REVIEW

The year 2017 was an eventful year. U. S. equity markets surged to new highs in December. There was also growth in global markets including emerging markets. Higher oil prices also contributed to the uptick in the economy. Jerome Powell was nominated to succeed Janet Yellen as chair of the Fed. The good news encouraged the Fed to increase rate hikes three times in 2017.

The Cumberland Presbyterian Endowment Fund, Retirement Fund and the Investment Loan Program benefitted from the growth in the domestic and international markets. The balance in the Endowment Fund ended the year at an all-time high of $62,548,692 including loans. The balance in the Investment Loan Program was also at an all-time high of $25,608,257.

While we can enjoy the success of 2017, we need to continue to be cautious about looking too far down the road. Sentiment and emotion rule the short term. The first quarter of 2018 is one example of the volatility investors can experience. We are confident that our investment manager, Gerber/Taylor can continue to help us navigate the turbulent ups and downs of the market. Since October 1981, Gerber/Taylor has done a wonderful job for the Cumberland Presbyterian Church.

C. BOARD OF STEWARDSHIP

The Board of Stewardship ended 2017 with an unrestricted surplus of $142,208. We are ever mindful of expenses incurred and try to be good stewards of what has been entrusted to the Board. We are grateful for the faithful support from congregations and individuals through their contributions to Our United Outreach.

D. MANAGEMENT OF FUNDS

At the end of 2017 the Endowment Fund portfolio was under the co-management of Gerber/Taylor Management, RREEF America II, Clarion, Tortoise, Headlands Capital and Eagle MLP. The funds of the Retirement Program were co-managed by Gerber/Taylor Management, RREEF America II, Tortoise, Headlands Capital and Eagle MLP.

The church loan portion of the endowment portion of the endowment portfolio and the investments of the Cumberland Presbyterian Church Investment Loan Program, Inc. were under the management of board staff with the help of Hilliard Lyons.

III. ENDOWMENT PROGRAM

Since 1836, the board and its corporate predecessors have sought to be faithful trustees of the funds given into their hands to provide a permanent financial foundation for the work of congregations, presbyteries, synods, and General Assembly agencies. The work of the Endowment Program is the oldest responsibility of the board and fulfills a portion of that task to which all Cumberland Presbyterians are called: "Christian stewardship acknowledges that all of life and creation is a trust from God, to be used for God's glory and service."—Confession of Faith for Cumberland Presbyterians 6:10.

A. COMMUNICATION

The Endowment Program report will be distributed to all endowment program participants, general assembly board members, churches, and individual contributors.

Agencies, other participants, and interested parties received quarterly detailed reports on the postings to all their endowments. With the addition of names supplied by the agencies during the year, the number of persons receiving these reports continues to expand. In addition, special reports were made as requested.

B. ASSETS, INVESTMENT MIX, AND PERFORMANCE

1. Assets and Investment Mix

The assets of the Endowment Fund totaled $59,134,640 for 2017 at market value. The following table provides a breakdown of the investment mix:

Investment Mix
Securities & Investments

15.1%	US Equity	$ 8,929,331
12.0%	Real Assets	$ 7,096,157
9.7%	Fixed Income	$ 5,736,060
16.7%	Hedged Equity	$ 9,875,485
16.8%	Multi-Strategy	$ 9,934,620
3.6%	Opportunistic	$ 2,128,847
14.4%	International Stocks	$ 8,515,388
8.5%	Emerging Markets	$ 5,026,444
2.0%	Private Equity	$ 1,182,693
1.2%	Cash	$ 709,615
100.0%	Total	$59,134,640

2. Performance of the Endowment Fund

The Endowment Fund generated $6,766,232 in investment earnings during 2017. Net contributions and withdrawals (including income distributions) were a negative $2,652,152. The change in market value was a positive of $4,114,080.

With the combining of the Growth/Income Fund and the Total Return Fund in January 2013, we also began paying out 5% (annualized) to the congregations, presbyteries and agencies. Previously agencies had difficulty in preparing budgets because of the unknown amount they would receive from endowment income. Now, they realize they will receive 5% in endowment income over a twelve-month period. With this information, they have a better idea how much endowment income they can expect. Earnings paid to congregations, presbyteries and agencies totaled $1,400,256 for 2017.

3. Total Rate of Return for the Endowment Fund

The following table gives the annualized rates of return as contained in the report from Gerber/Taylor Associates for year end 2017:

	One Year Period 01/01/17-12/31/17	Five Year Period 01/01/13-12/31/17	Since Inception 09/30/81-12/31/17
Endowment Fund	12.4%	7.8%	9.9%

C. ESTABLISHING AN ENDOWMENT AS A LEGACY

The Board of Stewardship, Foundation and Benefits manages 825 endowments established for the benefit of congregations, presbyteries, synods, agencies and other special ministries of the Cumberland Presbyterian denomination. Many of these endowments were established by individuals as a legacy to continue to benefit long after they are no longer with us. Some of the endowments were established by congregations, presbyteries and synods to help further their specific ministries. Some of the endowments were started with very little. Through the years these endowments have grown and the beneficiaries are reaping the gifts of the endowment income and using it in ministry in their local area or worldwide. Please consider establishing an endowment.

D. ENDOWMENT PROGRAM LOANS

Historical Review

Through investing up to 40% of the assets of the Endowment Program in the witness of the Church, the message of good news concerning Christ is strengthened both in the United States and overseas. A survey of old files in the Historical Foundation and in the vault of the Board of Stewardship reveals the important role played by this aspect of the investment policy. Over the past sixty-five years from 1944 to 2009, 841 loans were made to congregations, presbyteries, and synods. From 2010 through 2017 an additional 17 loans have been made. Through these loans, $42,714,405 has been provided in financing for expansion of facilities and extension of witness.

A look at the different periods during which loans have been made provides a picture of growing endowments (and of post-World War II inflation!).

Period	Loans	Total Loaned	Average
1944-49	35	$ 145,755	$ 4,164
1950-59	171	$ 1,360,441	$ 7,955
1960-69	208	$ 3,056,891	$ 14,697
1970-79	166	$ 3,609,084	$ 21,741
1980-89	101	$ 4,349,120	$ 43,061
1990-99	102	$ 14,440,837	$ 141,577
2000-09	58	$ 10,571,723	$ 182,271
2010-17	17	$ 5,180,554	$ 304,738

While looking at the table, it should be noted that the Cumberland Presbyterian Church Investment Loan Program began January 1, 2001. Since its creation most of the larger loans are made through the Investment Loan Program. At the end of the year the Endowment Loan Balance was $2,119,345.

Down through the years, donors to endowments have found satisfaction in the knowledge that the prudent investment of their gifts strengthened not only the work of particular churches, institutions, and causes which they designated to receive the income but also the broader witness of the Church.

E. OTHER CHURCH LOANS

In addition to loans from the Investment Loan Program and the Endowment Program there is another source available to the board for loans to churches.

1. Small Church Loan Fund

This fund, formerly known as the Revolving Church Loan Fund, was created through an endowment established by Lavenia Cole and gifts to the "Into the Nineties" Capital Gifts Campaign. All interest earned by the loans is added to the fund to increase the amount available for loans. There were five loans from the Small Church Loan Program at the end of 2017 totaling $135,820.

The rate of interest for the Small Church Loans made during 2017 was based on the loan rate established by the Cumberland Presbyterian Church Investment Loan Program at the beginning of each quarter. These loans are generally small loans of $70,000 or less and most are amortized over five years.

IV. CUMBERLAND PRESBYTERIAN CHURCH
INVESTMENT LOAN PROGRAM, INC.

In 1976, the board began a program to provide an opportunity for flexible investment of current temporary cash assets of congregations and agencies of the church. The primary purpose of the program is to provide income to participants as a foundation for ministry. On January 1, 2001, the assets of the original program, Cash Funds Management, were transferred to the new Cumberland Presbyterian Church Investment Loan Program, Inc.

For the year ending 2017, the assets for the Investment Loan Program were $25,608,257 compared to $22,407,583 in 2016. This is a 14% increase in assets in one year and over 57% in five years. There were 323 individual, congregation and agency accounts. At year end, deposits on account totaled $19,338,543. The total loans were $6,269,714 at year end.

For 2017, the corporation complied with the regulatory requirements in the states of Tennessee and Kentucky and was able to offer investment opportunities to individual Cumberland Presbyterians in the states of Tennessee, Kentucky, Texas, Missouri and New Mexico.

The board of directors is composed of the following: Mike St. John, president; Jim Shannon, vice-president and Debbie Shelton, secretary, and Gary Tubb. Robert Heflin serves as Treasurer and Executive Secretary. During the past year, the board met twice in regular session.

In order to simplify administration and focus on the strengths of the Investment Loan Program, the board took action to limit the offering of notes and depository accounts to "ready access accounts." All note holders (individuals) and depository account holders (churches and church agencies) with funds invested in these "on demand" accounts participated in the $622,498 which the program paid in interest. For 2017 the interest rate paid to account holders was 3%. The interest rate paid to account holders can fluctuate from one quarter to the next. In recent years there has been renewed interest for congregations to open new accounts because the interest paid is higher than current CD rates.

The table below provides a breakdown of the investment mix.

Investment Loan Program
Securities & Investments

20.6%	Cash Equivalents	$ 3,899,818
9.9%	Preferred Stocks	$ 1,783,695
0.9%	Mutual Funds	$ 1,386,711
68.6%	Taxable Fixed Income	$12,556,599
100.0%		$19,626,823

At the end of 2017 there were 22 loans to congregations made through the Investment Loan Program. The loan balance was $7,019,714. Every accountholder is investing in the future ministry of the Cumberland Presbyterian Church as well as receiving interest on that investment.

V. EMPLOYEE BENEFITS ADMINISTRATION AND RESEARCH

A. PURPOSE

The second of two broad areas of the work of the board is in employee benefits administration and research. The purpose of this program is as follows:

To support the lay and ordained employees of the church as they venture to be faithful under the call of Christ and the Church to the daily demands of providing leadership to congregations and Church agencies whom are the incarnation of the Body of Christ, the family of God at work in the world.

B. VISION

The board has a vision of uniform benefits for all Cumberland Presbyterian clergy, including group health insurance, group long-term disability coverage, and participation in the General Assembly's retirement plan. Ministers would then know what to expect when they are called to another church. No longer would some ministers have to do without what is considered in the secular world to be basic employee benefits. No longer would ministers and their families have to settle for being relegated to second class status. The reality is, as several General Assemblies have recognized, that this is possible if we work together in much the same manner that we send out missionaries and do a lot of other ministry. Good employee benefit plans are in place and they would be healthier and stronger if used and supported by all employees of the Cumberland Presbyterian Church.

VI. RETIREMENT PROGRAM

Since 1952, the board has provided a retirement program open to all church employees of the Cumberland Presbyterian Church. The program gives opportunity for churches and their employees to provide a source of retirement income based on voluntary contributions. In 1987, a new Cumberland Presbyterian Retirement Plan No. 2 was established as a qualified 403(b) defined contribution plan and in 1990 the General Assembly amended the plan to include the churches and employees of the Second Cumberland Presbyterian Church, now known as the Cumberland Presbyterian Church in America.

A. PLAN AMENDMENTS

As new needs arise or deficiencies in the original plan document for Cumberland Presbyterian Retirement Plan No. 2 become apparent, the General Assembly has the authority under Article IX Section 9.01 of the Plan to amend the same. In 2012 a revised plan document was approved by the General Assembly. Recently the IRS has adopted a pre-approved program for 403(b) plans, thus we have restated the plan to take advantage of the new regulations. At this time we are also able to make updates to the plan. The only update made, is the ability to contribute up to the IRS deferral limit each year. In 2018, this amount is $18,500 and may change in the coming years with no need to amend the plan. Below is the amended portion:

"As a Participant, you may elect to defer a percentage of your compensation each year instead of receiving that amount in cash. There are two types of pre-tax contributions that you can make under the plan: basic contributions and elective contributions. You may defer up to 5% of your pay as a basic contribution. Once you have reached the contribution limit for the basic contribution, you may defer an additional percentage or dollar amount of your pay as an elective contribution. However, the total deferrals that you can elect to defer from your pay in any taxable year may not exceed certain dollar limit which is set by law. The limit for 2018 is $18,500."

RECOMMENDATION 1: That the General Assembly approve the amended plan and updates of the Cumberland Presbyterian Retirement Plan #2.

B. YEAR END REPORT

On December 31, 2017, there were 309 active participants in the Retirement Plan. There were 15 receiving direct monthly payments as a result of their elections. In addition to these participants, there were 13 persons who were receiving annuity payments purchased through the Plan and for whom the Plan issues 1099-R's.

During 2017, $1,638,563 was dispersed to or for participants, an increase of 3.8% over 2016s $1,578,924. Contributions totaled $799,189 and were up 16.3 % over 2016s $686,942. Realized and unrealized gain on investments totaled $2,736,328 compared to 2016 gain of $1,256,899. The rate of return credited to the accounts for the year was 12.5% compared to 6.5% for 2016. (Comparative annual rates of return for: previous three years +6.1%, previous five years +7.5%, and from the beginning of professional management in March 1982, +9.4%.)

Effective January 1, 2011, Gerber/Taylor Management was retained to manage our stock portfolio. We have continued our relationship with Met West, a bond manager, and RREEF, a private real estate investment trust manager. Matt Robbins and Stacy Miller of Gerber/Taylor continue to be very helpful with keeping the board updated on market conditions and investment strategies.

VII. MINISTERIAL AID PROGRAM

A. MINISTERIAL AID

1. Full Benefit Recipients

As of March 2018, there are 6 Cumberland Presbyterian Church recipients of the full benefit of $531 (adjusted for inflation yearly) per month (increased from $300 on July 1, 2010), and 3 that receive partial benefits due to them having more income than the threshold established. The monthly total of these payments is $4,056.00; annually, $48,672.00 is paid. Beginning May 1, 2015, the method of distributing funds to overseas presbyteries was revised with the help of the Missions ministry team. Ministerial aid will now be offered in overseas presbyteries on an individual basis. Presently there are 6 recipients in Cauca Valley Presbytery and 5 recipients in Andes Presbytery that are receiving aid in the amount of $300 a month, for a total of $3,300 a month or $39,600 annually.

In October 2005, the board decided to distribute 75% of the previous year's surplus to the state side recipients. The Board of Stewardship has approved a cap of a maximum of $4,000 in lieu of large distributions that may have a negative effect on other benefits received, such as SSI, or state assistance.

2. Basic Requirements

The new basic requirements and amount for stateside recipients for the Ministerial Aid program were approved at the General Assembly of the Cumberland Presbyterian Church in June 2010. The poverty levels have been updated to the latest available figures. They are as follows:

Full Benefit of $531 a month for State Side Recipients

1. Minimum age is full retirement age set forth by the Social Security Administration.
2. Minimum years of service to the church - 15.
3. Can qualify for aid if a participant in the Cumberland Presbyterian Retirement Plan if income is below poverty level as established by the US Census Bureau.
4. Physical and/or mental disability (doctor's statement required) at any age, however, a minimum of ten years of service is required if less than 60 years of age.
5. Individuals' income cannot exceed federal poverty guidelines set forth for the year by the US Census Bureau. Poverty level is $12,140 a year or $1,012 a month for 2018.
6. Couples income cannot exceed federal poverty guidelines set forth for the year by the US Census Bureau. Poverty level is $16,460 a year or $1,372 a month for 2018.
(The GA Board of Stewardship is authorized to look at each case in light of unusual financial hardship; thus, application may be made even if income levels exceed the ceiling.)
7. Presbytery obtains information and approves (approval can be given by the committee or board charged by presbytery with this responsibility); certification of approval is sent to the General Assembly Board of Stewardship.
8. Surviving spouse is eligible if above items 2, 3 and 4 have been met.

Note: Recipient is responsible to verify if receiving Ministerial Aid would affect his or her SSI, Social Security or other benefits.

Cumberland Presbyterian Church applicants must submit to the Board a listing of assets and liabilities, so the net worth can be determined. The board urges presbyteries to maintain contact with persons under the Ministerial Aid Program who live within their bounds. Should there be serious unmet needs, the presbytery is urged to contact the board so that it may determine how the Ministerial Aid program can be of assistance in meeting those needs.

3. Cumberland Presbyterian Church in America

The CPCA currently has 3 participants who receive monthly payments. On June 1, 2015, the aid amount increased from $109 a month to $510 a month and the CPCA contributes 50% of the yearly aid and the CP Ministerial Aid Endowments 50%. The current amount received monthly per participant is $531. The CPCA normally pays its share in June or July following their General Assembly.

4. Ministers in Overseas Presbyteries

Since May 1, 2015, with the help of the Missions Ministry Team, Aid is available to those in overseas presbyteries who qualify on an individual basis. The Cumberland Presbyterian Church is present in 13 different countries and each country presents its unique legislation of how they manage pension plans according to laws and standards for salaries. The Mission Ministry Team will be the liaison between the Board of Stewardship and the Presbyteries outside of the United States aiding the Board in identifying the needs overseas and interpreting pension laws and standards for salaries. At present, aid is being sent to the Cauca Valley Presbytery and Andes Presbytery in Colombia, South America.

B. SPECIAL FINANCIAL NEEDS AID

At the Spring 2014 Board of Stewardship meeting, the Board approved the use of funds from the Ministerial Aid Cash Fund ILP to be used in special situations where illness has caused a financial hardship for those that are not eligible for Ministerial Aid. At present there are four individuals who have received payments.

VIII. INSURANCE PROGRAMS

The insurance programs of the board have been assigned by the General Assembly beginning in the middle of the previous century. Dental and Vision Insurance is the newest, begun in December 2008. Property and casualty insurance is the oldest, begun in 1951. While all of the insurance programs are important, group life and health insurance, begun in 1961, touches many lives in a personal way and often at times of deep anxiety. In all, about 202 men, women, and children depend on this program to meet their health care needs.

A. PROPERTY & CASUALTY INSURANCE

The Board of Stewardship, Foundation and Benefits secures property and casualty insurance coverage against accidental loss for the General Assembly Corporation, Board of Stewardship, Discipleship Ministry Team, Missions Ministry Team, Ministry Council, Communications Ministry Team, Pastoral Development Ministry Team, Memphis Theological Seminary, and Historical Foundation.

Our broker is Lipscomb & Pitts of Memphis, Tennessee. For 2018, Travelers Insurance carries our Property & Casualty policy and $2,500,000 in earth quake coverage, Evanston Insurance Company provides an additional $16,551,482 in earthquake coverage. Philadelphia carries our Directors & Officers coverage and Hanover carries our General Liability, Professional Liability, Crime, Automobile, and Umbrella policies. Beginning October 23, 2014, Workers Compensation coverage has been with Bridgefield Casualty.

B. GROUP LONG TERM DISABILITY INSURANCE

The presbyteries of Arkansas, Columbia, Covenant, Cumberland, del Cristo, East Tennessee, Missouri, Murfreesboro, Nashville, North Central, Red River, Robert Donnell, Trinity, West Tennessee and The Center have now established non-contributory long term disability programs insured currently through Cigna. This leaves only four stateside presbyteries (Choctaw, Hope, Grace and Tennessee Georgia) without a program. The quarterly rate applied to participant's salaries is .45 per $100 of salary.

There are three primary reasons for ministers to want the coverage and for presbyteries to want to provide the protection. The group rate is significantly lower than individual policy rates and does not require a large cash outlay to cover all full-time ministers in a presbytery; housing allowance and/or the fair rental value of a manse is included in the definition of salary for ministers; and, there is no medical qualification requirement in order to enroll. These advantages over individual policies make this coverage very attractive, especially to those who have previously purchased their own policies. In addition, a provision was negotiated with Cigna by the Board's consultant, whereby ministers, upon leaving a participating presbytery to serve in a non-participating presbytery, may continue the coverage if he or she so desires. The new employing church is then billed for the quarterly premium. There are now 10 ministers and two employees who are receiving or have received benefits from this insurance program. There are 170 participants as of January 1, 2018.

C. GROUP TRAVEL ACCIDENT INSURANCE

This policy provides twenty-four hour coverage on "named employees" for accidental death, dismemberment, or loss of sight while on business travel. The maximum benefit is $50,000 and there is also a $1,000 medical benefit. The annual premium is $900. We renew this policy every 3 years. Thirty-one named positions are covered under this policy.

D. GROUP HEALTH & LIFE INSURANCE

The board has used a fully-insured, managed care approach to provide group health insurance for Cumberland Presbyterian clergy and lay employees since March 1, 1999. Blue Cross / Blue Shield of Tennessee is our insurance carrier in 2018. In 2016, the group plan was split into 4 separate community rated groups which provided more competitive rates. For 2018, the plans realized a 2.5% increase due to premium increase of 5.4% and more funds being used from the Premium Stabilization Reserve due to higher returns of the endowments. Lipscomb & Pitts, a Memphis based insurance company, is our insurance broker, and Craig Wright, our agent.

1. Premiums

Efforts to maintain affordable premiums and comprehensive coverage are the biggest challenges we face. Premiums for 2018 are listed below and reflect the assistance from the Premium Stabilization Reserve. The goal for 2018 is to utilize approximately $167,000 from the Premiums Stabilization Reserve to help reduce the premiums participants pay for health insurance. In 2017 we utilized $123,521 from the Premium Stabilization Reserve.

Health Insurance Premiums for 2018

	Option 1	Option 2
Employee Only	$ 700	$ 564
Employee & Spouse	$1,385	$1,111
Employee & Child(ren)	$1,280	$1,027
Family	$1,977	$1,586

The Health Plans are on a calendar year as far as deductible and pricing is concerned. It is our objective with the new community rated plans to have the renewal pricing by no later than October 1, so presbyteries and agencies can have the figures for their fall meetings and better plan their budgets for the coming year. Periodically we seek bids from other carriers in an effort to keep premiums competitive. When this is done, we may not have the new premium information by October 1.

Open enrollment period is the month of December. It is during this time that an employee can enroll or change their health insurance coverage unless there are special circumstances.

2. Participation

As of February 1, 2018, 120 employees and 82 dependents for a total of 202 people depend on the Cumberland Presbyterian Church Health Insurance Program. A breakdown of family units by size at February 1, 2018 is listed below.

FAMILY UNITS BY SIZE

	Number of Units	Total
Emp. Only	77	77
Spouse Only	0	0
E & 1	2	4
E & 2	5	15
E & 3	0	0
E & S	19	38
Families of 3	6	18
Families of 4	6	24
Families of 5	4	20
Families of 6	1	6
Families of 7	0	0
Total	120	202

The following table shows the enrollment figures from January 2017 to December 2017. As one can see the numbers fluctuate from month to month.

MONTHLY GROUP INSURANCE ENROLLMENT

	EMPLOYEE COVERAGE	DEPENDENT COVERAGE	TOTAL
January	75	50	125
February	76	49	125
March	76	46	122
April	76	46	122
May	75	46	121
June	74	45	119
July	73	45	118
August	74	43	117
September	75	44	120
October	78	43	121
November	77	44	121
December	76	43	119

3. Premium Stabilization Reserve (Formerly Emergency Reserve)

The Premium Stabilization Reserve is invested in the Endowment Program Fund account which had a balance of $1,972,095 as of December 31, 2017. The Emergency Health Insurance Reserve was established in compliance with the 1992 General Assembly directive to be used in "emergency" situations to match presbyterial emergency fund disbursements. The 1998 General Assembly approved the Board's recommendation to allow the Board to use the Emergency Reserve to maintain the stability of the group health and life insurance plan. This allows these funds to be used for purposes outside of the original scope of the reserve. In 2017, the Board of Stewardship used $123,521 to help offset some of the cost of the health insurance premiums and have estimated that approximately $167,000 will be used in 2018 to help in reducing premiums for the health insurance participants.

4. Dental and Vision Insurance

On December 1, 2008, we began offering Dental and Vision insurance, on a voluntary basis, for anyone working at least 30 hours or more for any Cumberland Presbyterian Church, its agencies, boards, and institutions. Peter Whitely is the agent of record. At present there are 79 participating employees.

5. Jessie W. Hipsher Health Insurance Endowment

The Jesse W. Hipsher Health Insurance Endowment was created as the first step in the board's goal to raise $10,000,000 in endowments for the support of the Cumberland Presbyterian Health and Life Insurance Program. The endowment was established on March 6, 2004. At its establishment $11,450 had been raised. The balance of the endowment as of December 31, 2017 was $50,507.19.

6. Health Education / E-Mail Newsletter

To further educate participants in matters concerning healthcare, participants receive a monthly e-newsletter entitled, TopHealth, published by Oakstone Publishing. The monthly e-newsletter is full of health related tips that can be easily implemented by readers. The two page newsletter can be read within a matter of minutes. Also initiated in 2008 is the E-Mail newsletter that is designed as an information tool to help the participants of the Health and Retirement programs stay on top of happenings within the Board of Stewardship.

7. Wellness Program

Blue Cross offers a Preventive Health Guide and the Blue 365 discount program for a range of item from fitness, healthy eating, personal care and wellness and even information on financial health. Also offered are the Nurse chat 24/7/365 and Physician Now where you can speak to a physician on call.

Respectfully submitted,
Randy Davidson, Board Member
Robert Heflin, Executive Secretary

THE REPORT OF THE HISTORICAL FOUNDATION

I. GENERAL INFORMATION

A. OFFICERS OF THE BOARD

The officers of the board are as follows: Pat Ward, president; Reverend Mary Kathryn Kirkpatrick, vice-president; and Michael Fare, secretary. Susan Knight Gore is the director and treasurer of the Historical Library and Archives.

B. BOARD REPRESENTATIVES TO THE CPC & CPCA GENERAL ASSEMBLIES

The board's representative to the 188th General Assembly of the Cumberland Presbyterian Church and the 143rd General Assembly of the Cumberland Presbyterian Church in America is Reverend Lisa Oliver. The alternate is Pat Ward.

C. MEMBERSHIP AND MEETINGS OF THE BOARD

The board is currently composed of the following members: from the Cumberland Presbyterian Church in America—Jackie Cooper, Dorothy Hayden, Reverend Joe Howard III, Willie Lynk, and Pat Ward, from the Cumberland Presbyterian Church—Michael Fare, Robin McCaskey Hughes, Reverend Mary Kathryn Kirkpatrick, Ashley Lindsey, Lisa Oliver, and Sidney Swindle.

The Board of Trustees met, September 15, 2018, and February 23, 2018.

D. MEMBERS WHOSE TERMS EXPIRE

The first term of Reverend Lisa Oliver expires with the 2018 meeting of the Cumberland Presbyterian General Assembly, and she is eligible for reelection. The third term of Sidney Swindle expires with the 2018 meeting of the Cumberland Presbyterian General Assembly, and he is not eligible for reelection.

E. STAFF

Susan Knight Gore serves as the Archivist of the Historical Foundation. Missy Rose is the archival assistant for the Foundation.

II. ASSEMBLY REPORTING

As a matter of official structure, relative to the CPC, there is a Board of Trustees composed of members from both the CPC and CPCA, and relative to the CPCA, there is a committee composed of members from the CPCA.

III. PROGRAMS AND ACTIVITIES

A. HISTORY INTERPRETATION AND PROMOTIONAL ACTIVITIES

1. The 1810/1874 Circle

In order to enlist the financial support of interested members of our churches in the work of the Foundation, the 1810/1874 Circle was created. Membership is based on a financial contribution of $25 or more per year. Income through such gifts enables the Foundation to meet expenditures and is vital to the continued work of the Foundation.

We appreciate the support given to the Foundation by all members of the 1810/1874 Circle and encourage other members of the Cumberland Presbyterian Church and the Cumberland Presbyterian Church in America to join this donor group.

RECOMMENDATION 1: That the General Assembly instruct presbyteries to make congregations aware of the 1810/1874 Circle and encourage new members to support this endeavor annually.

2. Patrons

Persons who contribute $100 or more to one of the endowments of the Historical Foundation become patron members and receive a certificate. Patron memberships may also be given in honor or in memory of an individual.

3. Heritage Churches

Congregations contributing a minimum of $1,000 to an endowment of the Historical Foundation become Heritage Churches and receive a framed certificate. There are six categories of recognition and churches can move from one level to another.

Heritage Church $1,000 - $4,999
Silver Heritage Church $5,000 to $9,999
Golden Heritage Church $10,000 to $24,999
Platinum Heritage Church $25,000 to $49,999
Diamond Heritage Church $50,000 to $99,000
Jubilee Heritage Church $100,000 and up

4. Presbyterial Heritage Committees/Presbyterial Historians

To promote interest in the work of the Foundation and to nurture work in history on the presbyterial level, the Historical Foundation seeks to work cooperatively with the Presbyterial Heritage Committees/Presbyterial Historians of both general assemblies. The brochure, *Suggestions for Heritage Committees and Presbyterial Historians*, is available from the Foundation. The board expresses its appreciation to the presbyteries that have Heritage Committees/Presbyterial Historians.

5. Denomination Day Offering

The 2018 Denomination Day Offering was designated to fund the conversion of fragile and deteriorating analogue media to digital formats in order that it might better be preserved.

The Foundation expresses appreciation to congregations and others groups who received special offerings for the work of the Historical Foundation on Denomination Day. This special offering provides an opportunity for congregations to directly contribute to the support of the Historical Foundation as well as the Foundation supplying educational materials to each congregation.

RECOMMENDATION 2: That the General Assembly instruct presbyteries to encourage their congregations to have a special offering on the Sunday designated as Denomination Day to help support the special project designated for that year.

B. PUBLICATIONS

1. Promotional Materials

The Historical Foundation provides promotional materials describing its purpose and work, the various means of financially supporting this work, and listings of available publications and prints for sale through the Foundation. These materials are available on the Foundation's website.

2. Publication Series

The Foundation has a number of titles and prints available for purchase. Income from the sale of these items goes into the Historical Foundation Trust, a permanent endowment supporting the Foundation's work. Titles available are:

1883 Confession of Faith.

1895 Cumberland Cook Book.

Cumberland Presbyterianism and Arminianism Compared/Contrasted on Selected Doctrines by Joe Ben Irby.

Faith Once Delivered; Some Indispensable Doctrines of the Christian Faith by Joe Ben Irby.

Family of Faith: Cumberland Presbyterians in Harrison County [Texas], 1848-1998 by Rose Mary Magrill.

God So Loved by Roy Hall.

History of East Side Cumberland Presbyterian Church, Memphis, Tennessee, Memphis Tennessee: 1926-1986, by the Historical Committee.

History of the Cumberland Presbyterian Church by B. W. McDonnold.

Jerusalem Cumberland Presbyterian Church: A Documentary and Pictorial History by Anne Elizabeth Swain Odom.

Legacy of Grace: Louisiana and Texas Cumberland Presbyterian People & Places of Trinity Presbytery by Rose Mary Magrill.

Life and Thought of Finis Ewing by Joe Ben Irby.

Life and Thought of Milton Bird by Joe Ben Irby.

Life and Thought of Reuben Burrow by Joe Ben Irby.

Life and Thought of Robert Verrell Foster by Joe Ben Irby.

Life and Thought of Stanford Guthrie Burney by Joe Ben Irby.

Life and Times of Finis Ewing by F. R. Cossitt.

Soundings by Morris Pepper.

Theological Snippets by Joe Ben Irby.

This They Believed by Joe Ben Irby.

What Cumberland Presbyterians Believe by E. K. Reagin.

Women Shall Preach: Celebrating 125 Yeas of Ordained Women in Ministry in the Cumberland Presbyterian Church.

Prints of the *Samuel McAdow Home* and the *First Meeting of Cumberland Presbytery.*

These items are available for sale from Cumberland Presbyterian Resources.

RECOMMENDATION 3: That the General Assembly make presbyteries aware that the Historical Foundation is interested and has funds to publish books on topics concerning the Cumberland Presbyterian Church and Cumberland Presbyterian Church in America, and instruct them to share this information with the churches and individuals of their presbytery.

3. Denomination Day Resources

All the Past is but the Beginning of Beginning (Denomination Day resource) is available on the Foundation's web site under the Resources section:

http://www.cumberland.org/hfcpc/resource/

It includes eight dramas intended to present the birth of the Cumberland Presbyterian Church and the Cumberland Presbyterian Church in America. A hard copy may be requested from the Foundation office.

4. Online Promotion

Recognizing the increasing value of emerging social media, the Historical Foundation employs a Facebook group, "Historical Foundation of the CPC & CPCA," to engage an expanding audience of Cumberland Presbyterians in denominational history and heritage. By showcasing collection acquisitions, the Foundation expands the knowledge of those materials sought for preservation as well as the nature of archival development. The Foundation also employs a Facebook Page. The Facebook Page is somewhat more informal and is ideal for announcements.

C. HISTORICAL FOUNDATION AWARDS

1. Award in Cumberland Presbyterian History

The Foundation encourages the writing and publication of papers on all aspects of the history of the Cumberland Presbyterian Church in America and the Cumberland Presbyterian Church. One means of promoting such writing is the Historical Foundation Award in Cumberland Presbyterian History. A $300 prize is awarded to the author entering the best paper on any CPC or CPCA history subject which meets in form and content the requirements set by the Board of Trustees and judged by the board appointed awards committee. All manuscripts submitted to the competition become property of the Foundation and are added to the Historical Library and Archives.

The contest follows the calendar year, and entries for the 2018 competition are encouraged. All entries will be accepted through December 2018 for this year's contest. Any entries received following the deadline of December 31st will be automatically entered in the 2019 competition.

Guidelines and entry forms for submitting manuscripts to the competition are available from the Foundation office as well as on the internet, http://www.cumberland.org/hfcpc/Awards.htm. The Historical Foundation appreciates the participation of past and future CPCA and CP historians in this program.

The 2017 Award went to William R. Black of Bartlett, Tennessee for the paper "A Neutral Church?: Cumberland Presbyterians and the Problem of Slavery."

2. Awards of Recognition

Awards of recognition are certificates given to organizations or individuals in recognition of historic events or contributions to the preservation of our heritage as Cumberland Presbyterians. Appropriate applications for the award are: particular churches celebrating anniversaries of their organization; any judicatory or agency celebrating publication of a written history; celebrations of history or historic event in a creative or unusual manner; individuals who have provided continued service for 50 years or more as members of a local congregation or presbytery; individuals who have served for 40 years or more in a continuing leadership role (including pastors) within a local church. Individuals, churches, or presbyterial heritage committees may make application for the issuing of an award by contacting the Foundation office. Application forms are supplied by the Foundation office as well as the internet, http://www.cumberland.org/hfcpc/Awards.htm.

D. RELATIONSHIPS

Presbyterian Historical Society of the Southwest

The Presbyterian Historical Society of the Southwest is an agency of The Synod of the Sun, Presbyterian Church (USA) and Cumberland Presbyterian Churches in Arkansas, Louisiana, Oklahoma and Texas. Members of the Cumberland Presbyterian Church who serve on the board of this organization are Reverend Norlan Scrudder, Reverend Perryn Rice, and Doctor Rose Mary Magrill.

IV. HISTORICAL LIBRARY AND ARCHIVES

A. RESEARCH SERVICE

The Foundation's main research commitment is to the agencies, local congregations, and members of the Cumberland Presbyterian Churches. Since the Historical Library and Archives of the Historical Foundation serves as the official repository for the Cumberland Presbyterian General Assemblies, this is our focus. Although the separation of research into two types designated by their mode of access has been rapid and dramatic, both the traditional and "cyber" mode contribute to and enhance the other.

1. Traditional/Physical Access

Hands on access to primary source material remains the vital heart of historic and theological research. Rather than being diminished by increased electronic resources, traditional research has broadened due to heightened awareness of primary sources in an expanding information age. The Foundation receives research requests by personal visitors, mail, e-mail, and telephone. As time permits, requests are researched. Responses are sent to the requestor, as well as pertinent information on ministers, congregations, presbyteries and synods being placed on our website for future researchers.

2. Electronic Access

The Foundation's website continues to expand in order to provide greater access to the materials in the Historical Library and Archives. As well as being a research tool, the internet provides an invaluable and inexpensive means of promotion for the physical collections of the Historical Library and Archives, the activities of the Historical Foundation, and for the greater community of faith called Cumberland Presbyterians. Information at the site includes: general information about the Foundation, entire texts of important historical documents, historical information on particular congregations, ministers, presbyteries, and synods. Beginning in 2018, the Foundation added a YouTube Channel for historic films documenting the faith-life of Cumberland Presbyterians. The gateway URL to the Foundation's website is http://www.cumberland.org/hfcpc/. The YouTube Channel can be accessed directly at https://www.youtube.com/channel/UCTk4Wnc8b1T96d0L8Vkt4lg or through the gateway URL.

B. ACQUISITIONS

The Historical Library and Archives regularly receives items published by the two denominations, *Minutes of the General Assembly of the Cumberland Presbyterian Church, Preliminary Minutes of the General Assembly of the Cumberland Presbyterian Church, Yearbook of the General Assembly of the Cumberland Presbyterian Church, The Cumberland Presbyterian, Missionary Messenger, Minutes of the General Assembly of the Cumberland Presbyterian Church in America, Preliminary Minutes of the General Assembly of the Cumberland Presbyterian Church in America*, and *The Cumberland Flag.* Synods and presbyteries deposit four copies of their printed minutes in the Historical Library and Archives. In addition, books, pamphlets, theses, dissertations, records and publications of general assembly, boards, agencies, institutions, and task forces; records and publications of synods and presbyteries, session records and other materials of particular churches, biographical material of Cumberland Presbyterian and Cumberland Presbyterian Church in America ministers, photographs, audiovisual materials, and museum items were among the accessions received. The 2017 Accession List closed with 174 accession groups.

Some of the highlights added to the collection in 2017 include:

Audiovisual Items

Camp Lowrie. Fort Worth, Texas. Cumberland Presbyterian Church.
Film 16mm. *Camp Lowrie. History of Campsite 1949-1950.*

Rev. Roy Tinsley. Cassette Tape. Ohio Valley Presbytery.

Books

American Sunday-School Union. *The Gospel Story; or, The Story of Christ for the Young.* Revised by the Committee of Publication. Nashville, Tennessee: Cumberland Presbyterian Publishing House, 1887.

Kennedy, Nancy Wardlow. *New Bethel Cumberland Presbyterian Church, Brief History: Register of Elders, Deacons, Members, Adult Baptisms & Death 1870 to 1950.*

Lyle, John. *The Diary of the Rev. John Lyle 1801-1803; Together With a Narrative of J. Lyle's Mission in the Bounds of the Cumberland Presbytery During the Year 1805.* Bound typescript from the originals.

Morrison, James D., Joy Culbreath, and Kathy Carpenter. *Schools for the Choctaws.* Durant, Oklahoma: Ameba Publishing, 2016.

Wilson, Levin. *A Declaration of Principles and Church Policy, of the Independent Presbyterians.* Evansville, Ind.: A. N. Sanders, Printer, Daily Journal Office, 1855.

Periodicals
> *Cumberland Pearl.* June 2 and 9, 1929.
> *Our Lambs.* February 18, 1900, and October 6, 1902.
> *Senior Quarterly: An Aid to the Study of International Sunday School Lessons.* 1905.

Institutions
> Bethel College. McKenzie, Tennessee. Senior Token. A Presentation of the Class of '37.
> Cumberland University. Lebanon, Tennessee. Program. Dedication of the Chapel of Memorial Hall. Visit of the General Assembly of the Cumberland Presbyterian Church to Cumberland University, Lebanon, Tennessee, May 23, 1903.
> Waynesburg College. Waynesburg, Pennsylvania. Commencement Announcement. The Thirty-Seventh Annual Commencement of Waynesburg College, Thursday, June 28th, 1888, 9 A.M., in College Chapel. Compliments of the Class.

Museum Items
> Philadelphia Cumberland Presbyterian Church. Limestone, Washington county, Tennessee. Commemorative Plate. 150th Anniversary. Erected 1847.
> Sulphur Springs Cumberland Presbyterian Church. Dardanelle, Yell County, Arkansas. Time Capsule.
> Texas Synodic Encampment. Cumberland Presbyterian Church. Lathem Springs, Aquilla, Texas. August 23-30, 1938. Ribbon.
> Waukon Cumberland Presbyterian Church. Waukon, Allamakee county, Iowa. Commemorative Spoon.

Other Congregational Records
> Edgefield Cumberland Presbyterian Presbyterian Church. Nashville, Tennessee. *A Book of Favorite Recipes.* Ladies Bible Class, 1963.
> Jefferson Avenue Cumberland Presbyterian Church. Evansville, Indiana. Pastor's Aid Society and Ladies Aid Society. Minutes. January 29, 1897-January 22, 1904.
> Knoxville, First Cumberland Presbyterian Church. Knoxville, Knox county, Tennessee. Board of Deacons. Minutes. 1947-1978.
> Lewis Memorial Cumberland Presbyterian Church. Tampa, Florida. Church Directory. 1967.

Photographs
> General Assembly. Cumberland Presbyterian Church. May 15, 1930. Olney, Texas.
> Oakesdale Cumberland Presbyterian Church. Oakesdale, Whitman county, Washington. Rev. John C. Templeton, 1856-1934. Photograph of building and pastor. 1891.
> Rev. Clement Ester Wilkins. (1917-1982).
> YPGA. Young People's General Assembly. 1946. Photographs from an album.

Postcards
> Birthplace Shrine. Montgomery Bell State Park, Dickson County, Tennessee. McAdoo Spring. 1910.
> Cleveland Cumberland Presbyterian Church. Cleveland. Tennessee. About 1912.
> Elmira Chapel Cumberland Presbyterian Church. Longview, Texas. Bible School. July 27-August 1, 1942.
> General Assembly. Cumberland Presbyterian Church. Eightieth General Assembly, One Hundredth Anniversary. Dickson, Tennessee. 1910.

Presbyterial Records
> Brazos River Presbytery. Colored Cumberland Presbyterian Church.

Brazos River Presbytery. Colored Cumberland Presbyterian Church in the United States of America and Liberia, Africa.

Brazos River Presbytery. Colored Cumberland Presbyterian Church in the United States.

Brazos River Presbytery. Second Cumberland Presbyterian Church.

Sunday School Convention. Minutes. July 3-4, 1925-July 24, 1986.

> Clarksville Presbyterial Missionary Society. Cumberland Presbyterian Church. Minutes. March 28-29, 1944 in Clarksville, Tennessee. Also contains the minutes of September 26, 1944 at Mt. Denson in

Springfield, Tennessee.

Logan Presbytery. Cumberland Presbyterian Church. Minutes. April 4-5, 1892 and April 6-8, 1898.

Ohio Valley Presbytery. Cumberland Presbyterian Church in America. Minutes. October 16-17, 2015.

Sermons

Rev. Larry Chester Bagby (1940-2017)

Rev. La Royce Brown (1935-2006)

Session Records

Bethlehem Cumberland Presbyterian Church. Union City, Obion county, Tennessee. October 4, 1884-August 5, 1990.

Campbellsville Cumberland Presbyterian Church. Campbellsville, Taylor county, Kentucky. June 30, 1915-September 3, 1962.

Christ Church. Huntsville, Madison county, Alabama. October 17, 1999-December 9, 2012.

Clark's Grove Cumberland Presbyterian Church. Maryville, Blount county, Tennessee. Session Records. April 3, 1955-February 18, 1996.

Cookeville, First Cumberland Presbyterian Church. Cookeville, Putnam county, Tennessee. 1908-February 5, 1934; August 6, 1957-December 11, 1966; January 8, 1968-December 21, 1975; January 15, 1983-November 28, 1999.

El Paso, First Cumberland Presbyterian Church. El Paso, El Paso County, Texas. December 7, 2008-December 14, 2014.

Humboldt, First Cumberland Presbyterian Church. Humboldt, Gibson county, Tennessee. January 18, 1956-November 20, 2002.

Joywood Cumberland Presbyterian Church. Murfreesboro, Tennessee. November 28, 1984-December 1, 2005.

Knoxville, First Cumberland Presbyterian Church. Knoxville, Knox county, Tennessee. Session Records. January 14, 1959-December 6, 1967; January 7, 1970-December 11, 2005.

Synodical Records

Texas Synod and Auxiliaries. Cumberland Presbyterian Church in America. Minutes. August 8-11, 2007, Desoto, Texas; August 8-10, 2012, Tyler, Texas.

Synod of the Southeast. Cumberland Presbyterian Church. Stated Clerk Files. 1 box.

In all judicatories, from the session of the congregation through presbytery, synod, and the General Assemblies of both the Cumberland Presbyterian Church and the Cumberland Presbyterian Church in America, minutes form the legal record of the judicatory. Without these records there is often nothing to document persons joining the church, ordination as elder and clergy, disciplinary actions, etc. It is important to be aware that legally original minutes are always the property of the judicatory for which they are created. Should that judicatory cease to exist, the next higher judicatory becomes custodian responsible for securing and preserving the records of the extinct body. It can be difficult to convince persons that records kept by their relative are not family property but the General Assemblies of both denominations have ruled the only legal repository for the records of extinct judicatories is the Historical Foundation.

V. BIRTHPLACE SHRINE

The Birthplace Shrine located at Montgomery Bell State Park near Dickson, Tennessee was dedicated June 18, 1960. This site consists of the Memorial Chapel and a replica of the Reverend Samuel McAdow's log house. Since 1994, the Foundation has been responsible for the preservation and promotion of the Birthplace Shrine. Four endowments provide funds for maintenance and repairs: the Grace Johnson Beasley Birthplace Shrine Fund, the Birthplace Shrine Fund, the Henry Evan Harper Endowment for Cumberland Presbyterian History, and the P.F. Johnson Memorial Endowment. Gifts to these endowments provide for the continued preservation of the Birthplace Shrine. Interested donors are encouraged to contact the Foundation office. Another means of support are the fees collected from couples who use the chapel for their wedding ceremony. These funds are added to the Birthplace Shrine Fund and earnings are used for maintenance and special projects. The Board encourages individuals and groups to visit the Birthplace Shrine as an act of remembering our heritage and envisioning our future as Cumberland Presbyterians.

Recognizing the recognition and visibility that the Birthplace Shrine provides for the Cumberland Presbyterian denominations, the Foundation both sponsors and regularly participates in three activities at the Birthplace: Denomination Day, Easter Sunrise Service, and Christmas at the Bell. Both the Denomination Day and Christmas at the Bell events are costume re-enactments which interactively interpret denominational history for both Cumberland Presbyterians and other park visitors.

Groups and individuals are encouraged to contact the Foundation to set up work days and special projects. The Foundation thanks the Heritage Committee of Nashville Presbytery and the Charlotte Cumberland Presbyterian Church for their continuing volunteer upkeep of the property.

VII. FINANCIAL CONCERNS AND 2019 BUDGET

A. BUDGETS

The 2019 line-item budget of the Historical Foundation has been filed with the CPC General Assembly Office. (see page 120)

B. ENDOWMENTS

Anne Elizabeth Knight Adams Heritage Fund
Rosie Magrill Alexander Trust
Paul H. and Ann M. Allen Heritage Fund
Grace Johnson Beasley Birthplace Shrine Fund
Ethel Beal Benedict Heritage Fund
Birthplace Shrine Fund
James L. and Louise M. Bridges Heritage Fund
Mark and Elinor Swindle Brown Heritage Fund
Sydney and Elinor Brown Heritage Fund
Centennial Heritage Endowment
Walter Chesnut Heritage Fund
Lavenia Campbell Cole Heritage Fund
Cumberland Presbyterian Church in America Heritage Fund
Cumberland Presbyterian Women Archival Supplies Endowment
Bettye Jean Loggins McCaffrey Ellis Heritage Fund
Samuel Russell & Mary Grace (Barefoot) Estes Endowment
Family of Faith Endowment
Gettis and Delia Snyder Gilbert Heritage Fund
James C. and Freda M. Gilbert Heritage Fund
James C. and Freda M. Gilbert Trust
Mamie A. Gilbert Trust
Henry Evan Harper Endowment for Cumberland Presbyterian History
Ronald Wilson and Virginia Tosh Harper Endowment
Historical Foundation Trust
Donald and Jane Hubbard Heritage Fund
Cliff and Jill Hudson Heritage Fund
Robert and Kathy Hull Endowment
Into the Nineties Endowment
Joe Ben Irby Heritage Fund
P. F. Johnson Memorial Endowment
Irene A. Kiefer Endowment

Chow King Leong Endowment
Dennis Lawrence & Elmira Castleberry Magrill Trust
J. Richard Magrill Heritage Fund
Joe Richard and Mary Belle Magrill Trust
Gwendolyn McCaffrey McReynolds Heritage Fund
Jimmie Joe McKinley Heritage Fund
Edith Louise Mitchell Heritage Fund
Lloyd Freeman Mitchell Heritage Fund
Snowdy Clifton and Lillian Walkup Mitchell Heritage Fund
Rev. Charles and Paulette Morrow Endowment
Virginia Sue Williamson Morrow Heritage Fund
Anne Elizabeth Swain Odom Heritage Fund
Martha Sue Parr Heritage Fund
Florence Pennewill Heritage Fund
Morris and Ruth Pepper Endowment
Publishing House Endowment
Mable Magrill Rundell Trust
Samuel Callaway Rundell Heritage Fund
Paul and Mary Jo Schnorbus Heritage Fund
Roy and Mary Seawright Shelton Heritage Fund
Shiloh CPC Ellis County Texas Endowment
Hinkley and Vista Smartt Heritage Fund
John William Sparks Heritage Fund
Irvin Scott and Annie Mary Draper Swain Heritage Fund
F. P. Waits Historical Trust

Respectfully submitted,
Pat Ward, President
Susan Knight Gore, Archivist

THE REPORT OF THE BOARD OF TRUSTEES OF MEMPHIS THEOLOGICAL SEMINARY

Introduction

Memphis Theological Seminary is the only seminary of the Cumberland Presbyterian Church. Our history is traced back through the Cumberland Presbyterian Theological Seminary in McKenzie, Tennessee to the organization of the graduate School of Theology at Cumberland University and the Theological Department at Bethel College, both of which began in 1852. Those two schools of theology continued the legacy begun in the work of founder Reverend Finis Ewing, who educated candidates for the ministry in his home, and many other ministers, who trained young candidates in homes, churches, and on the trail. For one hundred sixty-six years, Cumberland Presbyterians have been providing formal theological education for the church's ministers. For two hundred years, the Cumberland Presbyterian Church has valued the importance of an educated ministry.

With the denomination's decision to move its seminary to Memphis, Tennessee in 1964, Memphis Theological Seminary of the Cumberland Presbyterian Church began to serve a larger and more diverse student body. Though students from other denominations were admitted during the McKenzie years, the move to a major metropolitan area opened the opportunity to attract more students from more denominations. Today, Memphis Theological Seminary has one of the most diverse student populations, in terms of denomination and race, of any seminary in the United States. This theological and denominational diversity provides a rich environment for educating pastors, chaplains, Christian educators, and other leaders for the church of Jesus Christ. The sign on our campus that faces Union Avenue reads: "Memphis Theological Seminary: an Ecumenical Mission of the Cumberland Presbyterian Church." Every Cumberland Presbyterian can be proud of the mission our seminary fulfills of educating our own church leaders, and leaders from more than 25 other denominations.

We, the trustees and administration of Memphis Theological Seminary, are privileged to be a part of this legacy, born out of and guided by the ecumenical and evangelical spirit of the Cumberland Presbyterian Church. We look forward to what God has in store for our ministry in the future. With gratitude for God's grace, guidance and provision in the past year, we make the following report to the 188th General Assembly of the Cumberland Presbyterian Church, meeting June 17-21, 2018, in Norman, Oklahoma.

I. BOARD OF TRUSTEES

A. OFFICERS

The following officers were elected by the Board of Trustees to serve during the past academic year: Moderator – Reverend Jennifer Newell (Cumberland Presbyterian minister, Tennessee-Georgia Presbytery); Vice-moderator – Reverend Nancy Cole (United Methodist minister, North Alabama Conference); Secretary – Mrs. Sondra Roddy (Cumberland Presbyterian elder, Clarksville, Tennessee); Treasurer – Mrs. Cassandra Price-Perry (Vice President of Operations and CFO, MTS). Jennifer Newell resigned from office and from the Board in January for personal reasons, and Reverend Nancy Cole assumed the office of Moderator. At the February meeting, Revernd Dr. Anne Hames was elected Vice-Moderator for the remainder of this academic year.

B. BOARD REPRESENTATIVE

Reverend Kevin Brantley, Cumberland Presbytery, was elected to serve as the Board's representative to this meeting of the General Assembly. Reverend Kip Rush, Nashville Presbytery, was elected alternate.

C. MEETINGS

The Board of Trustees has met twice since the last meeting of General Assembly: September 28-30, 2017 and February 8-9, 2018. The Board is scheduled to meet one more time before the meeting of General Assembly, on May 10-11, 2018. In addition to full Board meetings, standing committees meet on a regular schedule between Board meetings, usually by conference call.

Members of our Board of Trustees devote significant time and resources to their work on behalf of the seminary. By rule of the General Assembly, thirteen of the twenty-four members are Cumberland Presbyterians. The other eleven members of the Board represent five different denominations.

D. EXPIRATION OF TERMS

The terms of eight of twenty-four members of the Board of Trustees expire each year. Four of the eight whose terms expire this year are eligible to succeed themselves and have agreed to serve another three year term: Reverend Linda Howell (Cumberland Presbyterian, Keller, Texas); Ms. Sondra Roddy (Cumberland Presbyterian, Clarksville, Tennessee); Reverend Doctor Melvin Charles Smith (Baptist, Memphis, Tennessee), and Ms. Latisha Towns (Baptist, Memphis, Tennessee). All have served faithfully and contributed greatly to the life of the seminary. We are grateful for their willingness to continue serving if re-elected.

One trustee who was eligible to serve for another term resigned in 2017 after it was too late for him to be replaced, Reverend Dr. Kevin Henson (Cumberland Presbyterian, Keller, Texas).

Two other trustees resigned during the year because of family and work obligations that made it impossible for them to serve. Reverend Jennifer Newell (Cumberland Presbyterian, Chattanooga, Tennessee), and Mr. Craig White (Cumberland Presbyterian Church in America, Huntsville, Alabama) both of the class of 2020, will need to be replaced. Those resignations have been communicated to the Office of the General Assembly and the Nominating Committee.

Three trustees who complete their terms this year are ineligible for re-election, having been re-elected twice. Reverend Kevin Brantley (Cumberland Presbyterian, Sacramento, Kentucky), Mr. Mark Maddox (Cumberland Presbyterian, Dresden, Tennessee), and Mr. Takayoshi (Ted) Shirai (Cumberland Presbyterian, Yokohama, Japan), have served faithfully and well. We are grateful to God for all who have served in this important role on behalf of MTS and the Cumberland Presbyterian Church.

RECOMMENDATION 1: That the General Assembly express its gratitude to trustees Henson, Newell, White, Brantley, Maddox, and Shirai for their faithful service to Memphis Theological Seminary and the Cumberland Presbyterian Church.

E. WORK OF THE BOARD

In May, the Board adopted a new Strategic Plan to guide the work of the seminary over the next 3 to 5 years. The plan is organized around three strategic goals: Growing, Engaging, and Sustaining.

Memphis Theological Seminary Strategic Plan Imperatives are to:

1. Strengthen our ministry to the real world by growing our educational opportunities, our student body, our faculty, our ecumenical partnerships, and our facilities.

2. Create a culture of service that is engaging all barriers to community through intentional diversity, intentional multicultural educational experiences, and intentional internal and external communication.

3. Create a fiscal foundation for sustaining MTS today and into the future through enhancing existing revenue streams, creating new revenue streams, and balanced budgets.

These three broad, strategic imperatives cross all departments. Developing the objectives to reach these imperatives will necessitate collaboration and compromise. There will be need to be objectives for increasing enrollment, eliminating work silos, improving marketing, distance learning, and many others. Each department at MTS has developed goals and objectives to support the three imperatives and will track its progress toward attaining its goals on a regular basis.

F. "MINISTRY FOR THE REAL WORLD"

The 183rd General Assembly approved a recommendation from our Board granting us permission to engage in a major capital campaign for Memphis Theological Seminary. After two years in the quiet phase, the Board authorized a comprehensive campaign, titled, "Ministry for the Real World," which was launched publicly in October of 2015. The Board authorized a goal of $25 million to be raised through 2020, with approximately $10 million committed to operations, $10 million to capital improvements, including the construction of a new chapel, and $5 million for endowments.

As of the writing of this report, we have secured approximately $17 million in gifts and pledges toward the goal. Work has begun on the construction of Hamilton Chapel, and should be completed by June of 2019. What follows is the case statement for the campaign.

MINISTRY FOR THE REAL WORLD
Scholarship, Piety and Justice
MEMPHIS THEOLOGICAL SEMINARY

March 24, 2014

MINISTRY FOR THE REAL WORLD
TWO CENTURIES OF MAKING A DIFFERENCE.

"Academic scholarship is a major hallmark of Memphis Theological Seminary. The school feeds both the minds and spirits of its students. Rigorous scholastic study and intellectual discussion of the Bible from different points of view are encouraged. . . The goal is to foster informed critical thinkers. It is not to promote the agenda of Memphis Theological Seminary. When students graduate, they have the knowledge and practical tools to be effective ministers. They live their lives according to the teachings and values of the Bible. Graduates are well prepared to positively impact individuals, congregations and society." – Mrs. Ruby Wharton, Esq., Trustee.

In 1821, a pastor's dedication to theological education and inclusiveness gave rise to the first theological school west of the Mississippi. Thirty years later, out of the same Spirit, a theological department was established at Bethel College (now Bethel University) in McKenzie, Tennessee, an institution of the Cumberland Presbyterian Church.

Over one hundred years later, in 1964, in order to reach more ministers for the Gospel, the seminary was moved to Memphis, Tennessee and renamed Memphis Theological Seminary. It was intentionally opened as an ecumenical seminary that welcomes men and women of all faiths, cultures and ages. The philosophy and values of the seminary are as meaningful today as they were two centuries ago. The school focuses on scholarship, piety and justice. Inherent in these three words are powerful concepts that differentiate MTS from other seminaries.

• Scholarship implies disciplined, traditional study, but it also involves becoming a discerning critical thinker. Graduates are compelling spiritual servant leaders and thoughtful ministers. They are able to explain Biblical passages within both their historical context and their relevancy in today's world—and in such a way that lives are transformed.

• Piety involves our heart-felt devotion to God. True piety leads to compassion, selflessness, universal love and respect for all of God's creation. As Doctor Martin Luther King Jr. described so eloquently when he wrote, "Our goal is to create a beloved community, and this will require a qualitative change in our souls as well as a quantitative change in our lives."

• Justice does not refer to civil law. It is much more. Without the practice of justice as described in the Bible, love, liberty and even life cannot flourish. Love alone does not ensure equality. Biblical justice involves care for the poor and powerless and leads to inclusiveness, understanding and compassion. It is respecting all people, even those who are very different from you. It is actively participating in righting wrongs whenever and however they present themselves.

Our student population is very diverse and reflects the real world. There are no age, gender, economic, cultural, theological or racial barriers here. Our graduates will be ministering to many different populations and denominations. Their experience at MTS helps them understand how to work toward a beloved community.

Some of the most respected and influential ministers in the Mid-South are graduates of Memphis Theological Seminary. They are acknowledged for their depth of Biblical and religious knowledge and their ecumenism. They are respected for their ability to influence both religious and secular communities.

Wherever our graduates serve, they impact the lives of those they touch. They are formed to be ministers in the real world.

Our graduates touch thousands of lives in their chosen ministry. They become pastors, youth ministers, educators and chaplains in hospitals, prisons and the military.

For over fifty years, the seminary has occupied the magnificent turn-of-the-century Newburger Mansion in midtown Memphis, Tennessee. We have worked hard to maintain the original beauty of this grand home. Warmth and intimacy are created by cascading stairways, arched doorways, and handcrafted woodwork. It is the beautiful face we show to the public. In more recent years, we have added two adjoining mansions in response to a growing student body and the faculty and staff hired to serve them.

The three homes have served us well, but with enrollment reaching 325 students, we have outgrown them. Because of the reputation and impact of our graduates, our enrollment continues to grow. We believe we can reach an enrollment of 450 students in the not-too-distant future. Together students will represent over 30 denominations, several states and a few countries.

The Newburger Mansion's prized Ballroom is our makeshift chapel. Unfortunately it can only seat one-fifth of our student body. We are grateful to have resided in the homes on beautiful East Parkway during our time of growth. We will always maintain them. They will continue to serve us well as library space, offices and intimate gathering spaces for small discussion groups. But it is urgent that we expand our campus and construct a chapel and an academic building. We have acquired property adjacent to our campus for both structures. Now we must build. Our future depends on it.

PREPARING FOR ANOTHER TWO HUNDRED YEARS OF MINISTRY FOR THE REAL WORLD

The Board and administration of Memphis Theological Seminary have thought long and hard about the future of the seminary. We have prayed for God to guide us in our decision making. In order to ensure our future, we must undertake three important and much-needed projects without delay.

1. A new chapel is a top priority. We have made do with a small converted ballroom for too long.
2. We need a building to house our new, groundbreaking Methodist House of Studies. Methodists represent the single largest contingent of students at MTS. With faculty offices and meeting space, the Methodist House of Studies will relieve pressure on MTS's limited academic facilities.
3. Significantly increasing our endowment and underwriting an important faculty chair will enable MTS to prosper and grow. It will help us become financially stable and ready to withstand any potential financial crises for the next two hundred years. Like most seminaries, we are tuition dependent. At last report our endowment was $9.2 million. This does not generate sufficient interest income to meet the growing demands of our expanding student body. It is crucial that we double the endowment immediately. It will allow us to meet the increasing need for scholarships and financial aid. And it will be a cushion to protect MTS from unforeseen emergencies.

While MTS serves a variety of denominations, its' roots extend back to the Cumberland Presbyterian tradition. By fully endowing the Baird-Buck Chair in Cumberland Presbyterian Studies, we will ensure that our Cumberland Presbyterian students are fully prepared to serve the congregation to which they are sent.

Successfully completing these projects will enable MTS to aggressively pursue its mission well into the twenty-first century: To educate men and women for ordained and lay Christian ministry in the church and the world by shaping and inspiring lives devoted to scholarship, piety and justice.

Project One: Construct a new free-standing chapel

We are blessed to have already received two wonderfully generous gifts designated for our new chapel. The first is an extraordinary cash donation of $1 million. The same donors gave an additional $2 million in 2017 to help the project get started. These significant gifts are a vote of confidence in Memphis Theological Seminary. It recognizes the difference our graduates make in the world.

The second is one of the oldest and finest pipe organs in the South. It was donated to us by the Union Avenue United Methodist Church. It is an acknowledgement of the role we play in preparing strong spiritual leaders. The pipe organ was manufactured in 1924 by the M.P. Moller Organ Company. In today's dollars, it is estimated to be worth $550,000—a valuable and prestigious gift. Moller pipe organs are also installed in the chapels at Camp David and Lincoln Center.

Both gifts are true blessings and will enable MTS to construct a chapel that:
- Reflects our identity, purpose and excellence.
- Is large and adaptable enough for different denominations within the seminary to conduct worship services reflective of their cultures and expressions of faith.
- Provides a place of worship that will accommodate our entire student body.
- Replicates in a small way the churches in which graduates will preach. This will give students the experience of speaking from a real pulpit rather than a small podium.
- Has the proper acoustics to showcase the beautiful Moller pipe organ.
- Will allow us to offer certificates or degrees in church music and organ music.

Project Two: Construct a home for the Methodist House of Studies

There has long been a perceived gap between "the academy" and "the church." We at MTS have become convinced that such a binary way of thinking is deeply flawed. The relationship between seminary and church ought to be marked by an organic, mutually beneficial partnership. Within that partnership, it is the seminary's calling to be in service to the church—preparing women and men for pastoral leadership and resourcing the current ministry needs of pastors and congregations.

We at MTS believe that there is a point of intersection between the mission of the seminary and the mission of the church. Our commitment is to focus our resources and attention at that point of intersection. We are planning a major new initiative in the life of MTS—the Methodist House of Studies. Under the direction of faculty member Doctor Andrew C. Thompson, the Methodist House of Studies will serve as a "community within a community" where our Methodist students can take advantage of the best in Wesleyan theological formation within MTS' richly ecumenical context. The House of Studies will also serve as a vehicle for connecting the resources of MTS with the needs of the wider church. This link will offer pastors and congregations new avenues and contexts for mission and ministry.

The proposed building will house professors' offices and provide meeting space for this groundbreaking program. Given our facilities limitations, the additional space will contribute to the success of this important program.

The ecumenical partnership between Memphis Theological Seminary and the United Methodist Church goes back for decades. And from a strong foundation we believe a vital future can be cultivated and grown. At this crucial juncture in the life of both seminary and church, we are excited to anticipate advancing the relationship between the two with the creation of a home at MTS for the Methodist House of Studies.

**Project Three: Significantly increase our endowment including
fully endowing the Baird-Buck Chair in Cumberland Presbyterian Studies.**

Without a larger endowment, we cannot fully execute our mission. Cassandra Price-Perry, Vice President of Operations/CFO, explains this very well.

"I am here to use my financial skills to help students respond to their call by God to ministry. Because of our small endowment, the number and size of our scholarships and financial aid packages are limited. We are not able to enroll as many highly qualified and motivated students as we would like because they can't afford the cost of attendance—books, fees, travel, food and other miscellaneous expenses."

Our tuition is certainly not exorbitant, but nor is it cheap. Many students find it difficult to fund the entire three years required to receive a degree.

Sadly, this compromises our commitment to being an ecumenical school that welcomes everyone who meets our academic requirements. We have cut our operating expenses to the bone during the economic downturn. Still, we can only offer financial assistance to just a portion of the students who apply. Only with philanthropy will it be possible to provide financial assistance to the many motivated and qualified students who are called to serve.

Founded by the Cumberland Presbyterian Church, Memphis Theological Seminary has proclaimed the inclusiveness of the Gospel message for more than 150 years. A fully endowed Baird-Buck Chair in Cumberland Presbyterian Studies will ensure that the vibrant tradition which has guided MTS for eight generations will inspire seminarians for many years to come.

MAKING A REAL DIFFERENCE: MINISTRY FOR THE REAL WORLD

The graduates of Memphis Theological Seminary proclaim and embody God's message of redemption, justice and peace in service to others. Our graduates guide people in their faith and help them understand why they believe. This is powerful. They ignite people's hearts in love for Jesus Christ and support them in walking in His way. They model Christ-like behavior, and in doing so they transform the lives of those they touch—in church, in the grocery store, on a bus or in prisons. They shatter prejudice. They stand in the face of desperation and offer hope. They provide for those with nothing, and they teach others to do the same. The world is a better place because of their real world ministry—a ministry that is persuasive, practical and purposeful.

"Today, mainline religions are grappling with retaining membership. Our emphasis is on academics, practical application and an inclusive approach to theology. This prepares our graduates to be relevant and meaningful ordained and lay ministers in the real world today. This is the only way they can serve and embody God's mission of redemption, justice and peace in service to the New Creation of Jesus Christ. "My father attended this seminary, so it was only natural that I followed in his footsteps. Now that I am president, I am blessed to be leading the initiative to bring our facilities into the twenty-first century. We cannot wait. Our campus must reflect the extraordinary academic excellence within its walls." – Dr. Daniel J. Earheart-Brown, President

Angel, must I give again, I ask in dismay. And must I keep giving and giving and giving it away? Oh no, said the angel, his glance pierced me through. Just keep giving 'til the Lord stops giving to you.

THIS MINISTRY FOR THE REAL WORLD CAMPAIGN
IS NOT REALLY ABOUT NEW BUILDINGS

It is about the people.

It is about the highly qualified professors who work inside them. It is about the committed and passionate students who are following God's call to ministry. Sometimes they leave successful careers. Their families make significant economic and lifestyle changes. They do this to serve God, humanity and all of creation. Their lives are transformed. And as a result, our lives are changed. And the world is a better place because of them. Adequate classrooms and a student center will support students on their rigorous academic and spiritual journey. They deserve a real chapel in which to pray, preach, meditate and seek God's further counsel. A chapel filled with the music of a real pipe organ. And joyous voices joined in praise. Finally, Memphis Theological Seminary deserves facilities that truly reflect the excellence of its high academic standards. Its commitment to forming extraordinary ministers for the real world must be celebrated with quality facilities.

You have the power make a real and powerful difference. Your support ensures the success of our campaign. It also secures the future of Memphis Theological Seminary. With your support we will be able to continue to graduate outstanding ministers for the real world. Prayerfully consider your role in supporting our important undertaking. And as you do, please consider the wisdom of this poem. It reflects the insights of a very generous philanthropist.

YOUR SUPPORT HAS A POWERFUL RETURN

A donation to Memphis Theological Seminary means that your investment will be leveraged in extraordinary ways.

A message from Tim Orr, former Chair of the Board Trustees, Memphis Theological Seminary:

Dear Friends,

As you consider your participation in the Ministry for the Real World Campaign, you can rest assured that your investment will be leveraged in extraordinary ways. The check I write to Memphis Theological Seminary is multiplied many times over. I am not just writing a check for the seminary. My donation impacts global society.

Here is what I mean. People come here because they are called to ministry. MTS forms them into leaders—Christian leaders with Christian values. Their lives are changed forever. But it doesn't stop there. Everyone touched by one of our graduates is changed also. MTS prepares ministers to be relevant and compelling in the real world. In a world that is spiritually bankrupt, they are effective in their congregation and in all of society. Their lives are transformed, and they are given the tools and skills to transform the spirit of our global society— and they do. I ask you, 'what investment has this powerful a return?'

I hope you will join me at this turning point in the life of Memphis Theological Seminary. Your prayers and generosity will ensure that MTS continues to prepare men and women for transformation ministry to the real world.

Faithfully,
Tim Orr

RECOMMENDATION 2: That the General Assembly encourage individuals, churches, and groups across the Cumberland Presbyterian Church to consider investing in the development of future leaders through the "Ministry for the Real World" campaign.

II. ADMINISTRATION

A. PRESIDENT

Daniel J. (Jay) Earheart Brown, Ph.D., became the seventh President of Memphis Theological Seminary August 1, 2005. Jay had served on the faculty of MTS since August, 1997, having previously served as a pastor in Nashville, Tennessee, and Lexington, Kentucky. He is a life-long Cumberland Presbyterian and son of a Cumberland Presbyterian minister. He is a graduate of Bethel College (B.A.), Memphis Theological Seminary (M.Div.), and Union Theological Seminary in Richmond, Virginia (Ph.D.). He will complete his thirteenth year in this position at the end of the current academic year.

B. VICE PRESIDENT OF ACADEMIC AFFAIRS/DEAN

Reverend R. Stan Wood, D.Min., retired in July, 2017 as Vice President of Academic Affairs and Dean. The entire seminary community is grateful for the faithful service of Doctor Wood to the MTS community. In February, 2017, after a national search, Doctor Peter Gathje was elected by the Board of Trustees to become Vice President of Academic Affairs and Dean of the Seminary upon Doctor Wood's retirement.

Doctor Gathje served previously as Professor of Ethics at MTS and Associate Dean of Curriculum and Instruction. He is a lay Roman Catholic and is deeply committed to the mission of Memphis Theological Seminary, having taught on our faculty for the past ten years.

C. VICE PRESIDENT OF ADVANCEMENT

In October 2014, Doctor Keith Gaskin began work as Vice President of Advancement, coming to MTS after over twenty years of experience in development work for higher education, including service at Mississippi State University and the University of Alabama. He is a layman in the Presbyterian Church (USA). Keith holds a Ph.D. in higher education leadership from Mississippi State University.

Keith has brought to his work at MTS a proven track record of higher education fundraising, a commitment to the mission of MTS, and the ability to manage and build on the efforts of those who have gone before him. He has worked well with faculty and staff to encourage participation across the seminary in the work of development.

D. VICE PRESIDENT OF OPERATIONS/CFO

Ms. Cassandra Price-Perry began work with MTS in August 2010 as Vice President of Operations and Chief Financial Officer. She is a Certified Public Accountant with over 20 years of experience in business and accounting. Cassandra is an active laywoman in her Roman Catholic Church in Southaven, Mississippi. She has received high praise from our auditors and our Board for her work over the past almost seven years.

III. INSTRUCTION

A. DEGREE PROGRAMS

Memphis Theological Seminary offers five degree programs and three certificate programs, including the certificate offered through the Program of Alternate Studies. The Master of Divinity is the basic degree program for persons preparing for ordained ministry in many denominations. It continues to be our largest degree program, with over 70% of students enrolled. The M.Div. requires 84 semester hours and takes three years of full-time study to complete.

The Master of Arts (Religion) degree is an academic degree for persons seeking to pursue further graduate studies. The MAR requires 36 semester hours and takes two years of full-time study to complete. The faculty launched a major revision to the MAR in the fall of 2015 to clarify its role as an academic degree.

The Doctor of Ministry degree is a professional degree designed for pastors and other ministers who have at least three years of full-time work in ministry after their M.Div. and who want to engage in further theological reflection on the practice of ministry. The D.Min. is designed around five two-week residencies, in January and July, and the implementation of and report on a major project in ministry. It usually takes 3-5 years to complete.

In the spring of 2013, we awarded our first new degree in many years: the Master of Arts in Youth Ministry (MAYM). Through our partnership with the Center for Youth Ministry Training in Brentwood, Tennessee, and the new certificate program in youth ministry through the Cumberland Presbyterian Church, we have over 40 students enrolled in this degree program. MTS currently has, we believe, the largest master's program in youth ministry in the United States.

In the spring of 2016, we were approved by our accrediting bodies (The Southern Association of Colleges and Schools, and the Association of Theological Schools in the United States and Canada) to offer a new degree, the Master of Arts in Christian Ministry (MACM). This degree program began in the fall of 2016 with concentrations offered in Christian Education, Urban Ministry, and Social Justice Ministry. The MACM is a 42 hour degree for persons interested in pursuing specialized ministries. We plan to offer additional concentrations in the future (possibly rural ministry, counseling, etc.)

At Commencement in May of 2017, Memphis Theological Seminary awarded the Master of Arts in Youth Ministry degree to twelve graduates. Three persons were awarded the Master of Arts (Religion) degree. Three persons received the Master of Arts in Christian Ministry degree. Thirty-eight persons were awarded the Master of Divinity degree, and fourteen were awarded the Doctor of Ministry degree. Of these seventy graduates, fourteen were Cumberland Presbyterians.

Cumberland Presbyterian Master of Divinity graduates were:
Christopher Shane Anderson, Arkansas Presbytery
Deborah A. Chall-Hutchinson, Nashville Presbytery
Aaron Andrew Craig, East Tennessee Presbytery
Daniel Hopkins, Covenant Presbytery
Matthew Benjamin Ingram, Grace Presbytery
Leanne Rose Kerner, Murfreesboro Presbytery
Nathaniel Clay Mathews, Nashville Presbytery
Lacey Abigail Prevost, Hope Presbytery
Emily Claire Trapp, West Tennessee Presbytery
Kevin McKinley Twilla, Murfreesboro Presbytery
Paul Micah Watson, Murfreesboro Presbytery
Neal Wilkinson, Nashville Presbytery

Cumberland Presbyterian Master of Arts (Religion) graduate:
Rusuko Matsumoto, Japan Presbytery

Cumberland Presbyterian Doctor of Ministry graduate:
Choil Ma, Nashville Presbytery

B. CERTIFICATE PROGRAMS
In addition to the five degree programs, MTS offers the following certificates:
Program of Alternate Studies of the Cumberland Presbyterian Church
Drug and Alcohol Addiction Counseling Graduate Certificate
James Netters Certificate in Ministry
Certificate in Wesleyan Studies

C. FACULTY
For the current academic year, Memphis Theological Seminary has fifteen full-time teaching faculty and two administrative faculty members who teach part-time. In addition, the seminary curriculum is greatly enhanced by the work of ten to fifteen adjunct professors, most of whom are active in pastoral or other ministries.

Members of the MTS faculty continue to publish books and articles both for the academy and the church. Many faculty members preach in area churches on a regular basis, deliver lectures for local churches and judicatories, deliver papers at academic conferences, and write articles for a wide range of readers.

Under the leadership of VP/Dean Gathje, the faculty implemented our new M.Div. curriculum in the fall of 2016. Under the new curriculum, there will be greater emphasis on integration of learning for pastoral leadership. It will also continue to strengthen our focus on the practice of ministry as imaginative leadership drawing from the resources of scripture and tradition in particular cultural contexts.

D. ENROLLMENT
Total enrollment in Memphis Theological Seminary for the fall term of 2017 was 288, including all degree and certificate programs. We continued to see a drop in enrollment in our largest degree program,

the Master of Divinity. Declining enrollments led again to painful budget adjustments during the year, including the elimination of several part-time and full-time positions. Our largest number of students comes from the United Methodist Church, with 23.6% of total enrollment. Cumberland Presbyterians are the second largest denomination represented in the student body with about 12.3% of all students.

We continue to work to recruit Cumberland Presbyterian students, and to lift up the call of God to ordained ministry in the church. We call on all Cumberland Presbyterians to pray that God will continue to call men and women to the office of ministry, and that they will be well prepared through our educational institutions to lead growing and vibrant congregations in the ministry of Jesus Christ to the world.

RECOMMENDATION 3: That the General Assembly encourage all probationers to consider Memphis Theological Seminary and the Program of Alternate Studies as their first options for meeting educational requirements for ordained ministry.

D. PROGRAM OF ALTERNATE STUDIES (written by Doctor Michael Qualls, Director)

The Program of Alternate Studies currently has three foci:

1. Preparing for ministry those who are practically hindered from pursuing traditional theological education. We are working to provide integrity to the ordination process.

2. Delivering the denominational studies that enable persons with a Master of Divinity degree from an institution other than MTS to meet the constitutional requirements for ordination in the Cumberland Presbyterian Church.

3. Providing the critical education necessary for assimilation of potential Cumberland Presbyterian pastors in the expanding global church.

We are working to expand in a fourth area:

4. Becoming a reliable resource for foundational education of lay persons interested or involved in congregational leadership in the Cumberland Presbyterian Church.

MTS administration has approved a reduced tuition rate of $200 that would allow those not seeking ordination to take any of our online or face-to-face courses.

SES 2018

The 2018 Summer Extension School will be held on the Campus of Bethel University July 7-21. PAS Graduation will be July 7th at 11:00 am in Odom Hall.

ONLINE CLASSES

We held a class last summer that included in-class and remote students with live interactivity, debuting the new technology MTS is now employing from Academic Platforms. PAS is thrilled to be able to continue to develop our online offerings and find more students are accessible for the short-term intensive courses we offer when remote participation is an option. Most of our three online course offerings this winter have been asynchronous (at student's own schedule allows). Recently, a live synchronous online class was well received. Our instructors are now encouraged to use the tools available to enhance their learning outcomes.

PARTNERS IN MISSION

The opportunity to assist the global outreach of the Cumberland Presbyterian church has become an important aspect of PAS in recent years. Working with MMT personnel and PAS-Colombia we developed an experimental "distance" curriculum for a group of provisional pastors in Cuba. Doctor Stan Wood, retired academic dean of MTS, recently accompanied me to Haiti to complete the last course in the preparation for a group of six aspiring pastors from the Haiti Council of the Cumberland Presbyterian Church. I am extremely grateful for the gifts from several Cumberland Presbyterians to help defray the travel expense. This kind of ministry is done because the need is great, with no expectation that the students could pay tuition. I would like to call attention to the reality that there has been no increase from OUO for many years. Our tuition has continued to rise, sometimes working hardship on students and presbyteries, so that we will be able to meet the essential needs of the program without relying on MTS to make up shortfalls.

CPCA/CP COOPERATIVE WORK

The PAS Advisory Council approved the director to work out a plan for a reciprocal relationship of students in either PAS or the CPCA Certification program. This takes us one step closer to a synchronous mutual relationship.

SPECIAL RECOGNITION

We express appreciation to the planners of the 2018 General Assembly for a brief moment to make a presentation honoring the life and ministry of Reverend Dale Gentry, one of the last of the "circuit riding" pastors. An endowment has been inaugurated in his name with the income from the fund going to support the work of the Program of Alternate Studies. All who were impacted by Reverend Gentry's life and ministry are encouraged to contribute to this fund in his memory. A fuller narrative of his life will be shared at the MTS/PAS Luncheon on Wednesday.

It remains my great joy to serve in this vital ministry of the Cumberland Presbyterian Church. I covet your prayers for the continued success of our program. Please help us promote throughout the church the many ways that PAS can benefit individual clergy, lay persons, and congregations.

Respectfully,
Michael Qualls, Director

E. NEW ACADEMIC INITIATIVES

In the spring of 2016 we received word from our accreditors that we have been approved for a new degree program, the Master of Arts in Christian Ministry. This degree is designed for persons who are called to ministries other than ordained pastoral ministry. The new two-year degree will begin enrolling students in the fall of 2016. Students will choose between concentrations in Christian Education, Urban Ministry, and Social Justice. Additional concentrations to be added may include Children and Family Ministries, Rural Ministry, and other specialized ministries.

Our Master of Arts in Youth Ministry degree is, we think, now the largest graduate degree program in youth ministry in the United States. We continue to cooperate with the Center for Youth Ministry Training in Brentwood, Tennessee to offer a graduate residency in youth ministry.

In the fall of 2016 we implemented a major revision to our Master of Divinity curriculum. The revised curriculum will provide more opportunity for team teaching and cross-disciplinary work focused on integration of theology and practice for ministry.

With assistance from Bethel University leaders, we are planning to expand significantly our distance education offerings in the 2017-2018 academic year. New classroom technology was provided through a generous gift from one of our major donors and will provide educational services far beyond our geographic base. We are currently in the application process for approval for a hybrid online Master of Divinity degree using a cohort model of education. The application should be acted upon by the Association of Theological Schools in June of 2018.

F. ACCREDITATION

Memphis Theological Seminary holds dual accreditation by the Association of Theological Schools in the United States and Canada (ATS), and the Southern Association of Colleges and Schools (SACS). Every ten years, member schools go through an extensive process of re-accreditation review.

We completed our on-site visits from both accrediting bodies in March of 2018. Both bodies recommended reaffirmation of accreditation, with notations for areas of needed improvement, including financial stability, strategic planning and evaluation, and evaluation of educational outcomes in degree programs.

IV. FACILITIES

A. LEADERSHIP

Since the fall of 2015, our facilities and safety department has been ably led by Mr. Greg Spencer and a dedicated staff of facilities technicians. Mr. Spencer has more than twenty years of experience in construction and facilities management. He served in this role for two years previously, and after a brief stint in facilities management in corporate environment, Greg returned to our MTS leadership. We are grateful for his service.

B. DEBT ON PROPERTY

In 2015 we were able to secure a commercial loan to repay our debt to the Board of Stewardship for the purchase of properties adjacent to our campus. That long term debt now stands at approximately $2 million, less than half of our annual operating budget. This low debt allows us to operate as efficiently as possible.

C. COMMUTER HOUSING

MTS began to convert its student housing from individual rentals to commuter housing in 1998. Currently, MTS provides commuter housing, with very reasonable nightly rates, for about fifty students each week of the regular term. The need for such commuter housing has continued to grow, as has income from such rentals. Our ability to serve students from about a 250 mile radius around Memphis, through block scheduling of classes and provision of affordable commuter housing, has had a significant impact on the growth of the student body over the past ten years.

D. CAMPUS WORK GROUPS

We have been blessed in recent years by adult and youth work groups who have come to MTS during the summer months to help repair and maintain our campus housing. Groups have come from Trilla, Illinois, Greeneville, Tennessee, Florence, Alabama, Bowling Green, Kentucky, and Collierville, Tennessee, and the youth from West Tennessee Presbytery to volunteer their time in a variety of areas. We encourage work groups who would be willing to help the seminary in this way to contact Mr. Greg Spencer in the Facilities Office of the seminary.

E. SAFETY

The Office of Safety of MTS continues to explore ways to enhance the safety of our students in the context of our urban campus. Through the use of lighting, security officers, secure locks, and well articulated safety plans, the seminary seeks to provide a safe environment for students and visitors to our campus.

During the past seven years, MTS has contracted with a local security company to provide regular patrols around our neighborhood. This additional safety measure has been well received by our students and by our neighbors. We continue to seek ways to provide a safe environment for our campus community.

V. ADVANCEMENT AND FINANCE

A. BUDGET

Our Board of Trustees will approve a budget for the 2018-2019 academic year at its May meeting. Copies of that budget will be provided at the meeting of General Assembly.

Like seminaries across the country, we continue to face budget challenges from declining enrollments. The Board of Trustees in its February 2018 meeting imposed new budget discipline on the seminary to ensure the closing of our operating deficit over the next three years.

B. SCHOLARSHIPS AND GRANTS

We continue to cultivate relationships with foundations whose mission closely aligns with ours. The following grants for scholarships and other projects have been received in recent years:

1. The Eli Lilly Endowment, Inc. – "Thriving in Ministry"

In December 2017, MTS was notified that it had been selected to receive a grant of $1 million dollars from the Lilly Endowment, Inc., for use over five years to fund a Center for Pastoral Formation, Imagination, and Leadership at Memphis Theological Seminary. Working with partners including the Methodist Healthcare Clergy Coaching Network, the Center for Transforming Communities, the Cumberland Presbyterian Pastoral Ministry Development Team, and the Memphis Annual Conference of the UMC, the work of the Center will focus on supporting and sustaining clergy in their first five years of ministry post seminary. The new Center at MTS will provide services to our graduates to help them develop networks of support, encouragement, and spiritual depth to help them understand and survive the challenges of pastoral ministry in our time.

2. The Evelyn Alexander Scholarship

This scholarship is given annually to a PCUSA student. The scholarship fund is administered by First Presbyterian Church of Paragould, Arkansas.

3. The Kemmons Wilson Family Foundation

The Kemmons Wilson family, founders of the Holiday Inn hotel chain and noted philanthropists in Memphis, has renewed funding of the Wilson Scholarships at $15,000 for this year.

4. The H.W. Durham Foundation

In 2013, the Memphis-based H.W. Durham Foundation renewed its gift of $5,000 to provide 5 $1,000 scholarships for students who are 55+ years of age. These Durham Scholars will represent much of our student body who are second-career students.

C. ENDOWMENTS

1. The Reverend Dr. Stan Wood Endowment for Doctor of Ministry Students

Upon his retirement as Vice President of Academic Affairs and Dean of MTS, several friends of Doctor Stan Wood donated to begin an endowment in his honor. The Stan Wood Endowment, when it reaches a significant corpus, will provide D.Min. scholarships in gratitude for Stan's long and faithful service as Director of the D.Min. program at MTS.

2. The Young Kim Family Endowment for Excellence

Established by Doctor Yoong Kim and his wife, Ann, the $1 million commitment will provide unrestricted income to support areas of greatest need at the discretion of the President, including, but not limited to: operations, student and faculty support, technology, and campus infrastructure upgrades.

3. The James T. Freeman Endowed Scholarship

Established with gratitude for the life and ministry of MTS graduate, Reverend James T. Freeman, by MTS alumnus Doctor Randolph Meade Walker and the West Tennessee Baptist Missionary and Educational Association, the Freeman Scholarship will support African American Baptist students wishing to study at MTS. Rev. Freeman was a long-time pastor in the Memphis area who made regular trips to Kenya, West Africa, to dig wells, build schools and churches, and to provide support for some of the poorest communities in Kenya. Reverend Freeman was among the first African American students to enroll in MTS after the move to Memphis in 1964.

4. The Hughston R. and Lorraine Peyton Endowment

Reverend Hughston R. Peyton was a native of Hopkinsville, Kentucky. He grew up in the Cumberland Presbyterian Church and attended Bethel College. He went on to serve as a minister in the Presbyterian Church USA and as Field Director of Christian Education for the Synod of Southern California until his death at 100. Income from this endowment will support operations for the seminary.

5. The Baird-Buck Chair of Cumberland Presbyterian Studies

Doctor Clinton Buck, Professor Emeritus of Christian Education at MTS, knowing the need for more focused teaching in CP Heritage, has converted an existing endowment that was originally begun with the hopes of endowing a chair in Christian Education. Subsequent to Doctor Buck's decision, the late Mrs. Thalia Baird, widow of former President and Professor Doctor Colvin Baird, converted an endowment they had designated for general operations. Together with The Reverend J.T. Buck Scholarship Endowment Fund established in 1979 to provide scholarship assistance for Cumberland Presbyterian students at Memphis Theological Seminary, the new endowment was established with an initial principal balance of approximately $112,000. To-date, the fund has grown to almost $450,000 thanks to generous contributions from many Cumberland Presbyterians. The purpose of this endowment is to strengthen the Cumberland Presbyterian Church by establishing an endowed professorship with a primary focus of teaching Cumberland Presbyterian history, theology, church administration and the practice of ministry that is particular to the Cumberland Presbyterian Church. The goal is to raise $1.5 million to fully fund this endowed chair.

6. Reverend Hillman and Lorene Moore Endowed Scholarship Fund

Hillman Moore established this endowment fund on October 10, 2013, to be funded with a future gift of a bequest from his estate. We note with sadness and gratitude his passing in March of 2018. The endowment will be used to provide scholarship funds for training Cumberland Presbyterian students at Memphis Theological Seminary.

7. Wes and Susan Brantley Endowment

On October 15, 2013, the Brantley family of Ada, Oklahoma, was deeply saddened by the death of Susan Brantley, wife of former MTS trustee Wes Brantley, and mother of current trustee Kevin Brantley. In her memory, Wes has established the Wes and Susan Brantley Endowment to support general operating expenses of the seminary.

8. The Davis/Winston Scholarship for National Baptist Students

In the waning days of the spring semester 2013, one CP and one United Methodist student listened as three fellow students talked about the struggles they have in paying their seminary tuition. For these two students, all or most of their tuition is paid by their denomination. For the others, all National Baptists, humble servants with sweet spirits, the story is completely different.

Moved by the Holy Spirit through their student colleagues, they sought a way to establish a scholarship to help future National Baptist students. In recognition of the blessing received when seminary education is paid in full or in part by scholarship and/or denominational assistance, and in honor of exemplary and invigorating teaching by professors Doctor Christopher B. Davis and Doctor Eric Winston, they established a scholarship to support National Baptist students at MTS.

9. Reverend David and Leota Watson Scholarship Endowment Fund

A new endowment has been established to honor the ministry of the late Reverend David Watson.

His widow, Mrs. Leota Watson, has chosen to direct the endowment earnings to support scholarships for Cumberland Presbyterian students attending MTS. Those who knew and loved Reverend Watson and appreciate his and Leota's ministry are invited to send a gift to fully establish the Reverend David and Leota Watson Scholarship Endowment Fund. Every gift matters.

10. Rev. Walter (Pete) Palmer Endowment for the Program of Alternate Studies

This endowment was funded from a significant bequest from Reverend Palmer. The endowment will provide program support for the PAS summer extension school and scholarship aid for needy students.

11. Paul Blankenship Endowed Scholarship

Mrs. Nancy Blankenship, widow of former MTS Professor Doctor Paul Blankenship, has given a generous gift to endow a new scholarship for a United Methodist student in the Master of Divinity program, with preference to a student from the Memphis Annual Conference.

12. Rev. Henry Logan Starks Endowment

The Starks Endowment supports African American scholarships for students studying in the Masters level programs at MTS. Each year MTS holds a major fundraising luncheon to raise funds to build the Endowment.

13. Other Endowment funds

Many Cumberland Presbyterians and others continue to support endowments that have been established through the years to fund our work. Currently, the total MTS endowment, managed by the Board of Stewardship of the Cumberland Presbyterian Church, is just over $11 million. The Advancement Office and President are available at any time to discuss endowment gifts with potential donors.

D. ESTATE GIFTS

We continue to have conversations with friends and donors about the importance of remembering MTS (and their local churches, and other ministries they care deeply about) in their estate plans. We publish a list of those who have informed our office that they have included MTS in their will. That group is known as the Heritage Society. The Heritage Society is listed in every issue of The Lamp, our magazine for alumni and friends.

In the past year we have been notified of bequests from:

- Mrs. Edna Russell Jackson of Clarksville, Tennessee, a faithful member of the Clarksville Cumberland Presbyterian Church.
- Mrs. Alta Hensley, widow of Elder Floyd Hensley, former Moderator of the General Assembly. The Hensleys were long-time members of the Liberty Cumberland Presbyterian Church near Campbellsville, Kentucky.
- Reverend Hillman Moore, native of Jackson, Tennessee, retired Cumberland Presbyterian minister from Covenant Presbytery, who had lived for many years in the Paducah, Kentucky area. At the time of his death, Reverend Moore was living near his son, Morris, in the Austin, Texas area.

We are deeply grateful for the generosity that faithful Cumberland Presbyterians exhibit in remembering MTS, and other denominational ministries, in their estate planning. The MTS Advancement Staff and President are available to present programs on Planned Giving to churches, groups of churches, or presbyteries to encourage our members to remember their local churches and denominational ministries that are important to them in their wills and other planned giving vehicles.

F. SEMINARY/PAS SUNDAY

We have many churches in our denomination, and in other denominations we serve who recognize Seminary Sunday in their local churches. This provides time for education of members about the work of MTS and the Program of Alternate Studies and provides an opportunity for members to make a special one-time gift to support the work of the seminary. Please contact the seminary for more information on how you can recognize Seminary Sunday in your local church, and to request a speaker for the occasion.

RECOMMENDATION 4: That the third Sunday in August, (August 19, 2018 and August 18, 2019) be included in the General Assembly Calendar as Seminary/PAS Sunday, and that the General Assembly encourage all churches to share information about MTS and PAS and receive a special offering on that day, or on a more convenient day of the session's choosing.

G. ANNUAL FUND

Memphis Theological Seminary could not operate without the faithful contribution of its alumni and friends. Annual Fund contributions help us keep the cost of tuition down, so that students do not leave seminary with a large burden of debt to have to pay during their early years in ministry. Annual Fund contributions have grown steadily over the past fifteen years, as income from Our United Outreach has declined.

MTS friends and alumni are encouraged to consider joining the "1852 Society," a group of persons who pledge to give at least $18.52 per month to help support the work of the seminary. Information on the "1852 Society" is available at the MTS display table during the week of General Assembly, and can be accessed through our website: MemphisSeminary.edu.

In some respects, the income we receive from OUO puts us in a better position than many theological seminaries, whose income from denominational sources has declined significantly over the past twenty years. Our income from OUO has remained relatively steady over that time period. However, as a percentage of our total income, OUO has fallen from almost 20% to about 3% of our operating budget. We are grateful for the commitment of Cumberland Presbyterians to the ministry of MTS, and all our common ministries, expressed so tangibly through giving to Our United Outreach.

At the same time, we do not expect income from denominational contributions to increase significantly in the future. This means that we are required to put more time and energy into fund raising than ever before. We are grateful for the many alumni who have made a financial contribution to our ministry this year. We are also grateful for all the faithful laypersons who have given to the Annual Fund because they know the importance of an educated ministry to the life and health of our denomination.

H. AUDIT REPORT

The auditing firm of Zoccola Kaplan, P.C. has audited the books of Memphis Theological Seminary for the 2016-2017 fiscal year. The audit was unqualified. Copies of that report have been filed with the office of the Stated Clerk.

Respectfully submitted,
Nancy Cole, Moderator of the Board of Trustees
Daniel J. Earheart-Brown, President
Memphis Theological Seminary

THE REPORT OF THE
OUR UNITED OUTREACH COMMITTEE

The 2009 General Assembly established a denominational Our United Outreach Committee to be made up of 12 voting representatives, one from each Synod and the rest from the church programs and institutions. Executives from the church programs and institutions participate on the Committee as advisory members. This Committee meets annually unless there is a needed called meeting.

A goal of the Our United Outreach Committee is to encourage ALL churches to contribute to Our United Outreach. Approximately 30 percent of the churches do not give anything with a high percentage of other churches not giving at the 10 percent level. This past year, 2017, the budgeted goal for Our United Outreach was $2,800,000 – 86.89% giving was achieved. While this was an admirable achievement, the percentage is down from the 89% of 2016. The Committee seeks to involve ALL churches with Our United Outreach giving and at a greater level of giving.

I. OUR UNITED OUTREACH FUNDS ALLOCATION

The Our United Outreach Committee met March 2, 2018, to allocate the Our United Outreach funds for the 2019 year. The Our United Outreach allocation basis for 2019 is $2,600,000.

A line item of $25,000 for Legal Fees, $35,000 for Unification Task Force, and $92,044 for the OUO Development Coordinators have been approved as guaranteed amounts and are deducted from the goal amount prior to allocation purposes.

RECOMMENDATION 1: That General Assembly adopt the following Our United Outreach allocations for 2019:

The allocation is to be as follows:	$2,600,000.00		
Development Coordinator Office		92,044.00	
and OUO Committee			
Unification Task Force		35,000.00	
Sub-total	127,044.00		
(Amount to be allocated)	2,472,956.00		
Ministry Council	$ 1,236,478.00	50%	
Bethel University	123,648.00	5%	
Children's Home	74,189.00	3%	
Stewardship	148,377.00	6%	
General Assembly Office	197,836.00	8%	
Memphis Theological Seminary/	173,107.00	7%	
Program of Alternate Studies			
Historical Foundation	74,189.00	3%	
Shared Services	408,038.00	16.5%	
Contingency	12,365.00	.5%	
(Next four items total 1%)			
Comm. on Chaplains	9,570.00	.387%	
Judiciary Committee	9,026.00	.365%	
Theology/Social Concerns	3,363.00	.136%	
Nominating Committee	2,770.00	.112%	
	2,472,956.00		
Our United Outreach Goal	$2,600,000.00		

From the agencies listed above, all should be self-explanatory except maybe Shared Services. Maintenance, utilities, mowing, trash pick-up, pest extermination, and custodial are all examples of Shared Services for agencies sharing the Cumberland Presbyterian Center.

II. OUR UNITED OUTREACH COMMITTEE REQUESTS

In order to serve as better stewards of the funding that is guaranteed to the Unification Task Force and the Development Coordinator Office of OUO, our committee believes it would be helpful to have an accounting of these funds.

RECOMMENDATION 2: The OUO committee meeting in an executive session requests General Assembly to direct the Unification Task Force and Development Coordinator Office of OUO to account for expenditures to this committee.

Our committee believes that many across our denomination may not fully understand the ministry of OUO in supporting, and making possible, the many ministries of the Cumberland Presbyterian Church. We feel there is much work to do in educating individuals, congregations, and churches how their support of OUO makes a difference in the life of our church. We are searching for new ways to share the message, and promote the ministries that OUO makes possible in our denomination.

RECOMMENDATION 3: The OUO Committee request that General Assembly challenge churches to invite an OUO Representative or member of the OUO Committee to speak in their congregations.

III. OUR UNITED OUTREACH COMMITTEE

The Our United Outreach Committee is made up of individuals who possess the leadership abilities to identify the focus of the entities of the denomination. The denominational nominating committee always strives to find the best candidate for vacancies on denominational boards and agencies. The existing committee would like to express appreciation to Randy Weathersby- Synod of the Southeast, for his dedication and support of the goals of the Committee.

The Our United Outreach Committee members are enthusiastic in their approach to the development of total participation in this program of the church.

Respectfully submitted,
Reverend Bruce Hamilton, Chairperson
Randy Weathersby, Vice-Chairperson
Robin Wills, Secretary
and the Our United Outreach Committee

THE REPORT OF THE COMMISSION ON MILITARY CHAPLAINS AND PERSONNEL

The General Assembly Commission on Military Chaplains and Personnel is made up of three members, each serving terms of three years on the Commission. Those people are Reverend Tony Janner (2018), Reverend Cassandra Thomas (2019) and Reverend Charles McCaskey (2020). They can serve up to 9 years (3 three year terms). These three, along with the Stated Clerk, Reverend Michael Sharpe, are also members of the joint Presbyterian Council for Chaplains and Military Personnel (PCCMP), whose office is located at 4125 Nebraska Avenue NW, Washington DC. Other denominations that are a part of the PCCMP include the Presbyterian Church (USA), the Cumberland Presbyterian Church in America, and the Korean Presbyterian Church Abroad.

I. SUPPORT OF THE PCCMP

Financial support for the Presbyterian Council for Chaplains and Military Personnel (PCCMP) is received from the four member denominations and individuals, church judicatories and individual churches. The constant decrease of financial support is an issue that the PCCMP is constantly dealing with. The Cumberland Presbyterian Church has a budget line in the denominational budget to support the PCCMP. The Cumberland Presbyterian Church and the individual churches have traditionally received an offering on Memorial Day Sunday with those offerings being given directly to the PCCMP for it's budget. However, other special days may be considered to receive this special offering in the individual churches – the Sunday nearest Veterans day, "Four Chaplain's Sunday" (the first Sunday in February), the Sunday nearest the 4th of July or some other Sunday as a witness to support the men and women who have or are serving in the military, the Federal Bureau of Prisons, The Veterans Affairs and the Civil Air Patrol. These offering should be sent to the General Assembly Stated Clerk and are forwarded to the PCCMP for the outreach, mission, and maintenance of the PCCMP.

RECOMMENDATION 1: That each Cumberland Presbyterian Church provide an opportunity for their congregations to receive an offering on the last Sunday of May, or another special day, to support our ministry through the PCCMP.

RECOMMENDATION 2: That the budget line item of the Cumberland Presbyterian Church designated for the PCCMP be increased by 2 % beginning in 2020.

The PCCMP provides ecclesiastical endorsement for chaplains of the United States Armed Forces from the four member denominations who are serving on active duty or serving the Reserves/ National Guard. The PCCMP also endorses Ministers of Word and Sacrament who serve as chaplains in the Federal Bureau of Prisons and the Civil Air Patrol. The PCCMP also provides special training to chaplains and pastoral support to chaplains and their families who are endorsed for those positions from the four member denominations. The PCCMP provides an influential voice for the member denominations to the National Council on Ministry to the Armed Forces in matters relating to the ministry and welfare of the endorsed chaplains. The PCCMP also promotes a closer communications between chaplains and their denominational bodies.

RECOMMENDATION 3: That individual congregations of the Cumberland Presbytery determine and designate special days through the year to hold up the chaplains and their families in the service to which they have been endorsed.

II. MEETINGS AND DIRECTOR

The PCCMP, and the representatives of the member denominations normally meets at least once a year. This past year, the annual meeting was held at the denominational headquarters of the Cumberland Presbyterian Church in America in Huntsville, Alabama. The 2018 meeting is scheduled for California and is to be hosted by the Korean Presbyterian Church Abroad.

The PCCMP has just completed a director change. The new director of the PCCMP is retired Navy Chaplain Lyman M. Smith (CAPT, CHC, USN). His office is located in Washington D.C but his location is many times traveling to minister to the endorsed chaplains at their duty stations all over the World. He replaces retired chaplain Lawrence (Larry) Greenslit who retired as the director of the PCCMP this past year. The present chair of the PCCMP is the Reverend Cassandra Thomas (CP), the Vice-Chair is the Reverend John Kim (KPCA), the secretary is Army Daniel, Jr. (CPCA) and the treasurer is Kelly Wadsworth (PCUSA). Other Cumberland Presbyterian members Reverend Doctor Tony Janner and Reverend Doctor Charles McCaskey serve on various committees of the PCCMP. All three of the Cumberland Presbyterian members of the PCCMP are retired military chaplains. All member denominational Stated Clerks also serve as a member of the PCCMP – Reverend Michael Sharpe, the Cumberland Presbyterian Stated Clerk is a constant attender and valuable member of the PCCMP.

There are approximately 20 Cumberland Presbyterian Ministers of Word and Sacrament serving as military and federal chaplains. These chaplain's name and addresses are included in the Yearbook of the Cumberland Presbyterian Church. Information concerning the process of becoming a chaplain may be obtained by visiting the PCCMP website: www.pccmp.org.

Several meetings of the Endorsement Committee of the PCCMP is scheduled throughout the year to meet and endorse individuals who are applying for positions as chaplains.

Submitted:
Members of the Cumberland Presbyterian Commission on Chaplains and Personnel
Cassandra Thomas
Tony Janner
Charles McCaskey

THE REPORT OF THE PERMANENT JUDICIARY COMMITTEE

The Judiciary Committee met February 16, 2018 in Huntsville, Alabama. Present were Pam Brown, Annetta Camp, Harry Chapman, Andy McClung, Jan Overton, and Bill Tally. Also present were Mike Sharpe, stated clerk, and Jaime Jordan, legal counsel. Rachel Moses, Geoff Knight, and Kimberly Silvus were excused.

I. ORGANIZATION OF THE COMMITTEE

Annetta camp was elected chairperson, Jan Overton vice-chair, and Andy McClung secretary.

II. MEMORIAL

A memorial from Arkansas Presbytery regarding The Encounter curriculum was found to be properly formatted and therefore will be placed before General Assembly.

III. JOINT COMMITTEE ON AMENDMENTS

This committee elected Pam Brown and Jan Overton as representatives to serve on the Joint Committee on Amendments.

IV. GENERAL ASSEMBLY REPRESENTATIVES

Pam Brown will serve as this committee's representative to the 188th General Assembly. Andy McClung is the alternate.

V. PROPOSED AMENDMENT, PREAMBLE TO THE CONSTITUTION

The growth of the Cumberland Presbyterian Church outside of the United States is something to be celebrated. This committee has been informed that outside of the United States it is sometimes difficult to strictly apply the Cumberland Presbyterian Constitution, as different countries have different laws and social systems than that of the United States, in which our Constitution was formed. Therefore, this committee makes the following recommendation:

RECOMMENDATION 1: That the Preamble to the Constitution be amended by inserting the following paragraph between the first and second existing paragraphs: "Cumberland Presbyterian congregations are found around the world. While the mission of the church is the same everywhere, the forms and structures of the Constitution do not always fit seamlessly with the cultures, traditions, and legal systems of some countries. In countries other than the United States the provisions of the Constitution should be applied so far as possible, but the Constitution is, at its heart, a document which exists to promote spiritual objectives. If there are instances in which the letter of the Constitution cannot be applied without compromising the mission of the church and the spiritual objectives identified in the *Confession of Faith*, it is the spirit of the law, rather than the letter, which must prevail."

VI. PROPOSED AMENDMENTS, CONSTITUTION

Some of the language in our Constitution does not adequately reflect the intent of our structure or the actual practice of our judicatories in exercising pastoral care and authority between judicatories. Therefore, this committee recommends the following amendments to the Constitution (changes italicized):

RECOMMENDATION 2: That Constitution 3.03 be amended from "The authority of each level of church government is limited by the stated provisions of the church's constitution. Although each judicatory exercises exclusive original jurisdiction over all the matters specifically belonging to it, the lower judicatories are subject to the review and control of the higher judicatories in regular gradation." to read "The authority of each level of church government is limited by the stated provisions of the *Constitution*. Although each judicatory exercises exclusive original jurisdiction over all the matters specifically belonging to it, the lower judicatories are subject to the review *and appellate authority of the next higher judicatory.*"

This change clarifies the referenced constitution is the Constitution of the Cumberland Presbyterian Church/Cumberland Presbyterian Church in America, and that higher judicatories exercise their "review and control" of lower judicatories through appellate authority.

RECOMMENDATION 3: That Constitution 3.35 be amended from "A particular church shall not sell, nor lease its real property used for purposes of worship, nurture or ministry, without the written permission of the presbytery in which the particular church is located, transmitted through the session of the particular church." to read "A particular church shall not sell, *convey, lease, pledge, mortgage, or encumber* its real property used for purposes of worship, nurture, or ministry without the written permission of the presbytery in which the particular church is located, transmitted through the session of the particular church. *In granting its permission, the presbytery does not become a party to the church's agreement, nor a guarantor of any indebtedness.*"

RECOMMENDATION 4: That Constitution 7.06, which refers to the relationships of pastor, assistant/associate pastor, stated supply, and interim pastor, be amended from "A person shall enter into one of these relationships with a particular church only with the approval of the presbytery in the bounds of which the particular church is located. *The presbytery may authorize its board of missions to act on its behalf in examining the call and to give tentative approval to a relationship between a particular church and a minister, licentiate, or candidate, subject to formal approval at a meeting of the presbytery.*" to read "*A person shall enter into one of these relationships with a particular church only with the approval of the presbytery in the bounds of which the particular church is located. The church session shall bear responsibility for the selection of the person, and the presbytery's approval shall relate to the person's ministerial credentials, commitment to the theology and government of the Cumberland Presbyterian Church/Cumberland Presbyterian Church in America, and standing in his or her current presbytery, if any.* The presbytery may authorize its board of missions to act on its behalf in examining the call and to give tentative approval to a relationship between a particular church and a minister, licentiate, or candidate, subject to formal approval at a meeting of the presbytery."

The following recommendation deals with the responsibilities of synod.

RECOMMENDATION 5: That Constitution 8.5(f) be amended from "In general, to order with respect to the presbyteries, sessions, and churches under its care according to the government of the church, whatever may seem to edify the church;" to read "In general, to order with respect to the presbyteries, sessions, and churches under its care according to the government of the church, *whatever pertains to their spiritual welfare and the edification of* the church;".

This change recognizes the existing practice that synods do not become directly involved in the governance or operations of the local church, and that any authority of the synod over the local church is spiritual and ecclesiastical in nature.

The following three recommendations (6-8) deal with the responsibilities of General Assembly.

RECOMMENDATION 6: That Constitution 9.4 (d) be amended from "Institute and oversee the agencies necessary in its work;" to read "Institute and *review the work of denominational entities;*".

This change clarifies that the General Assembly's right to oversee the work of denominational commissions, committees, and incorporated entities is a right of review, and not necessarily a right to direct or control. The GA's relationship with committees and incorporated entities is not the same. Denominational entities are identified in GA Bylaw 10.01.

RECOMMENDATION 7: That Constitution 9.4(g) be amended from "Take care that the lower judicatories observe the government of the church and redress what they may have done contrary to order;" to read "Take care that the lower judicatories observe the government of the church and exercise its review and appellate authority to redress what they may have done contrary to order;".

This change recognizes that the General Assembly, like other judicatories, exercises its authority over lower judicatories through its power of review and appellate authority.

RECOMMENDATION 8: That Constitution 9.4(m) be amended from "Oversee the affairs of the whole church;" to read "*Keep watch over* the affairs of the whole church;".

This change indicates a relationship which is more pastoral than controlling, and clarifies the current overstatement of the relationship between the General Assembly and the other judicatories and denominational entities, as Merriam-Webster defines "oversee" as "to watch over and direct… in order to ensure a satisfactory outcome or performance: supervise." That is an overstatement in the church.

VII. AMENDMENT, GENERAL ASSEMBLY BYLAW

This bylaw deals with the composition of the Board of Trustees of Memphis Theological Seminary. This proposed change is only to clarify confusing and conflicting wording.

RECOMMENDATION 9: That Bylaw 10.06 of the General Assembly Corporation be amended from "The corporation shall elect the twenty-four (24) directors of Memphis Theological Seminary as provided in its charter. The corporation shall elect the directors in such a manner that, immediately following any election, there shall be at least eleven (11) directors who are members of ecumenical partners of the Seminary." to read "The corporation shall elect the twenty-four (24) directors of Memphis Theological Seminary as provided in its charter. The corporation shall elect the directors in such a manner that, immediately following any election, there shall be eleven (11) directors who are members of *denominations other than the Cumberland Presbyterian Church.*"

VIII. REVIEW OF SYNOD MINUTES

The 2017 minutes of Synod of the Midwest and Synod of the Southeast were reviewed and found to be in good order.

Respectfully submitted,
The Judiciary Committee

THE REPORT OF THE NOMINATING COMMITTEE

The Nominating Committee consists of a minister and a lay person from each synod, preferably from different presbyteries. Members may serve a three year term, but cannot succeed themselves. Cumberland Presbyterian members of any board or committee can be re-elected to the same board after a two year absence. Ecumenical representatives may be re-elected to the same board after a one year absence. With the exception of the Nominating Committee any person elected to serve on a denominational entity may serve three consecutive terms. Filling an unexpired term counts as one term, thus members of any entity do not always serve nine years before completing eligibility on a board/agency.

The members of the various Ministry Teams are no longer elected by the General Assembly, but are to be appointed by the Ministry Council.

The Committee submits the following list of nominees:

I. THE BOARD OF DIRECTORS OF THE GENERAL ASSEMBLY CORPORATION

(Members whose terms expire in 2021)

(2) MS. CALOTTA EDSELL, 7044 Woodsong Cove, Germantown, TN 38138, First Church Olive Branch Congregation, West Tennessee Presbytery, to succeed herself for a three-year term.

(2) REV. NORLAN SCRUDDER, 29688 S 534 Road, Park Hill, OK 74451, Red River Presbytery, to succeed himself for a three-year term.

II. MINISTRY COUNCIL

(Members whose terms expire in 2021)

(3) MR. KEN BEAN, 1035 Stonewall Street N, McKenzie, TN 38201, West Tennessee Presbytery, Synod of Great Rivers, to succeed himself for a three-year term.

(2) REV. KENNY BUTCHER, 4608 Cather Court, Nashville, TN, 4608 Cather Court, Nashville, TN 37214, Brush Hill Congregation, Tennessee Synod, Nashville Presbytery, for a three-year term.

(2) REV. PHILLIP LAYNE, 10699 Griffith Highway, Whitwell, TN 37397, Tennessee-Georgia Presbytery, Synod of the Southeast, to succeed himself for a three-year term.

(3) REV. RON MCMILLAN, 675 Kimberly Drive, Atoka, TN 38004, West Tennessee Presbytery, Synod of Great Rivers, to succeed himself for a three-year term.

(2) MS. VICTORY MOORE, 17388 Chandlerville Road, Virginia, IL 62691, Shiloh Congregation, North Central Presbytery, Synod of the Midwest, to succeed herself for a three-year term.

(Members whose terms expire in 2019)
YOUTH ADVISORY MEMBERS
(shall be between the ages of 15 and 17 years of age, elected for a one year term
and is eligible for an additional one term)

(1) MS. SYDNEY HOLDER, 6589 County Road 747, Cullman, AL 35055, Welti Congregation, Hope Presbytery, Synod of the Southeast, for a one-year term.

(1) MS. MADISON HOLLAND, 565 County Road 17, Scottsboro, AL 35768, Scottsboro Congregation, Robert Donnell Presbytery, Synod of the Southeast, for a one-year term.

(2) MS. LEIGHANNE MORGAN, 1468 Williams Cove Road, Winchester, TN 37398, Goshen Congregation, Tennessee Synod, Murfreesboro Presbytery, to succeed herself for a one-year term.

III. TRUSTEES OF HISTORICAL FOUNDATION

(Members whose terms expire in 2021)

(2) REV. LISA OLIVER, 110 Allen Drive, Hendersonville, TN 37075, Murfreesboro Presbytery, Tennessee Synod, to succeed herself for a three-year term.

(1) MS. KELLY SHANTON, 3932 W Beaver Creek Drive, Powell, TN 37849, Presbytery of East Tennessee, Synod of the Southeast, for a three-year term.

IV. TRUSTEES OF MEMPHIS THEOLOGICAL SEMINARY OF THE CUMBERLAND PRESBYTERIAN CHURCH

(Members whose terms expire in 2021)

(2) REV. LINDA HOWELL, PO Box 80050, Keller, TX, 76244, Red River Presbytery, Mission Synod, to succeed herself for a three-year term.

(3) MS. SONDRA RODDY, 2583 Hedgerow Lane, Clarksville, TN 37043, Nashville Presbytery, Tennessee Synod to succeed herself for a three-year term.

(3) +REV. MELVIN CHARLES SMITH, 1263 Haynes Street, Memphis, TN 38114, to succeed himself for a three-year term.

(3) +MS. LATISHA TOWNS, The Med, 877 Jefferson Avenue, Memphis, TN 38103, to succeed herself for a three-year term.

(1) REV. DANIEL BARKLEY, 2732 Rexford Street, Hokes Bluff, AL 35903, Grace Presbytery, Synod of the Southeast, for a three-year term.

(1) REV. RON FELL, 212 Ouachita 54, Camden, AR 71701, Arkansas Presbytery, Great Rivers Synod, for a three-year term.

(1) DR. YOONG KIM, 225 Bayswater Drive, Suwanee, GA 30024, Tennessee-Georgia Presbytery, Synod of the Southeast, for a three-year term.

(1) REV. RIAN PUCKETT, 55 Ham Street, Batesville, AR 72501, Arkansas Presbytery, Great Rivers Synod, for a three-year term.

(Members whose terms expire in 2020)

(1) +MS. VANESSA K MIDGETT, 118 Thunderbird Drive, Huntsville, AL 35749, to fill an unexpired two-year term.

(1) REV. JASON MIKEL, 410 Ramblewood Lane, Nolensville, TN 37135, Columbia Presbytery, Tennessee Synod, to fill an unexpired two-year term.

V. STEWARDSHIP, FOUNDATION AND BENEFITS

(Members whose terms expire in 2021)

(1) MS. DEBBIE SHANKS, 3997 N 100th Street, Casey, IL 62420, North Central Presbytery, Synod of the Midwest, for a three-year term

(2) MR. JAMES SHANNON, 2307 Littlemore Drive, Cordova, TN 38016, Germantown Congregations, West Tennessee Presbytery, Great Rivers Synod, to succeed himself for a three-year term.

(3) MR. MICHAEL ST. JOHN, 324 Carriage Place, Lebanon, MO 65536, White Oak Pond Congregation, Missouri Presbytery, Great Rivers Synod, to succeed himself for a three-year term

(Members whose terms expire in 2019)

(1) REV. KEN BYFORD, 23716 Highway 9 N, Piedmont, AL 36272, Grace Presbytery, Synod of the Southeast, for an unexpired one-year term.

GENERAL ASSEMBLY COMMISSIONS:

VI. MILITARY CHAPLAINS AND PERSONNEL

(Members whose terms expire in 2021)

(2) REV. TONY JANNER, 104 Northwood Drive, McKenzie, TN 38201, West Tennessee Presbytery, Great Rivers Synod, to succeed himself for a three-year term.

GENERAL ASSEMBLY COMMITTEES

VII. JUDICIARY

(Members whose terms expire in 2021)

(3) REV. ANNETTA CAMP, 2303 Mill Creek Road, Halls, TN 38040, West Tennessee Presbytery, Great Rivers Synod, to succeed herself for a three-year term.

(2) MR. BILL TALLY, 907 Tipperary Drive, Scottsboro, AL 35768, Scottsboro Congregation, Robert Donnell Presbytery, Synod of the Southeast, to succeed himself for a three-year term

(1) REV. JIM RATLIFF, 13 Hernando Drive, Cherokee Village, AR 72529, West Tennessee Presbytery, Great Rivers Synod, for a three-year term.

VIII. NOMINATING

(Members whose terms expire in 2021)

(1) MR. ETHAN MORGAN, 119 Mountain Top Lane, Cookeville, TN 38506, Murfreesboro Presbytery, Tennessee Synod, for a three-year term.

(1) REV. RANDY SHANNON, 30282 Highway H, Marshall, MO 65340, Missouri Presbytery, Great Rivers Synod, for a three year term.

IX. OUR UNITED OUTREACH COMMITTEE

(Members whose terms expire in 2021)

(1) MS. GWEN RODDYE, 3728 Wittenham Drive, Knoxville, TN 37921, Beaver Creek Congregation, Presbytery of East Tennessee, Synod of the Southeast, for a three-year term.

(3) MS. ROBIN WILLS, 4607 E Richmond Shop Road, Lebanon, TN 37090, Jerusalem Congregation, Murfreesboro Presbytery, Tennessee Synod, to succeed herself for a three-year term.

X. UNIFIED COMMITTEE ON THEOLOGY AND SOCIAL CONCERNS

(Members whose terms expire in 2021)

(1) REV. MITCH BOULTON, 80 Topsy Lane, Savannah, TN 38372, West Tennessee Presbytery, Great Rivers Synod, for a three-year term.

(1) REV. MICHAEL QUALLS, 5355 June Cove, Horn Lake, MS 38637, West Tennessee Presbytery, Great Rivers Synod, for a three-year term.

(1) MS. MELISSA WILSON, 107 Hillwood Drive, Dickson, TN 37055, Nashville Presbytery, Tennessee Synod, for a three-year term.

*Ecumenical Representative +Cumberland Presbyterian Church in America

THE REPORT OF THE
PLACE OF MEETING COMMITTEE

The Place of Meeting Committee consists of the Moderator, a representative of the Cumberland Presbyterian Women's Ministry, and the Stated Clerk who serves as the chairperson. The representative of the Cumberland Presbyterian Women's Ministry is the Convention Coordinator.

The 165th General Assembly, "authorized the committee to select meeting places up to five years in the future and that preference be given that keeps, insofar as possible, the General Assembly and the Convention of Cumberland Presbyterian Women's Ministry, and guest rooms in one facility. It is recognized that these places are hard to find and may cost some additional monies. The place of meeting committee will use its best judgment." The 173rd General Assembly approved exploring the use of college campuses and very large conference centers in addition to hotels/convention centers. When the Office of the General Assembly receives an invitation from a congregation or a presbytery, the Stated Clerk makes a site visit. If adequate facilities are discovered, a follow up visit is made by the Stated Clerk, the Assistant to the Stated Clerk, and the Convention Coordinator of the Cumberland Presbyterian Women's Ministry.

Unless the General Assembly sets aside Bylaw 14.02 Standing Rules 1 to allow for a different meeting time, the annual meeting is the third or the fourth week of June.

Commissioners, delegates to Conventions, and visitors are encouraged to stay at the General Assembly/Convention hotel, to assure meeting the contracted room block. Hotel contracts also include a commitment on food and beverages, thus it is important for boards/agencies to continue to sponsor special meal functions. The luncheons/dinners provide opportunities for the sponsoring agencies/boards to keep the church informed about their respective programs, thus enhancing support.

I. INFORMATION ABOUT FUTURE GENERAL ASSEMBLIES

Continued discussions with the leadership of the Cumberland Presbyterian Church in America regarding joint meetings of the General Assemblies in 2019 and 2020 may impact future meeting locations.

It is helpful to continue scheduling a few years in advance of the meeting to assure that adequate hotel/convention space is available and to negotiate a good rate. If a congregation or a presbytery is interested in hosting the General Assembly/Convention, the Office of the General Assembly will provide information on hosting responsibilities. Hosting the General Assembly/Convention is a service to the Church, allowing the Church to celebrate the good ministries occurring within a particular presbytery, and provides persons within a presbytery the opportunity to participate more fully in the annual meeting.

In the event that no invitation is received in a particular year or a situation arises requiring a change of venue for a particular year, the Corporate Board will be responsible for selecting a place of meeting.

The Office of the General Assembly has received an invitation from the Presbytery East Tennessee to host a future meeting of the General Assembly.

II. SCHEDULE OF FUTURE GENERAL ASSEMBLIES

189th   Huntsville, Alabama   June 10-14, 2019
(co-hosted by Robert Donnell Presbytery and Huntsville Presbytery CPCA)

IV. SCHEDULE OF MEETINGS BY PRESBYTERIES

The following schedule shows the annual meetings and the year that the General Assembly last met in the bounds of a particular presbytery.

Grace	2017	Red River	2004
Nashville	2016	East Tennessee	2003
Cauca Valley & Andes	2015	Covenant	2002
TN/GA	2014	del Cristo	2001
Murfreesboro	2013	Cumberland	2000
Hope & Robert Donnell	2012	Tennessee-Georgia	1998
Missouri	2011	Robert Donnell	1996
Nashville	2010	Nashville	1995
West Tennessee	2009	North Central	1980
Japan	2008	Trinity	1969
Arkansas	2007	Hope	1961
Grace	2006	Murfreesboro	1956
Columbia	2005		

Respectfully submitted,
Michael G. Sharpe
Pam Phillips Burk
David Lancaster

THE REPORT OF THE UNIFIED COMMITTEE ON THEOLOGY AND SOCIAL CONCERNS

I. MEETING AND OFFICERS

The Unified Committee on Theology and Social Concerns (UCTSC) met in Memphis, Tennessee on September 29-30, 2017 and by teleconference February 17, 2018. The following officers were elected during the fall meeting: Reverend Edmund Cox (CPCA) and Reverend Shelia O'Mara (CPC) Co-Chairs; and Reverend Nancy Fuqua (CPCA), Secretary.

II. EXPIRATION OF TERMS

The Committee notes that the terms of service for Reverend Shelia O'Mara, Reverend George Estes and David Phillips-Burk all expire in 2018. Each member is eligible to be reelected. All three members have declined to serve another term.

III. GENERAL ASSEMBLY REPRESENTATIVE

The Committee elected Reverend Richard Morgan (CPC) to serve as the representative to the meeting of the CPC/CPCA General Assembles in Norman, Oklahoma. Reverend Doctor Nancy Fuqua (CPCA) was elected as the alternate.

IV. GENERAL ASSEMBLY REFERRAL

The 142nd CPCA General Assembly memorial on "Why Union" was referred to the UCTSC. The Committee believes that the theological basis for union was addressed in the paper "Reflections on A Divided Church" and the opening paragraph in the 2016 Revised Plan for Union. If additional information/response is needed the Committee suggests that the Memorial be referred to the Unification Task Force.

"There is one, holy, universal, apostolic church. She is the body of Christ, who is her Head and Lord" (*Confession of Faith* 5.01). "The church is one because her head and Lord is one, Jesus Christ. Her oneness under her Lord is manifested in the one ministry of word and sacrament, not in any uniformity of covenantal expression, organization, or system of doctrine" (5.02). "The church, as the covenant community of believers who are redeemed, includes all people in all ages, past, present, and future, who respond in faith to God's covenant of grace, and all who are unable to respond, for reasons known to God, but who are saved by his grace" (5.06). It is on this belief that the Unification Task Force recommends the union of the Cumberland Presbyterian Church in America (CPCA) and the Cumberland Presbyterian Church (CPC). We are one in Christ by the grace of God and the power of the Holy Spirit! We believe that becoming one will strengthen our witness as Christian believers in the world, and that together we will be able to accomplish more for the glory of God. United together in Christ by faith, we are united to one another in love. In this communion we share the grace of Christ with one another, bear one another's burdens, and reach out to all other persons (*Confession of Faith* 5.10). [Revised Plan for Union June 2016]

"We can no longer accommodate ourselves to a comfortable religion at the expense of our souls being lost by our unwillingness to act. Cumberland Presbyterians must not merely **speak** of unity but **insist** on unity. As we were reminded by Martin Luther King, Jr. 'Either we learn how to live together as brothers and sisters, or die as fools.'" [Reflections on a Divided Church]

V. STUDY PAPERS

The Committee is currently reviewing a paper submitted by Reverend Chris Warren entitled "A Theological Statement on Inclusion of the LGBTQIA Community in the Cumberland Presbyterian Church." The Committee expects to complete its review this year for submission and recommendation to the 2019 General Assemblies.

VI. WORKS IN PROGRESS

The UCTSC has developed guidelines for a theological/social concerns panel made up of representatives of the CPC/CPCA to address emerging issues in a more timely way. Panel responses would not have the official sanction of the CPC or CPCA, but would provide useful reflections for persons in our two churches. The Committee expects to launch the panel during 2018. Communications announcing the panel and its work will be distributed to both churches.

Respectfully Submitted,
Unified Committee on Theology and Social Concerns

THE REPORT OF THE UNIFICATION TASK FORCE

I. MEETING AND OFFICERS

The Unification Task Force (UTF) of the Cumberland Presbyterian Church in America (CPCA) and the Cumberland Presbyterian Church (CPC) met once since the last meeting of the General Assemblies: April 5-6, 2018 in Nashville, Tennessee. Officers elected were Steve Mosley (CPC) and Elton Hall (CPCA), co-chairs; Craig White (CPCA) and Jay Earheart-Brown (CPC), secretaries. Other members of the UTF from the CPCA are Leon Cole, Lynne Herring, William Robinson, and Mitchell Walker. Other members of the UTF from the CPC are Perryn Rice, Robert Rush, Michael Sharpe, Gloria Villa-Diaz, and Joy Warren.

Joy Warren and Mitchell Walker were elected to serve as representatives of the Task Force to this meeting of the General Assemblies.

Pam Phillips-Burk submitted her resignation from the Task Force in early 2018. She has been a faithful and dedicated member of the Task Force, and has taken many leadership roles during her time of service. We will miss her contributions to our work.

RECOMMENDATION 1: That the General Assembly of the CPC accept, with gratitude for her faithful service to the Unification Task Force, the resignation of Pam Phillips-Burk from the UTF.

II. PROPOSED PLAN OF UNION

The 2014 General Assemblies, in concurrent session at Chattanooga, Tennessee, approved for study a Proposed Plan of Union. That plan has been distributed widely across both denominations, and has generated a great deal of discussion and feedback. For almost four years the plan has been studied. We are grateful for all the responses the Task Force has received, both positive and negative. The Task Force has carefully studied the responses, from the table discussions at Chattanooga, to the surveys distributed at Presbytery meetings and on-line, to individual letters received by the GA offices and by members of the Task Force. On the basis of all the responses to the proposed plan, and several meetings attended by members of the Task Force, we voted in our November meeting not to ask for a formal vote on the plan at the 2016 meetings of the General Assembly, which would have been the earliest possible date for such a vote.

We, instead, spent significant time revising the Proposed Plan of Union, and presented it to the concurrent meetings of the two General Assemblies in 2016, with the recommendation that the revised plan be approved for study in the two churches. At the 2017 General Assemblies, meeting concurrently near Tampa, Florida, we proposed that 2017-2019 both churches devote two years to relationship building and continued study of the Plan of Union. We then suggested that the plan be put to a vote at the concurrent General Assemblies meeting in Huntsville, Alabama in June of 2019. If approved by both Assemblies, the Plan of Union would be sent to the Presbyteries of both churches for approval of the Plan between the 2019 and 2020 Assemblies. If approved by a majority of Presbyteries of both churches, the 2020 Assemblies would meet briefly to finalize their business, adjourn sine die, and organize the new Assembly of the United Church.

While we do not know what the outcome of such a vote at next year's assemblies will be, we on the Task Force are convinced that the time is right for both churches to decide if we are ready to move forward with our union or not. If now is not the time, then we do not need to continue the work of the Task Force at the present, but put our energies into our cooperating when and where we can as brothers and sisters in Christ. It is our sincere desire as members of the Task Force to see this union happen, and we have been deeply enriched by our work together on this project for the past six years. But ultimately it is the churches who must decide this matter.

We urge the commissioners to the 2018 General Assemblies to read the Plan carefully and make any proposed amendments the Assemblies would like to see incorporated into the plan this year, so that the Task Force will have time to incorporate those changes before next year's vote. Of course, the 2019 Assemblies will have the opportunity to amend the Plan before approving it, but amendments made next year will have to be dealt with in a well-structured manner in order to receive consideration by both Assemblies.

At our April meeting, we decided to write, with consultation from our attorneys, draft Bylaws, Standing Rules, and Constitutional Amendments that will be circulated to both churches prior to the vote in 2019, so that there are as few details left hanging as possible. We hope to have those documents ready to distribute at least two months prior to the 2019 General Assembly meetings, so that commissioners and others will have ample time to study them prior to the vote.

With thanksgiving to God for the relationships we have developed as we have worked together for the past six years, and in hopes that all Cumberland Presbyterians may one day live and work together in one church, the UTF submits the following Proposed Plan of Union.

Proposed Plan for Union of the Cumberland Presbyterian Church and the Cumberland Presbyterian Church in America

"There is one, holy, universal, apostolic church. She is the body of Christ, who is her Head and Lord" (*Confession of Faith* 5.01). "The church is one because her head and Lord is one, Jesus Christ. Her oneness under her Lord is manifested in the one ministry of word and sacrament, not in any uniformity of covenantal expression, organization, or system of doctrine" (5.02). "The church, as the covenant community of believers who are redeemed, includes all people in all ages, past, present, and future, who respond in faith to God's covenant of grace, and all who are unable to respond, for reasons known to God, but who are saved by his grace" (5.06). It is on this belief that the Unification Task Force recommends the union of the Cumberland Presbyterian Church in America (CPCA) and the Cumberland Presbyterian Church (CPC). We are one in Christ by the grace of God and the power of the Holy Spirit! We believe that becoming one will strengthen our witness as Christian believers in the world, and that together we will be able to accomplish more for the glory of God. United together in Christ by faith, we are united to one another in love. In this communion we share the grace of Christ with one another, bear one another's burdens, and reach out to all other persons (*Confession of Faith* 5.10).

1.00 Mission Statement for the New Church

The Cumberland Presbyterian Church United affirms the great commission of Christ: "Go, therefore, and make disciples of all nations, baptizing them in the name of the Father, and of the Son, and of the Holy Spirit, and teaching them to obey everything that I have commanded you. And remember I am with you until the end of the age" (Matthew 28:19-20). We celebrate our oneness in faith. As disciples, we seek through worship, global witness, and service to be the hands and feet of Christ and to live out the love of Jesus Christ to the glory of God.

2.00 The *Confession of Faith and Government*

The Cumberland Presbyterian Church United will use the *Confession of Faith and Government* of the Cumberland Presbyterian Church and the Cumberland Presbyterian Church in America, approved by both General Assemblies of the former denominations in 1984 as its system of faith and government.

NOTE: It should be noted that in the Constitution (4.6, 5.6p) the CPC allows for a session to request permission from Presbytery for a designated elder to be trained and granted permission to serve communion for a one year period of time. This is an exception, NOT A RULE for general practice, for those presbyteries that have difficulty supplying each church with an ordained minister. The responsibility lies with presbytery for proper training and oversight of the designated elder. Again, is this an EXCEPTION. No presbytery is required to apply this exception.

2.01 The Cumberland Presbyterian Church United will use the *Catechism for Cumberland Presbyterians* (2008) for instruction in the faith and will include it in an updated edition of the *Confession of Faith and Government of the Cumberland Presbyterian Church United*.

2.02 The CP *Digest* (CPC) and Summaries of Actions (for both denominations) will continue to serve as resource tools. A new *Digest* will begin with the formation of the Cumberland Presbyterian Church United.

3.00 The Presbyteries and Synods

3.01 In an effort to make union something more than just an idea on paper, and to engage the grassroots in creating the new church, we recommend a restructure of the synod boundaries to create eight synods for the new church, with the following presbyteries in each –

Synod A*	Synod B*	Synod C	Synod D
Brazos River	Angelina	Covenant	Cleveland, Ohio
Del Christo	Arkansas	Missouri	Cumberland
Red River	Choctaw	New Hopewell	North Central
Hong Kong	East Texas	Purchase	Ohio Valley
Japan	Trinity	West Tennessee	
	Andes		
	Cauca Valley		

Synod E	Synod F	Synod G	Synod H
Columbia	East Tennessee	Florence	Birmingham
Elk River	Hiawassee	Hope	Grace
Murfreesboro	Tennessee-Georgia	Huntsville	South Alabama
Nashville	East Coast Korean	Robert Donnell	Tuscaloosa
	Tennessee Valley		

For relationship building during the first six years, all synods will be encouraged to hold an annual general meeting (*Constitution* 8.2) as opposed to a delegated meeting. Synods may petition General Assembly at any point for a change in boundaries.

* *NOTE: There are plans for organizing a new presbytery in Central and/or South America in the near future, as well as dreams for organizing a third presbytery in Asia. As soon as it is practical to do so, whether before or after union, two additional synods should be constituted. Synod I would include Andes, Cauca Valley, and any other presbyteries organized in Latin America. Synod J would include Hong Kong, Japan, and any other presbyteries organized in Asia.*

3.02 Presbyteries will remain as they are constituted at the time of union. During the first six years of the new church's life, synods will be encouraged to study the most beneficial presbyterial boundaries within their jurisdiction to fulfill of the mission of the church. Presbyteries may petition their synod at any time for a change in boundaries.

4.00 Commissioners and Youth Advisory Delegates to the General Assembly
4.01 Commissioners to the General Assembly

Each Presbytery will be entitled to send 2 minister commissioners and 2 elder commissioners to the General Assembly.

NOTE: If presbytery boundaries remain as currently constituted at the time of unification, this will allow for a total possible membership in the General Assembly of 152 commissioners. Of these potential commissioners, 60 would come from former presbyteries of the CPCA, and 92 would come from the former CPC.

4.02 Youth Advisory Delegates

Each presbytery will be entitled to send up to two Youth Advisory delegates to the General Assembly.

5.00 Moderator and Vice Moderator of General Assembly

5.01 The moderator/vice moderator will be elected each year during the first six years with the two offices alternating between persons from the two former denominations.

5.02 The moderator and vice moderator of the Cumberland Presbyterian Church United will reflect its diverse nature, to include international representatives. The church expects the moderator and vice moderator to travel within the denomination, sharing and gathering information among its local churches. Expenses and particular duties will be detailed in the Standing Rules of the Cumberland Presbyterian Church United.

6.00 Stated Clerk and Associate Stated Clerk of the General Assembly

6.01 The new church shall employ a Stated Clerk and an Associate Stated Clerk. Both positions will be full-time jobs. During the first six years of the Cumberland Presbyterian Church United, the Stated Clerk will serve six years and the Associate Stated Clerk will serve four years, after which each would be elected for a four-year period. One position will be filled by a former CPCA and the other position filled by a former CPC during their first terms. The subsequent election of each position will allow for continuity during transitions. Particular duties and responsibilities of the Stated Clerk and Associate Stated Clerk will be detailed in the Standing Rules of the Cumberland Presbyterian Church United.

7.00 Boards and Agencies of the General Assembly

7.01 Each church has programs in various stages of planning and implementation that are the result of commitment to ministry through the church. Insofar as possible, these plans and programs will be continued without interruption for a period of three years. The Cumberland Presbyterian Church has covenantal relationships with the Cumberland Presbyterian Children's Home in Denton, Texas and Bethel University in McKenzie, Tennessee. These covenantal relationships will remain in effect as they exist at the time of Unification, to be renewed every four years. The Cumberland Presbyterian Church United will continue ecumenical partnerships, such as with the World Communion of Reformed Churches.

7.02 Institutional Boards

The General Assembly shall have the following institutional boards: Trustees of Memphis Theological Seminary to include the Program of Alternate Studies and School of Continuing Education Committee, and Trustees of the Historical Foundation. Representation on each Board of Trustees will remain as they are constituted at the time of union.

7.03 Administrative Boards

The General Assembly shall have the following administrative Boards: The Board of Stewardship, Foundation and Benefits and The Board of Directors of the General Assembly Corporation. During the transition period, each of these boards will have equal number of members from each of the former denominations.

7.04 Commission

The General Assembly shall have the following commission: Chaplains and Military Personnel. Representation on the commission will be merged as they are constituted at the time of union until natural rotation occurs.

7.05 Standing Committees

The General Assembly shall have the following standing committees: Theology and Social Concerns, Judiciary, Our United Outreach, Nominating, and Multi-Cultural Ministry.

Committee representation on the Theology and Social Concerns Committee will remain as constituted at the time of union until natural rotations occurs.

Judiciary and Nominating committees in both denominations will each be merged at the time of union.

Committee representation for Our United Outreach will be expanded to include two elected representatives from each new synod (one voting representative from each of the former denominations until natural rotation occurs).

The Committee on Multi-Cultural Ministry is a new committee that will reflect the diversity of the Cumberland Presbyterian Church United. This committee will be comprised of eight (8) elected persons that will reflect the celebrative understanding of humanity in the areas of culture, language, heritage, and experience in the Cumberland Presbyterian Church United. Believing that all have been created in God's image, this committee works to answer the question of our sameness in God's image lived out in diverse ways.

7.06 The Cumberland Presbyterian Church United will have a Mission Programming Agency to provide coordination and oversight for those ministries formally planned and implemented by the two former denominations. After the three-year period, the new programming and denominational structure will consist of the following ministries and entities –

Christian Education & Nurture (Youth Convention & National Sunday School Convention
Missions (Evangelism, Missionary Auxiliary, Women's Ministry)
Clergy Care & Development
Communications (Cumberland Flag, Cumberland Presbyterian Magazine,
    Missionary Messenger, website)

Composition of each ministry entity will include equal number of persons from each of the former denominations in the new church at the time of union. Composition of the new Mission Programming Agency will include one staff person and one elected member from each ministry entity, along with one elected member representing each of the synods. The elected members will be equally representative of the two former denominations for the first six years. A Ministry Coordinator would provide executive leadership for the Mission Programming Agency.

8.00 Denominational Staff & Personnel

Currently, the CPCA employs two full time staff members; the CPC employs twenty-five staff members.

8.01 The new organizational structure will discontinue the positions of Administrative Director (CPCA) and the Director of Ministries (CPC) and will create the positions of Associate Stated Clerk and Ministry Coordinator. The Stated Clerk and Associate Stated Clerk will be elected during the General Assembly of 2018. The Implementation Task Force will make recommendations to the 2018 Assembly about the transition in staffing to be complete by the 2019 Assembly. The Ministry Coordinator will be employed by the Mission Programming Agency.

8.02 Staffing for the Cumberland Presbyterian Church United will reflect the diversity of the new church. As new staff positions become available, equal opportunity employment practices will prevail.

8.03 Denominational Offices

During the first six years, steps are to be taken to assure that regional sites be located in a minimum of three and a maximum of five locations. Thus, neither the Center in Huntsville nor the Center in Memphis will be designated as "the denominational center." By placing regional sites in a variety of locations this will assure that all areas of the church will be served equally. These regional sites can make use of offices in existing churches, or in homes of regional staff persons. Possible regional locations could be Memphis, Huntsville, Louisville, Texas, South America, Asia, etc.

8.04 Global Staff

There will be endorsed missionaries and partner missionaries in the new church. The new church will continue to support current and future missionaries and global work. Current missionaries include – Beth Wallace (Colombia, SA), Glenn Watts (Hong Kong), Anay Ortega (Guatemala), Phanor & Socorro Pejendino (Guatemala), Daniel & Kay Jang (Philippines), Kenneth & Delight Hopson (Uganda), Lawrence and Loretta Fung (Asian ministry USA), Carlos and Luz Dary Rivera (Mexico), Missionaries in undisclosed (6), CP missionaries supported by their presbyteries – Iwao Satoh and Keishi and Kazuko Ishitsuka

9.00 Stewardship and Finance

9.01 Legal control of assets of both churches will be transferred to the Cumberland Presbyterian Church United through appropriate legal transaction. The intent of all designated gifts and endowments will be honored.

9.02 The Cumberland Presbyterian Church United will develop an approach to the financing of the programs of the church that reflects the stewardship understanding of the new constituency. Such a unitary approach will be developed as soon as possible after formation and no later than the end of the first six years.

10.00 Recognition of Ordination

All ordinations, both clergy and lay (elders and deacons), of both denominations will be recognized by the Cumberland Presbyterian Church United. All future ordinations will be governed by the conditions specified in the Constitution. Persons who are recognized by their respective presbyteries as candidates and licentiates at the time the new church is formed will fulfill the requirements as specified by presbytery at the time they became probationers.

11.00 The Name of the New Denomination

The name of the denomination shall be the Cumberland Presbyterian Church United.

12.00 The Logo of the New Church

A new logo will be fashioned by the new church.

III. DETAILED TIMELINE FOR CONSIDERATION OF THE PLAN OF UNION

- **2018 General Assemblies** – Meeting concurrently in Norman, Oklahoma, the assemblies propose any changes to the Plan of Union that will need to be incorporated before the vote at the two General Assemblies in 2019.
- **2018-2019** – The Task Force makes final revisions to the Plan of Union, writes Draft Bylaws, Standing Rules, and Constitutional amendments based on the final version of the Plan to be distributed for study in April 2019.
- **2019** – Meeting concurrently in Huntsville, Alabama, the two assemblies vote on approving the Plan of Union, Bylaws, Standing Rules, and Constitutional Amendments, pending approval of a majority of presbyteries of the two churches. Any Constitutional amendments are sent to the Joint Committee on Amendments for review and preparation of final wording.
- **2019-2020** – If approved by a majority of both assemblies, the Plan is sent to the Presbyteries of both churches for approval.
- **2020** – The two Assemblies, meeting concurrently, announce the vote of their Presbyteries, and if approved by a majority of both, vote on final approval of Bylaws and Standing Rules for the General Assembly of the new church (2/3 vote of approval necessary). Constitutional amendments reviewed and prepared by the Joint Committee on Amendments are approved (3/4 vote of approval necessary to refer amendments to Presbyteries for approval, and 3/4 of presbyteries, voting by simple majority, needed to approve amendments). If both assemblies approve Bylaws, the two assemblies vote to adjourn sine die, and immediately meet to organize the new Assembly of the united Church. The Unification Task Force is

dismissed, and an Implementation Task Force is elected to guide the transition for the first few years to the new denomination.

RECOMMENDATION 2: That the General Assemblies of the CPCA and CPC approve the proposed timeline for action.

IV. COOPERATIVE WORK

The Task Force continues to be encouraged by cooperative work being done in many areas of our two denominations. At the General Assembly level, both churches cooperate in the work of the Historical Foundation, the Unified Committee on Theology and Social Concerns, the Cumberland Presbyterian Youth Conference and Presbyterian Youth Triennium, and the Presbyterian Council for Chaplains and Military Personnel. At the local and presbyterial levels, we continue to receive good reports from joint programs of camping and youth events, revivals, Vacation Bible Schools, joint worship and community meals. We encourage persons engaged in joint ministries to report those events to the Cumberland Presbyterian magazine, and on the Facebook page of the Unification Task Force.

The UTF will make available at its display table during the week of General Assembly a list of suggested activities that individuals and churches can try in their local areas, along with other materials to help promote the work of unification. All commissioners and visitors to the meeting of GA are encouraged to make use of these resources.

We are grateful for many volunteers who have worked as Unification Advocates, organizing joint meetings, praying for the work of Unification, and promoting deeper relationships between members of our two churches.

V. UNIFICATION SUNDAY

The 2017 General Assembly approved Unification Sunday as an official event on the calendars of our two churches. In 2018, that observation was scheduled for the fourth Sunday of June (June 24, 2018).

RECOMMENDATION 3: That the fourth Sunday in June 2019 be recognized in the CPC and the CPCA as Unification Sunday, and that all churches be encouraged to pray for our unity in Jesus Christ, and for discernment as we seek to express our unity more fully in the future.

VI. FINANCIAL REPORT

Our United Outreach Income in 2017:		$35,000.00
Expenditures in 2017:		
• Committee Expense	$ 6,514.63	
• 2017 GA Expense	$ 2,431.07	
• Communications/Printing	$ 3,401.00	
• Legal Fees	$ 405.60	
	$12,752.30	
Total Fund Balance as of 12/31/17:		$22,247.70

Note the balance of any funds not used by the Unification Task Force is held in an Investment Loan Account with the denominational Board of Stewardship and will be applied to any future costs associated with unification (e.g. legal fees).

Respectfully Submitted,
Unification Task Force
Steve Mosley and Elton Hall, co-chairs

THE REPORT OF BOARD OF TRUSTEES OF BETHEL UNIVERSITY

The Bethel University Board of Trustees is honored again to be able to report to the 2018 General Assembly of the Cumberland Presbyterian Church. Bethel University is now in its 176th year of existence and is the only university of the Cumberland Presbyterian Church. Our heritage has been rich and we are prayerfully hopeful for our future. We value our Cumberland Presbyterian connections as we move forward.

Our current Board of Trustee officers are as follows: Judge Ben Cantrell, Chair; Bill Dobbins, Vice-Chair; and Jeff Amrein, Secretary.

Bethel University in our covenant relationship with the General Assembly Corporation of the Cumberland Presbyterian Church has committed to no less than a majority of its total membership be active members of the Cumberland Presbyterian Church. Today, our Board of Trustees has 20 members of which 13 are active members of the Cumberland Presbyterian Church and 2 are active members of the Cumberland Presbyterian Church in America.

The current Bethel University Board of Trustees are: Ben Cantrell, Nashville, Tennessee; Bill Dobbins, Nashville, Tennessee; Jeff Amrein, Prospect, Kentucky; Charlie Garrett, Jackson, Tennessee; Reverend Elton C. Hall, Sr., Hewitt, Texas.; Dewana Latimer, Jackson, Tennessee; Doctor Ray Morris, Norcross, Georgia.; Steve Perryman, Rogersville, Missouri; Scott Conger, Jackson, Tennessee; Doctor Army Daniel, Huntsville, Alabama.; Doctor Robert Low, Springfield, Missouri; Doctor Brock Martin, Huntingdon, Tennessee; Doctor Nancy Bean, McKenzie, Tennessee; Lisa Cole, Nashville, Tennessee; Chet Dickson, Houston, Texas; Reverend Nancy McSpadden, Memphis, Tennessee; Doctor Ed Perkins, McKenzie, Tennessee; Ken Quinton, Sturgis, Kentucky; Tommy Surber, McKenzie, Tennessee; and Reverend Robert Watkins, Sun City, Arizona.

Since the General Assembly met in 2017 at Palm Harbor, Florida, our Board of Trustees have met on November 10-11, 2017, and April 6-7, 2018. Our next scheduled meeting will be July 20-1l, 2018 in McKenzie, Tennessee. At this July meeting, we will set our budget for the fiscal year of August 1, 2018 to July 31, 2019.

With this report we have enclosed our Fiscal Year Audit for the ending date of July 31, 2017. Bethel University had another balanced budget (5th in a row) of $447.929.00.

Yearly the Board of Trustees sets and approves the University's budget, selects its audit firm and receives the audit presentation every November, approves or rejects any new capital expenditures, reviews the mission of the University, approves policies, assesses the performance of the President and the Board among its many responsibilities.

The Board of Trustee members serve on various committees that include the: Executive Committee; Missions; Strategic Planning and Development Committee; Policy Committee; Finance and Budgeting Committee; Investment Committee; Committee on Trustees; and the By-Laws Committee.

At the 2017 meeting of the General Assembly we had just found out that our accrediting agency, SACSCOC, had removed us from probation for one item – the definition of online credit hours. We were able to satisfy SACSCOC in the shortest time possibly of 6 months.

We also reported last year that the Tennessee Board of Education in July, 2016, said they were removing Bethel University's ability to license teacher candidates. We felt this was unjust and carried it to Chancery Court in Davidson County, Tennessee. On June 13, 2017, Bethel presented its case and the Chancery Court ruled in Bethel's favor and overturned the Tennessee State Board of Education's decision. The State of Tennessee did appeal the decision to the middle Tennessee Court of Appeals and that case was heard on February 13, 2018. As of this writing, a decision has not been rendered, but Bethel University is able to grant licensure for qualified teacher applicants during the appeal.

2018 marks the year for our current reaccreditation with the Southern Association of Colleges and Schools Commission on Colleges (SACSCOC). Every 10 years schools in the SACSCOC jurisdiction must be examined and thoroughly vetted. Our official visit was in March and we will get the results in December of 2018. We are very optimistic.

This 2017-2018 school year has been another success for us. Our August 2017, December 2017 and May 2018 graduates watched 1,064 students walk across the stage and receive a Bethel University diploma.

U.S. News and World Reports recognized Bethel University as one of the five fastest growing private universities from 2000-2015.

Bethel University's fall enrollment 2016-2017 was 5513. That number includes both graduate and undergraduate enrollment.

Bethel University employs approximately 530 staff and faculty and is the second largest employer in Carroll County, Tennessee.

Our athletic teams have again received the highest possible ranking in the NAIA Champions of Character competition. This ranking included student grades, students and coach's public service work and other categories not related to wins and losses. We are in a very elite group for this honor.

Whether in the classroom, at plays, at concerts, or with the adult learner, Bethel University continues to be a leader in higher education.

Now in our 176th year, it is important to remember our Cumberland Presbyterian heritage that dates back to 1842 in McLemoresville, Tennessee. Bethel University treasures its Cumberland Presbyterian Heritage and its covenant relationship with the Cumberland Presbyterian Church.

We hope you will continue to pray for us and send us prospective high school students and possible adult online learners.

RECOMMENDATION 1: That the General Assembly of the Cumberland Presbyterian Church encourage churches and individuals to pray for Bethel University and send names of prospective students (both high schoolers and adults) to Bethel University.

The current Administration is:
- President – Doctor Walter Butler
- Vice President for Finance – Doctor David Huss
- Vice President for Development – Doctor Dale Henry
- Vice President for College of Arts and Sciences – Ms. Cindy Mallard
- Vice President for College of Professional Studies – Doctor Kimberly Martin
- Vice President for Health Sciences – Doctor Joe Hames
- Chief Academic Officer – Doctor Phyllis Campbell
- Special Assistant to President for Strategic Initiatives – Ms. Michelle Mitchell

Finally, it has been an honor this year to have one of our very own faculty, Doctor David Lancaster, to serve as the Moderator of the General Assembly. Dr. Lancaster represents all that is good and great at Bethel University.

THE REPORT OF THE BOARD OF TRUSTEES OF THE CUMBERLAND PRESBYTERIAN CHILDREN'S HOME

Introduction

Because of the life-giving grace through Jesus Christ, we at Cumberland Presbyterian Children's Home serve God by serving others. We accept individuals as they are and help them through their journey. We build relationships with those we serve through strength-based love and support. We want our children and families to be empowered as we strive to achieve excellence through our mission work. Our mission statement is:

In response to Christ's love and example,
we serve children and families
by providing healing and hope.

Cumberland Presbyterian Children's Home (CPCH) was established in 1904. Our ministry has continually focused on serving children and families for over 114 years. We use our guiding principles of faith, acceptance, care, and excellence in all we do at CPCH.

I. OUR GOAL

Our goal is for children to be protected and live free from abuse and neglect while healing from the devastating impacts of past trauma. We do this by providing safe residential care to youth in foster care, so they flourish in a safe place. Our goal is for single parent families who are experiencing crisis to find a new beginning and works towards independence and healing for their family. We do this by providing a transitional housing program while they receive case management and supportive resources to help rebuild their lives. Our goal is to offer an affordable mental health counseling clinic that serves individuals, couples, families, and children. We do this by operating a mental health counseling clinic that is affordable. Our goal is to engage our community by having a flourishing volunteer program and welcoming environment for all who support us in our mission. We do this by building relationships with our community partners and individuals who wish to make a difference in the lives of children and families. We serve to bring ourselves and others closer to God.

II. OUR VALUES

Our values of protection, preparation, prevention, education, and leadership provide a framework for our program design and are the building blocks for how we operate our ministry. The design of our programming allows us to help and support clients on a continuum; this allows us to meet clients where they are at and helps us serve a wide range of concerns and issues. This diagram is an example of our various services help clients on the continuum of our foundation values.

We created the Continuum of Care Model to help clients through a variety of situations and challenges. For example, we assess a family in crisis and based on our model they could be best served by taking a one of our parent education courses or they could be best served by living in our transitional housing program. Both quality interventions, but the needs of the of family varies based on the crisis the family is facing. We provide services to clients depending on their presenting needs. Providing these services places us in a unique leadership position to educate regarding the various needs and challenges faced by those we serve. The stronger our programs are; the more people we help.

III. OUR BOARD OF TRUSTEES AND GOVERNANCE

CPCH is a non-profit and tax exempt under IRS Code section 501(c)(3). Our board has 18 trustees and they meet twice per year in February and September. Ten of those seats must be filled by members of the Cumberland Presbyterian Church or the Cumberland Presbyterian Church of America.

IV. OUR CURRENT BOARD OF TRUSTEES

Chair - Mr. Richard Dean
Chair Emeritus - Mrs. Kay Goodman
Vice Chair - Mrs. Patricia Long
Secretary and Program Committee Chair - Rev. Joyce Merritt

Mr. Pete Carter
Rev. Duane Dougherty
Mrs. Carolyn Harmon
Mr. Charlie Harris

Rev. Melissa Knight
Mr. Cameron Marone
Mr. Brian Martin
Mr. Knight Miller

Rev. Dr. Perryn Rice
Mr. Jay Thomas
Mrs. Guin Tyus

V. FINANCIALS

Cumberland Presbyterian Children's Home depends on denominational support, OUO, donations, grants, planned giving, investments, fee for service revenue, and endowments to operate. Relationships with our donors are essential to growing and expanding our relationships to others who wish to be involved with our mission. We need your support. We need monetary donations, gifts in kind, and benefit from annual and legacy giving. Our goal is to provide the best care and the best environment for our children and families. The following is the breakdown in revenue received in these key categories.

Based on our annual audit, in 2016 CPCH received the following in donations and revenue for our home.
- Donations, Denominational Support, Grants, and Investment Revenue 71%
- Children's Residential and Emergency Care Services, CPS Revenue 25%
- Cumberland Family Services Counseling Clinic Revenue 3%
- Single Parent Family Transitional Housing Program Revenue 1%

In 2018, CPCH is working hard to decrease costs and ensure we are being good stewards of the donations and support we have received throughout our history. Continued giving allows us to fulfill our mission and build our endowment so CPCH's legacy continues to flourish. Cumberland spends approximately 87% of all revenue on our children and families. The small reminder is spent on administrative and fundraising costs.

VI. OUR SUCCESSES

CPCH has thousands of success stories over the course of our history. Annually, we serve approximately 150 children in our foster care programs and over 30 children and families in our transitional housing program. We serve hundreds of clients a year in our counseling clinic. We also have a growing volunteer base filled with individuals from churches, business organizations, educational institutes, and our community who wish to become involved in our ministry.

Our goal is for families to be healthy. One story of mother who worked hard to be reunited with her child is one that comes to mind as one of the biggest successes we were able to witness this past year. Christina, a single mother to a beautiful young 3 year old, has been sober for over one year and will be graduating from our program later this summer. Before coming to us, she had her child removed from her care by Child Protective Services when she was in a domestic violent relationship and struggling with her addiction. Through hard work and determination, she worked on her sobriety and was able to receive her toddler back into her care and move into our program. She was the first to graduate from our local drug court and is flourishing in our program. This is just one example of a family situation that we can help and support. Just one of our multiple success stories with a bright future.

A teenager in our care who has been living with us for approximately two years is going to be adopted by one of her teachers who she had a strong connection with in high school. This child came to us from a residential treatment center and she was challenging and defiant. Through our dedication and relationship building, she has learned how to use healthy coping skills and end her self-destructive tendencies that kept her down. This beautiful young woman was able to find success from the love and support she has at CPCH.

VII. OUR MISSION

Our mission helps others in crisis and we focus on helping them through life's most difficult challenges. Our counseling program specializes in treating trauma as healing from trauma is the gateway to finding a new-found sense of purpose and recovery. It is not often that you meet someone who has not been touched or impacted by issues related to mental health. We help clients through affordable mental health counseling, so counseling is affordable to everyone; just as it should be.

VIII. OUR STAFF

Our staff is passionate about the work they do. We work each day to carry out the mission that God has called us to do. We invite everyone to come and visit. Come and join us in our work so that we can make a difference in the lives of others together. We want to continue to share the news about the amazing work we do at Cumberland Presbyterian Children's Home. Thank you for making the lives of those we serve better and fulfilled. Thank you to our staff, our board, our donors, our supporters, and our friends. Please keep the Children's Home close in your prayers.

Respectfully submitted,
Dr. Jennifer Livings, LPC-S
Interim President

THE REPORT OF THE JOINT COMMITTEE ON AMENDMENTS

The Joint Committee on Amendments met February 16. 2018, in Huntsville, Alabama. Representing the CPCA were Willie Cowan and Vanessa Midgett. Representing the CPC were Pam Brown and Jan Overton. Also present were Craig White (Stated Clerk, CPCA), Mike Sharpe (Stated Clerk, CPC), Jaime Jordan (legal counsel, CPC), and Andy McClung (secretary).

I. PROPOSED AMENDMENT, JUDICATORY REPRESENTATION, CPCA

The Board of Judiciary of the CPCA will be proposing to the 2018 CPCA General Assembly an amendment to Constitution 5.4 and 8.2. The proposed change makes the representation formula for delegates to presbytery and synod consistent with the representation formula for delegates to General Assembly (9.2). If ratified, this amendment would affect only the CPCA.

II. UNION CPCA/CPC CHURCHES

This committee celebrates the possibility of union congregations being established by the Cumberland Presbyterian Church in America (CPCA) and the Cumberland Presbyterian Church (CPC). The stated clerk CPC and the administrative director CPCA will develop a step-by-step guide for the use of presbyteries in organizing or receiving such union churches.

III. PROPOSED CONSTITUTIONAL AMENDMENTS

The CPC representatives shared with the CPCA representatives of this committee the proposed constitutional amendments included in the Report of the Permanent Judiciary Committee. Because we share the Constitution, these amendments will go before the CPCA General Assembly as well.

Respectfully submitted,
The Joint Committee on Amendments

RESOLUTION

I. RESOLUTION FROM ARKANSAS PRESBYTERY REGARDING THE MISSION AND PURPOSE OF THE ENCOUNTER PUBLICATION

WHEREAS the Cumberland Presbyterian Church is founded on the teachings of Jesus Christ as expressed in Scripture and the Cumberland Presbyterian Confession of Faith.

WHEREAS the Encounter is a publication of the Cumberland Presbyterian and as such is considered as expressing the beliefs of the Cumberland Presbyterian Church.

WHEREAS the Encounter is in the position to influence Christians in their understanding of scripture and belief, and thus this position places its writers in a position of authority to speak on scripture and belief.

WHEREAS the writers of the Encounter Publications have at times spoken from this position of authority in ways that might be considered as expressing views that are not supported in the *Confession of Faith*.

WHEREAS in these writings, the author's may have had the desire to promote thought, they in turn failed to express the point of view found within the *Confession of Faith*. Such a failure never gave the readers the opportunity to think about the Cumberland Presbyterian View Point. The omission could be troubling because the writers are speaking from a positon of authority.

For many churches in Arkansas Presbytery, the most recent examples became quite troubling, as they see the Encounter Publication as a Cumberland Presbyterian Publication. These examples are listed below.

On page 16 of the June, July, August, 2017 *Encounter* has the following quote:

"For Christians, Jesus is the supreme example of loving kindness. To affirm this belief does not lessen the role of Moses for Judaism, Mohammed for Islam, or Buddha for Buddhism. It does not deny the positive influence of other important religious teachers. Buddha said often, "My religion is kindness." When anyone relates to the God of creative possibilities, transformation occurs, bringing harmony and peace. Gathering around the gentle teachings that are present in all religions offers a pathway to peace in our global, pluralistic age."

WHEREAS on page 17 of the June, July, August, 2017 *Encounter* has the following quote:

"Human kindness when grounded in the kindness of God revealed in Jesus' teachings and empowered by God's Spirit is a healing force for good. This healing kindness is also found in the teachings of Buddha."

WHEREAS the above two quotes may appear to elevate the teachings of Buddha and Islam to an equal position of Christ, and also as a way of salvation separate from that of Christ. If we are all kind, however we come to that kindness, then we are doing what God asks us to do, and thus we all find ourselves in a relationship with God.

There may be issues of interpretation and intent with these scriptures, but such interpretation and intent would have been unnecessary if a reference would have been made to our *Confession of Faith*.

Our *Confession of Faith* states in

3.07, "God's mighty act of reconciling love was accomplished in Jesus Christ, the divine Son who became flesh to be the means by which the sins of the world are forgiven."

4.10, "When persons repent of sin and in faith embrace God's salvation, they receive forgiveness for their sin and experience acceptance as God's children.

5.29, "Growth is natural to the church's life. The church is called into being and exists to reach out to those who have not experienced God's grace in Christ, and to nourish them with all the means of grace."

5:30, "In carrying out the apostolic commission, the covenant community has encouted and continues to encounter people who belong to religions which do not acknowledge Jesus Christ as Lord. While respecting persons who adhere to other religions, Christians are responsible to share with them the good news of salvation through Jesus Christ."

As Cumberland Presbyterians the "Who So Ever Will" doctrine is central to our faith, understanding, and practice as Cumberland Presbyterians. John 3:16-17 KJV states: *"For God so loved the world, that He gave His only begotten Son, that whosoever believeth in Him should not perish, but have everlasting life. For God sent not His Son into the world to condemn the world; but that that the world through Him might be saved.*

It is with a want for understanding of the Mission and Purpose of the Encounter Publication that Arkansas Presbytery petitions the 2018 General Assembly to take the following action.

Arkansas Presbytery petitions the 2018 General Assembly of the Cumberland Presbyterian Church to form a Committee to study the mission and purpose of the Encounter Publication in an effort to determine if this publication of the Cumberland Presbyterian is promoting a theology and understanding that supports and upholds our Confession of Faith. In an effort to gather this information the Committee will be asked to review the Adult Encounter Publications for the last 3 years. In this endeavor the Committee will also be instructed to study the subscription list of the Encounter Publication to determine how many of the Cumberland Presbyterian Churches listed in the Yearbook, subscribe to the Encounter. The Committee will also be instructed to inquire of at least 50% of the Cumberland Presbyterian Churches that do not scribe to the Encounter Material, as to why they do not.

After the Committee has completed its task, it will prepare a report to be presented at General Assembly in 2019 that includes all the information that it was asked to gather.

Respectfully submitted:,
Reverend Alan Meinzer, Arkansas Presbytery
Reverend Gordon Warren, Arkansas Presbytery
Reverend Jo Warren, Arkansas Presbytery

GENERAL ASSEMBLY AGENCIES

I. OFFICE OF THE GENERAL ASSEMBLY

A. GENERAL ASSEMBLY OFFICE

	Revised 2018	Proposed 2019
INCOME		
Our United Outreach	$211,836	$197,836
Endowments/Interest	20,000	20,000
Interest on Cash Funds Management	2,500	2,500
Sales of yearbook/digest	2,000	2,000
TOTAL INCOME	**$236,336**	**$222,336**
EXPENSE		
ECUMENICAL RELATIONS		
World Communion of Reformed Churches	$ 6,000	$ 6,000
CANAAC	2,000	2,000
Ecumenical Travel	1,000	1,000
Sub-Total	$ 9,000	$ 9,000
LIAISON WITH CHURCH		
General Assembly Meeting	$ 10,000	$ 10,000
Preliminary Minutes	5,000	5,000
GA Minutes/Mailing	500	500
Yearbook/Mailing	2,500	2,500
Travel/Moderator	8,500	8,500
Travel/Stated Clerk & Staff	8,500	8,500
Sub-Total	$ 35,000	$ 35,000
OFFICE		
Computer Supplies	$ 2,000	$ 2,000
Equipment/Supplies	2,500	2,500
Postage	2,000	2,000
Sub-Total	$ 6,500	$ 6,500
PERSONNEL		
Salaries/Housing	$139,420	$139,420
FICA (Asst to Stated Clerk)	4,300	4,300
Retirement	6,800	6,800
Health Insurance	30,000	30,000
Disability Insurance/Worker's Compensation	800	800
Sub-Total	$181,320	$181,320
STATED CLERK'S CONFERENCE/BOARD EXPENSE		
Legal Fees / Clerk's Conference	$ 1,963	$ 1,963
Corporate Board Expense	2,000	2,000
Sub-Total	$ 3,963	$ 3,963
TOTAL EXPENSE	**$235,783**	**$235,783**
From Reserves	$ 553	$ 13,447

B. GENERAL ASSEMBLY COMMISSIONS AND COMMITTEES

INCOME		
Contingency	$ 13,240	$ 12,365
Nominating Committee	2,966	2,770
Commission on Chaplains	10,247	9,570
Judiciary Committee	9,965	9,026
Theology and Social Concerns Committee	3,601	3,363
Our United Outreach Committee	92,044	92,044
TOTAL INCOME	**$132,065**	**$129,138**

	Revised 2018	Proposed 2019
EXPENSE		
Contingency	$ 13,240	$ 12,365
Nominating Committee	2,966	2,770
Commission on Chaplains	10,247	9,570
Judiciary Committee	9,965	9,026
Theology and Social Concerns Committee	3,601	3,363
Our United Outreach Committee	92,044	92,044
TOTAL EXPENSE	**$132,065**	**$129,138**

II. MINISTRY COUNCIL

	Revised 2018	Proposed 2019
INCOME		
Endowments	$ 0	$ 15,000
Grants	$ 0	$ 1,800
ILP Transfers		
MMT Budget Reserve Fund: out ILP	569,264	602,868
DMT Contingency Fund: in Wells Fargo	43,662	44,062
DMT Leader Development: out ILP	0	1,852
DMT Revolving Publication Fund: out ILP	4,000	7,500
CMT: out ILP	996	996
Contributions/Gifts		
Teacher of the Year	0	0
Patron Membership (DMT)	0	0
Christian Education Season Offering	0	0
DMT - General	3,100	2,889
MC - General	5,900	3,431
Our United Outreach		
OUO Income	1,053,642	1,104,837
In lieu of Our United Outreach	6,720	6,720
Birthplace Shrine Chaplaincy	3,750	3,750
Children's Fest	9,750	9,900
Clergy Crisis	6,000	6,000
CP Magazine Subscriptions	30,000	30,000
Cumberland Presbyterians Resources	69,360	69,360
CPWM		
Convention	8,000	8,000
Convention Offering	250	250
General	3,000	3,000
Sales Merchandise	700	700
CPYC	98,165	98,165
Discipleship Blueprints	2,400	2,400
Encounter	105,640	105,640
Family Week: Brochure Fees	150	0

	Revised 2018	Proposed 2019
Family Week: Brochure Fees	$ 150	$ 0
Global Missions Interns and Consultants: out ILP	0	0
Kaleo	0	13,500
Leader Development	5,492	5,492
Ministers Conference	0	6,000
Missionary Setup	15,000	15,000
Missionary Support	266,968	295,373
New Church Development (NCD) Subsidies	237,174	193,174
New Exploration Iniative - NCD	11,200	26,400
NPI: Children's CP Curriculum	500	500
Presbyterian Youth Triennium	5,000	5,000
Program Planning Calendar - Sales	920	920
Stir	1,500	1,500
Third Age Ministry	500	500
Young Adult Ministry	14,300	10,700
Youth Evangelism Conference	2,350	2,350
Youth Ministry Planning Council	2,500	2,500
Youth Workers Retreat	4,500	4,500
TOTAL INCOME	**$2,592,353**	**$2,699,818**

EXPENSES
Ministry Council Administration Salaries

	Revised 2018	Proposed 2019
Salaries	$ 759,473	$ 816,645
Clergy Housing Allowance	166,104	159,604
Health Insurance	130,500	146,688
Retirement	43,310	45,944
FICA	32,468	36,498
Tax Sheltered Annuity	6,287	6,287
Insurance/Disability	4,096	4,366

Ministry Council Administration General Expenses

	Revised 2018	Proposed 2019
Annual Credit Card Fees	$ 3,678	$ 3,678
Computer Equipment	0	0
Computer Software (Wufoo, Adobe, BaseCamp)	10,000	10,000
Educational Publications for Distribution	3,000	3,000
Employee Events	2,500	2,500

	Revised 2018	Proposed 2019
Employee Recognition	3,450	3,450
Foundation Direcory Online	500	500
Government Fees (annual reports)	40	40
Legal	2,000	2,000
MC Supplemental Report	5,000	5,000
P & C Insurance	19,090	16,090
Staff Resource Materials	1,997	1,197
Subscriptions/Membership	2,246	2,246
Telephone/Internet	624	840
Temporary Help	19,800	12,600
MC/Elected Team Member Recognition	1,040	1,040
Office Supplies	12,000	12,000
Postage	1,800	1,800
Relocation Expense	10,000	0
Beth-El Farmworker	$ 40,500	$ 40,500
Birthplace Shrine Chaplaincy: Chaplain's Stipend	3,750	3,750
Children's Fest	9,750	9,900
Clergy Crisis Support: Distribution	6,000	6,000
Coalition of Applachian Ministry	12,700	12,700
CP Magazine	54,033	54,033
Cumberland Presbyterian Resources	68,828	68,828
CPWM		
General	9,100	9,100
Sales Merchandise	2,000	2,000
Convention	11,950	11,950
Offering	250	250
CPYC	98,165	98,165
Cross-Culture Immigrant Leadership Training	4,000	4,000
Discipleship Blueprints	2,400	2,400
Ecumenical Stewardship Center	4,500	4,500
Encounter	36,812	36,812
Family Ministry	550	550
General Assembly	35,050	36,550
General Consultants	26,400	22,400
Kaleo	0	13,500
Leadership Referral Services	2,100	2,100

	Revised 2018	Proposed 2019
Leader Development	5,492	5,492
Ministers		
Conference	0	16,000
Encouragement & Recognition	3,818	3,818
Retreat	1,000	1,000
Missionary Messenger	59,480	59,480
Missionary Setup	0	30,000
Missionary Support	321,968	350,373
National Farm Worker	3,500	4,300
New Church Development (NCD) Subsidies	237,174	170,774
New Exploration Initiative	11,200	26,400
New Program Iniatives		
Children's Curriculum	1,000	1,000
CPWM Girls and Young Women Council	11,800	11,800
CP Learning Circles	0	0
DMT	0	0
PREP Staff Expenses	400	400
Presbyterian Youth Triennium	5,000	5,000
Presbyteries/Councils	129,820	144,820
Program Planning Calendar	5,150	5,150
Project Vida	8,500	8,500
Stir	5,000	5,000
Support Ministries	1,000	1,000
Third Age Ministry	500	500
Travel (includes elected member travel)	80,060	80,060
Web Development/Maintenance	2,000	2,000
Young Adult Ministry	14,300	14,661
Youth Evangelism Conference	7,350	7,350
Youth Ministry Planning Council - UBCD	2,500	2,500
Youth Workers Retreat	4,500	0
TOTAL EXPENSES	**$2,592,353**	**$ 2,699,818**
Surplus/(Deficit)	$ 0	$ 0

III. BOARD OF STEWARDSHIP

INCOME
    Contributions

	Revised 2018	Proposed 2019
Contributions/Gifts	$ 400	$ 3,000
ILP Contributions	2,600	2,000
Endowment Contributions	26,000	20,000
Total Contributions	**29,000**	**25,000**

	Revised 2018	Proposed 2019
Our United Outreach	136,000	135,000
Investment Earnings		
Endowment Earnings	90,000	96,000
ILP Earnings	16,000	8,000
Endowment WF Income	19,000	19,400
Total Investment Earnings	**125,000**	**123,400**
Realized Gain/Loss - Endowment	10,000	10,000
Unrealized Gain/Loss - Endowment	100,100	116,500
Total Investment Gains/Losses	**110,100**	**126,000**
Service Fees		
Management Fees - Acct Coordinator	1,600	1,600
Management Fees	55,000	61,000
Total Service Fees	**56,600**	**62,600**
TOTAL INCOME	**$456,700**	**$ 472,000**

EXPENSE

	Revised 2018	Proposed 2019
Salaries		
Salaries	$199,275	$ 205,783
Housing Allowance	21,000	21,000
Total Salaries	**220,275**	**226,783**
Benefits		
Health Insurance	70,000	70,500
Retirement	10,746	11,339
FICA	9,630	10,117
Insurance/Disability	800	1,000
Total Benefits	**91,176**	**92,956**
Events		
Conference/Events	500	500
Tax Guide for Ministers	3,700	4,100
Total Events	**4,200**	**4,600**
Board Expense		
Board/Agency Travel	15,000	15,000
Board/Agency Recognition	$ 600	$ 600
Total Board Expense	**15,600**	**15,600**
Resource Purchases		
Subscriptions	600	600
Total Resources Purchases	**600**	**600**
Contracted Services		
Legal	1,000	500
Audit	0	2,100
Temporary Help	1,000	1,000
Total Contracted Services	**2,000**	**3,600**
Insurance		
Insurance/Liability	4,000	4,200
	4,000	**4,200**
Professional Development		
Subscriptions & Membership	100	100
Total Professional Development	**100**	**100**
Payment/Subsidies		
ESC Stewardship Expense	3,500	3,500
ILP Withdrawal	2,500	2,500
Endowment Distribution	98,000	102,000
Total Payments/Subsidies	**104,000**	**108,000**
Equipment		
Office Equipment	800	800
Computer Equipment	2,000	2,000
Computer Maintenance	150	150
Computer Software	$ 500	$ 500

	Revised 2018	Proposed 2019
Total Equipment	**3,450**	**3,450**
Supplies		
Computer Supplies	500	500
Office Supplies	3,000	3,000
Total Supplies	**3,500**	**3,500**
Postage/Shipping		
Postage	1,000	1,486
Shipping	167	325
Total Postage/Shipping	**1,167**	**1,811**
Employee Recognition		
Employee Recognition	1,000	1,200
Total Employee Recognition	**1,000**	**1,200**
Travel		
Staff Travel	4,500	4,500
Total Travel	**4,500**	**4,500**
Miscellaneous		
Miscellaneous	1,032	1,000
Total Miscellaneous	**1,032**	**1,000**
Organization		
Organizational Expense	100	100
Total Organization	**100**	**100**
TOTAL EXPENSE	**$456,700**	**$ 472,000**

IV. HISTORICAL FOUNDATION

	Revised 2018	Proposed 2019
INCOME		
Our United Outreach	$ 72,439	$ 73,000
Endowments	73,000	75,000
Gifts	11,000	12,000
ILP Earnings	6,000	7,000
Denomination Day Offering	5,000	5,000
TOTAL INCOME	**$ 167,439**	**$ 172,000**
EXPENSE		
Salaries	$ 95,088	$ 97,128
FICA / Retirement	14,404	14,764
Insurance	10,034	10,034
Board Travel	6,000	7,000
Legal Fees	200	200
Continuing Education	2,000	2,000
Subscriptions/Memberships	2,000	2,000
Archival Equipment	2,000	2,000
Computer Supplies	500	500
Office Supplies	2,000	2,000
Postage	300	125
Acquisitions	10,313	11,649
Birthplace Shrine	8,000	8,000
Employee Recognition	600	600
Staff Travel	9,000	9,000
Denomination Day Project	5,000	5,000
TOTAL EXPENSE	**$ 167,439**	**$ 172,000**

V. MEMPHIS THEOLOGICAL SEMINARY

	Revised 2018	Proposed 2019
REVENUE		
Student Tuition Fees	$2,420,370	$ 2,023,950
Investment	306,608	303,431
Endowment Draw		200,000
Gifts and Grants	1,731,945	1,000,000
Other Revenues	128,700	102,009
TOTAL REVENUES	**$4,587,623**	**$ 3,629,390**
EXPENSES		
Business Office	$ 340,464	$ 332,733
Dean's Office	156,616	116,412
Chapel	44,316	1,900
Educational Development Committee	15,500	15,000
Advancement Office	389,775	335,951
Doctor of Ministry	60,200	61,550
Facilities	567,204	497,531
Faculty	940,017	815,646
Summer Classes	37,600	34,800
January Classes	11,000	8,000
Financial Aid	64,084	52,659
Information Technology	142,426	190,779
Library	255,496	238,664
President's Office	261,823	261,823
Admissions	156,603	110,881
Registrar & Institutional Research	134,161	99,125
Annual Fund/Alumni Affairs	100,779	0
Student Housing	91,642	120,695
Student Services	84,943	77,476
Certificate & Continuing Education	16,950	15,950
Methodist House of Studies	37,037	24,432
Student Government	2,775	2,700
Theology & Arts	37,359	0
Scholarships	423,208	347,483
Program of Alternate Studies	130,801	123,364
Formation For Ministry	92,605	89,556
Financial Leadership Ministry	93,435	0
Communications	49,825	0
Depreciation	185,891	197,752
TOTAL EXPENSES	**$4,926,535**	**$4,134,033**
Increase (decrease) in net assets	(338,912)	(504,643)

VI. SHARED SERVICES

	Revised 2018	Proposed 2019
REVENUE		
Our United Outreach	$ 343,420	346,967
TOTAL REVENUES	**$ 343,420**	**$ 346,967**
EXPENSES		
Salaries	$ 52,286	$ 53,332
Health Insurance	30,441	31,659
Retirement	2,614	2,667
FICA	4,000	4,080
Accounting Coordinator	1,600	1,600
Audit	21,000	22,500
Payroll Service	6,900	7,400
Bank Charges	17,500	14,000
Technology System Consultants - EMS	18,000	18,000
Software Maintenance Agreement - Blackbaud	15,700	17,000
Building & Maintenance	45,845	45,845
Pest Control	840	840
Lawn & Ground Maintenance	18,500	18,500
Lawn Treatment	1,500	1,500
Utilities - Building 1	24,650	24,650
Utilities - Building 2	18,500	17,000
Janitorial Service	8,100	8,100
Security System Monitoring	1,100	1,200
Trash Collection	1,850	2,500
Telephone/Internet	9,400	10,000
Heating & AC Maintenance Agreement	10,000	12,000
Insurance/Liability	11,844	11,844
Office Equipment Maintenance	14,000	14,000
Computer Maintenance	500	500
Computer Software	2,500	2,500
Office Supplies	2,500	2,000
Postage	750	750
Employee Events	1,000	1,000
TOTAL EXPENSE	$ 343,420	$ 346,967
Surplus/Deficit	$ 0	$ 0

The Proceedings of the

ONE HUNDRED EIGHTY-EIGHTH GENERAL ASSEMBLY

of the

CUMBERLAND PRESBYTERIAN CHURCH

session held in

NORMAN, OKLAHOMA
June 17-21, 2018

At Norman, Oklahoma and within the facilities of the Embassy Suites, there the seventeenth day of June in the year of our Lord, two thousand eighteen, at the appointed hour of seven o'clock in the evening, Minister and Elder Commissioners from the various presbyteries, youth advisory delegates and visitors assembled for concurrent meetings of the General Assemblies of the Cumberland Presbyterian Church and the Cumberland Presbyterian Church in America.

FIRST DAY – SUNDAY – JUNE 17, 2018

OPENING WORSHIP

At Norman, Oklahoma and within the Conference Center of the Embassy Suites Hotel, the one hundred eighty-eighth General Assembly of the Cumberland Presbyterian Church, the one hundred forty-third General Assembly of the Cumberland Presbyterian Church in America, the Convention of Cumberland Presbyterian Women's Ministry, and visitors gathered for worship at 7:00 p.m. Liturgists for the service were Ms. Yvonne Frierson, National Missionary Society President (CPCA), and Elder Lewis Leon Cole, Moderator (CPCA). The Music Leader was Ms. Brenda Ross, Red River Presbytery (CPC). Special Music was offered by Reverend Joe E. Howard, III, Brazos River Presbytery (CPCA) and Elder John Rainey, Cleveland Ohio Presbytery (CPCA). The Pianist was Ms. Robin McCaskey Hughes, Red River Presbytery (CPC). An offering of $2,870.94 was taken to be shared between the Choctaw Ministries (CPC) and Sickle Cell Disease Association of America, a designated CPCA project.

Reverend David Lancaster, Moderator, West Tennessee Presbytery (CPC) presented the sermon, "What About These Bones?," taken from the scripture passage Ezekiel 37:1-14. The Sacrament of Holy Communion was led by co-celebrants Reverend Melissa Malinoski, West Tennessee Presbytery (CPC) and Reverend Tramaine Snodgrass, Huntsville Presbytery (CPCA). Serving communion were Naomi King, Vanessa Midgett, Glenn Strain, Anthony Johnson, Michael T. Cooper, Kay Ward-Creer, Tom Jones (CPCA) and Ron Lewis, Chris Warren, Linda Drylie, Gloria Diaz, Hannah Bryan, Jerry Smyrl, and Christy Cooper (CPC).

SECOND DAY – MONDAY – JUNE 18, 2018

THE ASSEMBLY IS CONSTITUTED

The Moderator, the Reverend David Lancaster, called the assembly to order at 10:35 a.m. The constituting prayer was offered by Elder Roy Shanks, North Central Presbytery.

ADOPTION OF THE AGENDA

Moderator Lancaster asked for a motion that the agenda, as found in the Preliminary Minutes, be adopted. On Motion, the agenda was adopted.

REPORT OF THE CREDENTIALS COMMITTEE

Gloria Diaz presented the Report of the Credentials Committee. There were forty-four (44) ministers, forty-two (42) elders, for a total of eighty-six (86) commissioners present at 10:35 a.m. There were twenty (20) youth advisory delegates present. On motion, the report of the Credentials Committee was received, marked Appendix "A" and filed.

ELECTION OF THE MODERATOR

Moderator Lancaster declared the floor open for nominations for the office of moderator of the one hundred eighty-eighth General Assembly. Reverend Jay Earheart-Brown, Nashville Presbytery, and Reverend Lisa Scott, North Central Presbytery, were nominated. A Motion was made and seconded that nominations cease. Motion passed.

Reverend Ralph Blevins, North Central Presbytery, spoke on behalf of Reverend Lisa Scott. Reverend Perryn Rice, Red River Presbytery, by motion was granted permission to speak to the body. Reverend Rice spoke on behalf of Reverend Jay Earheart-Brown.

The Moderator called for delegates to cast their votes. The ballots were collected by the credentials committee who met with the Stated Clerk to count the ballots.

While the ballots were being counted, Mrs. Edith Old, Director of Ministries, introduced the two newest team leaders: Reverend Steven Shelton, Nashville Presbytery, Communications Team Leader and Reverend Pam Phillips-Burk, Pastoral Development Ministry Team Leader.

The Engrossing Clerk, Vernon Sansom, shared announcements and introduced the following Board/Agency Representatives:

Bethel University	Nancy Bean
Commission on Military Chaplains	Charles McCaskey
Children's Home	Duane Dougherty
Historical Foundation	Lisa Oliver
Judiciary	Pam Brown
Memphis Theological Seminary	Kevin Brantley
Ministry Council	Victory Moore
Our United Outreach	Bruce Hamilton
Stewardship	Randy Davidson
Theology & Social Concerns	Richard Morgan
Unification Task Force	Joy Warren (CPC)
	Mitchell Walker (CPCA)

Gloria Diaz, credentials committee chair, announced that by vote, Reverend Jay Earheart-Brown was elected Moderator of the 188th General Assembly of the Cumberland Presbyterian Church. Former Moderator, David Lancaster, was presented a replica of the Moderator's Cross, a gavel and stoles to newly elected Moderator, Reverend Jay Earheart-Brown. Moderator Earheart-Brown thanked the body for the honor of being elected and thanked the former Moderator for his service to the denomination.

Moderator Earheart-Brown introduced his family: wife, Mary; elder son, Paul; younger son, Carter (who was not present); step-mother Beth Brown; and nephew Houston Brown. The Moderator thanked the denomination for prayers that were offered for Houston who was seriously injured in an accident at Bethel University. He also thanked the faculty and staff of Memphis Theological Seminary for the support he received as president. He announced that he will leave Memphis Theological Seminary on July 31, 2018 and will become the pastor of Faith Cumberland Presbyterian Church, Bartlett, Tennessee.

ELECTION OF THE VICE-MODERATOR

Moderator Earheart-Brown opened the floor for nominations for Vice-Moderator. Reverend Charles (Buddy) Pope, Columbia Presbytery, was nominated to be Vice-Moderator of the 188th General Assembly of the Cumberland Presbyterian Church. There being no other nominations, a motion was made and seconded that nominations cease and that we move to elect. Motion passed. By vote, Reverend Charles (Buddy) Pope was elected vice-moderator of the of the 188th General Assembly of the Cumberland Presbyterian Church. Vice-Moderator Pope was escorted to the podium by Reverend Sherry Ladd, Columbia Presbytery. Vice-Moderator Pope thanked the body for the honor of being elected as Vice-Moderator of the General Assembly. He pledged to do his very best in service to the Cumberland Presbyterian Church.

PRESENTATION BY THE STATED CLERK

The Stated Clerk, Reverend Michael Sharpe, invited retiring Moderator David Lancaster to the podium. The Stated Clerk thanked Moderator Lancaster for his service to the 187th General Assembly. The Stated Clerk presented the former Moderator with replicas of the moderator's cross and gavel used in the 187th General Assembly of the Cumberland Presbyterian Church.

The former Moderator thanked the General Assembly for the opportunity to serve. He spoke about the important role that the Cumberland Presbyterian Church played in his family. First bringing his parents to faith before he was born, and all through his life as he was raised in the Cumberland Presbyterian Church.

COMMUNICATIONS

The Stated Clerk reported that there were no communications.

WELCOME, PASTOR HOST, LOCAL OFFICIALS

The Moderator introduced co-pastor hosts Reverend Marian Sontowski and Reverend Leslie Johnson, Red River Presbytery. Both co-pastor hosts welcomed the General Assembly to Oklahoma and thanked all who had worked hard to help with the organizing of this meeting.

COMMISSIONER RESOLUTIONS

A resolution was presented on the floor by Reverend Ron McMillan, West Tennessee Presbytery, calling for the 188th General Assembly to reaffirm and adopt the 1996 General Assembly Statement on Homosexuality as binding on presbyteries, sessions, ministers, elders, and deacons with listed adaptations. Reverend Chris Warren, Murfreesboro Presbytery, presented a resolution to the body dealing with the separation of immigrants from their children at the southern border.

The Stated Clerk advised that both resolutions as well as a copy of the 1996 statement dealing with homosexuality would be printed and distributed to all minister commissioners, elder commissioners and youth advisory delegates.

The Moderator referred both resolutions to the Theology and Social Concerns/Unification Task Force committee. Reverend Terra Sisco, Red River Presbytery, addressed the body and shared that there was a display table representing Oklahoma. She hoped all commissioners will stop by and take a look. There was also a free book available each day written by Reverend Tom Spence, Red River Presbytery.

Reverend Chris Warren, Murfreesboro Presbytery, presented a second resolution to the body calling for a study before taking action which was also referred to the Theology and Social Concerns/Unification Task Force committee. Copies of the resolution will be made available to all commissioners and youth advisory delegates.

RECESS

Moderator Earheart-Brown declared the General Assembly of the Cumberland Presbyterian Church in recess. The committees will begin meeting at 7 p.m. The General Assembly will reconvene on Thursday at 9:30 a.m.

AFTERNOON ACTIVITIES

At 2:00 p.m., a Joint Choctaw Anniversary Celebration which included: a Service of Celebration on the occasion of the 200th Anniversary of the Cumberland Presbyterian Church Ministry with the Choctaw as well as several cultural heritage demonstrations on breadmaking, pottery, Choctaw hymns and dancers. Participating in the service were Reverend Virginia Espinoza, song leader; Mrs. Robin McCaskey Hughes, pianist; Mr. Tim Maxville, Native American Flutist; and Choctaw Chief Gary Batton, guest speaker. Other participants were Reverend Hannah Bryan, Reverend Linda Scott, Ms. Faith Jacob Parra, Tvli Jacob, Mr. Dennis J. Parra, Elder Ronald Lewis, Councilman Tony Ward, and Roy Robinson. Also participating were members from the following churches: Coal Creek, Atoka, Oklahoma; Lone Star, Wardville, Oklahoma; McGee Chapel, Broken Bow, Oklahoma; Panki Bok, Eagletown, Oklahoma; Pigeon Roost, Boswell, Oklahoma; Pine Lake, Broken Bow, Oklahoma; Rock Creek, Honobia, Oklahoma; and Round Lake, Centrahoma, Oklahoma.

A joint moderator and anniversary reception was held at 4:30 p.m. honoring the moderators of the Cumberland Presbyterian Church in America and the Cumberland Presbyterian Church. The reception also included the Cumberland Presbyterian Church 500th Anniversary of Ministry with the Choctaw.

EVENING ACTIVITES

The Committees meetings began at 7:00 p.m.

SECOND DAY – TUESDAY – JUNE 19, 2018

The General Assembly began the day with a joint devotion and the FUN RUN & WALK at 7:00 a.m. at Legacy Park. The devotion was presented by Moderator Jay Earheart-Brown based on Proverbs 24:30-34.

The day was devoted to committee work from 10:00 a.m. until 5:00 p.m. and an evening session at 7:00 p.m. The attendance for the day: forty-four (44) Minister Commissioners, forty-two (42) Elder Commissioners for a total of eighty-six (86) Commissioners and nineteen (19) Youth Advisory Delegates.

EVENING PROGRAM

At 8:30 p.m. in Ballroom G & H, commissioners and visitors participated in a joint reception honoring Women in Ministry. Attendees enjoyed fellowship, refreshments, and wonderful door prizes.

THIRD DAY – WEDNESDAY – JUNE 20, 2018

The General Assembly and visitors began the day with a joint devotional at 8:30 a.m. led by the Women's Missionary Society (CPCA). The devotional, based on Isaiah 6:8, was presented by Reverend Michael Jones, Vice Moderator (CPCA).

Reverend Michael Qualls, Director of the Program of Alternate Studies made a presentation in memory of Reverend Dale Gentry, *"The Last of the Circuit Riders."* Reverend Gentry mentored scores of budding young ministers and built churches and strengthened churches in Arkansas, logging 40,000 miles each year in ministry. Reverend Gentry's ministry spanned 74 years.

Reverend Qualls introduced Reverend Gentry's son, Steve, and grandson Cody and presented them with a plaque from the Program of Alternate Studies recognizing Reverend Gentry's service to the Cumberland Presbyterian Church and his influence on those who entered the ministry. Steve and Cody Gentry addressed the gathering expressing their gratitude for recognizing Reverend Gentry.

Reverend Qualls announced that the Gentry Family and some of the churches that Reverend Gentry served have established a scholarship for ministers in Program of Alternate Studies in rural areas.

The session was closed by Moderator Reverend Jay Earheart-Brown who, after sharing some announcements, led the gathering in closing prayer remembering those who have had health concerns this week as well as the family of 3-year-old Levi Hughes, grandson of Reverend Richard and Marcia Hughes (Robert Donnell Presbytery) who died in a tragic accident.

The Committees used the remainder of the day in meetings, preparing and reviewing reports and collecting signatures. Attendance for the day: forty-two (42) minister commissioners, forty (40) elder commissioners for a total of eighty-two (82) and twenty-one (21) youth advisory delegates.

At 7:00 p.m., the 188th General Assembly and visitors gathered for worship led by the Young Adults. Participants included Reverend Neal Wilkinson and Joanna Wilkinson, Missouri Presbytery; A'An Parra, Choctaw Presbytery; Elea Forester, West Tennessee Presbytery; Reverend Paul Earheart-Brown, West Tennessee Presbytery; and youth advisory delegates: Abigail Mathis, Murfreesboro Presbytery; Callie Swindle, Grace Presbytery; Katy Barnes, Robert Donnell Presbytery; and Joseph Keenan, West Tennessee Presbytery.

FOURTH DAY – THURSDAY – JUNE 21, 2018

At 8:30 a.m., the General Assembly and visitors began the day with joyful singing and a devotional based on Isaiah 6:5-8, led by Youth Advisory Delegate Yahaira Patricio, Tennessee-Georgia Presbytery. Others taking part in the service were Reverend Melissa Malinoski, worship director, West Tennessee Presbytery; Ms. Robin McCaskey Hughes, pianist, Red River Presbytery; and Reverend Steven Shelton, guitarist, West Tennessee Presbytery.

CALL TO ORDER

The Moderator, Reverend Jay Earheart-Brown, called the assembly to order at 9:30 am. There were forty-one (41) ministers, forty-two (42) elders for a total of eighty-three (83) commissioners and twenty (20) youth advisory delegates present. The opening prayer was shared by Vice-Moderator Buddy Pope, Columbia Presbytery.

PARLIMENTARIAN APPOINTED

The Moderator appointed Pamela Brown, member of the Permanent Judiciary Committee, as Parliamentarian.

GREETINGS AND PRESENTATION

The body was greeted by Elder Leon Cole, Moderator of the Cumberland Presbyterian Church in America. Elder Cole stated that he looked forward to our joint meeting next year and the vote for unification.

Motion made and seconded to seat Elder Cole as an advisory member. Motion passed.

The Stated Clerk, Mike Sharpe, made a presentation to the Historical Foundation of a hand crafted commemorative Native American flute made by Elder Mikel Davis, Shiloh Cumberland Presbyterian Church, Red River Presbytery. Susan Gore, Archivist, Historical Foundation of the CPC and CPCA, received the flute with gratitude.

ANNOUNCEMENTS

The Moderator shared some "housekeeping" details.
- Reminder to invite the youth advisory delegates to vote prior to the commissioner vote.
- Instructed commissioners and youth advisory delegates wishing to address the Assembly to approach the microphone, introduce themselves by name and the presbytery they represent.
- To please write out any motions and give a copy to the Engrossing Clerk before returning to their seat.
- As committee reports are presented, committee members will come forward and be seated in the front rows of chairs.

The Stated Clerk explained the use indicator cards to convey responses toward content of speech and to indicate the mood of the General Assembly. Each commissioner received a copy of the Ten Essential Rules of Order to assist with following Robert's Rules of Order. He also announced that there are lost and found items at the clerk's table.

Reverend William Alas, Grace Presbytery, could not attend General Assembly as a minister commissioner because he had to appear before the Immigration Authorities and received word that his Visa would not be renewed. Johan Daza led the body in prayer for Reverend Alas and others who are facing deportation as well as our immigrant churches.

THE REPORT OF THE NOMINATING COMMITTEE

The Report of the Nominating Committee was presented by the Moderator as printed in the preliminary minutes. Those named in the report were placed in nomination. The Moderator opened the floor for further nominations. There was a nomination of Melinda Reams, Arkansas Presbytery, to the Ministry Council. This created a vote between Ken Bean, West Tennessee Presbytery; Ron McMillan, West Tennessee Presbytery; and Melinda Reams, Arkansas Presbytery. The body voted by paper ballot. While the vote was being tabulated, the body moved on to the Report of the Committee on Chaplains/Historic Foundation.

THE REPORT OF THE COMMITTEE ON CHAPLAINS/HISTORICAL FOUNDATION

The Report of the Committee on Chaplains/Historical Foundation was read by youth advisory delegates: Kennedy Holloway, Presbytery of East Tennessee and Callie Swindle, Grace Presbytery. A motion was made by Reverend Sherry Ladd, Columbia Presbytery, that the report be concurred in and the recommendations be adopted. Motion passed. The report was marked "B" and filed.

THE REPORT NOMINATING COMMITTEE-continued

The Credentials Committee reported that Mr. Ken Bean, West Tennessee Presbytery and Ms. Melinda Reams, Arkansas Presbytery were the nominees for the Ministry Council. The slate of nominees was elected. The report was marked "C" and filed.

THE REPORT OF THE COMMITTEE ON THEOLOGY AND SOCIAL CONCERNS/ UNIFICATION TASKFORCE

The Report of the Committee on Theology and Social Concerns/Unification Task force was read by Elder Ronald Lewis, Choctaw Presbytery; Elder Patricia Coleman, West Tennessee Presbytery; and Reverend Sandra Shepherd, Nashville Presbytery. A Motion was made by Reverend Randall Mayfield, Presbytery of East Tennessee, after noting editorial changes, to concur with the report and adopt its recommendations. Motion Seconded.

A motion was made by Reverend Ron McMillan, West Tennessee Presbytery, to amend the report to change the word "denied" to "adopted" in Recommendation 11. Motion seconded.

RECESS

Following discussion and while the motion to amend the report was still on the floor, the Moderator called for a 15-minute recess at 11:05 a.m.

The Moderator called the meeting back to order at 11:20 a.m. and called for the discussion to continue.

RECESS

Following further discussion on the motion, the Moderator called for a recess for lunch at 11:55 a.m. to reconvene at 2 p.m.

THE REPORT OF THE COMMITTEE ON THEOLOGY AND SOCIAL CONCERNS/ UNIFICATION TASKFORCE - continued

Moderator Earheart-Brown called the meeting back to order at 2:00 p.m. The Moderator shared prayer concerns from Reverend Buddy Pope concerning a death in the church he serves as well other calls for prayer. Prayer led by Reverend Jackson Tsui, Hong Kong Presbytery.

The Moderator called for discussion on the motion to amend Recommendation 11 to continue. After hearing the recommendation from one of the youth advisory delegates, who encouraged the body in a loving way, that further study of the issue rather than further discussion by the General Assembly would better serve the body, a motion was made and seconded to end debate and to proceed to vote by secret ballot. Motion passed.

GREETINGS AND ANNOUNCEMENTS

While the ballots were being tabulated, Cathy Littlefield, President of the Cumberland Presbyterian Women's Ministry Convention, brought greetings from the Convention and spoke of the projects that the Cumberland Presbyterian Women's Ministry would be sponsoring during the next year. She reported 35 new participants this year. Ms. Littlefield also reported on this year's Convention project. She reported that Pam Phillips-Burk has served wonderfully and would be missed by the Women's Ministry. The Cumberland Presbyterian Women's Ministry asks for prayers for a successor.

The Engrossing Clerk, Vernon Sansom, presented excuses for Reverend Courtney Kruger; Elder Sylvia Hall; and Elder Christy Cooper, representing Tennessee-Georgia Presbytery; Reverend Jerry Smyrl, Presbytery del Cristo; youth advisory delegate Callie Swindle, Grace Presbytery; and youth advisory delegate, Elena Riedell, Red River Presbytery. On motion, the excuses were granted.

An announcement was made that the Cumberland Presbyterian Children's Home is seeking a new President/CEO. Persons wishing to apply may do so at www.thecnm.org.

Permission was given to hear Reverend Michael Qualls, Director of the Program of Alternate Studies, who shared that a $500 donation had been given to the Gentry Scholarship Fund for PAS with a challenge to all graduates from the PAS program to do likewise.

THE REPORT OF THE COMMITTEE ON THEOLOGY AND SOCIAL CONCERNS/ UNIFICATION TASKFORCE - continued

The Credentials Committee announced that the tabulation of the ballots showed that the motion to amend Recommendation 11 failed.

Moderator Cole (CPCA) spoke to the report. He stated that the CPCA had voted to conduct a study dealing with the same issues that are being dealt with in the current report as well as getting direct input from persons who are directly affected by these issues.

A motion was made to amend Recommendation 13 to add the Ministry Council to the recommendation which would then read: *"Recommendation 13: That the Permanent Judiciary Committee, the Unified Committee on Theology and Social Concerns, and the Ministry Council work jointly to develop a position statement on the issues of human sexuality to be presented to the 189th General Assembly for it consideration."* Motion seconded. Following discussion, the motion was made to move the previous question. There was a second. The motion to move the previous question carried. The motion to amend Recommendation 13 passed.

A motion was made and seconded that all debate on this report end and proceed to vote. The motion passed. By vote, the Report of the Committee on Theology and Social Concerns/Unification Taskforce, as amended, was concurred in and the recommendations adopted. Report marked "D" and filed.

The Moderator asked Vice-Moderator Pope to moderate the meeting.

REPORT OF THE COMMITTEE ON MINISTRY COUNCIL

The Report of the Ministry Council was read by youth advisory delegate Dyllan Simmons, Covenant Presbytery; and Reverend Terra Sisco, Red River Presbytery. Reverend Sisco made the motion that the report be concurred in and the recommendations be adopted. Motion seconded.

A motion was made and seconded to divide the question to deal with Recommendation 1, and Recommendations 2 & 3 separately. Motion passed.

Following discussion, on motion and second, the question was called for Recommendation 1. By vote, Recommendation 1 was denied.

MODERATOR RETURNS TO PODIUM

The Moderator returned to the podium. A motion made to amend Recommendation 3 to read: *"That the 188th General Assembly assign a committee to work with the Discipleship Ministry Team in developing and conducting a census/survey disseminated through the stated clerks of each presbytery by the 190th General Assembly."* The motion passed.

Following discussion, a motion was made and seconded to end the debate. The motion passed. By vote, Recommendation 2 & Recommendation 3, as amended, carried. The Report on Ministry Council as amended was concurred in and the recommendations adopted. The report was marked "E" and filed. The Moderator will appoint the committee following recess.

RECESS

The Moderator called for a 15-minute recess at 3:30 p.m. to return at 3:45 p.m.

BUSINESS CONTINUED

The Moderator called the meeting to order at 3:45 p.m. and appointed the following to work with the Discipleship Ministry Team: Elder Vicki Goodwin, Missions Synod; Reverend Mike Reno, Great River Synod; Reverend Lisa Scott, Synod of the Midwest; Elder Grady Prevost, Synod of the South East; and Elder Ben Lindamood, Tennessee Synod.

THE VICE-MODERATOR RETURNED TO THE PODIUM

Vice-Moderator, Reverend Buddy Pope, returned to the podium.

THE REPORT OF THE COMMITTEE ON STEWARDSHIP/ELECTED OFFICERS

The Report of the Committee Stewardship/Elected Officers was presented by youth advisory delegates: Leigh Ann Morgan, Murfreesboro Presbytery; Kailey Sundstrom, Nashville Presbytery; Chloe Martin, Trinity Presbytery; and Elder Janis Wilson, Arkansas Presbytery. Editorial changes: in Recommendation 8 from "*Corporation*" to "*General Assembly*". Change calendar listing "*Middle School Event*" to "*The Meet Up.*" A motion was made by Reverend Andy McClung, West Tennessee Presbytery, and seconded, that the report be concurred in and the recommendations adopted. The motion passed. The report was marked "F" and filed.

MODERATOR EARHEART-BROWN RETURNED TO THE PODIUM

The Engrossing Clerk presented the following excuses: Youth Advisory Delegates: Jenna Snipes, Nashville Presbytery; Kailey Sundstrom, Nashville Presbytery; Emilee Jerrolds, West Tennessee Presbytery; Abigail Mathis, Murfreesboro Presbytery; Sydney Holder, Hope Presbytery; and Leigh Ann Morgan, Murfreesboro Presbytery. Reverends: Jimmy Byrd, Tennessee-Georgia Presbytery; Victor Jones, Arkansas Presbytery; and Sandra Shepherd, Nashville Presbytery. Elders Lisa Collins, Nashville Presbytery; Janis Wilson, Arkansas Presbytery; Vicki Goodwin, Red River Presbytery; and Ronald Lewis, Choctaw Presbytery. On motion, the excuses were granted.

THE REPORT OF THE COMMITTEE ON JUDICIARY

The Committee Chair, Reverend Buddy Pope, commended his committee members for their hard work. The Report of the Committee on Judiciary was presented by youth advisory delegates: Abigail Mathis, Murfreesboro Presbytery; Sydney Holder, Hope Presbytery; Joseph Keenan, West Tennessee; and Colten Lash, North Central Presbytery. A motion was made by Reverend Buddy Pope, Columbia Presbytery that the report be concurred in and the recommendations be adopted. Editorial change in Persons of Counsel to strike "*Elder*" from Pamela Brown's name. The motion passed. The report was marked "G" and filed.

THE REPORT OF THE COMMITTEE ON CHILDREN'S HOME/HIGHER EDUCATION

Committee Chair, Reverend Ron McMillian explained the workings of the committee and commended the committee members for their hard work. The Report of the Committee on Children's Home/Higher Education was presented by youth advisory delegates: Isaac Barkley, Grace Presbytery; Eden Seftail, Cumberland Presbytery; and Nathaniel Woods, Missouri Presbytery; and Elder Ben Brown, Red River Presbytery. Editorial changes were noted including Recommendation "*16*" should be "*15.*" A motion was made by Elder Mary Lyn Hunter, Missouri Presbytery, that the report, with editorial changes, be concurred in and the recommendations adopted. The motion passed. The report was marked "H" and filed.

RESOLUTION OF GRATITUDE

A Resolution of Gratitude was dramatically presented by Elder George Ladd, Columbia Presbytery, thanking many individuals and groups who made the 188th General Assembly of the Cumberland

Presbyterian Church a time of Spirit filled work for the Lord that we all might be sent. A motion was made to adopt the resolution. The Motion passed.

Resolution of Thanks for the 188th General Assembly

First of all, most of all, we thank God, our creator and sustainer, for all our many blessings.

We thank Jesus Christ, His Son, our Lord, who took our sins upon himself, saved us, who shows us the Way to live and to serve our Heavenly Father.

We thank the Lord for the work and service of retiring Vice-Moderator, the Reverend Lisa Scott and retiring Moderator, the Reverend David Lancaster, who charged us with the relevant question, "What about these bones?"

We thank God for the worship director, the Reverend Melissa Malinoski, and for the invigorating worship and fellowship that we experienced this week as we stand ready to be the hands and feet of Christ when the Lord blows his Holy Spirit over our lands, that as the hands and feet of Christ, we help these bones stand up and live. SEND US!

We thank God for the Reverend Mike Sharpe and the Office of the General Assembly who work so hard to plan, organize, and make General Assembly happen well, and for making what commissioners need readily available. SEND THEM to Huntsville, Alabama, to make 189th General Assembly even better.

We thank our Lord for our pastor hosts, the Reverend Leslie Johnson and the Reverend Marian Sontowski. We thank the East Lake Cumberland Presbyterian Church for the fellowship meal they provided, and we thank all the servants of Christ who are part of Red River Presbytery for welcoming us with their gifts of hospitality. SEND THEM!

We thank the Lord for Choctaw Presbytery, for 200 years of ministry, for sharing their rich culture, their beautiful clothing and jewelry, and their inspiring hymns, stories, and dances. Give us the tushka warrior spirit, not to slay perceived enemies, but to spread the Good News and bring souls to Christ. SEND THEM! SEND US!

We thank God for the Cumberland Presbyterian Women's Ministry—for their prodigious gifts, prayers, fellowship, and work in the church's ministry. SEND THEM!

We thank the Lord for all our sisters and brothers of the Cumberland Presbyterian Church in America, for their Moderator, Elder Leon Cole, and for the fellowship we all experienced this week. Bless us as we work together to minister and spread the Good News. SEND US!

We thank the Lord for our youth advisors and for all our youth, the future of our church. Lord, nurture them, inspire them, fill them with your Holy Spirit, and SEND THEM!

We thank God for Memphis Theological Seminary and the Program of Alternate Studies, their staff, students, and instructors. SEND THEM to prepare us.

We thank God for the Ministry Council and its teams. Bless them as they assist and enable us in doing ministry. SEND THEM to help SEND US!

We thank the Lord for the Cumberland Presbyterian Children's Home. To children and families suffering from crisis or trauma. SEND THEM! SEND US to help them!

We thank the Lord for sending us the Reverend Dale Gentry, who mentored so many ministers and whose sacrificial ministry brought so many to Christ. In that same selfless spirit, SEND US!

We praise God for calling the Reverend Doctor Jay Earheart-Brown to be our Moderator and the Reverend Buddy Pope to be our Vice-Moderator. Give them inspiration, wisdom, and traveling mercies in the coming year. SEND THEM!

Hear these Words of Isaiah again:

I heard the voice of the Lord, saying, Whom shall I send, and who will go for us? Then said I, Here I am; send me. And the Lord God said go . . . (Isaiah 6:8-9a)

And all of God's children said, "AMEN!"

The Resolution was marked "I" and filed.

OTHER BUSINESS

A Motion was made and seconded to approve the minutes of Sunday – Tuesday as printed in the packet. Motion passed.

READING OF THE MINUTES

The minutes for Wednesday and Thursday were read by the Engrossing Clerk. On motion, the minutes were approved as corrected.

RECESS

The Moderator announced a short recess to prepare for Closing Worship.

CLOSING WORSHIP

The Closing Worship was led by Reverend Melissa Malinoski, worship director, West Tennessee Presbytery, and the pianist was Ms. Robin McCaskey Hughes, Red River Presbytery.

A memorial roll of ministers who died during the past year was read during worship and a prayer was offered celebrating the witness, work and ministry of those remembered. The list was printed in the Preliminary Minutes on page 24.

The message was taken from John 10:11-18. The message challenged us to follow after Jesus' example. When called to lead, we should look to Jesus and his example. Reverend Malinoski closed the worship service and the 188th General Assembly with prayer.

ADJOURNMENT

A motion was made to adjourn the meeting of the 188th General Assembly of the Cumberland Presbyterian Church to meet June 9-14, 2019 at the Embassy Suites Hotel & Conference Center in Huntsville, Alabama. Motion passed at 6:12 p.m.

AUDITED FINANCIAL STATEMENTS OF

THE AGENCIES OF
THE CUMBERLAND PRESBYTERIAN
CHURCH CENTER

DECEMBER 31, 2017

THE AGENCIES OF
THE CUMBERLAND PRESBYTERIAN CHURCH CENTER

TABLE OF CONTENTS
DECEMBER 31, 2017

	PAGE
Independent Auditor's Report	1
Combined Statement of Financial Position	2
Combined Statement of Activity	3
Combined Statement of Cash Flows	4
Individual Statements of Financial Position	
Our United Outreach	5
General Assembly Corporation	6
Ministry Council	7
Shared Services	8
Historical Foundation	9
Board of Stewardship, Foundation, and Benefits	10
Small Church Loan Program	11
Insurance Program	12
Ministerial Aid	13
Investment Loan Program	14
Retirement Fund	15
Endowment Program	16
Individual Statements of Activity	
Our United Outreach	17
General Assembly Corporation	18
Ministry Council	19
Shared Services	20
Historical Foundation	21
Board of Stewardship, Foundation, and Benefits	22
Small Church Loan Program	23
Insurance Program	24
Ministerial Aid	25
Investment Loan Program	26
Retirement Fund	27
Endowment Program	28
Notes to Financial Statements	29 - 43

To the General Assembly Corporation
The Agencies of The Cumberland Presbyterian Church Center
Memphis, Tennessee

INDEPENDENT AUDITOR'S REPORT

We have audited the accompanying combined financial statements of The Agencies of The Cumberland Presbyterian Church Center, which comprise the combined statement of financial position as of December 31, 2017, and the related combined statements of activities and cash flows for the year then ended, and the related notes to the combined financial statements.

Management's Responsibility for the Financial Statements

Management is responsible for the preparation and fair presentation of these financial statements in accordance with accounting principles generally accepted in the United States of America; this includes the design, implementation, and maintenance of internal control relevant to the preparation and fair presentation of financial statements that are free from material misstatement, whether due to fraud or error.

Auditor's Responsibility

Our responsibility is to express an opinion on these combined financial statements based on our audit. We conducted our audit in accordance with auditing standards generally accepted in the United States of America. Those standards require that we plan and perform the audit to obtain reasonable assurance about whether the financial statements are free from material misstatement.

An audit involves performing procedures to obtain audit evidence about the amounts and disclosures in the combined financial statements. The procedures selected depend on the auditor's judgment, including the assessment of the risks of material misstatement of the combined financial statements, whether due to fraud or error. In making those risk assessments, the auditor considers internal control relevant to the entity's preparation and fair presentation of the combined financial statements in order to design audit procedures that are appropriate in the circumstances, but not for the purpose of expressing an opinion on the effectiveness of the entity's internal control. Accordingly, we express no such opinion. An audit also includes evaluating the appropriateness of accounting policies used and the reasonableness of significant accounting estimates made by management, as well as evaluating the overall presentation of the combined financial statements.

We believe that the audit evidence we have obtained is sufficient and appropriate to provide a basis for our audit opinion.

Opinion

In our opinion, the combined financial statements referred to above present fairly, in all material respects, the financial position of The Agencies of The Cumberland Presbyterian Church Center as of December 31, 2017, and the changes in their net assets and their cash flows for the year then ended in accordance with accounting principles generally accepted in the United States of America.

FOUTS & MORGAN
Certified Public Accountants

Memphis, Tennessee
May 23, 2018

THE AGENCIES OF
THE CUMBERLAND PRESBYTERIAN CHURCH CENTER

COMBINED STATEMENT OF FINANCIAL POSITION
DECEMBER 31, 2017

ASSETS

Cash	$ 591,531
Due from other agencies, boards, and divisions	6,311,353
Accounts receivable	33,362
Interest and dividends receivable, net of allowance for uncollectible interest	128,886
Health insurance tax credit receivable	879
Securities and investments	
Cash equivalents	6,132,568
Mortgage backed securities	15,727,005
Equity mutual funds	2,278,758
Real estate investment trusts	5,875,850
Private investment entities	74,824,663
Real estate	90,573
Inventory - at lower of cost or market	686
Prepaid expenses	38,145
Loans receivable, net of allowance for loan losses	8,184,030
Buildings and land	2,760,412
Furniture and equipment	156,745
Less: Accumulated depreciation	(809,640)
Total Assets	$ 122,325,806

LIABILITIES AND NET ASSETS

Liabilities:	
Accounts payable	$ 13,701
Accrued expenses	16
Notes payable to individual investors	2,908,522
Unearned subscriptions	6,869
Due to other agencies, boards, and divisions	6,407,206
Funds held in trust for others	33,603
Depository accounts held for church organizations	15,427,501
Total liabilities	24,797,418
Net Assets:	
Unrestricted	10,172,858
Temporarily restricted	1,411,522
Permanently restricted	60,754,139
Net assets available for benefits, at fair value	25,189,869
Total net assets	97,528,388
Total Liabilities and Net Assets	$ 122,325,806

See accompanying notes.

THE AGENCIES OF
THE CUMBERLAND PRESBYTERIAN CHURCH CENTER

COMBINED STATEMENT OF ACTIVITY
FOR THE YEAR ENDED DECEMBER 31, 2017

	Unrestricted	Temporarily Restricted	Permanently Restricted	Net Assets Available for Benefits	Totals
Revenues, gains, and other support:					
Contributions and gifts	$ 4,978,634	$ 1,102,576	$ 667,397	$ -	$ 6,748,607
Insurance program premium revenue	1,625,916	-	-	-	1,625,916
Endowment earnings	-	-	432,203	-	432,203
Interest and dividend income	532,194	45,217	16,231	112,941	706,583
Management service fees	52,130	-	-	(17,087)	35,043
Registration fees	2,422	-	-	-	2,422
Sales and subscription income	171,448	-	-	-	171,448
Net realized and unrealized gain on investments	874,905	-	6,415,535	2,736,327	10,026,767
Other income	21,788	-	-	-	21,788
Participant retirement contributions	-	-	-	799,189	799,189
Net assets released from restriction	2,138,768	(1,437,044)	(701,724)	-	-
Total revenues, gains, and other support	10,398,205	(289,251)	6,829,642	3,631,370	20,569,966
Recovery of provision for loan losses	259,000	-	-	-	259,000
Net revenues, gains, and other support - after provision for loan losses	10,657,205	(289,251)	6,829,642	3,631,370	20,828,966
Expenses:					
Our United Outreach	413,159	-	-	-	413,159
General Assembly Corporation	524,058	-	-	-	524,058
Ministry Council	4,841,957	-	-	-	4,841,957
Shared Services	430,994	-	-	-	430,994
Historical Foundation	200,497	-	-	-	200,497
Board of Stewardship, Foundation and Benefits	327,743	-	-	-	327,743
Small Church Loan Program	332,502	-	-	-	332,502
Insurance Program	1,790,829	-	-	-	1,790,829
Ministerial Aid	121,762	-	-	-	121,762
Investment Loan Program	67,646	-	-	-	67,646
Retirement Fund	-	-	-	1,639,108	1,639,108
Endowment Program	-	-	2,658,696	-	2,658,696
Total expenses	9,051,147	-	2,658,696	1,639,108	13,348,951
Change in net assets	1,606,058	(289,251)	4,170,946	1,992,262	7,480,015
Net assets at beginning of year	8,566,800	1,700,773	56,583,193	23,197,607	90,048,373
Net assets at end of year	$ 10,172,858	$ 1,411,522	$ 60,754,139	$ 25,189,869	$ 97,528,388

See accompanying notes.

THE AGENCIES OF
THE CUMBERLAND PRESBYTERIAN CHURCH CENTER

COMBINED STATEMENT OF CASH FLOWS
FOR THE YEAR ENDED DECEMBER 31, 2017

Cash flows from operating activities	
Combined change in net assets	$ 7,480,015
Adjustments to reconcile combined change in net assets to net cash used in operating activities:	
Depreciation	65,290
Net realized/unrealized (gain) loss on investments - Investment Loan Program	(671,447)
Net realized/unrealized (gain) loss on investments - Retirement Fund	(850,488)
Net realized/unrealized (gain) loss on investments - Endowment Program	1,293,401
Recovery of provision for loan losses	(259,000)
(Increase) decrease in operating assets:	
Due from other agencies, boards, and divisions	(157,169)
Accounts receivable	(31,049)
Interest and dividends receivable	(17,923)
Health insurance tax credit receivable	1,432
Prepaid assets	102,851
Increase (decrease) in operating liabilities:	
Accounts payable	(55,260)
Accrued expenses	16
Unearned subscriptions	(1,115)
Due to other agencies, boards, and divisions	(11,033)
Funds held in trust for others	185
Notes payable to individual investors	519,770
Depository accounts held for church organizations	1,309,503
Net cash provided by (used in) operating activities	8,717,979
Cash flows from investing activities	
Proceeds from sale of investments:	
Endowment Program	5,083,415
Retirement Fund	4,586,336
Investment Loan Program	13,374,387
Purchase of investments:	
Endowment Program	(10,565,680)
Retirement Fund	(5,727,818)
Investment Loan Program	(17,115,196)
Loan principal payments received	1,619,726
Net cash provided by (used in) investing activities	(8,744,830)
Net increase (decrease) in cash	(26,851)
Cash at the beginning of the year	618,382
Cash at the end of the year	$ 591,531

See accompanying notes.

THE AGENCIES OF
THE CUMBERLAND PRESBYTERIAN CHURCH CENTER
OUR UNITED OUTREACH
STATEMENT OF FINANCIAL POSITION
DECEMBER 31, 2017

ASSETS

Endowment earnings receivable	$ 32,623
Endowments - held by Endowment Program	2,802,076
Total Assets	$ 2,834,699

LIABILITIES AND NET ASSETS

Liabilities:	
Cash borrowed from other agencies, boards, and divisions	$ 14,890
Due to outside church organizations	34,924
Total liabilities	49,814
Net Assets:	
Unrestricted	(17,191)
Permanently restricted	2,802,076
Total net assets	2,784,885
Total Liabilities and Net Assets	$ 2,834,699

See accompanying notes.

THE AGENCIES OF
THE CUMBERLAND PRESBYTERIAN CHURCH CENTER
GENERAL ASSEMBLY CORPORATION
STATEMENT OF FINANCIAL POSITION
DECEMBER 31, 2017

ASSETS

Endowment earnings receivable	$	5,592
Inventory		686
Due from other agencies, boards, and divisions		482,194
		488,472
Endowments - held by Endowment Program		460,431
Total Assets	$	948,903

LIABILITIES AND NET ASSETS

Liabilities:		
Cash borrowed from other agencies, boards, and divisions	$	201,467
Due to other agencies, boards, and divisions		24,270
Funds held in trusts for others		33,603
Total liabilities		259,340
Net Assets:		
Unrestricted		229,132
Permanently restricted		460,431
Total net assets		689,563
Total Liabilities and Net Assets	$	948,903

See accompanying notes.

THE AGENCIES OF
THE CUMBERLAND PRESBYTERIAN CHURCH CENTER
MINISTRY COUNCIL
STATEMENT OF FINANCIAL POSITION
DECEMBER 31, 2017

ASSETS

Cash	$ 216,521
Accounts receivable	3,772
Endowment earnings receivable	168,171
Health insurance tax credit receivable	879
Due from other agencies, boards, and divisions	2,303,635
Securities and investments	
Real estate	51,818
	2,744,796
Endowments - held by Endowment Program	17,037,964
Total Assets	$ 19,782,760

LIABILITIES AND NET ASSETS

Liabilities:	
Accounts payable	$ 8,016
Accrued expenses	16
Unearned subscriptions	6,869
Total liabilities	14,901
Net Assets:	
Unrestricted	1,496,603
Temporarily restricted	1,233,292
Permanently restricted	17,037,964
Total net assets	19,767,859
Total Liabilities and Net Assets	$ 19,782,760

See accompanying notes.

THE AGENCIES OF
THE CUMBERLAND PRESBYTERIAN CHURCH CENTER
SHARED SERVICES
STATEMENT OF FINANCIAL POSITION
DECEMBER 31, 2017

ASSETS

Cash	$ 182,862
Accounts receivable	1,245
Buildings and land	2,760,412
Less: Accumulated depreciation	(652,895)
Furniture and equipment	156,745
Less: Accumulated depreciation	(156,745)
Total Assets	$ 2,291,624

LIABILITIES AND NET ASSETS

Liabilities:	
Accounts payable	$ 2,243
Net Assets:	
Unrestricted	2,289,381
Total Liabilities and Net Assets	$ 2,291,624

See accompanying notes.

THE AGENCIES OF
THE CUMBERLAND PRESBYTERIAN CHURCH CENTER
HISTORICAL FOUNDATION
STATEMENT OF FINANCIAL POSITION
DECEMBER 31, 2017

ASSETS

Cash	$	50,846
Endowment earnings receivable		18,167
Due from other agencies, boards, and divisions		172,576
Securities and investments		
Real estate		38,755
		280,344
Endowments - held by Endowment Program		1,628,574
Total Assets	$	1,908,918

LIABILITIES AND NET ASSETS

Liabilities:		
Accounts payable	$	1,078
Net Assets:		
Unrestricted		63,109
Temporarily restricted		178,230
Permanently restricted		1,666,501
Total net assets		1,907,840
Total Liabilities and Net Assets	$	1,908,918

See accompanying notes.

THE AGENCIES OF
THE CUMBERLAND PRESBYTERIAN CHURCH CENTER
BOARD OF STEWARDSHIP, FOUNDATION, AND BENEFITS
STATEMENT OF FINANCIAL POSITION
DECEMBER 31, 2017

ASSETS

Cash	$	696
Endowment earnings receivable		24,059
Due from other agencies, boards, and divisions		384,837
		409,592
Endowments - held by Endowment Program		2,067,234
Total Assets	$	2,476,826

LIABILITIES AND NET ASSETS

Liabilities:		
Cash borrowed from other agencies, boards, and divisions	$	3,718
Net Assets:		
Unrestricted		405,874
Permanently restricted		2,067,234
Total net assets		2,473,108
Total Liabilities and Net Assets	$	2,476,826

See accompanying notes.

THE AGENCIES OF
THE CUMBERLAND PRESBYTERIAN CHURCH CENTER
SMALL CHURCH LOAN PROGRAM
STATEMENT OF FINANCIAL POSITION
DECEMBER 31, 2017

ASSETS

Loans receivable, net of allowance for loan losses	$ 135,820
Due from other agencies, boards, and divisions	330,667
Total Assets	$ 466,487

LIABILITIES AND NET ASSETS

Net Assets:	
Permanently restricted	$ 466,487
Total Liabilities and Net Assets	$ 466,487

See accompanying notes.

THE AGENCIES OF
THE CUMBERLAND PRESBYTERIAN CHURCH CENTER
INSURANCE PROGRAM
STATEMENT OF FINANCIAL POSITION
DECEMBER 31, 2017

ASSETS

Cash	$	27,395
Accounts receivable		28,345
Prepaid expenses		38,145
Due from other agencies, boards, and divisions		2,051,204
Total Assets	$	2,145,089

LIABILITIES AND NET ASSETS

Liabilities:		
Accounts payable	$	2,364
Net Assets:		
Unrestricted		2,142,725
Total Liabilities and Net Assets	$	2,145,089

See accompanying notes.

THE AGENCIES OF
THE CUMBERLAND PRESBYTERIAN CHURCH CENTER
MINISTERIAL AID
STATEMENT OF FINANCIAL POSITION
DECEMBER 31, 2017

ASSETS

Cash	$	2,411
Endowment earnings receivable		22,357
Due from other agencies, boards, and divisions		315,271
		340,039
Endowment Funds - held by Endowment Program		3,396,485
Total Assets	$	3,736,524

LIABILITIES AND NET ASSETS

Net Assets:		
Unrestricted	$	340,039
Permanently restricted		3,396,485
Total net assets		3,736,524
Total Liabilities and Net Assets	$	3,736,524

See accompanying notes.

THE AGENCIES OF
THE CUMBERLAND PRESBYTERIAN CHURCH CENTER
INVESTMENT LOAN PROGRAM
STATEMENT OF FINANCIAL POSITION
DECEMBER 31, 2017

ASSETS

Interest and dividends receivable, net of allowance for uncollectible interest	$ 75,225
Securities and investments	
Cash equivalents	3,868,964
Bonds and mortgage backed securities	15,727,005
Loans receivable, net of allowance for loan losses	5,937,060
Total Assets	$ 25,608,254

LIABILITIES AND NET ASSETS

Liabilities:	
Notes payable to individual investors	$ 2,908,522
Due to other agencies, boards, and divisions	4,049,045
Depository accounts held for church organizations	15,427,501
Total liabilities	22,385,068
Net Assets:	
Unrestricted	3,223,186
Total Liabilities and Net Assets	$ 25,608,254

See accompanying notes.

THE AGENCIES OF
THE CUMBERLAND PRESBYTERIAN CHURCH CENTER
RETIREMENT FUND
STATEMENT OF FINANCIAL POSITION
DECEMBER 31, 2017

ASSETS

Interest and dividends receivable, net of allowance for uncollectible interest	$ 12,356
Securities and investments	
Cash equivalents	589,124
Equity mutual funds	693,200
Real estate investment trusts	1,448,740
Private investment entities	22,446,449
Total Assets	$ 25,189,869

LIABILITIES AND NET ASSETS

Net Assets:	
Net assets available for benefits, at fair value	$ 25,189,869
Total Liabilities and Net Assets	$ 25,189,869

See accompanying notes.

THE AGENCIES OF
THE CUMBERLAND PRESBYTERIAN CHURCH CENTER
ENDOWMENT PROGRAM
STATEMENT OF FINANCIAL POSITION
DECEMBER 31, 2017

ASSETS

Cash	$ 330,875
Interest and dividends receivable, net of allowance for uncollectible interest	41,305
Securities and investments	
Cash equivalents	1,674,480
Equity mutual funds	1,585,558
Real estate investment trusts	4,427,110
Private investment entities	52,378,214
Loans receivable, net of allowance for loan losses	2,111,150
	62,548,692
Less: Net endowment assets of The Agencies of The Cumberland Presbyterian Church Center, as reflected on separate statements of financial position	(27,392,764)
Total Assets	$ 35,155,928

LIABILITIES AND NET ASSETS

Liabilities:	
Due to other agencies, boards, and divisions	$ 2,298,967
Net Assets:	
Permanently restricted:	
Cumberland Presbyterian Children's Home	4,769,879
Discipleship Ministry Team	2,174,067
Missions Ministry Team	14,446,481
Memphis Theological Seminary	11,342,043
Board of Stewardship, Foundation, and Benefits	2,067,239
Our United Outreach	2,802,077
General Assembly Corporation	460,434
Communications Ministry Team	136,395
Pastoral Development Ministry Team	282,095
The Historical Foundation	1,627,491
Ministerial Aid	3,396,485
Bethel University	3,105,458
Other designated persons and organizations	13,639,581
Total net assets	60,249,725
Less: Net endowment assets of The Agencies of The Cumberland Presbyterian Church Center, as reflected on separate statements of financial position	(27,392,764)
Total Liabilities and Net Assets	$ 35,155,928

See accompanying notes.

THE AGENCIES OF
THE CUMBERLAND PRESBYTERIAN CHURCH CENTER
OUR UNITED OUTREACH
STATEMENT OF ACTIVITY
FOR THE YEAR ENDED DECEMBER 31, 2017

	Unrestricted	Temporarily Restricted	Permanently Restricted	Totals
Revenues, gains, and other support:				
Contributions	$ 2,293,514	$ -	$ 39,223	$ 2,332,737
Endowment earnings	-		17,195	17,195
Income from oil royalties	10,512	-	-	10,512
Net realized and unrealized gain on investments	-	-	285,776	285,776
Net assets released from restriction	131,438	-	(131,438)	-
	2,435,464	-	210,756	2,646,220
Expenses:				
Distribution to other agencies, boards, and divisions of The Cumberland Presbyterian Church:				
Bethel University	114,039	-	-	114,039
Board of Stewardship	136,846	-	-	136,846
Commission on Chaplains	8,827	-	-	8,827
Committee on Theology and Social Concern	3,102	-	-	3,102
Committee on Judiciary	8,325	-	-	8,325
Communications Ministry Team	119,927	-	-	119,927
Contingency Fund	11,154	-	-	11,154
Cumberland Presbyterian Children's Home	68,423	-	-	68,423
Discipleship Ministry Team	5,958	-	-	5,958
General Assembly Council	182,461	-	-	182,461
Historical Foundation	68,423	-	-	68,423
Legal Expense	25,000	-	-	25,000
Memphis Theological Seminary	130,916	-	-	130,916
Ministry Council	975,289	-	-	975,289
Missions Ministry Team	30,271	-	-	30,271
Nominating Committee	2,555	-	-	2,555
Pastoral Development Ministry Team	8,938	-	-	8,938
Program of Alternate Studies	28,738	-	-	28,738
Shared Service (Maintenance/Operations)	376,576	-	-	376,576
Shared Service (OUO Committee)	92,044	-	-	92,044
Unification Task Force	35,000	-	-	35,000
Property tax	2,015	-	-	2,015
	2,434,827	-	-	2,434,827
Change in net assets	637	-	210,756	211,393
Net assets at beginning of year	(17,828)	-	2,591,320	2,573,492
Net assets at end of year	$ (17,191)	$ -	$ 2,802,076	$ 2,784,885

See accompanying notes.

THE AGENCIES OF
THE CUMBERLAND PRESBYTERIAN CHURCH CENTER
GENERAL ASSEMBLY CORPORATION
STATEMENT OF ACTIVITY
FOR THE YEAR ENDED DECEMBER 31, 2017

	Unrestricted	Temporarily Restricted	Permanently Restricted	Totals
Revenues, gains, and other support:				
Our United Outreach	$ 182,461	$ -	$ -	$ 182,461
Contributions and gifts	361,498	-	-	361,498
Endowment earnings	22,457	-	-	22,457
Interest income	11,569	-	-	11,569
Other income	11,276	-	-	11,276
Net realized and unrealized gain on investments	-	-	47,656	47,656
Net assets released from restriction	22,977	-	(22,977)	-
	612,238	-	24,679	636,917
Expenses:				
Conferences and events	18,227	-	-	18,227
Employee benefits	31,533	-	-	31,533
Equipment maintenance	2,736	-	-	2,736
Grants made	264,657	-	-	264,657
Insurance	2,447	-	-	2,447
Miscellaneous	397	-	-	397
Payroll taxes	4,416	-	-	4,416
Postage and shipping	1,335	-	-	1,335
Printing and publications	1,384	-	-	1,384
Retirement	8,263	-	-	8,263
Salaries	171,426	-	-	171,426
Supplies	1,533	-	-	1,533
Travel	15,704	-	-	15,704
Total expenses	524,058	-	-	524,058
Change in net assets	88,180	-	24,679	112,859
Net assets at beginning of year	140,952	-	435,752	576,704
Net assets at end of year	$ 229,132	$ -	$ 460,431	$ 689,563

See accompanying notes.

18

THE AGENCIES OF
THE CUMBERLAND PRESBYTERIAN CHURCH CENTER
MINISTRY COUNCIL
STATEMENT OF ACTIVITY
FOR THE YEAR ENDED DECEMBER 31, 2017

	Unrestricted	Temporarily Restricted	Permanently Restricted	Totals
Revenues, gains, and other support:				
Our United Outreach	$ 1,257,362	$ -	$ -	$ 1,257,362
Contributions	-	1,068,467	60,153	1,128,620
Endowment earnings	(814,782)	-	104,856	(709,926)
Gifts - designated	2,174,654	-	-	2,174,654
Gifts - undesignated	127,575	-	-	127,575
Interest income	28,143	39,615	-	67,758
Registration fees	2,422	-	-	2,422
Sales of materials, literature, etc.	144,462	-	-	144,462
Subscription income	26,986	-	-	26,986
Net realized and unrealized gain on investments	-	-	1,742,997	1,742,997
Net assets released from restrictions	2,123,448	(1,391,801)	(731,647)	-
	5,070,270	(283,719)	1,176,359	5,962,910
Expenses:				
Computer	7,663	-	-	7,663
Conferences and events	97,486	-	-	97,486
Consulting fees	9,200	-	-	9,200
Contract labor	9,967	-	-	9,967
Dues and subscriptions	3,251	-	-	3,251
Employee benefits	126,778	-	-	126,778
Grants made	2,850,023	-	-	2,850,023
Honorariums	650	-	-	650
Insurance	21,235	-	-	21,235
Legal fees	1,851	-	-	1,851
Miscellaneous	21,264	-	-	21,264
Missionary support	360,902	-	-	360,902
Office	6,498	-	-	6,498
Payroll taxes	34,642	-	-	34,642
Postage and shipping	32,183	-	-	32,183
Printing and publications	112,700	-	-	112,700
Purchases for resale	29,857	-	-	29,857
Rent	700	-	-	700
Retirement	39,162	-	-	39,162
Salaries	896,713	-	-	896,713
Supplies	16,325	-	-	16,325
Telephone	1,924	-	-	1,924
Training	431	-	-	431
Travel	160,552	-	-	160,552
Total expenses	4,841,957	-	-	4,841,957
Change in net assets	228,313	(283,719)	1,176,359	1,120,953
Net assets at beginning of year	1,268,290	1,517,011	15,861,605	18,646,906
Net assets at end of year	$ 1,496,603	$ 1,233,292	$ 17,037,964	$ 19,767,859

See accompanying notes.

THE AGENCIES OF
THE CUMBERLAND PRESBYTERIAN CHURCH CENTER
SHARED SERVICES
STATEMENT OF ACTIVITY
FOR THE YEAR ENDED DECEMBER 31, 2017

	Unrestricted	Temporarily Restricted	Permanently Restricted	Totals
Revenues, gains, and other support:				
Our United Outreach	$ 376,576	$ -	$ -	$ 376,576
Expenses:				
Accounting fees	22,105	-	-	22,105
Bank fees	12,538	-	-	12,538
Computer	3,377	-	-	3,377
Consulting fees	42,274	-	-	42,274
Depreciation	65,289	-	-	65,289
Employee benefits	17,027	-	-	17,027
Equipment maintenance	27,241	-	-	27,241
Insurance	11,166	-	-	11,166
Miscellaneous	85,000	-	-	85,000
Occupancy	73,992	-	-	73,992
Payroll taxes	3,902	-	-	3,902
Postage and shipping	213	-	-	213
Property tax	1,029	-	-	1,029
Retirement	2,551	-	-	2,551
Salaries	51,011	-	-	51,011
Supplies	2,348	-	-	2,348
Telephone	9,931	-	-	9,931
Total expenses	430,994	-	-	430,994
Change in net assets	(54,418)	-	-	(54,418)
Net assets at beginning of year	2,343,799	-	-	2,343,799
Net assets at end of year	$ 2,289,381	$ -	$ -	$ 2,289,381

See accompanying notes.

THE AGENCIES OF
THE CUMBERLAND PRESBYTERIAN CHURCH CENTER
HISTORICAL FOUNDATION
STATEMENT OF ACTIVITY
FOR THE YEAR ENDED DECEMBER 31, 2017

	Unrestricted	Temporarily Restricted	Permanently Restricted	Totals
Revenues, gains, and other support:				
Our United Outreach	$ 68,423	$ -	$ -	$ 68,423
Contributions and gifts	10,716	34,109	34,144	78,969
Endowment earnings	-	-	9,924	9,924
Interest income	-	5,602	-	5,602
Net realized and unrealized gain on investments	-	-	164,911	164,911
Net assets released from restriction	117,491	(45,243)	(72,248)	-
	196,630	(5,532)	136,731	327,829
Expenses:				
Archival acquisitions	40,040	-	-	40,040
Archival equipment	3,679	-	-	3,679
Birthplace shrine	14,147	-	-	14,147
Contract labor	5,130	-	-	5,130
Dues and subscriptions	2,102	-	-	2,102
Employee benefits	9,858	-	-	9,858
Insurance	5,186	-	-	5,186
Miscellaneous	197	-	-	197
Payroll taxes	6,077	-	-	6,077
Postage and shipping	127	-	-	127
Printing and publications	1,218	-	-	1,218
Purchases for resale	287	-	-	287
Retirement	7,962	-	-	7,962
Salaries	79,439	-	-	79,439
Supplies	241	-	-	241
Training	10,612	-	-	10,612
Travel	14,195	-	-	14,195
Total expenses	200,497	-	-	200,497
Change in net assets	(3,867)	(5,532)	136,731	127,332
Net assets at beginning of year	66,976	183,762	1,529,770	1,780,508
Net assets at end of year	$ 63,109	$ 178,230	$ 1,666,501	$ 1,907,840

See accompanying notes.

THE AGENCIES OF
THE CUMBERLAND PRESBYTERIAN CHURCH CENTER
BOARD OF STEWARDSHIP, FOUNDATION AND BENEFITS
STATEMENT OF ACTIVITY
FOR THE YEAR ENDED DECEMBER 31, 2017

	Unrestricted	Temporarily Restricted	Permanently Restricted	Totals
Revenues, gains, and other support:				
Our United Outreach	$ 136,846	$ -	$ -	$ 136,846
Contributions and gifts	6,152	-	20,700	26,852
Endowment earnings	15,449	-	12,683	28,132
Interest income	12,152	-	-	12,152
Management service fees	52,130	-	-	52,130
Net realized and unrealized gain on investments	-	-	210,814	210,814
Net assets released from restriction	95,989	-	(95,989)	-
	318,718	-	148,208	466,926
Expenses:				
Accounting	2,036	-	-	2,036
Computer	284	-	-	284
Contract labor	1,800	-	-	1,800
Dues and subscriptions	632	-	-	632
Employee benefits	57,044	-	-	57,044
Grants made	28,071	-	-	28,071
Insurance	4,169	-	-	4,169
Legal	46	-	-	46
Miscellaneous	75	-	-	75
Payroll taxes	7,659	-	-	7,659
Postage and shipping	1,285	-	-	1,285
Printing and publications	4,056	-	-	4,056
Relocation	20	-	-	20
Retirement	9,457	-	-	9,457
Salaries	189,140	-	-	189,140
Stewardship fees	3,500	-	-	3,500
Stewardship materials and events	30	-	-	30
Supplies	2,961	-	-	2,961
Travel and board meetings	15,478	-	-	15,478
Total expenses	327,743	-	-	327,743
Change in net assets	(9,025)	-	148,208	139,183
Net assets at beginning of year	414,899	-	1,919,026	2,333,925
Net assets at end of year	$ 405,874	$ -	$ 2,067,234	$ 2,473,108

See accompanying notes.

THE AGENCIES OF
THE CUMBERLAND PRESBYTERIAN CHURCH CENTER
SMALL CHURCH LOAN PROGRAM
STATEMENT OF ACTIVITY
FOR THE YEAR ENDED DECEMBER 31, 2017

	Unrestricted	Temporarily Restricted	Permanently Restricted	Totals
Revenues, gains, and other support:				
Contributions	$ -	$ -	$ 332,502	$ 332,502
Interest income	-	-	16,231	16,231
Net assets released from restriction	332,502	-	(332,502)	-
	332,502	-	16,231	348,733
Expenses:				
Distribution to other agencies, boards, and divisions of The Cumberland Presbyterian Church:				
Investment Loan Program	332,502	-	-	332,502
Change in net assets	-	-	16,231	16,231
Net assets at beginning of year	-	-	450,256	450,256
Net assets at end of year	$ -	$ -	$ 466,487	$ 466,487

See accompanying notes.

THE AGENCIES OF
THE CUMBERLAND PRESBYTERIAN CHURCH CENTER
INSURANCE PROGRAM
STATEMENT OF ACTIVITY
FOR THE YEAR ENDED DECEMBER 31, 2017

	Unrestricted	Temporarily Restricted	Permanently Restricted	Totals
Revenues, gains, and other support:				
Premium revenue	$ 1,625,916	$ -	$ -	$ 1,625,916
Contributions	4,525	-	-	4,525
Interest income	14,483	-	-	14,483
Net realized gain on investments	1,879	-	-	1,879
Net unrealized gain on investments	201,579	-	-	201,579
	1,848,382	-	-	1,848,382
Expenses:				
Dues and subscriptions	716	-	-	716
Employee benefits	48	-	-	48
Insurance premiums	1,760,696	-	-	1,760,696
Payroll taxes	1,971	-	-	1,971
Postage and shipping	348	-	-	348
Retirement	1,288	-	-	1,288
Salaries	25,762	-	-	25,762
Total expenses	1,790,829	-	-	1,790,829
Change in net assets	57,553	-	-	57,553
Net assets at beginning of year	2,085,172	-	-	2,085,172
Net assets at end of year	$ 2,142,725	$ -	$ -	$ 2,142,725

See accompanying notes.

THE AGENCIES OF
THE CUMBERLAND PRESBYTERIAN CHURCH CENTER
MINISTERIAL AID
STATEMENT OF ACTIVITY
FOR THE YEAR ENDED DECEMBER 31, 2017

	Unrestricted	Temporarily Restricted	Permanently Restricted	Totals
Revenues, gains, and other support:				
Contributions	$ -	$ -	$ 1,100	$ 1,100
Endowment earnings	4,399	-	20,766	25,165
Interest income	8,438	-	-	8,438
Net realized and unrealized gain on investments	-	-	345,114	345,114
Net assets released from restriction	87,400	-	(87,400)	-
	100,237	-	279,580	379,817
Expenses:				
Ministerial aid	121,762	-	-	121,762
Change in net assets	(21,525)	-	279,580	258,055
Net assets at beginning of year	361,564	-	3,116,905	3,478,469
Net assets at end of year	$ 340,039	$ -	$ 3,396,485	$ 3,736,524

See accompanying notes.

THE AGENCIES OF
THE CUMBERLAND PRESBYTERIAN CHURCH CENTER
INVESTMENT LOAN PROGRAM
STATEMENT OF ACTIVITY
FOR THE YEAR ENDED DECEMBER 31, 2017

	Unrestricted	Temporarily Restricted	Permanently Restricted	Totals
Revenues, gains, and other support:				
Interest income	$ 1,079,907	$ -	$ -	$ 1,079,907
Interest expense	(622,498)	-	-	(622,498)
Net interest income	457,409	-	-	457,409
Recovery of provision for loan losses	259,000	-	-	259,000
Net interest income	716,409	-	-	716,409
Net gain (loss) on investments	671,447	-	-	671,447
	1,387,856	-	-	1,387,856
Expenses:				
Accounting fees	5,552	-	-	5,552
Legal fees	1,595	-	-	1,595
Management fee	51,000	-	-	51,000
Miscellaneous	6,234	-	-	6,234
Office	2,078	-	-	2,078
Postage and shipping	635	-	-	635
Supplies	552	-	-	552
Total expenses	67,646	-	-	67,646
Change in net assets	1,320,210	-	-	1,320,210
Net assets at beginning of year	1,902,976	-	-	1,902,976
Net assets at end of year	$ 3,223,186	$ -	$ -	$ 3,223,186

See accompanying notes.

THE AGENCIES OF
THE CUMBERLAND PRESBYTERIAN CHURCH CENTER
RETIREMENT FUND
STATEMENT OF ACTIVITY
FOR THE YEAR ENDED DECEMBER 31, 2017

	Net Assets Available for Benefits
Additions to Net Assets attributed to:	
Investment income:	
Interest and dividend income	$ 112,941
Management service fees	(17,087)
Net realized gain on investments	16,140
Net unrealized gain on investments	2,720,187
Net investment income	2,832,181
Contributions:	
Contributions by participants	799,189
	3,631,370
Deductions from Net Assets attributed to:	
Contract labor	545
Disbursements to participants	1,638,563
	1,639,108
Change in plan assets available for benefits	1,992,262
Net assets available for benefits at beginning of year	23,197,607
Net assets available for benefits at end of year	$ 25,189,869

See accompanying notes.

THE AGENCIES OF
THE CUMBERLAND PRESBYTERIAN CHURCH CENTER
ENDOWMENT PROGRAM
STATEMENT OF ACTIVITY
FOR THE YEAR ENDED DECEMBER 31, 2017

	Unrestricted	Temporarily Restricted	Permanently Restricted	Totals
Changes in Permanently Restricted Net Assets:				
Revenues, gains, and other support:				
Contributions	$ -	$ -	$ 667,397	$ 667,397
Interest and dividend income	-	-	432,203	432,203
Net realized gain on investments	-	-	56,404	56,404
Net unrealized gain on investments	-	-	6,358,752	6,358,752
	-	-	7,514,756	7,514,756
Expenses:				
Distribution for designated purposes	-	-	1,400,255	1,400,255
Distribution of earnings	-	-	1,919,294	1,919,294
Other expenses	-	-	39,412	39,412
	-	-	3,358,961	3,358,961
Change in net assets	-	-	4,155,795	4,155,795
Net assets at beginning of year	-	-	56,093,930	56,093,930
Net assets at end of year	$ -	$ -	$ 60,249,725	$ 60,249,725
Represented by funds held in trust for others:				
Bethel University	$ -	$ -	$ 3,105,458	$ 3,105,458
Cumberland Presbyterian Children's Home	-	-	4,769,879	4,769,879
Memphis Theological Seminary	-	-	11,342,043	11,342,043
Other designated persons and organizations	-	-	13,639,581	13,639,581
	-	-	32,856,961	32,856,961
Represented by funds held for The Agencies of The Cumberland Presbyterian Church Center:				
Discipleship Ministry Team	-	-	2,174,067	2,174,067
Missions Ministry Team	-	-	14,446,481	14,446,481
Board of Stewardship, Foundation, and Benefits	-	-	2,067,239	2,067,239
Our United Outreach	-	-	2,802,077	2,802,077
General Assembly Corporation	-	-	460,434	460,434
Communications Ministry Team	-	-	136,395	136,395
Pastoral Development Ministry Team	-	-	282,095	282,095
The Historical Foundation	-	-	1,627,491	1,627,491
Ministerial Aid	-	-	3,396,485	3,396,485
	-	-	27,392,764	27,392,764
Net assets at end of year	$ -	$ -	$ 60,249,725	$ 60,249,725

See accompanying notes.

THE AGENCIES OF
THE CUMBERLAND PRESBYTERIAN CHURCH CENTER

NOTES TO FINANCIAL STATEMENTS
DECEMBER 31, 2017

Note A - Nature of Activities and Significant Accounting Policies

Nature of Activities - By the covenant of Abraham and his descendants according to faith, God has established the church in the world through His Son Jesus Christ. This household of faith, the universal church, consists of all those persons in every nation and every age who confess Jesus Christ as Lord and Savior and who respond to His call for discipleship. The church in the world never exists for herself alone, but to glorify God and work for reconciliation through Christ. Christ claims the church and gives her the word and sacraments in order to bring God's grace and judgment to persons.

The General Assembly is the highest judicatory of this church and represents in one body all the particular churches thereof. It bears the title of the General Assembly of the Cumberland Presbyterian Church and constitutes the bond of union, peace, correspondence, and mutual confidence among all its churches and judicatories. The Agencies of The Cumberland Presbyterian Church Center have been established by the General Assembly and in 2000 it caused the Cumberland Presbyterian Church General Assembly Corporation to be formed. The Agencies consist of the following entities:

Cumberland Presbyterian Church General Assembly Corporation
Ministry Council of the Cumberland Presbyterian Church, Inc.
Board of Stewardship, Foundation, and Benefits of the Cumberland Presbyterian Church, Inc.
Historical Foundation of the Cumberland Presbyterian Church and the Cumberland Presbyterian Church in America

Contributions - Contributions received are recorded as unrestricted, temporarily restricted, or permanently restricted, depending on the existence and/or nature of any donor restrictions.

Support that is restricted by the donor is reported as an increase in unrestricted net assets if the restriction expires in the reporting period in which the support is recognized. All other donor restricted support is reported as an increase in temporarily or permanently restricted net assets depending on the nature of the restriction. When a restriction expires, temporarily restricted net assets are reclassified to unrestricted net assets.

Donated Equipment and Services - Donated equipment is reflected as contributions in the accompanying financial statements at their estimated values at the date of receipt. No equipment was donated to the Center during the year ended December 31, 2017. No amounts have been reflected in the statements for donated services because they did not meet the criteria for recognition under FASB ASC 958-605-25.

Use of Estimates - The preparation of financial statements in conformity with generally accepted accounting principles requires management to make estimates and assumptions that affect the reported amounts of assets and liabilities and disclosure of contingent assets and liabilities at the date of the financial statements and the reported amounts of revenues and expenses during the reporting period. Actual results could differ from these estimates.

NOTES CONTINUED

Note A - Nature of Activities and Significant Accounting Policies - Continued

The Cumberland Presbyterian Church Investment Loan Program, Inc.'s notes receivable consist of loans made to congregations, governing bodies, church organizations, and other qualifying related entities. The ability of each borrower to repay its loan generally depends upon the contributions received from its members. The number of members of each congregation and its revenue is likely to fluctuate.

The Program must rely on the borrower's or guarantor's continued financial viability for repayment of loans. If a borrower or guarantor experiences a decrease in contributions or revenues, payments on that loan may be adversely affected. Even though the loans are collateralized by real estate, realization of the appraised value upon default is not assured and is dependent upon the local economic conditions of the borrower. Therefore, the determination of the adequacy of the allowance for notes receivable losses is based on estimates that are particularly susceptible to significant changes in the economic environment and market conditions for the geographic areas where the borrowers are located.

While management uses available information to recognize losses on notes receivable, further reductions in the carrying amounts of notes receivable may be necessary based on changes in the economic conditions for the geographic area of the borrowers. It is therefore reasonably possible that the estimated losses on notes receivable may change materially in the near term. However, the amount of the change that is reasonably possible cannot be estimated.

Promises to Give - Unconditional promises to give are recognized as revenue or gains in the period received and as assets or decreases of liabilities depending on the form of the benefits received. Conditional promises to give are recognized when the conditions on which they depend are substantially met. The Center has no promises to give at December 31, 2017.

Inventory - Inventories are stated at the lower of cost or market. Cost is determined using the average cost method.

Depreciation - In years past, Shared Services has recorded property and equipment as assets and depreciated them. Depreciation of property and equipment was computed using the straight-line method over the estimated useful lives of the assets. Purchases of equipment after 1996 are not capitalized, but expensed when purchased; therefore, no depreciation expense has been recorded for items acquired in 1997 and thereafter. The difference between the cost of fixed assets expensed and depreciation expense that would be recorded is immaterial. In 2008, the Center purchased land and two incomplete office buildings. The cost of these plus the construction costs necessary to complete the new Center were capitalized and are being depreciated over an estimated useful life of 39 years. In 2009, the Shared Services agency purchased a large amount of computer equipment and capitalized these costs over four years. The computer equipment is now fully depreciated.

Property and Equipment - Property and equipment is recorded at historical cost. Donated property and equipment is recorded at fair market value at the date of donation. Such donations are reported as unrestricted support unless the donor has restricted the donated asset to a specific purpose. Assets donated with explicit restrictions regarding their use and contributions of cash that must be used to acquire property and equipment are reported as restricted support. Absent donor stipulations regarding how long those donated assets must be maintained, the Center reports expirations of donor restrictions when the donated or acquired assets are placed in service as instructed by the donor. The Center re-classes temporarily restricted net assets to unrestricted net assets at that time.

NOTES CONTINUED

Note A - Nature of Activities and Significant Accounting Policies - Continued

Investments - Investments are stated at fair value. Investments in private investment entities are valued based on the Center's proportional share of the net asset valuations reported by the general partners of the underlying entities. The reported values of all other investments (with the exception of notes receivable) are measured by quoted prices in active markets. Realized and unrealized gains and losses are reflected in the statement of activities. (See Note L)

The Center's investments include various types of securities in various companies within various markets. Investment securities are exposed to several risks, such as interest rate, market and credit risks. Due to the risks associated with certain investment securities, it is at least reasonably possible that changes in the values of investment securities will occur in the near term and those changes could materially affect the amounts reported in the Center's combined financial statements.

Fair Value Measurements - Fair value under accounting principles generally accepted in the United States of America is defined as the price that would be received to sell an asset or paid to transfer a liability in an orderly transaction between market participants at the measurement date. Generally accepted accounting principles establishes a three-tier fair value hierarchy that prioritizes the inputs used to measure fair value. These tiers include: Level 1, defined as observable inputs such as quoted prices available in active markets for identical assets or liabilities; Level 2, defined as pricing inputs other than quoted prices in active markets that are either directly or indirectly observable; and Level 3, defined as unobservable inputs about which little or no market data exists, therefore requiring an entity to develop its own assessment about the assumptions the market participants would use in pricing an asset or liability.

Income Tax Status - The Center is a not-for-profit organization exempt from federal income taxes under Internal Revenue Code (IRC) Section 501(c)(3); thus, no provision for federal income taxes has been made. The Center has a defined contribution retirement plan which is qualified under Internal Revenue Code Section 403(b); thus, no provision for income taxes has been included in the Plan's financial statements.

Cash and Cash Equivalents - For purposes of the statement of cash flows, all highly liquid investments with a maturity of three months or less are considered to be cash equivalents. However, cash and cash equivalents reported as securities and investments by the Endowment Program, Investment Loan Program and Retirement Fund are considered investments for purposes of the statement of cash flows.

Loans Receivable and Allowance for Losses - Loans receivable are stated at unpaid principal balances, less the allowance for notes receivable losses. Inter-agency loans are shown as due to/from other agencies, boards, and divisions.

The allowance for loans receivable is maintained at a level which, in management's judgment, is adequate to absorb credit losses inherent in the loans receivable portfolio. The amount of the allowance is based on management's evaluation of the collectability of the portfolio, including the nature of the portfolio, credit concentrations, trends in historical loss experience, economic conditions, and other risks inherent in the portfolio. Although management uses available information to recognize losses on notes receivable, because of uncertainties associated with the various local economic conditions of the borrowers and collateral values, it is reasonably possible that a material change could occur in the allowance for notes receivable in the near term. However, the amount of the change that is reasonably possible cannot be estimated. When considered necessary, the allowance is increased by a charge to expense and reduced by actual charge-offs, net of recoveries.

NOTES CONTINUED

Note B - Retirement Plan

General - The Cumberland Presbyterian Church Retirement Plan Number Two is available to certain employees of the Church and its agencies. All agencies, boards, and divisions match each employee's contribution up to five percent of the employee's salary. The total retirement contribution expense for The Agencies of The Cumberland Presbyterian Church Center for 2017 was $67,395.

The Plan obtained its latest determination letter on January 31, 1972, in which the Internal Revenue Service stated that the Plan, as then designed, was in compliance with the applicable requirements of the Internal Revenue Code. The Plan has been amended since receiving the determination letter. However, the Plan administrator and the Plan's tax counsel believe that the plan is currently designed and being operated in compliance with the applicable requirements of the Internal Revenue Code. The Plan is a "church plan" and is, therefore, not subject to ERISA.

Eligibility - Employees who are 18 years of age are immediately eligible to participate in the plan.

Vesting - Participants are immediately 100% vested in their accounts.

Investments - The Plan's investments are held by a bank-administered trust fund. The trust is the funding vehicle for the Plan, and all contributions are made to the trust. The cost and market value of the Plan's investments at December 31, 2017, are as follows:

	Cost	Market Value
Total	$ 17,141,957	$ 25,189,869

Note C - Endowment Program

The Endowment Program includes assets of The Agencies of The Cumberland Presbyterian Church Center and the assets of other agencies, boards, and divisions.

The Program's investments, other than notes receivable, real estate, and certificates of deposit, are held by a bank-administered trust fund. The costs and market value of the Program's investments held in trust at December 31, 2017, are as follows:

	Cost	Market Value
Total	$ 41,735,923	$ 60,106,667

The Center has interpreted the Uniform Prudent Management of Institutional Funds Act ("UPMIFA") requiring a portion of a donor restricted endowment of perpetual duration be classified as permanently restricted assets. The amount of the endowment that must be retained permanently is in accordance with explicit donor stipulations as outlined in their respective trust agreements.

NOTES CONTINUED

Note C - Endowment Program - Continued

The primary objective of these endowments is to provide a balance between capital appreciation, preservation of capital, and current income. This is a long-term goal designed to maximize returns without undue risk. The Board of Stewardship has set distribution rates with certain beneficiaries of the Endowment Program.

Unless otherwise stated in the donor agreement, the Board of Stewardship shall select the investment portfolio where the endowments will be invested as described in the Investment Policy of the Center. The Investment Policy of the Center outlines the asset allocations, permissible investments, and objectives of the portfolios.

Endowment Net Asset Composition by Type of Fund as of December 31, 2017:

	Permanently Restricted	Total
Donor-restricted endowment funds	$ 60,249,725	$ 60,249,725
Total funds	$ 60,249,725	$ 60,249,725

Changes in Endowment Net Assets for the year ended December 31, 2017:

	Permanently Restricted	Total
Endowment net assets, beginning of year	$ 56,093,930	$ 56,093,930
Investment return	6,807,947	6,807,947
Contributions	667,398	667,398
Appropriation of endowment assets for expenditures	(3,319,550)	(3,319,550)
Endowment net assets, end of year	$ 60,249,725	$ 60,249,725

Description of Amount Classified as Permanently Restricted Net Assets (Endowment Only):

Permanently Restricted Net Assets -

The portion of perpetual endowment funds that is required to be retained permanently either by explicit donor stipulation or by UPMIFA	$ 60,249,725
Total endowment funds classified as permanently restricted net assets	$ 60,249,725

NOTES CONTINUED

Note D - Investment Loan Program

Nature of Activities - On March 19, 1999, the State of Tennessee approved the charter for the Cumberland Presbyterian Church Investment Loan Program, Inc., a subsidiary corporation of the Board of Stewardship, Foundation and Benefits of the Cumberland Presbyterian Church, Inc. The Program is designed to allow participants to help provide the loans needed to finance the growth of Cumberland Presbyterian congregations in the 21st century.

1. It provides building loans secured by first mortgages to congregations, presbyteries, and church agencies.

2. It allows congregations, presbyteries, church agencies, and individual members of the Cumberland Presbyterian Church to invest their funds in interest bearing accounts from which withdrawals can be made "on demand" replacing the function of the Cash Funds Management Program.

3. All participants have the opportunity to invest funds for specific terms (such as three years or five years) in order to receive a higher rate of interest. A prospectus outlines the added investment options offered.

Securities and Investments - The cost and market values of Investment Loan Program investments at December 31, 2017, are as follows:

	Cost	Market Value
Total	$ 19,536,540	$ 19,595,969

Notes Payable to Individual Investors - Notes payable to individual investors are made through a general offering in the states of Kentucky, New Mexico, Tennessee, and Texas to eligible individual investors and must be purchased in minimum face amounts of $500. All notes payable to individual investors shown in these financial statements are Adjustable Rate Ready Access Notes. Adjustable Rate Ready Access Notes are payable on demand and pay an adjustable interest rate that may be adjusted each month. Additions of principal may be made to Adjustable Rate Ready Access Notes at any time. Withdrawals from Adjustable Rate Ready Access Notes may be made at any time and are payable upon written request of the investor; however, the Program reserves the right to require the investor to provide up to thirty (30) days written notice of any intended withdrawal before such withdrawal is made. Both additions to and withdrawals from Adjustable Rate Ready Access Notes must be made in minimum amounts of $250. The Program may review certain factors, such as investment gap analysis, loan demand, cash flow needs, and the current policy of the Federal Reserve, before establishing each month's rate of interest.

The notes are non-negotiable and may be assigned only upon the Program's written consent. The notes are unsecured and of equal priority with all other current indebtedness of the Program.

NOTES CONTINUED

Note D - Investment Loan Program - Continued

Depository Accounts Held for Church Organizations - The Cumberland Presbyterian Church Investment Loan Program, Inc. accepts depository accounts in which church organizations may place funds with the Program, in minimum amounts of $500. All depository accounts shown in these financial statements are Adjustable Rate Ready Access accounts. Like the Program's notes, depository accounts are general obligations of the Program, are unsecured and not insured, and are of equal priority with all other current indebtedness of the Program including notes. The interest rate on the depository accounts is adjusted pursuant to the policies of the Cumberland Presbyterian Church Investment Loan Program, Inc. as they may be adopted from time to time by its Board of Directors. The Cumberland Presbyterian Church Investment Loan Program, Inc. may terminate any depository account upon sixty (60) days written notice to the church organization.

Loans Receivable - Amounts that have been loaned are included on the Statement of Financial Position as loans receivable. There are 24 loans outstanding at December 31, 2017.

Loans receivable are collectible primarily through monthly payments based on up to a twenty-five year amortization period. Interest rates, as determined by the board, are based on the Prime Interest Rate as reported in the Wall Street Journal plus 1.5% per annum. On loans originated for $500,000 or less, the interest rate will be adjusted triennially. On loans originated for more than $500,000, the interest rate will be adjusted annually for the term of the loan.

The composition of loans is as follows:

Loans receivable (secured by real estate)	$	6,687,060
Less: allowance for loan losses		(750,000)
	$	5,937,060

A summary of changes in the allowance for loan losses is as follows:

Balance at beginning of year	$	1,009,000
Recovery of provision charged to operations		(259,000)
Balance at end of year	$	750,000

Estimated receipts of principal payments for the five years subsequent to 2017 are:

Year ending December 31,		Amount
2018	$	387,166
2019		398,065
2020		406,842
2021		426,749
2022		1,210,870
Thereafter		3,107,368
	$	5,937,060

NOTES CONTINUED

Note E - Funds Held in Trust

The Discipleship Ministry Team leader of the Ministry Council is responsible for certain funds held in trust for outside groups. Funds invested by the executive director in Investment Loan Program amounted to the following as of December 31, 2017:

P.R.E.M. $ 210,732

The General Assembly Corporation is responsible for funds held in trust for certain committees and commissions. These funds are shown as liabilities in the Statement of Financial Position of the General Assembly Corporation. Activity in these funds for the year ended December 31, 2017, is as follows:

	Nominating Committee	Committee on Judiciary
Balance January 1, 2017	$ 6,460	$ 3,050
Our United Outreach	2,462	9,579
Disbursements	(2,671)	(9,682)
Balance December 31, 2017	$ 6,251	$ 2,947

	Committee on Theology and Social Concerns	Commission on Chaplains
Balance January 1, 2017	$ 15,027	$ 8,881
Our United Outreach	3,168	9,331
Disbursements	(3,027)	(8,975)
Balance December 31, 2017	$ 15,168	$ 9,237

Note F - Insurance Program

The Cumberland Presbyterian Group Health and Life Insurance Program is a fully insured, experience-rated plan with a policy year ending on the last day of February. Any excess of premium over medical claims and other plan expenses is retained by the insurer; excess losses are no longer carried forward as a charge against the experience for subsequent policy years, as in the past, but must be absorbed by the insurer. The plan is the responsibility of the Board of Stewardship, Foundation, and Benefits.

The plan has one Investment Loan Program account and one account in the Endowment Program. Both are used as a stabilization reserve to provide some protection against unexpected medical claims volatility. The balance at December 31, 2017 of the Investment Loan Program account is $90,161. The balance at December 31, 2017 of the Endowment Program account is $1,972,095.

NOTES CONTINUED

Note G - Concentrations of Credit Risk Arising from Cash Deposits in Excess of Insured Limits

The Center maintains its cash balances in a financial institution located in Memphis, Tennessee. The balances are insured by the Federal Deposit Insurance Corporation up to $250,000 as of December 31, 2017. At various times, there were balances that exceeded these FDIC limits. Cash and cash equivalents classified as securities and investments are items held in equities backed by the Federal Government. These equities, while backed by the Federal Government, are not insured by the Federal Deposit Insurance Corporation. At December 31, 2017, a total of $164,017 exceeded the FDIC limits.

Note H - Real Estate

Real estate assets of both the Ministry Council and the Historical Foundation are held for investment and are therefore not depreciated. These assets amounted to the following at December 31, 2017:

Property Location	Ministry Council	Historical Foundation	Total
San Francisco, California	$ 51,818	$ -	$ 51,818
Birthplace Shrine Chapel, Dickson County, Tennessee	-	21,500	21,500
McAdow Home, Dickson County, Tennessee	-	17,255	17,255
Total	$ 51,818	$ 38,755	$ 90,573

Note I - Leases

The Ministry Council leases three copiers and two postage machines for use in its offices. Lease payments for the year ended December 31, 2017, totaled $11,199. The leases expire during 2018 and the minimum lease payments for the next year amount to $13,326.

NOTES CONTINUED

Note J - Combined Statement of Activities Expenses

The total expenses of various Agencies are included in the Combined Statement of Activities as follows:

Expense Description	Agencies
Our United Outreach	Our United Outreach
General Assembly Corporation	General Assembly Corporation
Ministry Council	Ministry Council
Shared Services	Shared Services
Historical Foundation	Historical Foundation
Board of Stewardship, Foundation, and Benefits	Board of Stewardship, Foundation, and Benefits
Small Church Loan Program	Small Church Loan Program
Insurance Program	Insurance Program
Ministerial Aid	Ministerial Aid
Investment Loan Program	Investment Loan Program
Retirement Fund	Retirement Fund
Endowment Program	Endowment Program

Costs originating from Shared Services (formerly Central Services - made up of Building and Maintenance, Computer Services Division, and Central Accounting Division) are now funded by Our United Outreach appropriations instead of being charged to the various applicable agencies based on usage.

Inter-agency revenue and expense items for Our United Outreach and endowment earnings have been eliminated on the combined statement of activity.

Note K - Fair Value Measurements

Prices for closed-end bond funds and equity mutual funds are readily available in the active markets in which those securities are traded, and the resulting fair values are categorized as level 1.

Prices for mortgage backed securities, bond mutual funds, and real estate investment trusts are determined on a recurring basis based upon inputs that are readily available in public markets or can be derived from information available in publicly quoted markets and are categorized as level 2.

NOTES CONTINUED

Note K - Fair Value Measurements - Continued

There is limited or no observable data for the prices of private investment entities that are held by the Center and the resulting fair values of these securities are categorized as level 3.

Fair values of assets measured on a recurring basis at December 31, 2017 are as follows:

	Fair Value	Fair Value Measurements at Reporting Date Using		
		Quoted Prices In Active Market for Identical Assets (Level 1)	Significant Other Observable Inputs (Level 2)	Significant Unobservable Inputs (Level 3)
December 31, 2017				
Mortgage backed securities	$ 15,727,005	$ -	$ 15,727,005	$ -
Equity mutual funds	2,278,758	2,278,758	-	-
Real estate investment trusts	5,875,850	-	5,875,850	-
Private investment entities	74,824,663	-	-	74,824,663
Total	$ 98,706,276	$ 2,278,758	$ 21,602,855	$ 74,824,663

Because of the multiple number and complexity of the calculations necessary, management does not believe it is practicable to estimate fair value of loans receivable, net of allowance for loan losses. Therefore, no adjustment has been made to the net carrying value of $8,184,030 listed on the Combined Statement of Financial Position.

NOTES CONTINUED

Note K - Fair Value Measurements - Continued

The following table provides information related to the previously mentioned investments that are valued based primarily on net asset value at December 31, 2017:

	Fair Value	Unfunded Commitments	Redemption Frequency (If Currently Eligible)	Redemption Notice Period
Private Investment Entities				
GT Emerging Markets (QP), L.P.	$ 7,228,577	None	Annual	90 Days
GT Offshore Fund, Ltd. (Class A)	8,879,462	None	Annual	90 Days
GT Offshore Fund, Ltd. (Class B)	9,844,523	None	Annual	90 Days
GT Institutional Fixed Income Fund LP	10,177,140	None	Annual	90 Days
GT ERISA Fund, Ltd. (Class A)	3,757,251	None	Annual	90 Days
GT ERISA Fund, Ltd. (Class B)	3,379,408	None	Annual	90 Days
GT Real Assets, L.P.	1,055,584	None	Annual	90 Days
GT Real Assets II, L.P.	474,106	None	Annual	90 Days
GT Special Opportunities III, L.P.	3,076,446	None	see note	see note
Palladian Partners VIII L.P.	1,017,900	None	Annual	90 Days
Headlands Capital Offshore, L.P.	638,088	None	Annual	90 Days
Midland Intl Equity QP Fund, L.P.	12,202,352	None	Quarterly	60 Days
Midland U.S. QP Fund, L.P.	13,093,826	None	Quarterly	60 Days
	$ 74,824,663			

The GT Special Opportunities III, L.P. provides for an annual redemption upon 90 days notice after an initial lock-up period of eighteen months.

NOTES CONTINUED

Note K - Fair Value Measurements - Continued

The following table summarizes fair value by fund for investments in private investment entities that are valued based primarily on net asset value at December 31, 2017:

Private Investment Entities	Retirement Fund	Endowment Program	Total Fair Value
GT Emerging Markets (QP), L.P.	$ 2,197,959	$ 5,030,618	$ 7,228,577
GT Offshore Fund, Ltd. (Class A)	-	8,879,462	8,879,462
GT Institutional Fixed Income Fund LP	3,380,950	6,796,190	10,177,140
GT Offshore Fund, Ltd. (Class B)	-	9,844,523	9,844,523
GT ERISA Fund, Ltd. (Class A)	3,757,251	-	3,757,251
GT ERISA Fund, Ltd. (Class B)	3,379,408	-	3,379,408
GT Real Assets, L.P.	327,595	727,989	1,055,584
GT Real Assets II, L.P.	135,459	338,647	474,106
GT Special Opportunities III, L.P.	921,373	2,155,073	3,076,446
Palladian Partners VIII LP	277,882	740,018	1,017,900
Midland Intl Equity QP Fund, L.P.	3,686,566	8,515,786	12,202,352
Headlands Capital Offshore, L.P.	192,608	445,480	638,088
Midland U.S. QP Fund, L.P.	4,189,398	8,904,428	13,093,826
	$ 22,446,449	$ 52,378,214	$ 74,824,663

NOTES CONTINUED

Note K - Fair Value Measurements - Continued

Assets measured at fair value on a recurring basis using significant unobservable inputs (Level 3):

Fair value at beginning of year	$	68,197,599
Investments and distributions, net		3,360,299
Realized/unrealized gains (losses)		3,266,765
Fair value at end of year	$	74,824,663

Gains and losses (realized and unrealized) for Level 3 assets included in net assets for the year are reported as follows:

On the Combined Statement of Activity, under Revenues, gains, and other support:

Permanently restricted net assets:		
Endowment program	$	3,053,632
Net assets available for benefits:		
Retirement fund		213,133
Total net assets	$	3,266,765

These investments without readily determinable values comprise approximately 61.17% of total assets at December 31, 2017.

All assets have been valued using a market approach.

A description of the Private Investment Entities and the investment objectives is as follows:

<u>GT Emerging Markets (QP), L.P.</u> - This fund is organized as a "fund of funds" which seek to achieve long-term capital appreciation through investments in limited partnerships, off-shore corporations, open-end mutual funds, closed-end mutual funds, commingled trust funds, and separately managed accounts that invest primarily in "emerging markets." Investments may also be made in industrialized nations such as the United States and Japan.

<u>GT Offshore Fund, Ltd. / GT ERISA Fund, Ltd.</u> - These are open-ended "umbrella" funds, incorporated as exempted companies in the Cayman Islands with multiple classes of Shares. Each class of share is separately valued and pursues its own clearly defined investment objective(s) and strategy(ies). These funds overall investment objectives are as follows:

Class A is broadly diversified among multiple investment managers and multiple investment strategies. The strategies employed may include multi-strategy arbitrage, capital structure arbitrage, distressed debt, long/short equity or niche financing.

Class B seeks to achieve a superior rate of return exceeding that of the MSCI World Index with less volatility while minimizing market risk through a hedged approach. The primary investment strategy will be a long/short equity strategy. This class is broadly diversified among multiple investment managers and multiple long/short equity strategies.

NOTES CONTINUED

Note K - Fair Value Measurements - Continued

GT Real Assets, L.P. - This fund is organized as a "fund of funds" investment vehicle that will pool and invest funds, generally through "Managed Investment Vehicles," for the purpose of generating attractive risk-adjusted returns by opportunistically investing in a broad spectrum of resources, real assets, and other investment strategies.

GT Special Opportunities, III, L.P. - This fund is organized as a "fund of funds" investment vehicle that will pool and invest funds, generally through "Managed Investment Vehicles," for the purpose of achieving a superior rate of return. The fund focuses on a very limited number of investment strategies that are considered to be opportunistic based upon prevailing market conditions. At times, the fund may only invest in one strategy and do so in a non-diversified manner, perhaps with only a single manager. The strategies sought by the fund will often be niche-focused. Accordingly, the risk level for the fund is anticipated to be extremely high.

Midland International Equity QP Fund, L.P. - This is an international equity fund which seeks to identify listed companies selling at a discount to intrinsic net worth on liquid stock exchanges of non-U.S. countries. The focus of this fund is long-term capital appreciation. This fund seeks to outperform the MSCI EAFE Index, net of fees and taxes, over a full market cycle.

Headlands Capital Offshore, L.P. - This is an offshore equity fund which seeks to outperform the broad U.S. equity market, net of fees and taxes over a full market cycle. The focus of this fund is long-term capital appreciation.

Midland U.S. QP Fund, L.P. - This fund's objective is to outperform the broad U.S. equity market, defined as the Russell 3000 Index, net of fees and taxes over a full market cycle. The fund seeks to compound capital at attractive rates through direct and indirect long-term ownership of publicly traded businesses domiciled in the United States.

Note L - Securities and Investments

Securities and investments at December 31, 2017 are as follows:

	Ministry Council	Historical Foundation	Investment Loan Program	Retirement Fund	Endowment Program	Total
Cash and cash equivalents	$ -	$ -	$ 3,868,964	$ 589,124	$ 1,674,480	$ 6,132,568
Mortgage backed securities	-	-	15,727,005	-	-	15,727,005
Equity mutual funds	-	-	-	693,200	1,585,558	2,278,758
Real estate investment trusts	-	-	-	1,448,740	4,427,110	5,875,850
Private investment entities	-	-	-	22,446,449	52,378,214	74,824,663
Real estate	51,818	38,755	-	-	-	90,573
	$ 51,818	$ 38,755	$ 19,595,969	$ 25,177,513	$ 60,065,362	$ 104,929,417

Note M - Subsequent Events

Subsequent events were evaluated through May 23, 2018, which is the date the financial statements were available to be issued.

BETHEL UNIVERSITY

FINANCIAL STATEMENTS
AND OTHER INFORMATION

JULY 31, 2017 AND 2016

BETHEL UNIVERSITY

Table of Contents

	Page
INDEPENDENT AUDITOR'S REPORT	1 - 3
FINANCIAL STATEMENTS	
Statements of Financial Position	4
Statements of Activities	5 - 6
Statements of Cash Flows	7 - 8
Notes to Financial Statements	9 - 31
SUPPLEMENTARY INFORMATION	
Financial Responsibility Composite Score	32 - 33
University Key Financial Ratios	34 - 36
Unrestricted Net Assets Exclusive of Plant, Property, Equipment, and Related Debt and Obligation Under Financing Arrangement	37
OTHER INFORMATION	
Schedule of Expenditures of Federal Awards	38
Notes to Schedule of Expenditures of Federal Awards	39
INDEPENDENT AUDITOR'S REPORT ON INTERNAL CONTROL OVER FINANCIAL REPORTING AND ON COMPLIANCE AND OTHER MATTERS BASED ON AN AUDIT OF FINANCIAL STATEMENTS PERFORMED IN ACCORDANCE WITH *GOVERNMENT AUDITING STANDARDS*	40 - 41
INDEPENDENT AUDITOR'S REPORT ON COMPLIANCE FOR EACH MAJOR PROGRAM AND ON INTERNAL CONTROL OVER COMPLIANCE REQUIRED BY UNIFORM GUIDANCE	42 - 44
SCHEDULE OF FINDINGS AND QUESTIONED COSTS	45 - 46
SCHEDULE OF PRIOR YEAR FINDINGS AND QUESTIONED COSTS	47

-i-

Independent Auditor's Report

The Board of Trustees
Bethel University
McKenzie, Tennessee

Report on the Financial Statements

We have audited the accompanying financial statements of Bethel University (the "University"), which comprise the statements of financial position as of July 31, 2017 and 2016, and the related statements of activities and cash flows for the years then ended, and the related notes to the financial statements.

Management's Responsibility for the Financial Statements

Management is responsible for the preparation and fair presentation of these financial statements in accordance with accounting principles generally accepted in the United States of America; this includes the design, implementation, and maintenance of internal control relevant to the preparation and fair presentation of financial statements that are free from material misstatement, whether due to fraud or error.

Auditor's Responsibility

Our responsibility is to express an opinion on these financial statements based on our audits. We conducted our audits in accordance with auditing standards generally accepted in the United States of America and the standards applicable to financial audits contained in *Government Auditing Standards*, issued by the Comptroller General of the United States. Those standards require that we plan and perform the audit to obtain reasonable assurance about whether the financial statements are free from material misstatement.

An audit involves performing procedures to obtain audit evidence about the amounts and disclosures in the financial statements. The procedures selected depend on the auditor's judgment, including the assessment of the risks of material misstatement of the financial statements, whether due to fraud or error. In making those risk assessments, the auditor considers internal control relevant to the entity's preparation and fair presentation of the financial statements in order to design audit procedures that are appropriate in the circumstances, but not for the purpose of expressing an opinion on the effectiveness of the entity's internal control. Accordingly, we express no such opinion. An audit also includes evaluating the appropriateness of accounting policies used and the reasonableness of significant accounting estimates made by management, as well as evaluating the overall presentation of the financial statements.

 Bethel University

We believe that the audit evidence we have obtained is sufficient and appropriate to provide a basis for our audit opinion.

Opinion

In our opinion, the financial statements referred to above present fairly, in all material respects, the financial position of Bethel University as of July 31, 2017 and 2016, and the changes in its net assets and its cash flows for the years then ended in accordance with accounting principles generally accepted in the United States of America.

Other Matters

Other Information

Our audits were conducted for the purpose of forming an opinion on the financial statements as a whole. The accompanying schedule of expenditures of federal awards, as required by Title 2 U.S. *Code of Federal Regulations* (CFR) Part 200, *Uniform Administrative Requirements, Cost Principles, and Audit Requirements for Federal Awards* (Uniform Guidance), is presented for purposes of additional analysis and is not a required part of the financial statements. Such information is the responsibility of management and was derived from and relates directly to the underlying accounting and other records used to prepare the financial statements. The information has been subjected to the auditing procedures applied in the audit of the financial statements and certain additional procedures, including comparing and reconciling such information directly to the underlying accounting and other records used to prepare the financial statements or to the financial statements themselves, and other additional procedures in accordance with auditing standards generally accepted in the United States of America. In our opinion, the information is fairly stated, in all material respects, in relation to the financial statements as a whole.

Disclaimer of Opinion on Supplementary Information

Our audits were conducted for the purpose of forming an opinion on the financial statements as a whole. The Schedules of Financial Responsibility Composite Score, University Key Financial Ratios, and Unrestricted Net Assets Exclusive of Property, Buildings, Equipment, Related Debt and Obligation Under Financing Arrangement, which are the responsibility of management, are presented for purposes of additional analysis and are not a required part of the financial statements. Such information has not been subjected to the auditing procedures applied in the audit of the financial statements and, accordingly, we do not express an opinion or provide any assurance on it.

 Bethel University

Other Reporting Required by Government Auditing Standards

In accordance with *Government Auditing Standards*, we have also issued our report dated September 29, 2017, on our consideration of the University's internal control over financial reporting and on our tests of its compliance with certain provisions of laws, regulations, contracts, and grant agreements and other matters. The purpose of that report is to describe the scope of our testing of internal control over financial reporting and compliance and the results of that testing, and not to provide an opinion on internal control over financial reporting or on compliance. That report is an integral part of an audit performed in accordance with *Government Auditing Standards* in considering the University's internal control over financial reporting and compliance.

Crosslin, PLLC

Nashville, Tennessee
September 29, 2017

BETHEL UNIVERSITY
STATEMENTS OF FINANCIAL POSITION

ASSETS

	July 31,	
	2017	2016
Cash and cash equivalents	$ 1,320,193	$ 1,494,925
Perkins loan cash	64,895	78,214
Receivables:		
Contributions, net (Note B)	15,215,442	12,113,005
Students, net of allowances of $828,078 and $1,422,292 respectively	1,450,507	1,333,506
Perkins loans, net of allowances of $216,345 and $237,841, respectively	157,823	188,367
Other	70,930	918,376
Inventories	292,688	260,658
Prepaid expenses, deposits, and other assets (Note F)	254,041	243,576
Investments (Note C)	3,742,992	3,556,561
Beneficial interest in assets held by others (Note D)	3,710,652	3,552,714
Cash value life insurance	451,432	-
Property, buildings, and equipment:		
Land	260,851	260,851
Buildings and improvements	87,098,384	85,468,815
Equipment, furniture and automobiles	8,190,729	8,566,821
Library books	1,284,514	1,284,514
Construction in progress	274,289	274,289
	97,108,767	95,855,290
Less: Accumulated depreciation	(24,202,696)	(21,691,537)
Total property and equipment, net	72,906,071	74,163,753
Total assets	$ 99,637,666	$ 97,903,655

LIABILITIES AND NET ASSETS

Liabilities:		
Accounts payable and accrued liabilities	$ 3,310,684	$ 6,438,104
Accrued payroll and benefits	970,029	443,545
Deferred tuition revenue	3,331,149	2,793,384
Annuities payable	-	385
Debt (Note E)	9,525,377	5,547,696
Obligation under financing arrangement, net (Note F)	46,460,584	47,050,260
Advances from the federal government	308,557	346,924
Total liabilities	63,906,380	62,620,298
Net Assets:		
Unrestricted	24,132,550	22,874,163
Temporarily restricted (Notes G and H)	838,973	2,074,644
Permanently restricted (Notes G and H)	10,759,763	10,334,550
Total net assets	35,731,286	35,283,357
Total liabilities and net assets	$ 99,637,666	$ 97,903,655

See accompanying notes to financial statements.

BETHEL UNIVERSITY
STATEMENTS OF ACTIVITIES

	Year Ended July 31, 2017			
	Unrestricted	Temporarily Restricted	Permanently Restricted	Total
Revenue, gains and other support:				
Regular tuition and fees	$ 49,810,522	$ -	$ -	$ 49,810,522
Degree completion tuition	5,541,903	-	-	5,541,903
Institutional scholarships and grants	(12,327,341)	-	-	(12,327,341)
Net tuition and fees	43,025,084	-	-	43,025,084
Bookstore income	1,101,073	-	-	1,101,073
Private gifts and contracts	4,208,952	534,636	267,275	5,010,863
Investment gain	458,650	-	-	458,650
Unrealized gain on beneficial interests in assets held by others	-	-	157,938	157,938
Auxiliary fund revenues	7,146,440	-	-	7,146,440
Government grants	166,127			166,127
Other income	1,394,994	-	-	1,394,994
Net assets released from restrictions	1,763,359	(1,763,359)	-	-
Reclassification	6,948	(6,948)	-	-
Total revenue, gains and other support	59,271,627	(1,235,671)	425,213	58,461,169
Expenses:				
Education and general:				
Instruction	27,856,245	-	-	27,856,245
Academic support	6,705,595	-	-	6,705,595
Student services	9,347,740	-	-	9,347,740
Institutional support	10,883,726	-	-	10,883,726
Auxiliary enterprises	3,219,934	-	-	3,219,934
Total expenses	58,013,240	-	-	58,013,240
Net increase (decrease) in net assets	1,258,387	(1,235,671)	425,213	447,929
Net assets, beginning of year	22,874,163	2,074,644	10,334,550	35,283,357
Net assets, end of year	$ 24,132,550	$ 838,973	$ 10,759,763	$ 35,731,286

	Year Ended July 31, 2016			
	Unrestricted	Temporarily Restricted	Permanently Restricted	Total
	$ 51,512,171	$ -	$ -	$ 51,512,171
	7,480,380	-	-	7,480,380
	(13,071,993)	-	-	(13,071,993)
	45,920,558	-	-	45,920,558
	1,324,252	-	-	1,324,252
	10,461,052	612,551	12,975	11,086,578
	(15,480)	(12,262)	-	(27,742)
	-	-	(107,711)	(107,711)
	7,264,067	-	-	7,264,067
	2,163,269	-	-	2,163,269
	1,648,420	-	-	1,648,420
	776,627	(776,627)	-	-
	159,591	(1,662)	(157,929)	-
	69,702,356	(178,000)	(252,665)	69,271,691
	27,466,606	-	-	27,466,606
	10,325,896	-	-	10,325,896
	10,008,562	-	-	10,008,562
	6,493,886	-	-	6,493,886
	4,608,195	-	-	4,608,195
	58,903,145	-	-	58,903,145
	10,799,211	(178,000)	(252,665)	10,368,546
	12,074,952	2,252,644	10,587,215	24,914,811
	$ 22,874,163	$ 2,074,644	$ 10,334,550	$ 35,283,357

See accompanying notes to financial statements.

BETHEL UNIVERSITY
STATEMENTS OF CASH FLOWS

	Year Ended July 31,	
	2017	2016
CASH FLOWS FROM OPERATING ACTIVITIES:		
Increase in net assets	$ 447,929	$ 10,368,546
Adjustments to reconcile increase in net assets to net cash (used in) provided by operating activities		
Non-cash:		
Allowance for doubtful student accounts, contributions and Perkins loans receivable	(615,710)	(207,322)
Loss (gain) on disposal of property and equipment	29,190	(28,168)
Unrealized gain on investments and beneficial interests in assets held by others	(337,337)	(218,454)
Non-cash contributions	(7,032)	(45,000)
Cash value life insurance	(451,432)	-
Depreciation and amortization	2,952,779	2,588,126
(Increase) decrease in:		
Contributions receivable	(3,102,437)	(9,017,048)
Student accounts receivable	477,213	781,739
Perkins loans receivable	52,040	30,500
Other receivables	847,447	(615,331)
Inventories	(32,030)	(24,182)
Prepaid expenses, deposits, and other assets	(10,465)	(986,996)
Increase (decrease) in:		
Accounts payable and student account deposits	(3,127,420)	(251,674)
Accrued payroll and benefits	526,484	(315,290)
Deferred tuition revenue	537,765	(1,579,735)
Advances from federal government	(38,367)	(64,857)
Contributions restricted for long-term investments	(267,275)	(12,975)
Total adjustments	(2,566,587)	(9,966,667)
Net cash (used in) provided by operating activities	(2,118,658)	401,879
CASH FLOWS FROM INVESTING ACTIVITIES:		
Payments received on note receivable	-	7,792,839
Payment of accounts payable for property, buildings and equipment	-	(1,602,512)
Purchases of property, buildings and equipment	(1,743,917)	(14,628,089)
Proceeds from disposal of property and equipment	42,500	31,589
Net cash used in investing activities	(1,701,417)	(8,406,173)
CASH FLOWS FROM FINANCING ACTIVITIES:		
(Decrease) increase in annuity obligations	(385)	385
Proceeds from notes payable and line-of-credit	13,823,082	8,378,862
Proceeds from financing arrangement, net	-	48,300,000
Payments on notes payable and line-of-credit	(9,845,401)	(48,456,409)
Repayments of financing arrangement and capital lease obligations, net	(612,547)	(409,293)
Contributions restricted for long-term investments	267,275	12,975
Net cash provided by investing activities	3,632,024	7,826,520

See accompanying notes to financial statements.

BETHEL UNIVERSITY
STATEMENTS OF CASH FLOWS - Continued

	Year Ended July 31,	
	2017	2016
Net decrease in cash and cash equivalents	(188,051)	(177,774)
Cash and cash equivalents at beginning of year	1,573,139	1,750,913
Cash and cash equivalents at end of year	$ 1,385,088	$ 1,573,139
Supplemental disclosures of cash flow information:		
Interest paid	$ 1,915,695	$ 2,416,773
Non-cash financing and investing activities:		
Purchases of property and equipment	1,743,917	16,593,084
Amount financed through capital leases, accounts payable, debt, or received through donations	-	(1,964,995)
Total paid for property and equipment	$ 1,743,917	$ 14,628,089

Property held for investment of $3,185,000 was placed in service during fiscal 2016 and transferred to property and equipment.

See accompanying notes to financial statements.

BETHEL UNIVERSITY
NOTES TO FINANCIAL STATEMENTS
JULY 31, 2017 AND 2016

A. SUMMARY OF SIGNIFICANT ACCOUNTING POLICIES

Organization and Business Purpose

Bethel University (the "University") is a private, residential, coeducational University affiliated with the Cumberland Presbyterian Church, dedicated primarily to educating students in the liberal arts and science while also offering select pre-professional programs, a graduate teacher education program, a master of business administration program, a master of criminal justice program, and a master of physician's assistant program. In addition to its traditional academic programs, the University also offers a degree-completion program. The University is accredited by the Southern Association of Colleges and Schools, Commission on Colleges, and its education emphasizes academic excellence, high achievement, intellectual and personal integrity, and participation in community life. Its Christian heritage finds expression in commitment to the values of personal growth, justice, community, and service.

Accrual Basis and Financial Statement Presentation

The financial statements of the University have been prepared on the accrual basis of accounting.

The University classifies its revenues, expenses, gains, and losses into three classes of net assets based on the existence or absence of donor-imposed restrictions. Net assets of the University and changes therein are as follows:

Unrestricted net assets - Net assets that are not subject to donor-imposed stipulations and net assets where donor-imposed stipulations have been met within the reporting period.

Temporarily restricted net assets - Net assets subject to donor-imposed stipulations that may or will be met by actions of the University.

Permanently restricted net assets - Net assets subject to donor-imposed stipulations that the University is required to maintain permanently. Generally, the donors of these assets permit the University to use all or a part of the income earned on related investments for general or specific purposes.

The amount of each of these classes of net assets is displayed in the statements of financial position and the amount of change in each class of net assets is displayed in the statements of activities.

BETHEL UNIVERSITY
NOTES TO FINANCIAL STATEMENTS
JULY 31, 2017 AND 2016

A. SUMMARY OF SIGNIFICANT ACCOUNTING POLICES - Continued

Use of Estimates in the Preparation of Financial Statements

The preparation of financial statements in conformity with accounting principles generally accepted in the United States of America requires management to make assumptions that affect the reported amounts of assets and liabilities, disclosure of contingent assets and liabilities at the date of the financial statements, and the reported amounts of revenues and expenses during the reporting period. The more significant areas include the recovery period for property and equipment, the allocation of certain operating expenses to functional categories, the collection of contributions receivable, and the adequacy of the allowance for doubtful student receivables. Management believes that such estimates have been based on reasonable assumptions and that such estimates are adequate. Actual results could differ from those estimates.

Contributions

The University reports gifts of cash and other assets as restricted support if received with donor-imposed stipulations that limit the use of the donated assets. When a donor-imposed restriction expires, *i.e.*, when the purpose of the restriction is accomplished, temporarily restricted net assets are reclassified to unrestricted net assets and reported in the statement of activities as net assets released from restrictions. The University has elected to report contributions received with donor-imposed restrictions as an increase to unrestricted net assets if the restrictions are met in the same fiscal year that the contributions are received.

The University reports gifts of land, equipment, and other assets as unrestricted support unless explicit donor-imposed stipulations specify how the donated assets must be used. Gifts of long-lived assets with explicit restrictions that specify how the assets are to be used and gifts of cash or other assets that must be used to acquire long-lived assets are reported as restricted support. Absent explicit donor-imposed stipulations regarding how long the long-lived assets must be maintained, the University reports expirations of donor-imposed restrictions when the donated or acquired long-lived assets are placed in service.

Contribution of services are recognized if the services received (a) create or enhance non-financial assets or (b) require specialized skills, provided by individuals possessing those skills and would typically need to be purchased if not provided by donation.

In the event a donor makes changes to the nature of a restricted gift, which affects its classification among the net asset categories, such amounts are reflected as reclassifications in the statements of activities.

BETHEL UNIVERSITY
NOTES TO FINANCIAL STATEMENTS
JULY 31, 2017 AND 2016

A. SUMMARY OF SIGNIFICANT ACCOUNTING POLICIES - Continued

Perkins Loan - Cash

As required by federal regulations, cash related to the Federal Perkins Loan Program is maintained in a separate bank account.

Student Accounts Receivable

The University records accounts receivable at their estimated net realizable value. An allowance for doubtful accounts is recorded based upon management's estimate of uncollectible accounts determined by analysis of specific student balances and a general reserve based upon agings of outstanding balances. Past due balances and delinquent receivables are charged against the allowance when they are determined to be uncollectible by management.

Notes Receivable - Students

Notes receivable from students at July 31, 2017 and 2016, totaled $157,823 and $188,367, respectively, net of allowances of $216,345 and $237,841, respectively. Student loans are granted by the University under the federally funded Perkins loan program. These funds are disbursed based upon the demonstration of financial need on the Perkins loan, at which time the loan will also begin accruing interest. Perkins loan amounts are then repaid through a third party billing service. Student loans are considered past due when payment has not been received within 30 days. At July 31, 2017 and 2016, student loans represented 0.16% and 0.19%, respectively, of total assets.

The allowance for doubtful accounts is established based on prior collection experience and current economic factors which, in management's judgment, could influence the ability of loan recipients to repay the amounts per the loan terms. Loan balances are written off only when they are deemed to be permanently uncollectible.

Contributions Receivable

Contributions receivable are recorded at their estimated fair value using a discount rate commensurate with the rate on U.S. Government Securities whose maturities correspond to the maturities of the contributions. Contributions receivable are considered to be either conditional or unconditional promises to give. A conditional contribution is one which depends on the occurrence of a specified uncertain future event to become binding on the donor. Conditional contributions are not recorded as revenue until the condition is met, at which time they become unconditional. Unconditional contributions are recorded as revenue at the time verifiable evidence of the promise to give is received.

BETHEL UNIVERSITY
NOTES TO FINANCIAL STATEMENTS
JULY 31, 2017 AND 2016

A. SUMMARY OF SIGNIFICANT ACCOUNTING POLICIES - Continued

Inventories

Inventories consist primarily of books and supplies and are stated at the lower of cost or market. Cost is determined using the average cost method.

Investments

Investments in marketable equity securities with readily determinable fair values and investments in debt securities are stated at their fair values in the statements of financial position. Fair value of investments is determined based on quoted market prices or using Level 2 or 3 inputs as described in Note I. All gains and losses (both realized and unrealized) and other investment income are reported in the statements of activities.

Property and Equipment

Property and equipment are recorded at cost at the date of acquisition or fair value at the date of donation in the case of gifts. Depreciation on property and equipment is calculated on the straight-line method over estimated useful lives of 20 - 40 years for buildings and improvements, 5 - 7 years for equipment and furniture, 5 years for automobiles, and 20 years for other property. Property held under capital leases are depreciated on the straight-line method based on the shorter of the estimated useful life of the property to the University or the life of the capital lease. Library books and repairs/renovations to buildings and equipment that do not add value or extend the useful life of the assets are expensed as incurred. Depreciation, operation, and maintenance charges are allocated to appropriate functional expense categories.

The estimate to complete construction in progress is $2,925,711 as of July 31, 2017.

Deferred Revenue

Deferred revenue consists primarily of charges and cash receipts collected prior to year-end for services rendered after year-end. These receipts pertain to upcoming tuition and fees.

BETHEL UNIVERSITY
NOTES TO FINANCIAL STATEMENTS
JULY 31, 2017 AND 2016

A. SUMMARY OF SIGNIFICANT ACCOUNTING POLICIES - Continued

Debt Issuance Cost

Costs incurred in connection with the issuance of the University's obligation under financing arrangement have been capitalized and are being amortized using the straight-line method. Effective August 1, 2016, The University adopted the provisions of FASB ASU 2015-03, *Imputation of Interest (Subtopic 835-30): Simplifying the Presentation of Debt Issuance Costs*. ASU 2015-03 requires entities to present issuance costs related to a recognized debt liability as a direct deduction from the carrying amount of the debt liability. The adoption required retrospective application. Unamortized debt issuance costs in the amount of $878,624 and $901,495 as of July 31, 2017 and 2016, respectively, have been netted against obligations, under financing arrangement on the statement of financial position.

Advances from the Federal Government for Student Loans

The Perkins Loan Program is a campus-based program providing revolving loan funds for financial assistance to eligible postsecondary school students based on financial need. The Department of Education provides funds along with the University, which are used to make loans to eligible students at low interest rates. Refundable government advances for Perkins at July 31, 2017 and 2016 were $308,557 and $346,924, respectively.

Advertising Costs

Advertising costs are expensed as incurred and totaled approximately $1,343,236 and $1,294,097 for the years ended July 31, 2017 and 2016, respectively.

Tax Status

The University is exempt from Federal income taxes under §501(a) of the Internal Revenue Code ("IRC") as an organization described in IRC §501(c)(3). Accordingly, no provision for income taxes has been made in the accompanying financial statements. The University is not classified as a private foundation.

BETHEL UNIVERSITY
NOTES TO FINANCIAL STATEMENTS
JULY 31, 2017 AND 2016

A. SUMMARY OF SIGNIFICANT ACCOUNTING POLICIES - Continued

The University accounts for the effect of any uncertain tax positions based on a more likely than not threshold to the recognition of the tax positions being sustained based on the technical merits of the position under examination by the applicable taxing authority. If a tax position or positions are deemed to result in uncertainties of those positions, the unrecognized tax benefit is estimated based on a cumulative probability assessment that aggregates the estimated tax liability for all uncertain tax positions. Tax positions for the University include, but are not limited to, the tax-exempt status and determination of whether certain income is subject to unrelated business income tax; however, the University has determined that such tax positions do not result in an uncertainty requiring recognition.

Fair Value Measurements

Assets and liabilities recorded at fair value in the statements of financial position are categorized based on the level of judgment associated with the inputs used to measure their fair value. Related disclosures are included in Note I. Level inputs, as defined by Financial Accounting Standards Board Accounting Standards Codification ("ASC") 820, *Fair Value Measurements and Disclosures,* are as follows:

Level 1 - Values are unadjusted quoted prices for identical assets and liabilities in active markets accessible at the measurement date.

Level 2 - Inputs include quoted prices for similar assets or liabilities in active markets, quoted prices from those willing to trade in markets that are not active, or other inputs that are observable or can be corroborated by market data for the term of the instrument. Such inputs include market interest rates and volatilities, spreads and yield curves.

Level 3 - Certain inputs are unobservable (supported by little or no market activity) and significant to the fair value measurement. Unobservable inputs reflect the University's best estimate of what hypothetical market participants would use to determine a transaction price for the asset or liability at the reporting date.

Classification of Expenses

Expenses are classified functionally as a measure of service efforts and accomplishments. Direct expenses incurred for a single function are allocated entirely to that function. Joint expenses applicable to more than one function are allocated on the basis of objectively summarized information or management estimates.

Reclassifications

Certain reclassifications have been made to the 2016 financial statements in order for them to conform to the 2017 presentation.

BETHEL UNIVERSITY
NOTES TO FINANCIAL STATEMENTS
JULY 31, 2017 AND 2016

B. CONTRIBUTIONS RECEIVABLE

Contributions receivable at July 31, 2017 and 2016 consist of the following:

	2017	2016
Contributions receivable (present value)	$ 15,385,535	$ 12,283,098
Less: allowance for doubtful contributions	(170,093)	(170,093)
	$ 15,215,442	$ 12,113,005

Expected maturities of contributions receivable at July 31, 2017 are as follows:

Fiscal Year Ending July 31,	Amount
2018	$ 4,593,335
2019	1,825,869
2020	1,824,854
2021	1,824,686
2022	1,814,510
Thereafter	4,125,760
Total expected contributions	16,009,014
Less: allowance for net present value using a weighted average discount rate of 1.00%	(623,479)
Present value of contributions receivable	$ 15,385,535

BETHEL UNIVERSITY
NOTES TO FINANCIAL STATEMENTS
JULY 31, 2017 AND 2016

C. INVESTMENTS

The investments of the University are principally administered by the University or by the Board of Stewardship of the Cumberland Presbyterian Church, Inc. (the "Board"). The funds administered by the Board are co-mingled with funds of other agencies of the Church. The University's portion represents approximately 5.2% of the funds administered by the Board at July 31, 2017 and 2016. The investments of the University, including investment property with a book value of $472,810 as of July 31, 2017 and 2016, are invested as follows:

	2017	2016
Administered by the Board:		
Marketable equity and debt securities	$3,064,954	$2,880,910
Administered by the University:		
Marketable equity and debt securities	6,883	6,948
Certificates of deposits	100,492	100,292
Investment Property and Other	570,663	568,411
	$3,742,992	$3,556,561

D. BENEFICIAL INTEREST IN ASSETS HELD BY OTHERS

Beneficial interest in assets held by others represents arrangements in which a donor establishes and funds a perpetual trust administered by an individual or organization other than the University. The fair value of perpetually held trusts in which the University had a beneficial interest as of July 31, 2017 and 2016, was $3,710,652 and $3,552,714, respectively. The University records these trusts at estimated fair value. Income distributed to the University from the beneficial interest assets is temporarily restricted for scholarships.

BETHEL UNIVERSITY
NOTES TO FINANCIAL STATEMENTS
JULY 31, 2017 AND 2016

E. DEBT

The University has the following debt obligations at July 31, 2017 and 2016:

	2017	2016
Note payable to Kubota Credit Corporation, U.S.A., 0% interest, collateralized by specified equipment.	$ -	$ 185
Line-of-credit totaling $2,000,000 with Centennial Bank; bearing variable interest calculated as Prime Rate as published by The Wall Street Journal plus 1.00 % with a floor of 5.00%; line-of-credit matures and full payment due February 1, 2018; collateralized by accounts receivable, equipment, and inventory; paid in full August 29, 2016.	-	2,000,000
Construction line-of-credit totaling $607,800 (maximum) with Centennial Bank, bearing interest at 5.00% with the principal draws due in full on January 31, 2017; collateralized by future grant Payments; paid in full February 14, 2017.	-	184,998
Line-of-credit totaling $2,000,000 with Centennial Bank; bearing variable interest calculated as Prime Rate as published by The Wall Street Journal plus 1.00 % with a floor of 5.00%; line-of-credit matures and full payment due August 15, 2018; collateralized by accounts receivable, equipment, and inventory.	1,999,861	-
Line-of-credit totaling $1,000,000 with Centennial Bank; bearing variable interest calculated as Prime Rate as published by The Wall Street Journal plus 1.00 % with a floor of 5.00%; line-of-credit matures and full payment due December 12, 2017; collateralized by accounts receivable, equipment, and inventory.	1,000,000	-

BETHEL UNIVERSITY
NOTES TO FINANCIAL STATEMENTS
JULY 31, 2017 AND 2016

E. DEBT - Continued

	2017	2016
Note payable to City of Paris, bearing interest at 0.00%, with monthly principal payments of $8,663 due beginning on September 30, 2014, through final maturity on August 31, 2022.	528,413	632,363
Note payable to Carroll Bank & Trust, bearing interest at 5.25%, with the full principal balance maturing February 17, 2017; collateralized by certain real Property; paid in full January 18, 2017.	-	2,000,150
Note payable to Carroll Bank & Trust, bearing interest at 5.25%, with the full principal balance maturing August 25, 2018; collateralized by certain real property.	2,000,141	-
Note payable to Carroll Bank & Trust, bearing interest at 5.25%, with the full principal balance maturing August 10, 2018; collateralized by certain real property.	1,000,150	-
Note Payable to First Bank, bearing interest at 5.00%, with the full principal balance maturing August 31, 2017; paid in full on August 31, 2017.	400,000	-
Line-of-credit with a related party private company totaling $5,000,000, bearing interest at 5.00%, payable in monthly installments of interest only, continuing until July 31, 2021; at which time the balance is due; paid in full August 28, 2017.	2,000,000	
Note payable to Renasant Bank, payable in monthly installments of $13,609 including interest of 4.50% through June 12, 2018, with a final payment of $469,356 due July 12, 2018; collateralized by an agreement not to transfer or encumber certain real property.	596,812	730,000
	$9,525,377	$5,547,696

- 18 -

BETHEL UNIVERSITY
NOTES TO FINANCIAL STATEMENTS
JULY 31, 2017 AND 2016

E. DEBT - Continued

The anticipated maturities of the University's notes payable are as follows:

Fiscal Year Ending July 31,	Amount
2018	$4,100,762
2019	5,104,102
2020	103,950
2021	103,950
2022	103,950
Thereafter	8,663
	$9,525,377

Interest Expense

For the years ending July 31, 2017 and 2016, Bethel University incurred interest expense of $1,915,695 and $2,416,773, respectively.

Compliance with Covenants

The Renasant Bank loan agreement contains a debt service coverage ratio that requires the University to maintain a debt coverage ratio of 1.25x, tested annually by the bank. Based on the University's calculations as of July 31, 2017, the University was in compliance with this covenant and ratio.

F. OBLIGATIONS UNDER FINANCING ARRANGEMENT

On December 28, 2015, the United States Department of Agriculture (USDA) funded a Campus Facility Acquisition through a Rural Development Communities Facilities Loan with NCCD - Bethel Properties LLC, a separate legal entity independent of the University. The loan to NCCD - Bethel Properties LLC totaled $48,300,000, bearing a fixed interest of 3.25% with a repayment term of 40 years. NCCD - Bethel Properties LLC utilized the proceeds of the loan to lease certain University buildings, in which the University leased back from NCCD - Bethel Properties LLC. The University remits the lease payments to NCCD - Bethel Properties LLC, who in turn repays USDA. The monthly lease payments equal the monthly note payment. The agreement expires December 28, 2055. Due to easement and right of way concerns, substantially all of the McKenzie campus is incorporated into the lease, lease-back transaction ("financing arrangement"). Buildings held under the capital lease at July 31, 2017 totaled $57,998,848, net of accumulated depreciation of $7,512,613.

- 19 -

BETHEL UNIVERSITY
NOTES TO FINANCIAL STATEMENTS
JULY 31, 2017 AND 2016

F. OBLIGATIONS UNDER FINANCING ARRANGEMENT - Continued

Minimum future lease payments under capital leases as of July 31, 2017, are as follows:

Fiscal Year Ending July 31,	Amount
2018	$ 2,161,908
2019	2,161,908
2020	2,161,908
2021	2,161,908
2022	2,161,908
Thereafter	72,025,997
	82,835,537
Less: Amount representing interest	(35,496,329)
Amount representing debt-refinancing costs, net	(878,624)
Present value of net minimum lease payments	$46,460,584

Annually, the University will incur amortization expense on debt-refinancing costs of $22,871, until the lease expires December 28, 2055.

Compliance with Covenants

The Sublease Agreement between NCCD - Bethel Properties LLC, as sublessor, and Bethel University, as sublessee, contains a covenant that requires the University to maintain a debt service coverage ratio of at least 1.0. This ratio is defined as earnings before interest, taxes, depreciation, and amortization divided by the annual lease payments due to NCCD – Bethel Properties LLC. Based on the University's calculations as of July 31, 2017, the University was in compliance with this covenant and ratio.

G. TEMPORARILY AND PERMANENTLY RESTRICTED NET ASSETS

At July 31, 2017 and 2016, temporarily restricted net assets are available for the following purposes:

	2017	2016
Scholarships	$ 578,235	$ 457,896
Time restrictions and other	260,738	1,616,748
	$ 838,973	$2,074,644

BETHEL UNIVERSITY
NOTES TO FINANCIAL STATEMENTS
JULY 31, 2017 AND 2016

G. TEMPORARILY AND PERMANENTLY RESTRICTED NET ASSETS - Continued

At July 31, 2017 and 2016, permanently restricted net assets are as follows:

	2017	2016
Beneficial interest in assets held by others	$ 3,710,652	$ 3,552,714
Endowments	7,049,111	6,781,836
	$10,759,763	$10,334,550

The endowments represent nonexpendable funds that are subject to restrictions requiring the principal to be invested and only the income used as specified by the donors.

Net assets were released from donor restrictions by incurring expenses satisfying the restricted purposes. The following is a summary of the assets released from restrictions for the years ended July 31, 2017 and 2016:

	2017	2016
Institutional support expenditures	$1,385,669	$ 373,745
Scholarship and grant expenditures	377,690	402,882
	$1,763,359	$ 776,627

H. ENDOWMENT

The University's endowment consists of individual donor-restricted funds established for a variety of purposes. As required by U.S. generally accepted accounting principles, net assets associated with endowment funds are classified and reported based on the existence or absence of donor-imposed restrictions.

BETHEL UNIVERSITY
NOTES TO FINANCIAL STATEMENTS
JULY 31, 2017 AND 2016

H.   ENDOWMENT - Continued

Interpretation of Relevant Law

The Board of Trustees of the University has interpreted the applicable state laws as requiring the preservation of the original gift as of the gift date of the donor-restricted endowment funds absent explicit donor stipulations to the contrary. As a result of this interpretation, the University classified as permanently restricted net assets (a) the original value of gifts donated to the permanent endowment, (b) the original value of subsequent gifts to the permanent endowment, and (c) accumulations to the permanent endowment made in accordance with the direction of the applicable donor gift instrument at the time the accumulation is added to the fund. The remaining portion of the donor-restricted endowment fund that is not classified in permanently restricted net assets is classified as temporarily restricted net assets until those amounts are appropriated for expenditure by the University in a manner consistent with the standard of prudence prescribed by applicable state laws. In accordance with applicable state laws, the University considers the following factors in making a determination to appropriate or accumulate donor-restricted endowment funds:

- The duration and preservation of the fund
- The purposes of the University and the donor-restricted endowment fund
- General economic conditions
- The possible effect of inflation and deflation
- The expected total return from income and the appreciation of investments
- Other resources of the University
- The investment policy of the University

- 22 -

BETHEL UNIVERSITY
NOTES TO FINANCIAL STATEMENTS
JULY 31, 2017 AND 2016

H.   ENDOWMENT - Continued

Changes in Endowment Net Assets

	Temporarily Restricted	Permanently Restricted	Total
Endowment net assets, August 1, 2015	$ 660,004	$ 10,587,215	$ 11,247,219
Reclassification	(1,662)	(157,929)	(159,591)
Investment return:			
Investment income	(12,262)	-	(12,262)
Net depreciation (realized and unrealized)	-	(107,711)	(107,711)
Total investment return	(12,262)	(107,711)	(119,973)
Contributions	-	12,975	12,975
Appropriation of endowment assets for expenditure (scholarships)	-	-	-
Endowment net assets, July 31, 2016	646,080	10,334,550	10,980,630
Reclassification	(6,948)	-	(6,948)
Investment return:			
Investment income	-	-	-
Net appreciation (realized and unrealized)	-	157,938	157,938
Total investment return	-	157,938	157,938
Contributions	-	267,275	267,275
Appropriation of endowment assets for expenditure (scholarships)	-	-	-
Endowment net assets, July 31, 2017	$ 639,132	$ 10,759,763	$ 11,398,895

BETHEL UNIVERSITY
NOTES TO FINANCIAL STATEMENTS
JULY 31, 2017 AND 2016

H. ENDOWMENT - Continued

Return Objectives and Risk Parameters

The University has adopted an investment and spending policy for endowment assets that attempt to provide a predictable stream of funding to programs supported by its endowment while seeking to maintain the purchasing power of the endowment assets. Endowment assets include those assets of donor-restricted funds that the University must hold in perpetuity or for a donor-specified period(s). Under this policy, as approved by the Board of Trustees, the endowment assets are invested with an overall total return objective as established for each time horizon: 1) Short Term, 2) Intermediate, and 3) Long Term according to the funding needs of the University. The returns will be compared with the generally accepted indices, *i.e.*, the S&P 500, certain Bond Indices, MSCI EAFE stock indices, and an index of U.S. Treasury Bills depending on the time horizon in place. At July 31, 2017 and 2016, the endowment assets consist of investments in certificates of deposit, marketable debt and equity securities, and beneficial interests in assets held by others.

Strategies Employed for Achieving Objectives

To satisfy its rate-of-return objectives, the University relies on a total return strategy in which investment returns are achieved through both capital appreciation (realized and unrealized) and current yield (interest and dividends). The University targets an investment allocation based on the three time horizons described above and that places emphasis on diversification of assets within prudent risk constraints.

Spending Policy and How the Investment Objectives Relate to Spending Policy

During fiscal year 2009, the University's Board of Trustees adopted a spending policy, which is based on the "Total Return" concept of determining the amount available for distribution. Total Return takes into consideration all of the elements of long-term investment return. The appropriate spending amount is based on the projected long-term Total Return of the funds, less an estimate of future inflation. The goal of the Total Return approach is to provide for a level of current income that protects the future purchasing power of the fund, thereby providing for increasing amounts of future income. The University anticipates that this percentage will be in the range of 3 to 5% of market value based on historical measurements of Total Return and Inflation. The market value of the fund will be noted each year on a specific date and a three-year rolling average market value will be established. The rolling three-year market value will be multiplied by the approved spending percentage which will be set annually.

BETHEL UNIVERSITY
NOTES TO FINANCIAL STATEMENTS
JULY 31, 2017 AND 2016

I. FAIR VALUES OF FINANCIAL INSTRUMENTS

Required disclosures concerning the estimated fair values of financial instruments are presented below. The estimated fair value amounts have been determined based on the University's assessment of available market information and appropriate valuation methodologies. The following table summarizes required fair value disclosures under ASC 825, *Financial Instruments*, and measurements at July 31, 2017 and 2016 for the assets and liabilities measured at fair value on a recurring basis under ASC 820, *Fair Value Measurements and Disclosures*:

	Carrying Amount	Estimated Fair Value	Measured at Fair Value	Fair Value Measurements Using		
				Level 1	Level 2	Level 3
July 31, 2017						
Assets:						
Investments:						
Cash and cash equivalents	$ 196,383	$ 196,383	$ 196,383	$196,383	$ -	$ -
Certificates of deposits	100,492	100,492	100,492	100,492	-	-
Equity funds:						
U.S. Equities	121,856	121,856	121,856	121,856	-	-
Venture Capital	2,851,451	2,851,451	2,851,451	-	-	2,851,451
Investment Property	472,810	472,810	472,810	-	-	472,810
Total Investments	$3,742,992	$3,742,992	$3,742,992	$418,731	$ -	$3,324,261
Beneficial interests in trusts	3,710,652	3,710,652	3,710,652	-	3,710,652	-
Liabilities:						
Debt and financing arrangement	$55,985,961	$62,258,702	-	-	-	-

BETHEL UNIVERSITY
NOTES TO FINANCIAL STATEMENTS
JULY 31, 2017 AND 2016

I. FAIR VALUES OF FINANCIAL INSTRUMENTS - Continued

	Carrying Amount	Estimated Fair Value	Measured at Fair Value	Fair Value Measurements Using		
				Level 1	Level 2	Level 3
July 31, 2016						
Assets:						
Investments:						
Cash and cash equivalents	$ 223,019	$ 223,019	$ 223,019	$223,019	$ -	$ -
Certificates of deposits	100,292	100,292	100,292	100,292	-	-
Equity funds:						
U.S. Equities	130,212	130,212	130,212	130,212	-	-
Venture Capital	2,630,228	2,630,228	2,630,228	-	-	2,630,228
Investment Property	472,810	472,810	472,810	-	-	472,810
Total Investments	$3,556,561	$3,556,561	$3,556,561	$453,523	$ -	$3,103,038
Beneficial interests in trusts	3,552,714	3,552,714	3,552,714	-	3,552,714	-
Liabilities:						
Debt and financing arrangement	$53,499,451	$59,493,600	-	-	-	-

Changes in Level 3 assets are as follows:

	Fair Value Measurements Using Significant Unobservable Inputs (Level 3)	
	2017	2016
Beginning Balance	$3,103,038	$ 5,539,794
Purchases and sales, net	221,223	(2,436,756)
Ending Balance	$3,324,261	$ 3,103,038

- 26 -

BETHEL UNIVERSITY
NOTES TO FINANCIAL STATEMENTS
JULY 31, 2017 AND 2016

I. FAIR VALUES OF FINANCIAL INSTRUMENTS - Continued

The following methods and assumptions were used to estimate the fair value of each class of financial instruments:

Cash equivalents, receivables, accounts payable and accrued payroll and benefits, deferred revenue and advances from the Federal government for student loans

The carrying values of these items approximate their fair values due to the short maturities of these instruments.

Investments

Fair values are based on quoted market prices, where available, and Level 2 and 3 inputs. The carrying amounts and the fair values of the University's investments are presented in Note C.

Notes payable and obligations under financing arrangement and capital leases

For fixed rate debt, fair value was estimated using discounted cash flow analyses based on the University's current incremental borrowing rates for similar types of borrowing arrangements.

J. FUND RAISING ACTIVITIES

The University conducts fundraising activities each year. The total cost of these activities for fiscal years 2017 and 2016, was $670,030 and $896,376, respectively.

K. RETIREMENT PLAN

The University's full-time employees may participate in a retirement plan administered by the Branch Banking and Trust Company (BB&T). The University makes payments to the plan by withholding an employee-elected percentage from the employee's salary with the University matching the employee's deduction up to five percent (5%). Total matching contributions were made by the University for fiscal years 2017 and 2016, of $521,024 and $449,299, respectively.

BETHEL UNIVERSITY
NOTES TO FINANCIAL STATEMENTS
JULY 31, 2017 AND 2016

L. CONCENTRATION OF RISKS

Concentration of Risk

The University generates revenue predominantly from tuition and fees, investment income, gifts, auxiliary enterprises and contributions. In planning and budgeting during a fiscal year, significant reliance is placed on meeting tuition, gift, auxiliary, investment earnings and contribution goals in order for the University to sustain successful operations. In the event that enrollment or gifts and contributions significantly decrease in any one year, operations could be adversely affected.

Financial instruments that potentially subject the University to concentrations of credit risk and market risk consist principally of cash equivalents, investments, and student receivables.

The University, in connection with its activities, grants credit to students that involves, to varying degrees, elements of credit risk. The maximum accounting loss from credit risk is limited to the amounts that are recognized in the accompanying statements of financial position as student accounts receivable at July 31, 2017 and 2016.

The University also has three bank deposits in excess of those insured under regulatory insurance limits.

M. OPERATING LEASES

The University leases office and classroom space for satellite campuses for programs offered through its College of Professional Studies, office space for University services, and an activities space for a University athletic program. These leases expire at various dates through fiscal year 2023. Minimum future rental payments under non-cancelable operating leases as of July 31, 2017 are as follows:

Fiscal Year Ending July 31,	Amount
2018	$1,274,301
2019	1,153,500
2020	247,165
2021	96,000
2022	49,800
Thereafter	57,000
	$2,877,766

- 28 -

BETHEL UNIVERSITY
NOTES TO FINANCIAL STATEMENTS
JULY 31, 2017 AND 2016

M. OPERATING LEASES - Continued

Operating lease payments under the non-cancelable leases totaled $1,409,902 and $2,078,036 for the years ended July 31, 2017 and 2016, respectively.

On August 10, 2011, the University entered into a ten (10) year lease, which expires August 31, 2021, with a related party. The building leased provides office space for University services to students. Operating lease payments under the non-cancelable lease totaled $50,400 for each of the years ended July 31, 2017 and 2016, respectively.

N. FUNCTIONAL ALLOCATION OF EXPENSES

During the years ended July 31, 2017 and 2016, the University allocated the cost of certain professional fees and the operation and maintenance of physical plant, including depreciation and amortization expense of $2,952,779 and $2,588,126 respectively, over the cost of providing instruction, academic support, student services, institutional support, and auxiliary enterprises as follows:

	2017	2016
Instruction	$4,497,539	$ 4,690,617
Academic support	1,082,654	1,763,408
Student services	1,509,242	1,709,215
Institutional support	1,757,235	1,108,995
Auxiliary enterprises	519,875	786,965
Total operation and maintenance of physical plant	$9,366,545	$10,059,200

O. LITIGATION AND CONTINGENCIES

The University is a defendant in legal actions from time to time in the normal course of operations. It is not currently possible to state the ultimate liability, if any, in these matters. In the opinion of management, any resulting liability from these actions will not have a material adverse effect on the financial position of the activities of the University.

BETHEL UNIVERSITY
NOTES TO FINANCIAL STATEMENTS
JULY 31, 2017 AND 2016

P. RELATED PARTY TRANSACTIONS

During fiscal years 2017 and 2016, the University had an agreement with a company owned by a member of the University's faculty. Under the agreement, the company developed and is maintaining the following online programs of study for the University:

- Master of Business Administration
- Master of Arts in Education
- Master of Science in Criminal Justice
- Bachelor of Science in Organizational Leadership
- Bachelor of Science in Criminal Justice
- Bachelor of Science in Emergency Services Management
- Associates of Arts
- Associates of Science
- Dual Enrollment

Specifically, the company is responsible for developing course work, producing lectures and graphic presentations, and maintaining student records. Fees under the agreement range from $149 to $319 per student, per course. The most recent agreement was executed effective April 1, 2015 for twelve (12) months, and automatically renews for an additional term of twelve (12) months unless terminated in accordance with the agreement. Total fees incurred during fiscal years 2017 and 2016 were $5,944,319 and $6,473,190, respectively.

During fiscal years 2017 and 2016, the University entered into an agreement with a company co-founded by a member of the Board of Trustees. Under the agreement, the company was granted rights as the University's exclusive technology supplier for the Registered Nurse to Bachelor of Science in Nursing (RN to BSN) online program of study. The company has developed a learning management system (LMS) that is used as a platform for online curriculum delivery for the Colleges of Arts and Sciences and Health Sciences. The curriculum is developed by and remains the property of the University. Additionally, the company provides online support for students and faculty and has developed a process within the LMS to obtain other analytical data. Fees under the agreement are $50 per user per class for licensing rights to the product, including all enhancements, modifications, and new releases or modules. The agreement was executed March 9, 2015 and shall continue for five (5) years, which will automatically extend for an additional two (2) years unless terminated in accordance with the agreement. Total fees incurred during fiscal years 2017 and 2016 were $743,075 and $419,750 respectively.

BETHEL UNIVERSITY
NOTES TO FINANCIAL STATEMENTS
JULY 31, 2017 AND 2016

P. RELATED PARTY TRANSACTIONS - Continued

The University entered into a line-of-credit with a private company owned by a member of the Board of Trustees. Total outstanding balance as of July 31, 2017 was $2,000,000 (See Note E).

At various times throughout the fiscal year, the University transacts business with a related party as part of the normal business operations of the University.

The University entered into leasing arrangements with related parties as described in Note M.

Q. SUBSEQUENT EVENTS

The University has evaluated subsequent events through September 29, 2017, the issuance date of the University's financial statements, and has determined that there are no subsequent events requiring disclosure, except the subsequent payment of certain debt as disclosed in Note E, and those events discussed in the following paragraph. On August 1, 2017, the University entered into a loan agreement. The agreement provided for a line of credit facility with borrowings up to $700,000. On August 1, 2017, The University received an initial advance from the line of credit for the full amount. Interest will accrue on the unpaid principal balance at a rate of 5.00%. Interest and principal are due at maturity on November 1, 2017.

SUPPLEMENTARY INFORMATION

BETHEL UNIVERSITY
SUPPLEMENTARY INFORMATION
YEAR ENDED JULY 31, 2017

FINANCIAL RESPONSIBILITY COMPOSITE SCORE

As explained on the United States Department of Education's website (https://studentaid.ed.gov/sa/about/data-center/school/composite-scores),

Section 498(c) of the Higher Education Act of 1965, as amended, requires for-profit and non-profit institutions to annually submit audited financial statements to the Department to demonstrate they are maintaining the standards of financial responsibility necessary to participate in the Title IV programs. One of many standards, which the Department utilizes to gauge the financial responsibility of an institution, is a composite of three ratios derived from an institution's audited financial statements. The three ratios are a primary reserve ratio, an equity ratio, and a net income ratio. These ratios gauge the fundamental elements of the financial health of an institution, not the educational quality of an institution.

The composite score reflects the overall relative financial health of institutions along a scale from negative 1.0 to positive 3.0. A score greater than or equal to 1.5 indicates the institution is considered financially responsible.

Schools with scores of less than 1.5 but greater than or equal to 1.0 are considered financially responsible, but require additional oversight. These schools are subject to cash monitoring and other participation requirements.

For the fiscal years ended July 31, 2015, 2016, and 2017, management calculated the University's financial responsibility composite scores as follows:

BETHEL UNIVERSITY
SUPPLEMENTARY INFORMATION
YEAR ENDED JULY 31, 2017

FINANCIAL RESPONSIBILITY COMPOSITE SCORE - Continued

Ratios:		2015		2016		2017
Primary Reserve Ratio:	0.0207		0.0356		0.1147	
Expendable Net Assets		$ 1,312,554		$ 2,099,357		$ 6,651,413
Total Expense		$ 63,528,037		$ 58,903,145		$ 58,013,240
Equity Ratio:	0.3008		0.3571		0.3586	
Modified Net Assets		$ 24,914,811		$ 35,283,357		$ 35,731,286
Modified Assets		$ 82,834,615		$ 98,805,150		$ 99,637,666
Net Income Ratio:	0.0435		0.1549		0.0212	
Change in Unrestricted Net Assets		$ 2,891,998		$ 10,799,211		$ 1,258,387
Total Unrestricted Revenue		$ 66,420,035		$ 69,702,356		$ 59,271,627
Strength Factor Scores:						
Primary Reserve strength factor score	0.2066		0.3564		1.1465	
Equity strength factor score	1.8047		2.1426		2.1517	
Net Income strength factor score	3.0000		3.0000		2.0615	
Composite Score:						
Primary Reserve Weighted Score	0.0826		0.1426		0.4586	
Equity Weighted Score	0.7219		0.8570		0.8607	
Net Income Weighted Score	0.6000		0.6000		0.4123	
Total Composite Score (Rounded):		1.4		1.6		1.7

UNIVERSITY KEY FINANCIAL RATIOS

The financial health of the University can be evaluated through the use of ratios. The following ratios are customarily utilized by higher education institutions to measure financial condition. There are four fundamental financial questions addressed by analysis of four core ratios.

- Are resources sufficient and flexible enough to support the mission? - Primary Reserve Ratio
- Do operating results indicate the institution is living within available resources? - Net Operating Revenues Ratio
- Does asset performance and management support the strategic direction? - Return on Net Assets
- Are financial resources, including debt, managed strategically to advance the mission? - Viability Ratio

When combined, these four ratios deliver a single measure of the University's overall financial health, referred to as the Composite Financial Index. The following charts analyze the aforementioned ratios for the fiscal year ended July 31, 2015, 2016, and 2017:

BETHEL UNIVERSITY
SUPPLEMENTARY INFORMATION
YEAR ENDED JULY 31, 2017

UNIVERSITY KEY FINANCIAL RATIOS - Continued

Composite Financial Index

The Composite Financial Index (CFI) is calculated based upon the values of its four component ratios: 1) Primary Reserve, 2) Net Operating Revenue, 3) Return on Net Assets, and 4) Viability Ratio. Once each of the four ratios is calculated, further weighting is conducted to measure the relative strength of the score and its importance in the composite score. The CFI combines the four core ratios identified below into a single score. The combination, using a prescribed weighting plan, allows a weakness or strength in one ratio to be offset by another ratio result. The CFI reflects a picture of the financial health of the institution at a point in time.

COMPOSITE FINANCIAL INDEX (CFI)

FY15	FY16	FY17
1.1	3.0	0.7

Primary Reserve Ratio

The Primary Reserve Ratio is intended to address the question of sufficiency and flexibility for support of the mission. The ratio measures the financial strength of the University by comparing expendable net assets, which includes those assets the University can access and spend quickly to meet obligations, to total expenses at the end of every fiscal year. This ratio identifies the University's financial strength and flexibility by identifying how long the University can function by using reserves without the generation of any new net assets. A primary reserve ratio of .40 or 40% is advisable, implying that the university has the ability to cover over 4 ½ months of expenses. Key items that can impact this ratio include principal payments on debt, using net assets to fund capital construction projects, endowment returns, and total operating expenses. Although not reaching the benchmark, the University's ratio is trending in a positive direction.

PRIMARY RESERVE RATIO

FY15	FY16	FY17	EXPLANATION
$12,074,952	$22,874,163	$24,132,550	+ unrestricted net assets EOY
$ 2,252,644	$ 2,074,644	$ 838,973	+ temporarily restricted net assets EOY
$57,283,818	$74,163,753	$72,906,071	-- land, building, and equipment, net of depreciation EOY
$42,019,386	$49,314,303	$55,464,585	+ long-term debt EOY
$63,528,037	$58,903,145	$58,013,240	total expenses
-0.01	0.00	0.13	Ratio
-0.11	0.01	0.98	strength factor
0.0	0.0	0.3	weighted value

BETHEL UNIVERSITY
SUPPLEMENTARY INFORMATION
YEAR ENDED JULY 31, 2017

UNIVERSITY KEY FINANCIAL RATIOS - Continued

Net Operating Revenues Ratio

The Net Operating Revenues Ratio is intended to indicate if the University is living within its available resources. The University needs to generate some level of surplus over long periods of time because operations are one source for reinvestment in future initiatives. Short-term deficits may occur as a result of strategic decisions. It is when deficits are unplanned or unmanaged and occurring as a result of core operations that evaluation of operations is necessitated. A positive ratio indicates the University is in good financial condition. An organization should establish a target percentage, and establishing a benchmark should be in line with operating growth. A ratio of 2 to 4 percent indicates the University operated within its means and should be maintained over time; however, fluctuations from year to year are normal. A large ratio identifies an operating surplus and a stronger financial position. While a negative ratio indicates an operating loss for the year, universities need to be careful about too large of a positive ratio, indicating under spending on mission critical initiatives.

NET OPERATING REVENUES RATIO (%):
Using Change in Unrestricted Net Assets

FY15	FY16	FY17	EXPLANATION
$ 2,891,998	$10,799,211	$ 1,258,387	change in unrestricted net assets
$66,420,035	$69,702,356	$59,271,627	total unrestricted revenue
4.4	15.5	2.1	ratio
3.35	10.00	1.63	strength factor
0.3	1.0	0.2	weighted value

Return on Net Assets Ratio

The Return on Net Assets Ratio is intended to assess if the asset performance and management support the strategic direction. The ratio measures whether the University is financially better off than in the previous year by measuring total economic return or the level of change in total net assets. This ratio is the most comprehensive measure of growth or decline in wealth over time. There is not a specific threshold; however, 3 to 4 percent is a generally acceptable real rate of return. An improving trend in this ratio indicates the university is increasing its net assets and is likely to be in a position to set aside financial resources to strengthen its future financial flexibility. Key items that may impact this ratio include changes in the net operating revenue ratio, endowment returns, capital gifts and grants, capital transfers, and endowment gifts. This indicator can be greatly impacted when borrowing money for a capital project and when the capital item is added to Net Assets. Looking at the trend will even out the anomalies.

BETHEL UNIVERSITY
SUPPLEMENTARY INFORMATION
YEAR ENDED JULY 31, 2017

UNIVERSITY KEY FINANCIAL RATIOS - Continued

Return on Net Assets Ratio - Continued

RETURN ON NET ASSETS RATIO (%)

FY15	FY16	FY17	EXPLANATION
$ 1,924,274	$10,368,546	$ 447,929	change in net assets
$22,990,537	$24,914,811	$35,283,357	total net assets BOY
8.4	41.6	1.3	ratio
4.18	10.00	0.63	strength factor
0.8	2.0	0.1	weighted value

Viability Ratio

The Viability Ratio is intended to address the question of whether financial resources are being strategically managed to advance the mission of the University. It measures availability of expendable net assets for coverage of debt should the University be required to settle its obligations as of the date on the balance sheet. A 1:1 ratio is desired, indicating adequate net assets to meet obligations. This ratio is one of the most basic determinants of clear financial health and is regarded as governing the University's ability to assume new debt. A ratio of 1.25 or greater indicates a strong creditworthy University with sufficient resources to satisfy debt obligations; however, each university should identify the ratio that is right for its mission specific needs. A viability ratio that falls below 1:1 hinders the university's ability to respond to adverse condition, to secure external capital, and to have flexibility to fund new objectives. Key items that may impact this ratio include principal payments on debt, using net assets for capital construction projects, issuance of new debt, and endowment returns. Although not reaching the benchmark, the University's ratio is trending in a positive direction.

VIABILITY RATIO

FY15	FY16	FY17	EXPLANATION
$12,074,952	$22,874,163	$24,132,550	+ unrestricted net assets EOY
$ 2,252,644	$ 2,074,644	$ 838,973	+ temporarily restricted net assets EOY
$57,283,818	$74,163,753	$72,906,071	-- land, building, and equipment, net of depreciation EOY
$42,019,386	$49,314,303	$55,464,585	+ long-term debt EOY
$42,019,386	$49,314,303	$55,464,585	long-term debt EOY
-0.02	0.00	0.14	ratio
0.05	0.00	0.33	strength factor
0.0	0.0	0.1	weighted value

BETHEL UNIVERSITY
SUPPLEMENTARY INFORMATION
YEAR ENDED JULY 31, 2017

UNRESTRICTED NET ASSETS EXCLUSIVE OF PLANT, PROPERTY, EQUIPMENT, RELATED DEBT AND OBLIGATION UNDER FINANCING ARRANGEMENT

The Southern Association of School and Colleges, Commission on Colleges (SACSCOC), has various core requirements for meeting standards. One such standard is core requirement 2.11.1 requiring, among other things, the University to present a statement of financial position of unrestricted net assets, exclusive of plant assets and plant-related debt, which represents the change in unrestricted net assets attributable to operations. The chart below is provided to meet this SACSCOC requirement. Although the University's net unrestricted assets, excluding plant, property, equipment, and related debt is negative, the trend over the past three fiscal years is positive, indicating the University has taken measures to strengthen its financial stability.

**Statements of Financial Position of
Unrestricted Net Assets, Exclusive of Plant
Assets and Plant-Related Debt**

	July 31,		
Restatement of Net Assets without plant and plant-related debt	2017	2016	2015
Unrestricted Net Assets	$ 24,132,550	$ 22,874,163	$ 12,074,952
Less: property, plant, and equipment, net	(72,906,071)	(74,163,753)	(57,283,818)
Add: plant-related debt	48,464,433	49,499,301	36,624,268
URNA not including plant and debt	$ (309,088)	$ (1,790,289)	$ (8,584,598)

OTHER INFORMATION

BETHEL UNIVERSITY
SCHEDULE OF EXPENDITURES OF FEDERAL AWARDS
YEAR ENDED JULY 31, 2017

Federal Grantor/Pass-through Grantor/ Program or Cluster Title	Federal CFDA Number	Federal Expenditures
U.S. Department of Education - Direct Awards		
Student Financial Assistance - Cluster: (1)		
Federal Direct Student Loans Program (Note C)	84.268	$49,598,721
Federal Perkins Loan Program (Note B)	84.038	374,168
Federal Work-Study Program (Note D)	84.033	154,312
Federal Supplemental Educational		
Opportunity Grants Program (Note D)	84.007	329,784
Federal Pell Grant Program	84.063	11,706,632
Teacher Education Assistance for University and		
Higher Education Grant	84.379	63,338
Total Student Financial Assistance - Cluster		63,226,955
U.S. Department of Education - Pass-through		
Program from:		
Special Education: Grants to States		
Tennessee Teachers Assistants Grant	84.027A	30,500
Total U.S. Department of Education		63,257,455
U.S. Department of Homeland Security – Pass-through		
Program from:		
State Department of Military:		
Hazard Mitigation Grant (1) (Note D)	97.039	3
Total Expenditures of Federal Awards		$63,257,458

(1) Tested as a major program

See independent auditor's report.

BETHEL UNIVERSITY
NOTES TO SCHEDULE OF EXPENDITURES OF FEDERAL AWARDS
YEAR ENDED JULY 31, 2017

A. BASIS OF PRESENTATION

The accompanying schedule of expenditures of federal awards is presented in accordance with the requirements by Title 2 U.S. *Code of Federal* Regulations (CFR) Part 200, *Uniform Administrative Requirements, Cost Principles, and Audit Requirements for Federal Awards* (Uniform Guidance), on the accrual basis of accounting consistent with the basis of accounting used by the University in the preparation of its financial statements.

The University has elected not to use the 10-percent de minimis indirect cost rate allowed under the Uniform Guidance.

B. FEDERAL PERKINS LOAN PROGRAM - CFDA #84.038

The outstanding loan balance for the Federal Perkins Loan Program at July 31, 2017 was $157,823, net of the allowance for uncollectible loans of $216,345. Total loan disbursements for the program for the year ended July 31, 2017, were $8,500. Other disbursements include an expenditure for repayment of fund capital in the amount of $38,367.

C. FEDERAL DIRECT LOANS PROGRAM - CFDA #84.268

During the fiscal year ending July 31, 2017, the University processed $49,598,721 of new loans under the Federal Direct Loans program (which includes subsidized and unsubsidized Stafford Loans, Parents for Undergraduate Students, and Supplemental Loans for Students)

D. MATCHING FUNDS

The University provided matching funds of $155,433 for the Federal Supplemental Educational Opportunity Grants program during the fiscal year ended July 31, 2017. The University received a waiver from the U.S. Department of Education and elected not to provide matching funds for the Federal Work Study program during the fiscal year ended July 31, 2017.

Independent Auditor's Report on Internal Control Over
Financial Reporting and on Compliance and Other Matters
Based on an Audit of Financial Statements Performed in
Accordance with *Government Auditing Standards*

The Board of Trustees
Bethel University
McKenzie, Tennessee

We have audited, in accordance with the auditing standards generally accepted in the United States of America and the standards applicable to financial audits contained in *Government Auditing Standards* issued by the Comptroller General of the United States, the financial statements of Bethel University (the "University"), which comprise the statements of financial position as of July 31, 2017, and the related statements of activities and cash flows for the year then ended, and the related notes to the financial statements, and have issued our report thereon dated September 29, 2017.

Internal Control Over Financial Reporting

In planning and performing our audit of the financial statements, we considered the University's internal control over financial reporting (internal control) to determine the audit procedures that are appropriate in the circumstances for the purpose of expressing our opinion on the financial statements, but not for the purpose of expressing an opinion on the effectiveness of the University's internal control. Accordingly, we do not express an opinion on the effectiveness of the University's internal control.

A *deficiency in internal control* exists when the design or operation of a control does not allow management or employees, in the normal course of performing their assigned functions, to prevent, or detect and correct misstatements on a timely basis. A *material weakness* is a deficiency, or a combination of deficiencies, in internal control such that there is a reasonable possibility that a material misstatement of the entity's financial statements will not be prevented, or detected and corrected on a timely basis. A *significant deficiency* is a deficiency, or a combination of deficiencies, in internal control that is less severe than a material weakness, yet important enough to merit attention by those charged with governance.

The Board of Trustees
Bethel University

Our consideration of the internal control was for the limited purpose described in the first paragraph of this section and was not designed to identify all deficiencies in internal control that might be material weaknesses or significant deficiencies. Given these limitations, during our audit we did not identify any deficiencies in internal control that we consider to be material weaknesses. However, material weaknesses may exist that have not been identified.

Compliance and Other Matters

As part of obtaining reasonable assurance about whether the University's financial statements are free from material misstatement, we performed tests of its compliance with certain provisions of laws, regulations, contracts, and grant agreements, noncompliance with which could have a direct and material effect on the determination of financial statement amounts. However, providing an opinion on compliance with those provisions was not an objective of our audit, and accordingly, we do not express such an opinion. The results of our tests disclosed no instances of noncompliance or other matters that are required to be reported under *Government Auditing Standards*.

Purpose of this Report

The purpose of this report is solely to describe the scope of our testing of internal control and compliance and the results of that testing, and not to provide an opinion on the effectiveness of the University's internal control or on compliance. This report is an integral part of an audit performed in accordance with *Government Auditing Standards* in considering the University's internal control and compliance. Accordingly, this communication is not suitable for any other purpose.

Crosslin, PLLC

Nashville, Tennessee
September 29, 2017

Independent Auditor's Report on Compliance For Each Major
Programs and on Internal Control Over Compliance
Required by Uniform Guidance

The Board of Trustees
Bethel University
McKenzie, Tennessee

Report on Compliance for Each Major Federal Program

We have audited Bethel University's (the "University") compliance with the types of compliance requirements described in the *OMB Compliance Supplement* that could have a direct and material effect on the University's major federal programs for the year ended July 31, 2017. The University's major federal programs are identified in the summary of auditor's results section of the accompanying schedule of findings and questioned costs.

Management's Responsibility

Management is responsible for compliance with federal statutes, regulations, and the terms and conditions of its federal awards applicable to its federal programs.

Auditor's Responsibility

Our responsibility is to express an opinion on compliance for each of the University's major federal programs based on our audit of the types of compliance requirements referred to above. We conducted our audit of compliance in accordance with auditing standards generally accepted in the United States of America; the standards applicable to financial audits contained in *Government Auditing Standards*, issued by the Comptroller General of the United States; and the audit requirements of Title 2 U.S. *Code of Federal Regulations* (CFR) Part 200, *Uniform Administrative Requirements, Cost Principles, and Audit Requirements for Federal Awards* (Uniform Guidance). Those standards and the Uniform Guidance require that we plan and perform the audit to obtain reasonable assurance about whether noncompliance with the types of compliance requirements referred to above that could have a direct and material effect on a major federal program occurred. An audit includes examining, on a test basis, evidence about the University's compliance with those requirements and performing such other procedures as we considered necessary in the circumstances.

We believe that our audit provides a reasonable basis for our opinion on compliance for each major federal program. However, our audit does not provide a legal determination of the University's compliance.

The Board of Trustees
Bethel University

Opinion on Each Major Federal Program

In our opinion, the University complied, in all material respects, with the types of compliance requirements referred to above that could have a direct and material effect on each major federal program for the year ended July 31, 2017.

Report on Internal Control Over Compliance

Management of the University is responsible for establishing and maintaining effective internal control over compliance with the types of compliance requirements referred to above. In planning and performing our audit of compliance, we considered the University's internal control over compliance with the types of requirements that could have a direct and material effect on each major federal program to determine the auditing procedures that are appropriate in the circumstances for the purpose of expressing an opinion on compliance for each major federal program and to test and report on internal control over compliance in accordance with the Uniform Guidance, but not for the purpose of expressing an opinion on the effectiveness of internal control over compliance. Accordingly, we do not express an opinion on the effectiveness of the University's internal control over compliance.

A *deficiency in internal control over compliance* exists when the design or operation of a control over compliance does not allow management or employees, in the normal course of performing their assigned functions, to prevent, or detect and correct, noncompliance with a type of compliance requirement of a federal program on a timely basis. A *material weakness in internal control over compliance* is a deficiency, or combination of deficiencies, in internal control over compliance, such that there is a reasonable possibility that material noncompliance with a type of compliance requirement of a federal program will not be prevented, or detected and corrected, on a timely basis. A *significant deficiency in internal control over compliance* is a deficiency, or a combination of deficiencies, in internal control over compliance with a type of compliance requirement of a federal program that is less severe than a material weakness in internal control over compliance, yet important enough to merit attention by those charged with governance.

Our consideration of internal control over compliance was for the limited purpose described in the first paragraph of this section and was not designed to identify all deficiencies in internal control over compliance that might be material weaknesses or significant deficiencies. We did not identify any deficiencies in internal control over compliance that we consider to be material weaknesses. However, material weaknesses may exist that have not been identified.

The Board of Trustees
Bethel University

The purpose of this report on internal control over compliance is solely to describe the scope of our testing of internal control over compliance and the results of that testing based on the requirements of the Uniform Guidance. Accordingly, this report is not suitable for any other purpose.

Crosslin, PLLC

Nashville, Tennessee
September 29, 2017

BETHEL UNIVERSITY
SCHEDULE OF FINDINGS AND QUESTIONED COSTS
YEAR ENDED JULY 31, 2017

I. SUMMARY OF INDEPENDENT AUDITOR'S RESULTS

Financial Statements

Type of auditor's report issued: Unmodified

Internal control over financial reporting:

- Material weakness(es) identified? ___Yes _X_ No
- Significant deficiency(ies) identified? ___Yes _X_ None Reported

Noncompliance material to financial statements noted? ___Yes _X_ No

Federal Awards

Internal control over major program:

- Material weakness(es) identified? ___Yes _X_ No
- Significant deficiency(ies) identified? ___Yes _X_ None Noted

Type of auditor's report issued on compliance for major program: Unmodified

Any audit findings disclosed that are required to be reported in accordance with 2 CFR 200.516(a)? ___Yes _X_ No

BETHEL UNIVERSITY
SCHEDULE OF FINDINGS AND QUESTIONED COSTS
YEAR ENDED JULY 31, 2017

I. SUMMARY OF INDEPENDENT AUDITOR'S RESULTS - Continued

Major Programs:

CFDA Number	Name of Federal Program	Amount Expended
SFA Cluster:		
84.063	Federal Pell Grant Program	$11,706,632
84.268	Federal Direct Student Loans Program	49,598,721
84.038	Federal Perkins Loan Program	374,168
84.007	Federal Supplemental Educational Opportunity Grants Program	329,784
84.033	Federal Work-Study Program	154,312
84.038	Perkins Loans	374,168
84.379	TEACHER Education Assistance for College and Higher Education Grant	63,338

Dollar threshold used to distinguish between type A
and type B programs $1,898,078

Auditee qualified as low-risk auditee   X Yes ___ No

II. FINANCIAL STATEMENT FINDINGS

    A. Material Weakness in Internal Control

       None Reported.

    B. Compliance Findings

       None Reported.

III. FINDINGS AND QUESTIONED COSTS FOR FEDERAL AWARDS

    None Reported.

BETHEL UNIVERSITY
SCHEDULE OF PRIOR YEAR FINDINGS AND QUESTIONED COSTS
YEAR ENDED JULY 31, 2017

The University had no prior audit findings related to the testing of its federal award programs.

**CUMBERLAND PRESBYTERIAN
CHILDREN'S HOME**

FINANCIAL STATEMENTS
AND
AUDITORS' REPORT

DECEMBER 31, 2017

CUMBERLAND PRESBYTERIAN CHILDREN'S HOME

TABLE OF CONTENTS

	Page
Independent Auditors' Report	1
Statement of Financial Position	3
Statement of Activities	4
Statement of Cash Flows	5
Statement of Functional Expenses	6-7
Notes to the Financial Statements	8-14
Supplemental Information	
Schedule of Board of Stewardship Endowments	16-17

HANKINS, EASTUP, DEATON, TONN & SEAY
A PROFESSIONAL CORPORATION
CERTIFIED PUBLIC ACCOUNTANTS

Members:
AMERICAN INSTITUTE OF CERTIFIED PUBLIC ACCOUNTANTS
TEXAS SOCIETY OF CERTIFIED PUBLIC ACCOUNTANTS

902 NORTH LOCUST
P.O. BOX 977
DENTON, TX 76202-0977

TEL. (940) 387-8563
FAX (940) 383-4746

Independent Auditors' Report

Cumberland Presbyterian Children's Home
Denton, Texas

We have audited the accompanying financial statements of Cumberland Presbyterian Children's Home (a nonprofit organization), which comprise the statement of financial position as of December 31, 2017 and the related statements of activities and cash flows for the year then ended, and the related notes to the financial statements.

Management's Responsibility for the Financial Statements

Management is responsible for the preparation and fair presentation of these financial statements in accordance with accounting principles generally accepted in the United States of America; this includes the design, implementation, and maintenance of internal control relevant to the preparation and fair presentation of financial statements that are free from material misstatement, whether due to fraud or error.

Auditor's Responsibility

Our responsibility is to express an opinion on these financial statements based on our audit. We conducted our audit in accordance with auditing standards generally accepted in the United States of America. Those standards require that we plan and perform the audit to obtain reasonable assurance about whether the financial statements are free of material misstatement.

An audit involves performing procedures to obtain audit evidence about the amounts and disclosures in the financial statements. The procedures selected depend on the auditor's judgment, including the assessment of the risks of material misstatement of the financial statements, whether due to fraud or error. In making those risk assessments, the auditor considers internal control relevant to the entity's preparation and fair presentation of the financial statements in order to design audit procedures that are appropriate in the circumstances, but not for the purpose of expressing an opinion on the effectiveness of the entity's internal control. Accordingly, we express no such opinion. An audit also includes evaluating the appropriateness of accounting policies used and the reasonableness of significant accounting estimates made by management, as well as evaluating the overall presentation of the financial statements. We believe that the audit evidence we have obtained is sufficient and appropriate to provide a basis for our audit opinion.

Opinion

In our opinion, the financial statements referred to above present fairly, in all material respects, the financial position of Cumberland Presbyterian Children's Home as of December 31, 2017, and the changes in its net assets and its cash flows for the year then ended in accordance with accounting principles generally accepted in the United States of America.

Hankins, Eastup, Deaton, Tonn & Seay

Hankins, Eastup, Deaton, Tonn & Seay
Denton, Texas
June 8, 2018

CUMBERLAND PRESBYTERIAN CHILDREN'S HOME

STATEMENT OF FINANCIAL POSITION
DECEMBER 31, 2017

ASSETS:

Cash and cash equivalents	$ 254,264
Due from Board of Stewardship	71,269
Other receivables	60,904
Prepaid expenses	1,256
Land, buildings and equipment, net	3,541,703
Other long-term investments	9,192,787
TOTAL ASSETS	**$ 13,122,183**

LIABILITIES AND NET ASSETS:

Liabilities:	
Accounts payable	$ 24,080
Accrued liabilities	75,935
Line of credit - First United Bank	100,190
Total Liabilities	200,205
Net Assets:	
Unrestricted	7,250,175
Temporarily restricted	34,267
Permanently restricted	5,637,536
Total Net Assets	12,921,978
TOTAL LIABILITIES AND NET ASSETS	**$ 13,122,183**

See Accompanying Notes to the Financial Statements.

CUMBERLAND PRESBYTERIAN CHILDREN'S HOME

STATEMENT OF ACTIVITIES
FOR THE YEAR ENDED DECEMBER 31, 2017

	Unrestricted	Temporarily Restricted	Permanently Restricted	Total
Revenues, Gains and Other Support:				
Contributions and grants	$ 677,829	$ -	$ 28,297	$ 706,126
CPS revenue	634,578	-	-	634,578
Other program fees	70,241	-	-	70,241
Denominational support	68,939	-	-	68,939
Income on long-term investments	108,721	588	31,311	140,620
Unrealized gains on investments	365,686	5,245	507,345	878,276
Oil and gas royalties	3,701	-	-	3,701
Rents	44,172	-	-	44,172
Subtotal	1,973,867	5,833	566,953	2,546,653
Net assets released from Restrictions	769,479	-	(769,479)	-
Total Revenue, Gains and Other Support	2,743,346	5,833	(202,526)	2,546,653
Expenses:				
Program services:				
Children's residential program	962,586	-	-	962,586
Emergency shelter program	845,010	-	-	845,010
Single parent family program	214,780	-	-	214,780
Cumberland family services	337,855	-	-	337,855
Management and general	196,660	-	-	196,660
Fundraising	241,122	-	-	241,122
Total Expenses	2,798,013	-	-	2,798,013
Change in net assets	(54,667)	5,833	(202,526)	(251,360)
Net assets at beginning of year	7,304,842	28,434	5,840,062	13,173,338
Net assets at end of year	$ 7,250,175	$ 34,267	$ 5,637,536	$12,921,978

See Accompanying Notes to the Financial Statements.

CUMBERLAND PRESBYTERIAN CHILDREN'S HOME

STATEMENT OF CASH FLOWS
FOR THE YEAR ENDED DECEMBER 31, 2017

Cash Flows from Operating Activities:	
Change in net assets	$ (251,360)
Adjustments to reconcile change in net assets to net cash provided by operating activities:	
Depreciation	197,904
(Increase) Decrease in receivables	28,918
(Increase) Decrease in prepaid expenses	2,461
Increase (Decrease) in accounts payable/accrued liabilities	(69,514)
Unrealized losses (gains) on investments	(878,276)
Contributions restricted for long-term investment	(28,297)
Net Cash Provided (Used) by Operating Activities	(998,164)
Cash Flows from Investing Activities:	
Purchase of fixed assets	(24,702)
Investment withdrawals	903,404
Net Cash Provided by Investing Activities	878,702
Cash Flows from Financing Activities:	
Line of credit proceeds	565,891
Payments on line of credit	(465,701)
Proceeds from contributions restricted for investment in endowment	28,297
Net Cash Provided by Financing Activities	128,487
Net Increase in Cash and Cash Equivalents	9,025
Cash and Cash Equivalents at Beginning of Year	245,239
Cash and Cash Equivalents at End of Year	$ 254,264
Supplemental Data:	
Interest paid during the year	$ 4,619

See Accompanyin Notes to the Financial Statements.

CUMBERLAND PRESBYTERIAN CHILDREN'S HOME

STATEMENT OF FUNCTIONAL EXPENSES
FOR THE YEAR ENDED DECEMBER 31, 2017

	Program Services				
	Children's Residential Program	Emergency Shelter Program	Single Parent Family Program	Cumberland Family Services	Total
Salaries and Wages	$ 430,405	$ 460,961	$ 118,690	$ 211,519	$ 1,221,575
Employee Benefits	54,744	58,630	15,096	26,904	155,374
Payroll Taxes	35,487	38,006	9,786	17,440	100,719
Total Salaries and Related Expenses	520,636	557,597	143,572	255,863	1,477,668
Activities and travel	21,496	12,956	2,208	4,458	41,118
Clothing and supplies	18,601	17,500	67	6,753	42,921
Food and dining out	79,115	17,756	2,532	357	99,760
Training and education	25,299	10,878	1,310	3,647	41,134
Medical and dental	989	4,172	7,243	-	12,404
Other program expenses	-	-	-	1,698	1,698
Utilities	58,218	44,018	11,359	12,779	126,374
Property, liability insurance	33,374	25,235	6,512	7,324	72,445
Repairs and maintenance	66,233	50,078	12,923	14,540	143,774
Supplies, postage, printing	13,505	10,215	2,637	2,968	29,325
Computer software, maintenance	10,174	7,693	1,986	2,233	22,086
Permits and fees	880	665	172	193	1,910
Special events expense	-	-	-	-	-
Vehicle expenses	4,400	3,328	859	967	9,554
General assembly	-	-	-	-	-
Professional fees	20,376	15,406	3,977	4,473	44,232
Contract labor	8,149	6,163	1,591	1,790	17,693
Public relations/communications	-	-	-	-	-
Investment management fees	-	-	-	-	-
Board expense	-	-	-	-	-
Interest	-	-	-	-	-
Total Expenses Before Depreciation	881,445	783,660	198,948	320,043	2,184,096
Depreciation	81,141	61,350	15,832	17,812	176,135
TOTAL EXPENSES	$ 962,586	$ 845,010	$ 214,780	$ 337,855	$ 2,360,231

The accompanying notes are an integral part of this statement.

	Supporting Services			
Fundraising	Administration	Total		Total Expenses
$ 90,216	$ 106,275	$ 196,491		$ 1,418,066
11,475	13,517	24,992		180,366
7,438	8,762	16,200		116,919
109,129	128,554	237,683		1,715,351
5,752	-	5,752		46,870
-	-	-		42,921
736	10,183	10,919		110,679
-	20,459	20,459		61,593
-	-	-		12,404
-	-	-		1,698
7,100	8,521	15,621		141,995
4,069	4,884	8,953		81,398
8,077	9,695	17,772		161,546
30,886	1,971	32,857		62,182
1,240	1,491	2,731		24,817
107	128	235		2,145
3,990	-	3,990		3,990
537	642	1,179		10,733
-	591	591		591
2,487	2,984	5,471		49,703
995	1,189	2,184		19,877
11,660	-	11,660		11,660
-	25,109	25,109		25,109
-	8,228	8,228		8,228
-	4,619	4,619		4,619
186,765	229,248	416,013		2,600,109
9,895	11,874	21,769		197,904
$ 196,660	$ 241,122	$ 437,782		$ 2,798,013

CUMBERLAND PRESBYTERIAN CHILDREN'S HOME

NOTES TO FINANCIAL STATEMENTS
DECEMBER 31, 2017

NOTE A - SUMMARY OF SIGNIFICANT ACCOUNTING POLICIES

Organization

Cumberland Presbyterian Children's Home (CPCH) is a nonprofit organization originally chartered in Kentucky in 1904 and moved to Denton, Texas in 1932. Its purpose is to provide long-term residential basic child care for children between the ages of 3 and 17. CPCH is licensed to care for up to 40 children. CPCH's primary sources of revenue are income from child care, donations and income from long-term investments.

Basis of Presentation

The accompanying financial statements have been prepared on the accrual basis of accounting in accordance with accounting principles generally accepted in the United States of America. Net assets and revenues, expenses, gains, and losses are classified based on the existence or absence of donor-imposed restrictions. Accordingly, net assets of CPCH and changes therein are classified and reported as follows:

Unrestricted Net Assets – not subject to donor-imposed restrictions. Unrestricted net assets may be designated for specific purposes by action of the Board of Directors.

Temporarily Restricted Net Assets – subject to donor-imposed stipulations that may be fulfilled by actions of CPCH to meet the stipulations or that become unrestricted at the date specified by the donor.

Permanently Restricted Net Assets – subject to donor-imposed stipulations that they be retained and invested permanently by CPCH to use all or part of the investment return on these net assets for specified or unspecified purposes.

Income Taxes

CPCH is exempt from Federal income taxes under Section 501(c)(3) of the Internal Revenue Code. In addition, CPCH has been determined by the Internal Revenue Service not to be a private foundation within the meaning of Section 509(a)(1) and 170 (b)(1)(A)(vi) of the Code.

Fixed Assets

All acquisitions of property and equipment in excess of $5,000 and all expenditures for repairs, maintenance, or improvements that significantly prolong the useful lives of the assets are capitalized. Prior to 1/1/13 CPCH used an acquisition cost threshold of $1,000 but increased the threshold to $5,000 at that date in order to reduce the administrative costs of recording and tracking items of furniture and equipment. Purchases of property and equipment are recorded at cost. Donations of property and equipment are recorded as support at their estimated fair value at the date of gift. Such donations are reported as unrestricted support unless the donor has restricted the donated asset to a specific purpose. Assets donated with explicit restrictions regarding their use and contributions of cash that must be used to acquire property and equipment are reported as restricted support. Absent donor stipulations regarding how long those donated assets must be maintained, CPCH reports expirations of donor restrictions when the donated or acquired assets are placed in service as instructed by the donor. CPCH reclassifies temporarily restricted net assets to unrestricted net assets at that time. Property and equipment are depreciated using the straight-line method over the estimated useful life of assets.

CUMBERLAND PRESBYTERIAN CHILDREN'S HOME

NOTES TO FINANCIAL STATEMENTS
DECEMBER 31, 2017

The class lives of the more significant items within each property classification are as follows:

Vehicles	5 years
Equipment	5 to 10 years
Furniture and fixtures	5 to 10 years
Buildings	20 to 40 years

Investment Securities

Investments in marketable securities with readily determinable fair values and all investments in debt securities are valued at their fair values in the statement of financial position. Unrealized gains and losses are included in the change in net assets.

Estimates

The preparation of financial statements in conformity with generally accepted accounting principles requires management to make estimates and assumptions that affect the reported amounts of assets and liabilities at the date of the financial statements and the reported amounts of revenues and expenses during the reporting period. Accordingly, actual results could differ from those estimates.

FASB 116 and 117

In accordance with Statement of Financial Accounting Standards ("SFAS") No. 116, *Accounting for Contributions Received and Contributions Made*, contributions received are recorded as unrestricted, temporarily restricted, or permanently restricted support depending on the existence and/or nature of donor restrictions. CPCH reports gifts of cash and other assets as restricted support if they are received with donor stipulations that limit the use of the donated assets. When a donor restriction expires, that is, when a stipulated time restriction ends or purpose restriction is accomplished, temporarily restricted net assets are reclassified to unrestricted net assets and reported in the statement of activities as net assets released from restrictions. Contributions that are restricted by the donor are reported as increases in unrestricted net assets if the restrictions expire in the fiscal year in which the contributions are recognized.

Unconditional promises to give are recorded as revenue when received. Unconditional promises to give that are due within one year are recorded at the face amount of the commitment. Unconditional promises to give that are due beyond one year are not reflected at the face amount of the commitment, but when material are discounted to a present value, or net realizable value, using a 3% discount rate. Unconditional promises to give that are determined to be uncollectible are written off as an expense at that time. At December 31, 2017, CPCH had no outstanding unconditional promises to give.

CPCH reports gifts of land, buildings, and equipment as unrestricted support unless explicit donor stipulations specify how the donated assets must be used. Gifts of long-lived assets with explicit restrictions that specify how the assets are to be used and gifts of cash or other assets that must be used to acquire long-lived assets are reported as restricted support. Absent explicit donor stipulations about how long those long-lived assets must be maintained, CPCH reports expirations of donor restrictions when the donated or acquired long-lived assets are placed in service.

CUMBERLAND PRESBYTERIAN CHILDREN'S HOME

NOTES TO FINANCIAL STATEMENTS
DECEMBER 31, 2017

Contributed Services and Materials

In addition to receiving cash contributions, CPCH occasionally receives in-kind contributions from various donors. It is the policy of CPCH to record the estimated fair market value of certain in-kind donations as an asset or expense in its financial statements, and similarly increase donations by a like amount.

A substantial number of volunteers have donated significant amounts of time to CPCH's programs and supporting services. Contributions of donated services that create or enhance non-financial assets or that require specialized skills, are provided by individuals possessing these skills, and would typically need to be purchased if not provided by donation, are recorded at their fair values in the period received. For the year ended December 31, 2017, there were no amounts recorded for contributed services and materials.

Cash and Cash Equivalents

For purposes of the statement of cash flows, CPCH considers all highly liquid investments with a maturity of three months or less to be cash equivalents.

NOTE B – INVESTMENTS

Investments in equity securities with readily determinable fair values and all investments in debt securities are measured at fair value. All non cash contributions are recorded at fair value at the date of receipt. Stock is recorded at the average of the high and low selling price on the date received. Investments sold are recorded at amount received on the trade date.

Investment income and realized gains and losses are reported as increases in unrestricted net assets unless the donor placed restrictions on the income's use. The change in fair value between years along with realized gains or losses are reflected in the statement of activities in the year of the change.

Some investments are held and managed by the Board of Stewardship, Finance and Benefits of the Cumberland Presbyterian Church, while other investments are held in an investment brokerage account in the name of CPCH, and are managed by investment managers of the brokerage firm. No single investment exceeds five percent of CPCH's net assets.

NOTE C – ENDOWMENTS

CPCH's endowments consist of 88 individual donor-restricted funds established by individual donors for a variety of purposes. Net assets associated with endowments are classified and reported based on the existence or absence of donor-imposed restrictions.

A reconciliation of the beginning and ending balances of endowment funds is as follows:

	Permanently Restricted
Balance, 12/31/16	$ 5,013,906
Contributions	28,297
Earnings	31,311
Investment gains	521,390
Distributions	(768,257)
Balance, 12/31/17	$ 4,826,647

CUMBERLAND PRESBYTERIAN CHILDREN'S HOME

NOTES TO FINANCIAL STATEMENTS
DECEMBER 31, 2017

Funds with Deficiencies

From time to time, the fair value of assets associated with individual donor restricted endowment funds may fall below the level that the donor requires CPCH to retain as a fund of perpetual duration. CPCH did not have any net deficiencies of this nature as of December 31, 2017.

Return Objectives and Risk Parameters

CPCH has adopted investment and spending policies for endowment assets that attempt to provide a predictable stream of funding to programs supported by its endowment while seeking to maintain the purchasing power of the endowment assets. Under this policy, as approved by the board of trustees, the endowment assets are invested in equity securities, fixed-income securities and short-term reserves with asset allocation within defined acceptable ranges, while assuming a moderate level of investment risk. CPCH expects its endowment funds, over time, to provide an average rate of return sufficient to provide operating funds as needed. Actual returns in any given year may vary from this amount.

Strategies Employed for Achieving Objectives

To satisfy its long-term rate-of-return objectives, CPCH relies on a total return strategy in which investment returns are achieved through both capital appreciation (realized and unrealized) and current yield (interest and dividends). CPCH targets a diversified asset allocation that places a greater emphasis on equity-based investments to achieve its long-term return objectives within prudent risk constraints.

Spending Policy and How the Investment Objectives Relate to Spending Policy

CPCH has no written spending policy that commits it to annual distributions from any of the endowment's fund balances. CPCH normally appropriates for distribution each year sufficient earnings needed to fund its operating budget. Accordingly, over the long term, CPCH expects the current spending policy to allow its endowment to continue to grow. This is consistent with CPCH's objective to maintain the purchasing power of the endowment assets held in perpetuity or for a specified term as well as to provide additional real growth through new gifts and investment return.

NOTE D – FAIR VALUE OF FINANCIAL INSTRUMENTS

CPCH's financial instruments, none of which are held for trading purposes, include cash, securities and receivables. CPCH has estimated fair value of financial instruments in accordance with requirements of SFAS No. 157. The estimated fair value amounts have been determined by CPCH, using available market information and appropriate valuation methodologies. However, considerable judgment is necessarily required in interpreting market data to develop the estimates of fair value. Accordingly, the estimates presented herein are not necessarily indicative of the amounts that CPCH could realize in a current market exchange. The use of different market assumptions and estimation methodologies may have a material effect on the estimated fair value amounts. The carrying amount of cash and cash equivalents, and receivables approximated fair market value at December 31, 2017 because of their relatively short maturity and market terms. The fair value of long term investments at December 31, 2017 is determined based on quoted market values for U.S. government securities, fixed income securities and equity securities.

CUMBERLAND PRESBYTERIAN CHILDREN'S HOME

NOTES TO FINANCIAL STATEMENTS
DECEMBER 31, 2017

NOTE D – FAIR VALUE OF FINANCIAL INSTRUMENTS (CONT'D)

Financial instruments are considered Level 1 when their values are determined using quoted prices in active markets for identical assets that the reporting entity has the ability to access at the measurement date. Level 2 inputs are inputs other than quoted prices included within Level 1, such as quoted prices for similar assets in active or inactive markets, inputs other than quoted prices that are observable for the asset, or inputs that are derived principally from or corroborated by observable market data by correlation or other means.

Financial instruments are considered Level 3 when their values are determined using pricing models, discounted cash flow methodologies or similar techniques and at least one significant model assumption or input is unobservable. Level 3 financial instruments also include those for which the determination of fair value requires significant management judgment or estimation.

In accordance with these definitions, the following table represents CPCH's fair value hierarchy for its investments measured at fair value as of December 31, 2017:

	Quoted Prices for Active Markets for Identical Assets (Level 1)	Significant Other Observable Inputs (Level 2)	Total
Equity securities	$ 7,299,433	$ -	$ 7,299,433
Fixed income securities	-	1,641,363	1,641,363
Certificate of deposit	-	251,991	251,991
Total	$ 7,299,433	$ 1,893,354	$ 9,192,787

The estimated fair value of investments was determined by CPCH in accordance with its investment policy. Estimated fair value is determined by CPCH based on a number of factors, including: comparable publicly traded securities, the costs of investments to CPCH, as well as the current and projected operating performance. Changes in unrealized appreciation or depreciation of the investments are recognized as unrealized gains and losses in the statement of activities. Because of the inherent uncertainty of these valuations, the estimated values may differ from the actual fair values that may or may not be ultimately realized.

NOTE E - LAND, BUILDINGS AND EQUIPMENT

Land, buildings and equipment at December 31, 2017 consist of the following:

	Cost	Accumulated Depreciation	Book Value
Land	$ 23,477		$ 23,477
Buildings	5,870,217	$ 2,717,162	3,153,055
Campus infrastructure	583,513	282,885	300,628
Furniture & equipment	346,640	327,842	18,798
Vehicles	196,463	150,718	45,745
Total	$ 7,020,310	$ 3,478,607	$ 3,541,703

CUMBERLAND PRESBYTERIAN CHILDREN'S HOME

NOTES TO FINANCIAL STATEMENTS
DECEMBER 31, 2017

NOTE F - TEMPORARILY RESTRICTED NET ASSETS

Temporarily restricted net assets are available for the following purposes or periods:

Lena Hart Educational Fund	$ 4,703
Humphrey Scholarship Endowment	1,557
Walker Trimble Scholarship Fund	3,276
David Long Memorial Fund	431
Sybil V. Cockerham College Fund	1,627
Eleanor Sargeant Endowment	933
For periods after December 31, 2017 - term endowment to be received in a future year – Naomi Locke Trust	21,740
Total	$ 34,267

NOTE G - OTHER LONG-TERM INVESTMENTS

	Total	Unrestricted	Temporarily Restricted	Permanently Restricted
Endowments held by the Board of Stewardship	$ 4,769,879	$ -	$ -	$ 4,769,879
Certificates of deposit – First United Bank	251,991	251,991		
Mutual funds held by First National Bank – Virginia Ekiss Trust	365,529	-	-	365,529
Mutual funds held by Regions Bank – Laura Harpole Trust	110,800	-	-	110,800
Mutual funds held by Fairfield Natl. Bank - Naomi Locke Trust	21,740	-	21,740	-
Funds held at J P Morgan:				
Lena Hart Educational Fund	7,203	-	4,703	2,500
Humphrey Scholarship Endowment	5,038	-	1,557	3,481
Walker Trimble Scholarship Fund	11,556	-	3,276	8,280
David Long Memorial Fund	1,431	-	431	1,000
Sybil V. Cockerham College Fund	3,627	-	1,627	2,000
Eleanor Sargeant Endowment	3,513	-	933	2,580
Operating Reserve	3,303,703	3,303,703	-	-
Funds held at Charles Schwab:				
Operating Reserve	2,217	2,217	-	-
4,000 shares Exxon-Mobil held by CPCH - Jessie DiCarlo Endowment	334,560	-	-	334,560
Total	$ 9,192,787	$ 3,557,911	$ 34,267	$ 5,600,609

CUMBERLAND PRESBYTERIAN CHILDREN'S HOME

NOTES TO FINANCIAL STATEMENTS
DECEMBER 31, 2017

NOTE H - PERMANENTLY RESTRICTED NET ASSETS

Permanently restricted net assets are restricted as follows:

Investments in perpetuity, the income from which is expendable to support any activities of CPCH	$ 5,637,536
Total	$ 5,637,536

NOTE I – SUBSEQUENT EVENTS

Management evaluates subsequent events through the date of the report, which is the date the financial statements were available to be issued.

NOTE J – COMPONENTS OF INVESTMENT RETURN

Investment return for the year ended December 31, 2017, including interest and dividends on investments and interest earned on cash balances is summarized as follows:

Unrestricted investment return:	
Interest and dividend income:	
JP Morgan investments	$ 81,612
Exxon Mobil stock investment	12,240
Other	14,869
Unrealized gains on investments	365,686
Total unrestricted investment return	474,407
Restricted investment return:	
Interest income:	
Board of Stewardship investments	31,311
Other	588
Unrealized gains on investments	512,590
Total restricted investment return	544,489
Less investment management fees	(25,109)
Total Investment Return	$ 993,787

NOTE K – BANK LINE OF CREDIT

From time to time CPCH draws on a $200,000 line of credit established at First United Bank of Texas for working capital purposes. A total of $565,891 was borrowed and repaid on the line of credit during 2017, with $100,190 owed at the end of the year. Total interest paid during 2017 on the line of credit was $4,619.

SUPPLEMENTAL SCHEDULE

CUMBERLAND PRESBYTERIAN CHILDREN'S HOME

SCHEDULE OF BOARD OF STEWARDSHIP ENDOWMENTS
DECEMBER 31, 2017

Donor-established Endowments:

	Balance
Merlyn & Joann Kitterman Alexander	$ 983
W.A. and Elizabeth Bearden Trust	11,190
Grace Johnson Beasley Memorial Endowment	26,054
Bethlehem CPC Memorial Endowment	4,258
Bridges Scholarship Fund	29,409
J.T. and Dorothy Britt Trust	7,879
Children's Home Endowment	227,295
Lavenia Campbell Cole Trust 20%	14,332
Lavenia Campbell Cole Annuity Endowment	58,204
Lavenia Cole Testamentary Trust 25%	471,703
Mrs. A.L. Colvin Memorial Fund	1,210
John W. and Eva Cox Trust Fund	21,814
Steve Curry Trust	382,922
Daniel Class, First Cumberland Presbyterian Church	22,528
Donnie Curry Davis Memorial	131,031
Mary Elberta Davis Memorial	14,067
Fred and Mattie Mae Dwiggins Memorial Trust	56,482
J.S. Eustis Memorial Trust Fund	8,917
Clester H. Evans, Sr., Trust	14,888
John M. Friedel Trust	15,400
Joyce C. Frisby Memorial Endowment	19,845
Vaughn and Mary Elizabeth Fults Trust	14,205
Garner-Miller Memorial Trust	8,764
James C. and Freda M. Gilbert Endowment	81,773
Henry and Jayne Glaspy Memorial Fund	5,813
Rev. W.J. Gregory Memorial	73,070
Glenn Griffin Endowment	31,151
Rev. and Mrs. Henry M. Guynn Memorial	3,237
Chad Harper Endowment	13,644
Newsome and Imogene Harvey Endowment	1,787
Clarence & Lula Herring Endowment	4,253
Kenneth and Clara Holsopple Trust	37,652
George and Lottie M. Hutchins Trust	800,755
Norma K. Johnson Memorial Library	8,036
P.F. Johnson Memorial Endowment	13,340
Robert and Genevie Johnson Endowment	3,894
Mr. and Mrs. Robert L. Johnson	8,406
Violet Louise Jolly Endowment	849
Eulava Joyce Memorial Trust	7,014
Ruth Cypert and Harlie Klugler Memorial Fund	14,125
Blanche R. Lake Endowment	10,179
Wade P. Lane/Maude Dorough Memorial Trust	6,700
Adolphus M. Latta Memorial Trust	36,151
Mr. and Mrs. Robert F. Little Endowment Fund	25,526
Charles E. and Addie Mae Lloyd Endowment Fund	15,923
Tony and Ann Martin Endowment	2,878
Mrs. Lucille (Lucy) Mast Endowment	2,926

CUMBERLAND PRESBYTERIAN CHILDREN'S HOME

SCHEDULE OF BOARD OF STEWARDSHIP ENDOWMENTS (CONT'D)
DECEMBER 31, 2017

Donor-established Endowments:

	Balance
W.B. and Azales McClurkan, Sr. Memorial	$ 13,614
Williams J. McCall Memorial Trust	7,014
McEwen Church Trust	5,388
McKinley and Barnett Families Endowment	600,477
J.C. McKinley Endowment	13,282
Velma McKinley Trust	13,282
Mary McKnight Memorial Trust	7,974
Kenneth and Mae Moore Endowment Fund	4,959
Operational Trust Fund	104,340
Bert and Pat Owen Endowment	1,103
Hamilton & Merion Parks Family Trust #3	13,345
Joe Parr Trust Fund	55,137
Martha Sue Parr Endowment	1,126
Mary M. Poole Endowment Fund	674,583
Jack and Mary Proctor Memorial Trust Fund	44,977
SQ&K Maurine Proctor Trust	3,984
Mary Acena Prewitt Trust Fund	63,584
Rev. and Mrs. Joe Reed Memorial	3,289
Marguerite D. Richards Endowment	17,914
Agnes Durbin Richardson Trust	21,249
Pat N. & Essie H. Roberts Memorial	41,475
Frances Benefield Roberts Trust Fund	1,643
Rev. and Mrs. John A. Russell Memorial	3,207
John Ann and Mary Shimer	10,558
Rev. W.B. and Lydia Snipes Memorial Trust	22,788
Don M. & Nancy Tabor Endowment Trust	24,271
Townsend Trust Fund	27,070
Hattie A. Wheeless Fund	13,925
Whitfield Family Endowment	8,490
Porter and Hattie S. Williamson Memorial Trust	120,778
Helen Wynn Endowment Fund	12,634
Maxie and Will Young Memorial Endowment	14,620
Dixie Campbell Zinn Memorial Trust	4,395
Dr. John P. Austin Endowment	20,142
Total	$ 4,769,879

**Memphis Theological Seminary
of the Cumberland Presbyterian Church
Financial Statements
July 31, 2017 and 2016**

MEMPHIS THEOLOGICAL SEMINARY OF THE CUMBERLAND PRESBYTERIAN CHURCH

Table of Contents — *July 31, 2017 and 2016*

	Page
Independent Auditor's Report	3
Financial Statements	
Statements of Financial Position	5
Statement of Activities	6
Statement of Functional Expenses	7
Statements of Cash Flows	8
Notes to the Financial Statements	9
Supplementary Information	
Schedule of Expenditures of Federal Awards	19
Non-Financial Section	
Independent Auditor's Report on Internal Control over Financial Reporting and on Compliance and Other Matters Based on an Audit of Financial Statements Performed in Accordance with *Government Auditing Standards*	21
Independent Auditor's Report on Compliance for a Major Program and on Internal Control over Compliance Required by the Uniform Guidance	23
Schedule of Findings and Questioned Costs	25
Summary Schedule of Prior Audit Findings	26

INDEPENDENT AUDITOR'S REPORT

To the Board of Trustees
Memphis Theological Seminary of the Cumberland Presbyterian Church
Memphis, Tennessee

Report on the Financial Statements

We have audited the accompanying financial statements of Memphis Theological Seminary of the Cumberland Presbyterian Church (a nonprofit organization), which comprise the statement of financial position as of July 31, 2017, and the related statements of activities, functional expenses, and cash flows for the year then ended, and the related notes to the financial statements.

Management's Responsibility for the Financial Statements

Management is responsible for the preparation and fair presentation of these financial statements in accordance with accounting principles generally accepted in the United States of America; this includes the design, implementation, and maintenance of internal control relevant to the preparation and fair presentation of financial statements that are free from material misstatement, whether due to fraud or error.

Auditor's Responsibility

Our responsibility is to express an opinion on these financial statements based on our audit. We conducted our audit in accordance with auditing standards generally accepted in the United States of America and the standards applicable to financial audits contained in *Government Auditing Standards*, issued by the Comptroller General of the United States. Those standards require that we plan and perform the audit to obtain reasonable assurance about whether the financial statements are free from material misstatement.

An audit involves performing procedures to obtain audit evidence about the amounts and disclosures in the financial statements. The procedures selected depend on the auditor's judgment, including the assessment of the risks of material misstatement of the financial statements, whether due to fraud or error. In making those risk assessments, the auditor considers internal control relevant to the entity's preparation and fair presentation of the financial statements in order to design audit procedures that are appropriate in the circumstances, but not for the purpose of expressing an opinion on the effectiveness of the entity's internal control. Accordingly, we express no such opinion. An audit also includes evaluating the appropriateness of accounting policies used and the reasonableness of significant accounting estimates made by management, as well as evaluating the overall presentation of the financial statements.

We believe that the audit evidence we have obtained is sufficient and appropriate to provide a basis for our audit opinion.

Opinion

In our opinion, the financial statements referred to above present fairly, in all material respects, the financial position of Memphis Theological Seminary of the Cumberland Presbyterian Church as of July 31, 2017, and the changes in its net assets and its cash flows for the year then ended in accordance with accounting principles generally accepted in the United States of America.

Other Matters

Other Information

Our audit was conducted for the purpose of forming an opinion on the financial statements as a whole. The accompanying schedule of expenditures of federal awards, as required by Title 2 U.S. *Code of Federal Regulations* (CFR) Part 200, *Uniform Administrative Requirements, Cost Principles*, and *Audit Requirements for Federal Awards*, is presented for purposes of additional analysis and is not a required part of the financial statements. Such information is the responsibility of management and was derived from and relates directly to the underlying accounting and other records used to prepare the financial statements. The information has been subjected to the auditing procedures applied in the audit of the financial statements and certain additional procedures, including comparing and reconciling such information directly to the underlying accounting and other records used to prepare the financial statements or to the financial statements themselves, and other additional procedures in accordance with auditing standards generally accepted in the United States of America. In our opinion, the information is fairly stated, in all material respects, in relation to the financial statements as a whole.

Other Reporting Required by *Government Auditing Standards*

In accordance with *Government Auditing Standards*, we have also issued our report dated November 8, 2017, on our consideration of Memphis Theological Seminary of the Cumberland Presbyterian Church's internal control over financial reporting and on our tests of its compliance with certain provisions of laws, regulations, contracts, and grant agreements and other matters. The purpose of that report is to describe the scope of our testing of internal control over financial reporting and compliance and the results of that testing, and not to provide an opinion on internal control over financial reporting or on compliance. That report is an integral part of an audit performed in accordance with *Government Auditing Standards* in considering Memphis Theological Seminary of the Cumberland Presbyterian Church's internal control over financial reporting and compliance.

Report on Summarized Comparative Information

We have previously audited Memphis Theological Seminary of the Cumberland Presbyterian Church's 2016 financial statements, and we expressed an unmodified audit opinion on those audited financial statements in our report dated November 15, 2016. In our opinion, the summarized comparative information presented herein as of and for the year ended July 31, 2016, is consistent, in all material respects, with the audited financial statements from which it has been derived.

Cannon Wright Blount PLLC

Memphis, Tennessee
November 8, 2017

MEMPHIS THEOLOGICAL SEMINARY OF THE CUMBERLAND PRESBYTERIAN CHURCH

Statements of Financial Position — *July 31, 2017 and 2016*

ASSETS

	2017	2016
Cash and cash equivalents	$ 2,442,549	$ 417,767
Investments, at fair value	11,202,716	10,272,557
Tuition and fees receivable, net of allowance of $89,146 in 2017 and $80,448 in 2016	50,000	125,517
Pledges receivable, net of discounts on pledges	460,261	715,178
Other receivables	159,164	242,364
Capital assets, net of accumulated depreciation	3,124,753	3,153,924
Cash value of life insurance	31,970	36,692
Land held for sale	27,448	27,448
Other assets	38,763	43,437
Total assets	$ 17,537,624	$ 15,034,884

LIABILITIES AND NET ASSETS

	2017	2016
Liabilities		
Accounts payable and accrued expenses	$ 375,061	$ 303,359
Line of credit	910,000	100,000
Note payable	1,588,012	1,647,333
Total liabilities	2,873,073	2,050,692
Net Assets		
Unrestricted		
Board designated	125,290	74,114
Other unrestricted	2,378,689	2,965,501
Temporarily restricted	5,413,312	3,247,881
Permanently restricted	6,747,260	6,696,696
Total net assets	14,664,551	12,984,192
Total liabilities and net assets	$ 17,537,624	$ 15,034,884

See independent auditor's report and notes to the financial statements

MEMPHIS THEOLOGICAL SEMINARY OF THE CUMBERLAND PRESBYTERIAN CHURCH

Statement of Activities

For the Year Ended July 31, 2017
(with summarized comparative totals for the year ended July 31, 2016)

	Unrestricted	Temporarily Restricted	Permanently Restricted	2017 Total	2016 Total
Operating Revenues and Support					
Tuition and fees, net of scholarships of $420,331 and $472,805	$ 1,718,815	$ -	$ -	$ 1,718,815	$ 1,862,835
Contributions and grants	637,066	2,250,869	118,579	3,006,514	2,093,891
Other revenue and support	150,818	-	-	150,818	220,307
Net assets released from restrictions	727,578	(659,563)	(68,015)	-	-
Total operating revenues and support	3,234,277	1,591,306	50,564	4,876,147	4,177,033
Expenses					
Educational program services					
Instruction	1,900,920	-	-	1,900,920	1,771,063
Library	361,995	-	-	361,995	360,000
Student services	290,504	-	-	290,504	298,726
Financial leadership for ministry	65,576	-	-	65,576	71,546
Program for alternative studies	105,404	-	-	105,404	130,849
Academic support	122,457	-	-	122,457	120,725
Supporting services					
Institutional support	1,064,921	-	-	1,064,921	1,191,013
Development and fundraising	554,817	-	-	554,817	585,630
Total expenses	4,466,594	-	-	4,466,594	4,529,552
Increase (decrease) in net assets from operations	(1,232,317)	1,591,306	50,564	409,553	(352,519)
Non-operating revenues and expenses					
Investment income (loss)	696,681	574,125	-	1,270,806	(14,891)
Change in net assets	(535,636)	2,165,431	50,564	1,680,359	(367,410)
Net assets, beginning of year	3,039,615	3,247,881	6,696,696	12,984,192	13,351,602
Net assets - end of year	$ 2,503,979	$ 5,413,312	$ 6,747,260	$ 14,664,551	$ 12,984,192

See independent auditor's report and notes to the financial statements

MEMPHIS THEOLOGICAL SEMINARY OF THE CUMBERLAND PRESBYTERIAN CHURCH

Statement of Functional Expenses

For the Year Ended July 31, 2017
(with summarized comparative totals for the year ended July 31, 2016)

	Educational Program Services					Supporting Services					
	Instruction	Library	Student Services	Financial Leadership for Ministry	Program for Alternative Studies	Academic Support	Facilities Operations	Security Services	Institutional Support	Development and Fund Raising	2017 Total	2016 Total
Salaries and Wages	$1,223,041	$124,183	$209,292	$39,865	$70,882	$90,390	$ -	$ -	$434,925	$251,463	$2,603,386	$2,537,692
Benefits	207,047	34,550	21,941	664	13,086	21,113	-	-	87,832	50,609	483,607	459,097
Professional Development	19,638	-	1,585	250	-	811	-	-	1,178	1,101	24,563	40,876
Travel/Auto Expense	5,802	1,003	3,945	514	5,494	2,695	-	-	9,509	8,564	39,589	25,603
Office Supplies and Expense	14,674	53,395	6,669	1,884	2,551	2,067	7,352	-	38,559	80,245	207,396	185,123
Consultants / Professional	13,625	-	-	1,689	-	-	584	61,281	71,054	-	148,233	161,978
Special Events	61,621	-	4,894	4,490	7,362	-	-	-	39,380	82,378	200,125	179,061
Student / Covenant Groups	33,875	-	-	-	-	-	-	-	-	-	33,875	40,550
Repairs and Maintenance	195	1,226	-	-	-	-	110,761	-	2,446	-	114,628	146,569
Utilities	-	-	-	-	-	-	71,137	-	-	-	71,137	77,328
Insurance Expense	-	-	-	-	-	-	99,992	-	-	3,146	103,138	108,704
Property Taxes	-	-	-	-	-	-	20,395	-	-	-	20,395	12,051
Other Expense	18,933	708	6,460	7,942	235	-	(807)	-	87,544	32,558	153,573	204,429
Interest Expense	-	-	-	-	-	-	76,657	-	-	-	76,657	70,126
Capital Campaign Expense	-	-	-	-	-	-	-	-	-	35,440	35,440	97,056
Depreciation	-	-	-	-	-	-	150,852	-	-	-	150,852	183,309
Allocation of Facilities Operations & Security	302,469	146,930	35,718	8,278	5,794	5,381	(745,096)	(61,281)	292,494	9,313	-	-
	$1,900,920	$361,995	$290,504	$65,576	$105,404	$122,457	$ -	$ -	$1,064,921	$554,817	$4,466,594	$4,529,552

See independent auditor's report and notes to the financial statements

MEMPHIS THEOLOGICAL SEMINARY OF THE CUMBERLAND PRESBYTERIAN CHURCH

Statements of Cash Flows *For the Years Ended July 31, 2017 and 2016*

	2017	2016
Cash Flows from Operating Activities		
Change in net assets	$ 1,680,359	$ (367,410)
Adjustments to reconcile change in net assets to net cash provided by (used in) operating activities:		
Depreciation	150,852	183,309
Capital (gains) losses on investments	(1,155,210)	89,914
Bad debt expense	18,000	100,656
Discount on pledges	(20,129)	(10,893)
Changes in operating assets and liabilities:		
(Increase) decrease in assets		
Tuition, fees and other receivables	140,717	(209,388)
Pledges receivable	275,046	96,455
Other assets	4,674	34,774
Increase (decrease) in liabilities		
Accounts payable and accrued expenses	71,702	17,253
Prepaid revenue	-	(123,667)
Net cash provided by (used for) operating activities	1,166,011	(188,997)
Cash Flows from Investing Activities		
Purchases of investments	(472,585)	(190,139)
Reinvestments of investment earnings	(69,070)	(67,542)
Sale of investments	766,706	314,752
(Increase) decrease in cash surrender value of life insurance	4,722	280
Purchases of property and equipment	(121,681)	(118,021)
Net cash flows from (used for) investing activities	108,092	(60,670)
Cash Flows from Financing Activities		
Increase (decrease) in line of credit	810,000	(70,000)
Proceeds from issuance of notes payable	-	1,680,262
Principal payments on notes payable	(59,321)	(1,548,180)
Net cash flows from (used for) financing activities	750,679	62,082
Net increase (decrease) in cash and cash equivalents	2,024,782	(187,585)
Cash and cash equivalents, beginning of year	417,767	605,352
Cash and cash equivalents, end of year	$ 2,442,549	$ 417,767
Supplemental Disclosure:		
Interest paid during the year	$ 76,095	$ 69,059

See independent auditor's report and notes to the consolidated financial statements

MEMPHIS THEOLOGICAL SEMINARY OF THE CUMBERLAND PRESBYTERIAN CHURCH
Notes to the Financial Statements *July 31, 2017 and 2016*

Note 1 – Organization and Purpose

The Memphis Theological Seminary of the Cumberland Presbyterian Church (the "Seminary") is an ecumenical Protestant seminary serving the Mid-South region from its campus in Memphis, Tennessee. Memphis Theological Seminary of the Cumberland Presbyterian Church provides postgraduate theological education to clergy and church leaders of the parent denomination and qualified students from other denominations. Memphis Theological Seminary of the Cumberland Presbyterian Church is governed by a Board of Trustees elected by the General Assembly of the Cumberland Presbyterian Church.

Note 2 – Significant Accounting Policies

Financial Statement Presentation

Memphis Theological Seminary of the Cumberland Presbyterian Church prepares its financial statements in accordance with accounting principles generally accepted in the United States of America, which involves the application of accrual accounting. Under generally accepted accounting principles, Memphis Theological Seminary of the Cumberland Presbyterian Church reports information regarding its financial position and activities according to three classes of net assets as follows:

Unrestricted Net Assets — Net assets that are not subject to donor-imposed stipulations. Unrestricted net assets may be designated for specific purposes by action of the Board of Trustees or may otherwise be limited by contractual agreements with outside parties.

Temporarily Restricted Net Assets — Net assets whose use by the Seminary is subject to donor-imposed stipulations that can be fulfilled by actions of the Seminary pursuant to those stipulations or that expire by the passage of time.

Permanently Restricted Net Assets — Net assets subject to donor-imposed stipulations that they be maintained permanently by the Seminary. Generally, the donors of these assets permit the Seminary to use all or part of the investment return on these assets.

Contributions

Contributions received by Memphis Theological Seminary of the Cumberland Presbyterian Church are recorded as unrestricted, temporarily restricted, or permanently restricted support depending on the existence and/or nature of any donor restrictions. Temporarily restricted net assets are reclassified to unrestricted net assets upon satisfaction of the time or purpose restrictions.

Investment Valuation and Income Recognition

Investments are reported at fair value. Fair value is the price that would be received to sell an asset or paid to transfer a liability in an orderly transaction between market participants at the measurement date. See Notes 3 and 4 for discussion and computation of fair value.

Unrealized holding gains and losses are included in current year revenue and support as a component of investment income. Realized gains and losses are computed using the specific identification method.

Capital Assets

All acquisitions of property and equipment and expenditures for repairs and maintenance that prolong the useful lives of assets in excess of $1,000 are capitalized at cost. Expenditures for normal repair and maintenance are expensed to operations as they occur. Depreciation is provided through the straight-line method over the assets' estimated useful lives which range from three to ten years for equipment, fifteen years for library books and twenty-five to forty years for buildings.

Cash Equivalents

Cash equivalents are defined as short term, highly liquid investments that are both readily convertible to known amounts of cash and are so near maturity that they present insignificant risk of changes in value because of changes in interest rates.

MEMPHIS THEOLOGICAL SEMINARY OF THE CUMBERLAND PRESBYTERIAN CHURCH
Notes to the Financial Statements *July 31, 2017 and 2016*

Note 2 – Significant Accounting Policies (continued)

Use of Estimates in the Preparation of Financial Statements

The preparation of financial statements in conformity with generally accepted accounting principles requires management to make estimates and assumptions that affect the amounts reported in the financial statements and accompanying notes. Actual results could differ from those estimates.

Income Taxes

Memphis Theological Seminary of the Cumberland Presbyterian Church is a not-for-profit organization that is exempt from income taxes under Internal Revenue Code Section 501(c)(3) and is also exempt from state income taxes. The Seminary is generally no longer subject to federal and state audit for tax years prior to the year ended July 31, 2014.

Donated Property, Equipment and Services

Donations of property and use of property are recorded as support at their estimated fair value at the date of donation. Such donations are reported as unrestricted support unless the donor has restricted the donated asset to a specific purpose. The value of donated property was $-0- in 2016 and 2015.

Donated services are recognized as contributions if the services (a) create or enhance non-financial assets or (b) require specialized skills, are performed by people with those skills, and would otherwise be purchased by the Organization. There were no contributed services recorded for accounting and consulting in 2016 and 2015.

Functional Allocation of Expenses

The cost of providing the various educational programs and supporting services has been summarized on a functional basis in the statement of functional expenses. Accordingly, certain costs have been allocated among the programs and services benefited.

Subsequent Events

Memphis Theological Seminary of the Cumberland Presbyterian Church evaluated all events or transactions that occurred through November 8, 2017, the date Memphis Theological Seminary of the Cumberland Presbyterian Church approved these financial statements for issuance.

Note 3 – Fair Value Measurement

FASB ASC Subtopic 820-10 *Fair Value Measurements*,(formerly SFAS No. 157), defines fair value as the exchange price that would be received for an asset or paid to transfer a liability in the principal or most advantageous market for the asset or liability in an orderly transaction between market participants at the measurement date. SFAS No. 157 established a three-level fair value hierarchy that prioritizes the inputs used to measure fair value. This hierarchy requires entities to maximize the use of observable inputs and minimize the use of unobservable inputs.

The three levels of inputs used to measure fair value are as follows:

- Level 1 – Quoted prices in active markets for identical assets or liabilities.

- Level 2 – Observable inputs other than quoted prices included in Level 1, such as quoted prices for similar assets and liabilities in active markets; quoted prices for identical or similar assets or liabilities in markets that are not active; or inputs that are observable or can be corroborated by observable market data.

- Level 3 – Unobservable inputs that are supported by little or no market activity and that are significant to the fair value of the assets or liabilities. This includes certain pricing models, discounted cash flow methodologies and similar techniques that use significant unobservable inputs.

MEMPHIS THEOLOGICAL SEMINARY OF THE CUMBERLAND PRESBYTERIAN CHURCH
Notes to the Financial Statements — *July 31, 2017 and 2016*

Note 3 – Fair Value Measurement (continued)

The estimated fair value of Memphis Theological Seminary of the Cumberland Presbyterian Church's financial instruments has been determined by management using available market information. However, considerable judgment is required in interpreting market data to develop the estimates of fair value. Accordingly, the fair values are not necessarily indicative of the amounts that Memphis Theological Seminary of the Cumberland Presbyterian Church could realize in a current market exchange. The use of different market assumptions may have a material effect on the estimated fair value amounts.

The carrying amounts of cash and cash equivalents, net receivables, cash value of life insurance, payables, accrued liabilities, and debt are a reasonable estimate of their fair value, due to their short term nature, method of computation and interest rates for current debt.

All financial assets that are measured at fair value on a recurring basis (at least annually) have been segregated into the most appropriate level within the fair value hierarchy based on the inputs used to determine the fair value at the measurement date.

The following table sets forth by level, within the fair value hierarchy, the Seminary's financial instruments at fair value as of July 31, 2017:

	Total	Level 1	Level 2	Level 3
Investment securities				
Cash/cash equivalents	$ 110,737	$ 110,737	$ -	$ -
Money market funds	3,262	3,262	-	-
Bonds and bond funds	22,698	22,698	-	-
Common and preferred stocks	146,615	146,615	-	-
Real estate investment funds	841,094	-	841,094	-
Mutual funds	601,257	601,257	-	-
Private investment entities	9,477,053	-	-	9,477,053
Total investments	$ 11,202,716	$ 884,569	$ 841,094	$ 9,477,053
Land held for sale	$ 27,448	$ -	$ -	$ 27,448

MEMPHIS THEOLOGICAL SEMINARY OF THE CUMBERLAND PRESBYTERIAN CHURCH

Notes to the Financial Statements *July 31, 2017 and 2016*

Note 3 – Fair Value Measurement (continued)

The following table sets forth by level, within the fair value hierarchy, the Seminary's financial instruments at fair value as of July 31, 2016:

	Total	Level 1	Level 2	Level 3
Investment securities				
Cash/cash equivalents	$ 728,900	$ 728,900	$ -	$ -
Money market funds	10,046	10,046	-	-
Bonds and bond funds	25,434	25,434	-	-
Common and preferred stocks	120,713	120,713	-	-
Real estate investment funds	736,330	-	736,330	-
Mutual funds	214,288	214,288	-	-
Private investment entities	8,436,846	-	-	8,436,846
Total investments	$ 10,272,557	$ 1,099,381	$ 736,330	$ 8,436,846
Land held for sale	$ 27,448	$ -	$ -	$ 27,448

The private investment entities are investments entered into by the Board of Stewardship to achieve greater rates of return. They include funds whose inputs used to determine fair value are considered unobservable and are therefore Level 3 inputs.

The carrying value of the above land held for sale is based on expected recoverability at the time of sale. Memphis Theological Seminary of the Cumberland Presbyterian Church uses appraised values and other information available to determine the carrying value. The inputs used to determine fair value are considered unobservable and are therefore Level 3 inputs.

Transactions in Level 3 assets for the years ended July 31, 2017 and 2016, were as follows:

	2017	2016
Private investment entities		
Beginning balance	$ 8,436,846	$ 7,236,272
Change in allocation of investments	896,525	(250,521)
Reinvestments	94,174	1,409,870
Realized/unrealized gains (losses)	49,508	41,225
Ending balance	$ 9,477,053	$ 8,436,846
Land held for sale		
Beginning balance	$ 27,448	$ 27,448
Ending balance	$ 27,448	$ 27,448

MEMPHIS THEOLOGICAL SEMINARY OF THE CUMBERLAND PRESBYTERIAN CHURCH
Notes to the Financial Statements — *July 31, 2017 and 2016*

Note 3 – Fair Value Measurement (continued)

Investment income (loss) was as follows for the years ended July 31, 2017 and 2016:

	2017	2016
Investment income	$ 115,596	$ 75,023
Realized investment gains (losses)	51,964	59,487
Unrealized investment gains (losses)	1,103,246	(149,401)
Net investment income (loss)	$ 1,270,806	$ (14,891)

Note 4 – Endowments

Nearly all of Memphis Theological Seminary of the Cumberland Presbyterian Church's investments, which contain endowments, are managed by the Board of Stewardship, Foundation and Benefits of the Cumberland Presbyterian Church, Inc., and maintained in pooled investment accounts with other funds. The investments generally originate from gifts and contributions for which separate identifiable investment accounts are created that indicate the source of the funds and/or the purpose for which the funds are to be used. Many of these accounts are designated for monthly distributions to Memphis Theological Seminary of the Cumberland Presbyterian Church based on one-twelfth of 5% of the rolling average value. The Board of Stewardship, Foundation and Benefits, issues an aggregate amount to Memphis Theological Seminary of the Cumberland Presbyterian Church and charges the applicable accounts for their proportionate share. In addition, Memphis Theological Seminary of the Cumberland Presbyterian Church can request on an as needed basis, additional distributions that will be used for the purpose for which the account was created.

The Seminary has interpreted the Uniform Prudent Management of Institutional Funds Act ("UPMIFA") requiring a portion of a donor restricted endowment of perpetual duration be classified as permanently restricted assets. The amount of the endowment that must be retained permanently is in accordance with explicit donor stipulations as outlined in their respective endowment agreements. The Seminary has other endowment funds that are temporarily restricted by the donor as to purpose and are classified as temporarily restricted until they are expended on their respective purposes. Investment income and net appreciation on these permanently and temporarily restricted endowments is classified as temporarily restricted or permanently restricted if so directed by the donor in the respective endowment agreements or as unrestricted in the absence of donor instructions. The Seminary has other donated funds and board designated funds that are included in investments and are not restricted as to use. These funds, as well as investment income and net appreciation on these funds are classified as unrestricted. Expenditures (withdrawals) of the temporarily restricted and unrestricted funds are approved by management. The funds held by the Board of Stewardship, Foundation and Benefits of the Cumberland Presbyterian Church, Inc. are invested with the primary objective of providing a balance between capital appreciation, preservation of capital, and current income. This is a long-term goal designed to maximize returns without undue risk. The Board of Stewardship selects the investment portfolio where the endowments will be invested as described in the Investment Policy of The Cumberland Presbyterian Church Center, which outlines the asset allocations, permissible investments, and objectives of the portfolios.

MEMPHIS THEOLOGICAL SEMINARY OF THE CUMBERLAND PRESBYTERIAN CHURCH
Notes to the Financial Statements *July 31, 2017 and 2016*

Note 4 – Endowments (continued)

Changes in endowment net assets for the years ended July 31, 2017 and 2016, were as follows:

	Unrestricted Board Designated	Unrestricted Other	Temporarily Restricted	Permanently Restricted	Total
Balance at July 31, 2015	$ 79,437	$ 1,781,704	$ 2,096,696	$ 6,461,705	$ 10,419,542
Investment return:					
Investment income	595	31,864	35,083	-	67,542
Change in market value	3,487	(42,950)	(50,451)	-	(89,914)
Total investment return	4,082	(11,086)	(15,368)	-	(22,372)
Contributions	-	105,148	-	84,991	190,139
Appropriation of endowment assets for expenditure	(4,945)	(179,699)	(130,108)	-	(314,752)
Balance at July 31, 2016	78,574	1,696,067	1,951,220	6,546,696	10,272,557
Investment return:					
Investment income	998	35,175	32,897	-	69,070
Change in market value	16,338	597,645	541,228	-	1,155,211
Total investment return	17,336	632,820	574,125	-	1,224,281
Contributions	100,000	104,006	-	268,579	472,585
Appropriation of endowment assets for expenditure	144,592	442,937	179,178	-	766,707
Reclassifications	73,972	(5,957)	-	(68,015)	-
Balance at July 31, 2017	$ 125,290	$ 1,983,999	$ 2,346,167	$ 6,747,260	$ 11,202,716

Note 5 – Capital Assets

Capital assets are as follows at July 31, 2017 and 2016:

	2017	2016
Building and improvements	$ 4,379,338	$ 4,357,318
Furniture and equipment	903,709	892,587
Library books	1,885,318	1,853,526
Vehicles	44,014	44,014
	7,212,379	7,147,445
Less accumulated depreciation	4,747,257	4,597,189
	2,465,122	2,550,256
Land	208,650	208,650
Construction in progress	450,981	395,018
Capital assets, net	$ 3,124,753	$ 3,153,924

Depreciation expense for the years ended July 31, 2017 and 2016, was $150,852 and $183,309, respectively.

MEMPHIS THEOLOGICAL SEMINARY OF THE CUMBERLAND PRESBYTERIAN CHURCH
Notes to the Financial Statements   *July 31, 2017 and 2016*

Note 6 – Concentration of Credit Risk

Memphis Theological Seminary of the Cumberland Presbyterian Church has cash equivalents invested by the Board of Stewardship, Foundation and Benefits. At July 31, 2017, these funds total $2,274,236 and are not insured by the Federal Deposit Insurance Corporation (FDIC).

In addition, Memphis Theological Seminary of the Cumberland Presbyterian Church maintains cash balances in accounts at a well-established financial institution located in Memphis, Tennessee. These balances are insured by the Federal Deposit Insurance Corporation up to certain limits. At July 31, 2017, Memphis Theological Seminary of the Cumberland Presbyterian Church had no uninsured balances.

Memphis Theological Seminary of the Cumberland Presbyterian Church's tuition and fees receivable are from students for which the majority receive some form of financial assistance. Management maintains an allowance for uncollectible based on periodic reviews of each individual student's account.

Note 7 - Pledges Receivable

Pledges receivable primarily represent pledges from numerous donors to be used for a capital campaign which was initiated in a prior year. The campaign has three purposes: 1) to help fund the construction of a new free-standing chapel; 2) to fund construction of a new classroom/office building; and 3) to increase endowments. At the beginning of the prior fiscal year, the fund raising campaign was changed from a capital campaign to a comprehensive campaign in which pledges made could still be designated to the capital campaign, but could also be designated to support facilities maintenance, support the annual fund, or be undesignated. Pledges receivable for the capital/comprehensive campaign totaled $379,596 and $604,642 at July 31, 2017 and 2016, respectively. Pledges receivable also include a pledge to offset the cost of a faculty member. Pledges receivable to offset the cost of the faculty member totaled $100,000 and $150,000 as of July 31, 2017 and 2016, respectively. These amounts have been discounted to present value using a rate of 3.07%. Management considers all pledges receivable at July 31, 2017 and 2016, to be fully collectible.

The pledges, net of the discount, are due to be received as follows:

	2017	2016
Less than one year	$ 308,396	$ 310,345
One year to five years	171,200	444,297
Gross contributions receivable	479,596	754,642
Less: discount to present value	(19,335)	(39,464)
Contributions receivable, net	$ 460,261	$ 715,178

Note 8 – Line of Credit

Memphis Theological Seminary of the Cumberland Presbyterian Church has a $1,000,000 unsecured revolving line of credit agreement with a local bank that matures December 2017. Borrowings outstanding under the agreement ($910,000 at July 31, 2017 and $100,000 at July 31, 2016) bear interest at the bank's prime rate (4.25 percent at July 31, 2017). The line is guaranteed by the Board of the Stewardship, Foundation and Benefits of the Cumberland Presbyterian Church.

MEMPHIS THEOLOGICAL SEMINARY OF THE CUMBERLAND PRESBYTERIAN CHURCH
Notes to the Financial Statements *July 31, 2017 and 2016*

Note 9 – Note Payable

Notes payable consist of the following at July 31, 2017 and 2016:

	2017	2016
Note payable, due in monthly installments of $10,052 bearing interest at 3.85% through November 2025 and a single balloon payment of the remaining unpaid balance in December 2025	$ 1,588,012	$ 1,647,333

The note payable is secured by property owned by the Seminary and located at 168 East Parkway South, Memphis, Tennessee.

Scheduled principal payments required for the years ending July 31 are as follows:

	Amount
2018	$ 60,498
2019	62,869
2020	65,180
2021	67,887
2022	70,547
Thereafter	1,261,031
Total notes payable	$ 1,588,012

Note 10 – Retirement Plan

Memphis Theological Seminary of the Cumberland Presbyterian Church sponsors a qualified defined contribution retirement plan for eligible employees as defined by the plan under IRC Section 403(b). Employees are eligible to participate in the plan immediately upon hire and contributions to the plan are vested immediately. Each participant in the plan may make voluntary contributions to the plan of up to the lesser of twenty percent (20%) of annual compensation received by the participant during the plan year, or the maximum allowed by law. Memphis Theological Seminary of the Cumberland Presbyterian Church matches participant's contributions to a maximum of 3.5%. Contributions to the plan by Memphis Theological Seminary of the Cumberland Presbyterian Church for the years ended July 31, 2017 and 2016, were $61,162 and $54,380, respectively.

MEMPHIS THEOLOGICAL SEMINARY OF THE CUMBERLAND PRESBYTERIAN CHURCH
Notes to the Financial Statements *July 31, 2017 and 2016*

Note 11 – Related Party Transactions

Memphis Theological Seminary of the Cumberland Presbyterian Church and the Board of Stewardship are separate corporations but both are affiliated with the Cumberland Presbyterian Church in that the governing board of the Church elects the members of the Board of Trustees of Memphis Theological Seminary of the Cumberland Presbyterian Church and the Board of Stewardship. There are no common board members between Memphis Theological Seminary of the Cumberland Presbyterian Church and the Board of Stewardship. Amounts due to and from the Board of Stewardship as of July 31, 2017 and 2016, are as follows:

	2017	2016
Seminary assets held by the Board of Stewardship:		
Seminary cash held	$ 2,274,236	$ 246,559
Seminary investments held	$ 11,100,096	$ 10,116,325
Other Receivables	$ 148,612	$ 69,689

Note 12 – Temporarily Restricted Net Assets

Temporarily restricted net assets consist of the following at July 31, 2017 and 2016:

	2017	2016
Endowment restrictions	$ 2,346,167	$ 1,951,220
Capital campaign restriction	839,276	920,229
Comprehensive campaign restriction	1,983,482	42,142
Faculty salary restriction	96,116	141,722
Financial Leadership for Ministries	143,271	152,567
Other restrictions	5,000	40,001
	$ 5,413,312	$ 3,247,881

Note 13 – Concentration of Revenue

In the years ended July 31, 2017 and 2016, approximately 32% and 15%, respectively, of total operating revenues and support was received from one individual.

Note 14 – Future Operations

Memphis Theological Seminary of the Cumberland Presbyterian Church has sustained losses from operations in each of the last four fiscal years. Over this same period, tuition revenue has decreased due to declining student enrollment. Contributions over that period have fluctuated, but a significant portion of contributions have been restricted by the donors as to use other than for operations. Unrestricted contributions for the year ended July 31, 2017, decreased significantly from the prior year thereby producing an even greater loss from unrestricted operations than in previous years. Continued losses could increase the use of unrestricted endowment funds and cause significant cash shortages. Management is committed to taking steps to increase enrollment, seek additional contributions, and bring expenses in line with revenues.

Note 15 – Commitment

On March 1, 2017, Memphis Theological Seminary of the Cumberland Presbyterian Church entered into an agreement with an architectural firm to construct a building to be used by the Seminary as a chapel/classroom area. The cost of the building has been initially established as $2,750,000. Groundbreaking for the new building occurred in September 2017. The construction cost is expected to be completely funded through contributions designated for the purpose of the project.

Supplementary Information

MEMPHIS THEOLOGICAL SEMINARY OF THE CUMBERLAND PRESBYTERIAN CHURCH

Schedule of Expenditures of Federal Awards *For the Year Ended July 31, 2017*

Federal Grantor/ Pass-Through Grantor/ Program or Cluster Title	CFDA Number	Total Expended
U.S. Department of Education Federal Family Education Loan Program	84.032	$ 1,863,116

Basis of Presentation

The accompanying schedule of expenditures of federal awards (the "Schedule") includes the federal award activity of Memphis Theological Seminary of the Cumberland Presbyterian Church under programs of the federal government for the year ended July 31, 2017. The information in this Schedule is presented in accordance with the requirements of Title 2 CFR U.S. *Code of Federal Regulations* Part 200, *Uniform Administrative Requirements, Cost Principles, and Audit Requirements for Federal Awards* (Uniform Guidance). Because the Schedule presents only a selected portion of the operations of Memphis Theological Seminary of the Cumberland Presbyterian Church, it is not intended to and does not present the financial position, changes in net assets or cash flows of Memphis Theological Seminary of the Cumberland Presbyterian Church.

Summary of Significant Accounting Policies

Expenditures reported on the Schedule are reported on the accrual basis of accounting. Such expenditures are recognized following the cost principles contained in OMB Circular A-21, *Cost Principles for Educational Institutions*, wherein certain types of expenditures are not allowable or are limited as to reimbursement. Memphis Theological Seminary of the Cumberland Presbyterian Church elected not to use the ten per cent de minimis indirect cost rate option.

Non-Financial Information

CANNON WRIGHT BLOUNT

INDEPENDENT AUDITOR'S REPORT ON INTERNAL CONTROL OVER FINANCIAL REPORTING AND ON COMPLIANCE AND OTHER MATTERS BASED ON AN AUDIT OF FINANCIAL STATEMENTS PERFORMED IN ACCORDANCE WITH *GOVERNMENT AUDITING STANDARDS*

To the Board of Trustees
Memphis Theological Seminary of the Cumberland Presbyterian Church
Memphis, Tennessee

We have audited, in accordance with the auditing standards generally accepted in the United States of America and the standards applicable to financial audits contained in *Government Auditing Standards* issued by the Comptroller General of the United States, the financial statements of Memphis Theological Seminary of the Cumberland Presbyterian Church (a nonprofit organization), which comprise the statement of financial position as of July 31, 2017, and the related statements of activities, functional expenses, and cash flows for the year then ended, and the related notes to the financial statements, and have issued our report thereon dated November 8, 2017.

Internal Control over Financial Reporting

In planning and performing our audit of the financial statements, we considered Memphis Theological Seminary of the Cumberland Presbyterian Church's internal control over financial reporting (internal control) to determine the audit procedures that are appropriate in the circumstances for the purpose of expressing our opinion on the financial statements, but not for the purpose of expressing an opinion on the effectiveness of Memphis Theological Seminary of the Cumberland Presbyterian Church's internal control. Accordingly, we do not express an opinion on the effectiveness of Memphis Theological Seminary of the Cumberland Presbyterian Church's internal control.

A *deficiency in internal control* exists when the design or operation of a control does not allow management or employees, in the normal course of performing their assigned functions, to prevent, or detect and correct, misstatements on a timely basis. A *material weakness* is a deficiency, or a combination of deficiencies, in internal control, such that there is a reasonable possibility that a material misstatement of the entity's financial statements will not be prevented, or detected and corrected on a timely basis. A *significant deficiency* is a deficiency, or a combination of deficiencies, in internal control that is less severe than a material weakness, yet important enough to merit attention by those charged with governance.

Our consideration of internal control was for the limited purpose described in the first paragraph of this section and was not designed to identify all deficiencies in internal control that might be material weaknesses or significant deficiencies. Given these limitations, during our audit we did not identify any deficiencies in internal control that we consider to be material weaknesses. However, material weaknesses may exist that have not been identified.

Compliance and Other Matters

As part of obtaining reasonable assurance about whether Memphis Theological Seminary of the Cumberland Presbyterian Church's financial statements are free from material misstatement, we performed tests of its compliance with certain provisions of laws, regulations, contracts, and grant agreements, noncompliance with which could have a direct and material effect on the determination of financial statement amounts. However, providing an opinion on compliance with those provisions was not an objective of our audit, and accordingly, we do not express such an opinion. The results of our tests disclosed no instances of noncompliance or other matters that are required to be reported under *Government Auditing Standards*.

CANNON WRIGHT BLOUNT PLLC   756 RIDGE LAKE BLVD   MEMPHIS TN 38120

PHONE *901.685.7500*   FAX *901.685.7569*   *WWW.CANNONWRIGHTBLOUNT.COM*

Purpose of this Report

The purpose of this report is solely to describe the scope of our testing of internal control and compliance and the results of that testing, and not to provide an opinion on the effectiveness of the organization's internal control or on compliance. This report is an integral part of an audit performed in accordance with *Government Auditing Standards* in considering the organization's internal control and compliance. Accordingly, this communication is not suitable for any other purpose.

Cannon Wright Blount PLLC

Memphis, Tennessee
November 8, 2017

INDEPENDENT AUDITOR'S REPORT ON COMPLIANCE FOR A MAJOR PROGRAM AND ON INTERNAL CONTROL OVER COMPLIANCE REQUIRED BY THE UNIFORM GUIDANCE

To the Board of Trustees
Memphis Theological Seminary of the Cumberland Presbyterian Church
Memphis, Tennessee

Report on Compliance for a Major Federal Program

We have audited Memphis Theological Seminary of the Cumberland Presbyterian Church's compliance with the types of compliance requirements described in the *OMB Compliance Supplement* that could have a direct and material effect on Memphis Theological Seminary of the Cumberland Presbyterian Church's major federal program for the year ended July 31, 2017. Memphis Theological Seminary of the Cumberland Presbyterian Church's major federal program is identified in the summary of auditor's results section of the accompanying schedule of findings and questioned costs.

Management's Responsibility

Management is responsible for compliance with federal statutes, regulations, and the terms and conditions of its federal awards applicable to its federal program.

Auditor's Responsibility

Our responsibility is to express an opinion on compliance for Memphis Theological Seminary of the Cumberland Presbyterian Church's major federal program based on our audit of the types of compliance requirements referred to above. We conducted our audit of compliance in accordance with auditing standards generally accepted in the United States of America; the standards applicable to financial audits contained in *Government Auditing Standards*, issued by the Comptroller General of the United States; and the audit requirements of Title 2 U.S. *Code of Federal Regulations* Part 200, *Uniform Administrative Requirements, Cost Principles,* and *Audit Requirements for Federal Awards* (Uniform Guidance). Those standards and the Uniform Guidance require that we plan and perform the audit to obtain reasonable assurance about whether noncompliance with the types of compliance requirements referred to above that could have a direct and material effect on a major federal program occurred. An audit includes examining, on a test basis, evidence about Memphis Theological Seminary of the Cumberland Presbyterian Church's compliance with those requirements and performing such other procedures as we considered necessary in the circumstances.

We believe that our audit provides a reasonable basis for our opinion on compliance for the major federal program. However, our audit does not provide a legal determination of Memphis Theological Seminary of the Cumberland Presbyterian Church's compliance.

Opinion on a Major Federal Program

In our opinion, Memphis Theological Seminary of the Cumberland Presbyterian Church complied, in all material respects, with the types of compliance requirements referred to above that could have a direct and material effect on its major federal program for the year ended July 31, 2017.

Report on Internal Control over Compliance

Management of Memphis Theological Seminary of the Cumberland Presbyterian Church is responsible for establishing and maintaining effective internal control over compliance with the types of compliance requirements referred to above. In planning and performing our audit of compliance, we considered Memphis Theological Seminary of the Cumberland Presbyterian Church's internal control over compliance with the types of requirements that could have a direct and material effect on a major federal program to determine the auditing procedures that are appropriate in the circumstances for the purpose of expressing an opinion on compliance for a major federal program and to test and report on internal control over compliance in accordance with the Uniform Guidance, but not for the purpose of expressing an opinion on the effectiveness of internal control over compliance. Accordingly, we do not express an opinion on the effectiveness of Memphis Theological Seminary of the Cumberland Presbyterian Church's internal control over compliance.

A *deficiency in internal control over compliance* exists when the design or operation of a control over compliance does not allow management or employees, in the normal course of performing their assigned functions, to prevent, or detect and correct, noncompliance with a type of compliance requirement of a federal program on a timely basis. A *material weakness in internal control over compliance* is a deficiency, or combination of deficiencies, in internal control over compliance, such that there is a reasonable possibility that material noncompliance with a type of compliance requirement of a federal program will not be prevented, or detected and corrected, on a timely basis. A *significant deficiency in internal control over compliance* is a deficiency, or a combination of deficiencies, in internal control over compliance with a type of compliance requirement of a federal program that is less severe than a material weakness in internal control over compliance, yet important enough to merit attention by those charged with governance.

Our consideration of internal control over compliance was for the limited purpose described in the first paragraph of this section and was not designed to identify all deficiencies in internal control over compliance that might be material weaknesses or significant deficiencies. We did not identify any deficiencies in internal control over compliance that we consider to be material weaknesses. However, material weaknesses may exist that have not been identified.

The purpose of this report on internal control over compliance is solely to describe the scope of our testing of internal control over compliance and the results of that testing based on the requirements of the Uniform Guidance. Accordingly, this report is not suitable for any other purpose.

Cam Wright Blount PLLC

Memphis, Tennessee
November 8, 2017

MEMPHIS THEOLOGICAL SEMINARY OF THE CUMBERLAND PRESBYTERIAN CHURCH

Schedule of Findings and Questioned Costs *For the Year Ended July 31, 2017*

SECTION I - SUMMARY OF AUDITOR'S RESULTS

Financial Statements

Type of auditor's report issued:	Unmodified
Internal control over financial reporting:	
- Material weakness(es) identified?	___ yes _X_ no
- Significant deficiencies identified that are not considered to be material weaknesses?	___ yes _X_ none noted
- Noncompliance material to financial statements noted?	___ yes _X_ no

Federal Awards:

Internal control over major programs:	
- Material weakness(es) identified?	___ yes _X_ no
- Significant deficiencies identified that are not considered to be material weaknesses?	___ yes _X_ none noted
Type of auditor's report issued on compliance for major program:	Unmodified
Any audit findings disclosed that are required to be reported in accordance with 2 CFR section 200.516(a)?	___ yes _X_ no

Identification of major programs:

CFDA 84.032	U.S. Department of Education Federal Family Education Loan Program
Threshold for distinguishing type A and B programs:	$750,000
Auditee qualified as low risk auditee:	_X_ yes ___ no

SECTION II - FINANCIAL STATEMENT FINDINGS

There are no financial statement findings for the year ended July 31, 2017.

SECTION III - FEDERAL AWARD FINDINGS AND QUESTIONED COSTS

There are no federal award findings or questioned costs for the year ended July 31, 2017.

MEMPHIS THEOLOGICAL SEMINARY OF THE CUMBERLAND PRESBYTERIAN CHURCH

Summary Schedule of Prior Audit Findings **For the Year Ended July 31, 2017**

There were no findings or questioned costs for the year ended July 31, 2016.

November 8, 2017

To the Board of Trustees
Memphis Theological Seminary of the Cumberland Presbyterian Church
Memphis, Tennessee

We have audited the financial statements of the Memphis Theological Seminary of the Cumberland Presbyterian Church for the year ended July 31, 2017, and have issued our report thereon dated November 8, 2017. Professional standards require that we provide you with information about our responsibilities under generally accepted auditing standards, *Government Auditing Standards* and the Uniform Guidance, as well as certain information related to the planned scope and timing of our audit. We have communicated such information in our letter to you dated May 26, 2017. Professional standards also require that we communicate to you the following information related to our audit.

Significant Audit Findings

Qualitative Aspects of Accounting Practices

Management is responsible for the selection and use of appropriate accounting policies. The significant accounting policies used by the Memphis Theological Seminary of the Cumberland Presbyterian Church are described in Note 2 to the financial statements. No new accounting policies were adopted and the application of existing policies was not changed during 2017. We noted no transactions entered into by the Organization during the year for which there is a lack of authoritative guidance or consensus. All significant transactions have been recognized in the financial statements in the proper period.

Accounting estimates are an integral part of the financial statements prepared by management and are based on management's knowledge and experience about past and current events and assumptions about future events. Certain accounting estimates are particularly sensitive because of their significance to the financial statements and because of the possibility that future events affecting them may differ significantly from those expected. The most sensitive estimate affecting the financial statements was:

> Investments are reported at fair value as of the end of the fiscal year. The fluctuation of market value causes uncertainty in the ultimate realizable value of the investments.

The financial statement disclosures are neutral, consistent, and clear.

Difficulties Encountered in Performing the Audit

We encountered no significant difficulties in dealing with management in performing and completing our audit.

Corrected and Uncorrected Misstatements

Professional standards require us to accumulate all misstatements identified during the audit, other than those that are clearly trivial, and communicate them to the appropriate level of management. The attached schedule summarizes uncorrected misstatements of the financial statements. Management has determined that their effects are immaterial, both individually and in the aggregate, to the financial statements taken as a whole. In addition, none of the misstatements detected as a result of audit procedures and corrected by management were material, either individually or in the aggregate, to the financial statements taken as a whole.

Disagreements with Management

For purposes of this letter, a disagreement with management is a financial accounting, reporting, or auditing matter, whether or not resolved to our satisfaction, that could be significant to the financial statements or the auditor's report. We are pleased to report that no such disagreements arose during the course of our audit.

Management Representations

We have requested certain representations from management that are included in the management representation letter dated November 8, 2017.

Management Consultations with Other Independent Accountants

In some cases, management may decide to consult with other accountants about auditing and accounting matters, similar to obtaining a "second opinion" on certain situations. If a consultation involves application of an accounting principle to the Organization's financial statements or a determination of the type of auditor's opinion that may be expressed on those statements, our professional standards require the consulting accountant to check with us to determine that the consultant has all the relevant facts. To our knowledge, there were no such consultations with other accountants.

Other Audit Findings or Issues

We generally discuss a variety of matters, including the application of accounting principles and auditing standards, with management each year prior to retention as the Organization's auditors. However, these discussions occurred in the normal course of our professional relationship and our responses were not a condition to our retention.

Other Matters

With respect to the supplementary information accompanying the financial statements, we made certain inquiries of management and evaluated the form, content, and methods of preparing the information to determine that the information complies with U.S. generally accepted accounting principles, the method of preparing it has not changed from the prior period, and the information is appropriate and complete in relation to our audit of the financial statements. We compared and reconciled the supplementary information to the underlying accounting records used to prepare the financial statements or to the financial statements themselves.

This information is intended solely for the use of board of trustees and management of the Memphis Theological Seminary of the Cumberland Presbyterian Church and is not intended to be, and should not be, used by anyone other than these specified parties.

Very truly yours,

Cannon Wright Blount PLLC

Client: **Memphis Theological Seminary of the Cumberland**
Engagement: **2017 - Memphis Theological Seminary 2017**
Period Ending: **7/31/2017**
Trial Balance: **2210 - Trial Balance**
Workpaper: **2240 - Proposed JE Report**

Account	Description	W/P Ref	Debit	Credit
Proposed JE # 17		4632		
To recognize prior year and current year suspense account liabilities as income				
21098-000-000	Endowment Suspense		30,731.00	
43024-280-000	Endowment Gifts - Permanently Restricted		2,137.00	
32210-000-000	Net Assets - Unrestricted			32,868.00
Total			32,868.00	32,868.00
Proposed JE # 18		4510		
To adjust for prior year cumulative overaccrual of accumulated depreciation that was corrected in the current year				
69000-000-000	Depreciation Expense		31,429.00	
32210-000-000	Net Assets - Unrestricted			31,429.00
Total			31,429.00	31,429.00
Proposed JE # 19		5123		
To reverse accrual of audit fees at July 31, 2016, that was corrected in the current year				
61250-010-000	Audit Expenses		23,469.00	
32210-000-000	Net Assets - Unrestricted			23,469.00
Total			23,469.00	23,469.00

APPENDICES

REPORT OF THE CREDENTIALS COMMITTEE
(Appendix A)

The Credentials Committee certifies the list of commissioners on pages 5 and 6 of the Preliminary Minutes with the following change:

On the part of Minister Delegates, Reverend William Alas, Grace Presbytery, is not present.

On the part of the Elder Commissioners, Elder Brittney Stevens, Nashville Presbytery, is not present.

On the part of Youth Advisory Delegates, Carley Bell, Cumberland Presbytery is not present.

Enrollment as of 10:30 a.m. is certified as forty-four (44) ministers, forty-two (42) elders and twenty (20) youth advisory delegates.

Respectfully submitted,
Reverend Gloria Diaz, Chair
Elder Richard Snowden
Elder Diann Phelps
Youth Advisory Delegate Isaac Barkley

REPORT OF THE COMMITTEE ON CHAPLAINS/HISTORICAL FOUNDATION
(Appendix B)

I. REFERRALS

Referrals to this committee are as follows: The Report of the Board of Trustees of the Historical Foundation and the Report of the Commission on Chaplains and Military Personnel.

II. PERSONS OF COUNSEL

Appearing before this committee were: Ms. Susan Knight Gore, Archivist, Historical Foundation; Reverend Lisa Oliver, Board Representative, Historical Foundation; Navy Chaplain Lyman M. Smith (CAPT, CHC, USN), Director of the Presbyterian Council for Chaplains and Military Personnel, and Reverend Charles McCaskey, representative to the Presbyterian Council for Chaplains and Military Personnel.

III. CONSIDERATION OF REFERRALS

A. REPORT OF THE BOARD OF TRUSTEES OF THE HISTORICAL FOUNDATION

The Chaplains/Historical Foundation Committee commends the work of the Historical Foundation, giving thanks for their passionate leadership and dedication to the preservation of the history of the Cumberland Presbyterian Church in America and the Cumberland Presbyterian Church. The committee recognizes the difficulties in attempting to retrieve and preserve all kinds of history and memorabilia from the ministry of these churches, and we applaud the dedication of the Historical Foundation for their tireless service. We are especially thankful for Mrs. Susan Knight Gore and Reverend Lisa Oliver for appearing before and sharing with our committee.

1. History Interpretation And Promotional Activities A. 1810/1874 Circle

RECOMMENDATION 1: That Recommendation 1 of the Report of the Historical

Foundation, "that the General Assembly instruct presbyteries to make congregations aware of the 1810/1874 circle and encourage new members to supprt this endeavor annually," be adopted.

2. Denomination Day Offering

RECOMMENDATION 2: That Recommendation 2 of the Report of the Historical Foundation, "that General Assembly instruct presbyteries to encourage their congregations to have a special offering on the Sunday designated as denomination day to help support the special project designated for that year," be adopted.

3. Publication Series

RECOMMENDATION 3: That Recommendation 3 of the Report of the Historical Foundation, "that the General Assembly make presbyteries aware that the Historical Foundation is interested and has funds to publish books on topics concerning the Cumberland Presbyterian Church and the Cumberland Presbyterian Church in America, and instruct them to share this information with the churches and individuals of their presbytery," be adopted.

B. REPORT OF THE COMMISSION ON MILITARY CHAPLAINS AND PERSONNEL

The Chaplains/Historical Foundation committee was grateful to hear from the new leadership of the PCCMP, Navy Chaplain Lyman M. Smith, and wishes to thank Chaplain Smith for appearing before the committee, especially given his tight schedule and many other responsibilities. We applaud the work of the PCCMP and are grateful for their role as "Chaplain to our Chaplains," serving the role of pastoral care for the women and men called by God to serve as chaplains in the military.

We discussed the global nature of the Cumberland Presbyterian Church and the different ways military is viewed in ecclesiastical bodies outside the United States. For this reason, and for the reason that the observations suggested by the report are important historical days for the United States and not for other nations, and the PCCMP endorses chaplains to United States military only and not to other military bodies in the world, the committee felt it was appropriate to encourage the observation of the date suggested to be only for congregations in the United States.

1. Support of the PCCMP

RECOMMENDATION 1: That Recommendation 1 of the Report of the Commission on Military Chaplains and Personnel, "that each Cumberland Presbyterian Church provide an opportunity for their congregations to receive an offering on the last sunday of May, or another special day, to support our ministry through the PCCMP," be denied.

RECOMMENDATION 2: That General Assembly instruct presbyteries to encourage congregations in the United States to receive an offering on the last Sunday of May, or another special day, to support our ministry through the PCCMP.

The committee recognized that we are not empowered to make changes to the budget of the Cumberland Presbyterian Church, and felt it was not appropriate to pass a resolution that suggested we had that authority.

RECOMMENDATION 3: That Recommendation 2 of the Report of the Commission on Military Chaplains and Personnel, "that the budget line item of the Cumberland Presbyterian Church designated for the PCCMP be increased by 2% beginning in 2020," be denied.

RECOMMENDATION 4: That the office of Our United Outreach be encouraged to increase the 2019 budget designated to the PCCMP by 2% for fiscal year 2020.

RECOMMENDATION 5: That Recommedation 3 of the Report of the Commission on Military Chaplains and Personnel, "that individual congregations of the Cumberland Presbyterian Church determine and designate special days through the year to hold up the Chaplains and their families in the service to which they have been endorsed," be denied.

RECOMMENDATION 6: That the General Assembly instruct presbyteries to encourage congregations in the United States to determine and designate special days through the year to hold up the Chaplains and their families in the service to which they have been endorsed.

Respectfully submitted,
The Chaplains/Historical Foundation committee

REPORT OF THE COMMITTEE ON
THEOLOGY AND SOCIAL CONCERNS/ UNIFICATION TASK FORCE
(Appendix C)

I. REFERRALS

Referrals to this committee are as follows: The Report of the Ministry Council, Section 1.B.6 and Appendix A Questions for the Unification Task Force; The Report of the Unified Committee on Theology and Social Concerns; and The Report of the Unification Task Force.

II. PERSONS OF COUNSEL

Appearing before this committee were: Reverend Mitchell Walker (CPCA) and Reverend Joy Warren (CPC), representatives of the Unification Task Force; Reverend Byron Forester, board member and Reverend Richard Morgan, representative, Theology and Social Concerns (CPC); Reverend Carolyn Goins and Reverend Mike Cooper, Theology and Social Concerns (CPCA); Reverend Ron McMillan; Reverend Chris Warren; Mr. Ben Diaz; Elder Leon Cole, Moderator (CPCA); Ms. Edith Old, Director of Ministries; and Ms. Victory Moore, representative Ministry Council.

III. CONSIDERATION OF REFERRALS

A. REPORT OF THE MINISTRY COUNCIL, SECTION 1.B.6 AND APPENDIX A QUESTIONS FOR THE UNIFICATION TASK FORCE

The committee considered the reports, and after consultation with representatives of the Unification Task Force and the Ministry Council, the committee believes better communication between the Ministry Council and the Unification Task Force is needed.

RECOMMENDATION 1: That the Ministry Council and the Unification Task Force be encouraged to meet together as early as the August 2018 meeting of the Ministry Council and no later than the end of 2018 to establish a viable network of communication between those entities so that they may continue to work for a successful unification of the CPC and the CPCA.

RECOMMENDATION 2: That Item I.B.6 and Appendix A be referred to the Unification Task Force for its continued work.

B. UNIFIED COMMITTEE ON THEOLOGY AND SOCIAL CONCERNS

The committee concurs in the report. The committee questions the wisdom of including mention of specific unpublished study papers.

RECOMMENDATION 3: That the Unified Committee on Theology and Social Concerns make available to the church at large its guidelines for the panel described in its report.

C. UNIFICATION TASK FORCE

The committee received the report. The committee shares the concerns of the Ministry Council over legal and logistical issues. We affirm the care and thought that have already been put into the work of unification by the task force and have full confidence that they will provide appropriate answers to the council's questions.

We would affirm the formation of a separate Implementation Task Force might be helpful with the creation of the new denomination after unification occurs.

We affirm the steps already taken by the CPCA in amending its constitution to facilitate a move toward unification.

RECOMMENDATION 5: That Recommendation 1 of the Report of the Unification Task Force, "that the General Assembly of the CPC accept, with gratitude for her faithful service to the Unification Task Force, the resignation of Pam Phillips-Burk from the UTF," be adopted.

RECOMMENDATION 6: That Recommendation 2 of the Report of the Unification Task Force, "that the General Assemblies of the CPCA and CPC approve the proposed timeline for action," be adopted.

The detailed timeline for consideration of the plan of union reads as follows:
- 2018 General Assemblies – Meeting concurrently in Norman, Oklahoma, the assemblies propose any changes to the Plan of Union that will need to be incorporated before the vote at the two General Assemblies in 2019.
- 2018-2019 – The Task Force makes final revisions to the Plan of Union, writes Draft Bylaws, Standing Rules, and Constitutional amendments based on the final version of the Plan to be distributed for study in April 2019.
- 2019 – Meeting concurrently in Huntsville, Alabama, the two assemblies vote on approving the Plan of Union, Bylaws, Standing Rules, and Constitutional Amendments, pending approval of a majority of presbyteries of the two churches. Any Constitutional amendments are sent to the Joint Committee on Amendments for review and preparation of final wording.
- 2019-2020 – If approved by a majority of both assemblies, the Plan is sent to the Presbyteries of both churches for approval.
- 2020 – The two Assemblies, meeting concurrently, announce the vote of their Presbyteries, and if approved by a majority of both, vote on final approval of Bylaws and Standing Rules for the General Assembly of the new church (2/3 vote of approval necessary). Constitutional amendments reviewed and prepared by the Joint Committee on Amendments are approved (3/4 vote of approval necessary to refer amendments to Presbyteries for approval, and 3/4 of presbyteries, voting by simple majority, needed to approve amendments). If both assemblies approve Bylaws, the two assemblies vote to adjourn sine die, and immediately meet to organize the new Assembly of the United Church. The Unification Task Force is dismissed, and an Implementation Task Force is elected to guide the transition for the first few years to the new denomination.

RECOMMENDATION 7: That Recommendation 3 of the Report of the Unification Task Force, "that the fourth Sunday in June 2019 be recognized in the CPC and the CPCA as Unification Sunday, and that all churches be encouraged to pray for our unity in Jesus Christ, and for discernment as we seek to express our unity more fully in the future," be denied.

RECOMMENDATION 8: That the 4th Sunday in June 2019 be recognized in the CPC and the CPCA as Unification Sunday, and that all presbyteries encourage their churches to pray for our unity in Jesus Christ, and for discernment as we seek to express our unity more fully in the future.

IV. RESOLUTIONS

A. RESOLUTION FROM REVEREND CHRIS WARREN OF MURFREESBORO PRESBYTERY REGARDING THE IMPORTANCE OF WELCOME FOR THOSE WHO ARE "STRANGERS IN THE LAND" AT THE SOUTHERN BORDER OF THE UNITED STATES.

The committee heard and questioned Reverend Warren regarding the resolution. The committee supports the intent of the resolution but questions the author's use of the phrase "demand that those with the authority to do so" in the final paragraph.

RECOMMENDATION 9: That the resolution from Reverend Chris Warren that states:

"WHEREAS the foundational texts of the Christian Church, found in the Old and New Testaments of the Holy Bible emphasize the importance of welcome for those who are strangers in the land;

Deuteronomy 10:17-19 "For the LORD your God is God of gods and Lord of lords, the great God, mighty and awesome, who is not partial and takes no bribe, who executes justice for the orphan and the widow, and who loves the strangers providing them with food and clothing. You shall also love the stranger, for you were strangers in the land of Egypt."

Job 29:11-16 "When the ear heard, it commended me, and when the eye saw, it approved; because I delivered the poor who cried and the orphan who had no helper. The blessing of the wretched came upon me, and I caused the widow's heart to sing for joy. I put on righteousness, and it clothed me; my justice was like a robe and a turban. I was eyes to the blind, and feet to the lame. I was father to the needy, and I championed the cause of the stranger."

Psalm 146:7b-9 "The LORD sets the prisoners free; the LORD opens the eyes of the blind. The LORD lifts up those who are bowed down; the LORD loves the righteous. The LORD watches over the strangers; he upholds the orphan and the widow, but the way of the wicked he brings to ruin."

Matthew 25 :34-40 "Then the king will say to those at his right hand, 'Come, you that are blessed by my Father, inherit the kingdom prepared for you from the foundation of the world; for I was hungry and you gave me food, I was a stranger and you welcomed me, I was naked and you gave me clothing, I was sick and you took care of me, I was in prison and you visited me.' The the righteous will answer him, 'Lord, when was it that we saw you hungry and gave you food, or thirsty and gave you something to drink? And when was it that we saw you a stranger and welcomed you, or naked and gave you clothing? And when was it that we saw you sick or in prison and visited you?' And the king will answer them, 'Truly I tell you, just as you did it to one of the least of these who are members of my family, you did it to me.'"

WHEREAS the Scripture teaches that people of God should love our neighbors as ourselves (Leviticus 19:18, Matthew 22:39) and Christians have interpreted this command to apply to people both near and far away, and Romans 13:10 teaches "Love does no wrong to a neighbor; therefore love is the fulfillment of the law;"

WHEREAS our Lord Jesus taught the Golden Rule, "In everything do to others as you would have them do unto you; for this is the law and the prophets;"

WHEREAS the Cumberland Presbyterian Church is a global church, with members in many different countries, all members of which, from whatever place they come, are loved and cherished by God;

WHEREAS the Confession of Faith of the Cumberland Presbyterian Church states in section 6:15 that "God created the family as the primary community in which persons experience love, companionship, support, protection, discipline, encouragement, and other blessings ... "

WHEREAS the Confession of Faith of the Cumberland Presbyterian Church states in sections 6.30-6.31 that "The covenant community, governed by the Lord Christ, opposes, resists, and seeks to change all circumstances of oppression--political, economic, cultural, racial-by which persons are denied the essential dignity God intends for them in the work of creation. The covenant community affirms the lordship of Christ who sought out the poor, the oppressed, the sick, and the helpless. In her corporate life and through her individual members, the church is an advocate for all victims of violence and all those who the law or society treats as less than persons for whom Christ died. Such advocacy involves not only opposition to all unjust laws and forms of injustice but even more support for those attitudes and actions which embody the way of Christ, which is to overcome evil with good.

WHEREAS the current policy at the southern border of the United States is to detain adults who approach the border whether seeking asylum or other entry into the United States and to separate the children of those adults from their parents without any indication when their children will be restored to them, thus violating the command to welcome the stranger and the importance of the family life as the primary place in which people find love, including the love of God;

WHEREAS the way of Christ, overcoming evil with good, is violated by these denials of human rights and essential dignity; and

WHEREAS the Cumberland Presbyterian Church serves the one true God who is not limited or biased in love to people of any race, creed, nation, or any other factor used by humanity to divide;

BE IT RESOLVED that the 188th General Assembly of the Cumberland Presbyterian Church denounces the abhorrent treatment of those attempting to apply for asylum to the United States or enter the United States from its southern border;

BE IT RESOLVED that an attempt to justify this treatment of any human by use of the scripture of the Holy Bible is a gross misuse of scripture;

BE IT FURTHER RESOLVED that the 188th General Assembly of the Cumberland Presbyterian Church demands that those with the authority to do so stop these practices, particularly the practice of dividing children from their parents, contributing to terror, uncertainty, and unnecessary cruel suffering to families of God's beloved.

Respectfully Submitted, Reverend Chris Warren, Minister Commissioner to the 188th General Assembly of the Cumberland Presbyterian Church, Murfreesboro Presbytery," be denied.

RECOMMENDATION 10: That the 188th General Assembly of the Cumberland Presbyterian Church joins with the chorus of other denominations denouncing the abhorrent treatment of those attempting to apply for asylum or enter into the United States from our southern border, particularly the practice of dividing children from their parents, contributing to terror, uncertainty and unnecessary cruel suffering to families of God's beloved.

B. RESOLUTION FROM REVEREND RON MCMILLAN OF WEST TENNESSEE PRESBYTERY REGARDING HUMAN SEXUALITY.

The committee heard and questioned Reverend McMillan regarding the resolution. The committee affirms the need for a timely loving, Biblical response from the church on the issues presented. We further affirm that the Confession of Faith and Constitution holds us all to seek to support one another. Following lengthy discussion and deliberation, the committee recognizes that there are several judicial implications and a great many theological questions which deserve proper study and consultation before an informed vote can occur.

RECOMMENDATION 11: That the resolution from Reverend Ron McMillan regarding human sexuality, which states:

"WHEREAS in 1996 the General Assembly adopted a theological and judicial statement on homosexuality (General Assembly Minutes, page 313), and

WHEREAS since that time the cultural conversation and judicial decisions about marriage, sexuality, and gender identity have expanded well beyond homosexuality to include the broader LGBTQ+ movement since the 1996 General Assembly Statement on Homosexuality, necessitating a loving biblical response from the church, and

WHEREAS the general revelation of Creation reveals the binary sexuality (despite certain genetic anomalies) of human beings in the natural world; the specific revelation of the Scriptures (Gen. 1:27; 2:18-23) affirms the creation of humanity as male and female in God's image as being very good and consistently treats biological sex and gender as the same; and our Confession of Faith affirms "Among all forms of life, only human beings are created in God's own image. In the sight of God, male and female are created equal and complementary" (1.11), and

WHEREAS the connectional nature of our church, as defined by the Confession of Faith and Constitution, and demonstrated in meetings of the judicatories, churches, and lives of our members, holds us all to seek to live and support one another, holding one another accountable according to the Scriptures and our understanding of its truths as expressed in the above documents, and

BE IT RESOLVED that the General Assembly of the Cumberland Presbyterian Church reaffirm and adopt the resolutions made in the 1996 General Assembly Statement on Homosexuality as binding on our presbytery, sessions, ministers, elders, and deacons with the following adaptations:

BE IT FURTHER RESOLVED that the General Assembly of the Cumberland Presbyterian Church go on record affirming that Biblical teaching makes it clear that the practice of homosexuality or any sex act outside of monogamous marriage between a man and a woman is a sin, yet with the understanding that while God loves the sinner, He hates the sin, and His grace is available to all, 'For God did not send His Son into the world to condemn the world, but to save the world through Him' (John 3:17)

BE IT FURTHER RESOLVED, that since the practice of homosexuality or any sex act outside of monogamous marriage between a man and a woman is incompatible with a Christian life style and since officers of the church must be 'examples to the flock', General Assembly affirms that the Cumberland Presbyterian Church does not condone the ordination of practicing homosexuals or those practicing a lifestyle other than monogamous marriage or celibate singleness as Deacons, Elders or Ministers of Word and Sacrament, nor does it condone or allow the officiating of such weddings by ministers, nor the official sanctioning of such weddings by sessions/ churches, and

BE IT FURTHER RESOLVED, that the General Assembly, state as its position that we, as Christians who are ourselves sinners redeemed by the grace of God and who continue to struggle with temptation and sin in our own lives (Phil. 2:12-13; 1 Car. 10:12), must reach out to those persons who are struggling with homosexuality or any LGBTQ+ identity, offering them Christian love, education, friendship, therapy and intercession to the end that they and we may experience true wholesomeness through the freeing, renewing grace of God in Jesus Christ (Gal. 6:1-3; Jude 22-23)," be denied.

C. RESOLUTION FROM REVEREND CHRIS WARREN OF MURFREESBORO PRESBYTERY REGARDING HUMAN SEXUALITY.

Received the resolution. The committee heard and questioned Reverend Warren regarding the resolution. The committee affirms the need to take time to think, study, learn and reflect before developing a position statement on issues of human sexuality.

RECOMMENDATION 12: That the resolution presented by Reverend Chris Warren which states:

"WHEREAS Cumberland Presbyterians do not agree on interpretation of scriptural passages, few as they are, that refer to sexuality;
WHEREAS Biblical scholars have offered many different interpretations that are inclusive of sexuality outside a traditional male/female binary;
WHEREAS a resolution to exclude based on sexuality is mean spirited;
BE IT RESOLVED that the General Assembly of the Cumberland Presbyterian Church take time to think, study, learn, and reflect before taking a step to disenfranchise and exclude persons who have a heart to serve Christ and persons who are already serving in leadership roles in the Church.

Respectfully Submitted, Reverend Chris Warren, Minister Commissioner, Murfreesboro Presbytery," be denied.

V. FURTHER ACTIONS

A. CPC STATEMENT ON HUMAN SEXUALITY

The committee recognizes deficiencies and potential constitutional issues in the resolutions for which we recommend denial. Furthermore, the committee believes there is a need for a great deal more study prior to a vote on issues regarding human sexuality. Yet, it is our desire that the Cumberland Presbyterian Church develop an appropriate response to these critical issues. We strongly urge the denomination to begin with the Statement on Homosexuality adopted by General Assembly in 1996 and consider other pertinent information from various perspectives in order to set forth a loving, Biblical and theologically sound response to these very important questions. Therefore, we make the following recommendation:

RECOMMENDATION 13: That the Permanent Judiciary Committee, Unified Committee on Theology and Social Concerns, and the Ministry Council work jointly to develop a position statement on issues of human sexuality to be presented to the 189th General Assembly for its consideration.

B. The committee recognizes the miscommunication regarding joint meetings of the Committees on Theology and Social Concerns of each denomination that were to take place during our General Assemblies. We deeply regret the miscommunication and look forward to future meetings together with our sisters and brothers in Christ.

Respectfully Submitted,
Committee on Theological and Social Concerns/Unification Task Force

REPORT OF THE COMMITTEE ON MINISTRY COUNCIL

I. REFERRALS

Referrals to this committee are as follows: The Report of the Ministry Council, except shaded section 1.B.6 and Appendix A Questions for the Unification Task Force, which are referred to the Committee on Theology & Social Concerns/ Unification Task Force; and the Resolution from Arkansas Presbytery Regarding the Mission and Purpose of the Encounter Publication.

II. PERSONS OF COUNSEL

Appearing before this committee were: Mrs. Edith Old, Director of Ministries; Ms. Victory Moore, Representive from Ministry Council; Reverend Elinor Brown, Discipleship Ministry Team; Reverend Milton Ortiz, Missions Ministry Team; Reverend Drew Gray, member of the Ministry Council; and Reverend Alan Meinzer, Reverend Gordon Warren, Reverend Jo Warren from Arkansas Presbytery.

III. CONSIDERATION OF REFERRALS

A. REPORT OF THE MINISTRY COUNCIL

We commend the Ministry Council for all of their hard work and make the following recommendation:

RECOMMENDATION 1: That Recommendation 1 of the Report of the Ministry Council, "that the 188th General Assembly interpret the phrase "a degree in a graduate school of theology" Constitution 6.34 to be inclusive of Master's degrees in other forms of Christian ministry (for example MA Youth Ministry, MA Christian Ministry) and not restricted to Master of Divinity," be denied.

B. RESOLUTION FROM ARKANSAS PRESBYTERY REGARDING THE MISSION AND PURPOSE OF THE ENCOUNTER PUBLICATION

After reviewing the resolution by Arkansas Presbytery regarding the mission and purpose of the Encounter Publication. We, the Ministry Council Committee, would like to commend Arkansas Presbytery on their heartfelt desire to make the Encounter Publication the best tool that it can be for the growth of the CPC Church. We would also like to commend the DMT for having an open-door policy and encourage all congregations to communicate directly with the DMT when concerns arise.

RECOMMENDATION 2: That the Resolution from Arkansas Presbytery which reads:

WHEREAS the Cumberland Presbyterian Church is founded on the teachings of Jesus Christ as expressed in Scripture and the Cumberland Presbyterian Confession of Faith.
WHEREAS the Encounter is a publication of the Cumberland Presbyterian and as such is considered as expressing the beliefs of the Cumberland Presbyterian Church.
WHEREAS the Encounter is in the position to influence Christians in their understanding of scripture and belief, and thus this position places its writers in a position of authority to speak on scripture and belief.
WHEREAS the writers of the Encounter Publications have at times spoken from this position of authority in ways that might be considered as expressing views that are not supported in the Confession of Faith.

WHEREAS in these writings, the author's may have had the desire to promote thought, they in turn failed to express the point of view found within the Confession of Faith. Such a failure never gave the readers the opportunity to think about the Cumberland Presbyterian View Point. The omission could be troubling because the writers are speaking from a positon of authority. For many churches in Arkansas Presbytery, the most recent examples became quite troubling, as they see the Encounter Publication as a Cumberland Presbyterian Publication. These examples are listed below.

On page 16 of the June, July, August, 2017 Encounter has the following quote:
"For Christians, Jesus is the supreme example of loving kindness. To affirm this belief does not lessen the role of Moses for Judaism, Mohammed for Islam, or Buddha for Buddhism. It does not deny the positive influence of other important religious teachers. Buddha said often, "My religion is kindness." When anyone relates to the God of creative possibilities, transformation occurs, bringing harmony and peace. Gathering around the gentle teachings that are present in all religions offers a pathway to peace in our global, pluralistic age."

WHEREAS on page 17 of the June, July, August, 2017 Encounter has the following quote: "Human kindness when grounded in the kindness of God revealed in Jesus' teachings and empowered by God's Spirit is a healing force for good. This healing kindness is also found in the teachings of Buddha."

WHEREAS the above two quotes may appear to elevate the teachings of Buddha and Islam to an equal position of Christ, and also as a way of salvation separate from that of Christ. If we are all kind, however we come to that kindness, then we are doing what God asks us to do, and thus we all find ourselves in a relationship with God.

There may be issues of interpretation and intent with these scriptures, but such interpretation and intent would have been unnecessary if a reference would have been made to our Confession of Faith.

Our Confession of Faith states in
3.07, "God's mighty act of reconciling love was accomplished in Jesus Christ, the divine Son who became flesh to be the means by which the sins of the world are forgiven."
4.10, "When persons repent of sin and in faith embrace God's salvation, they receive forgiveness for their sin and experience acceptance as God's children."
5.29, "Growth is natural to the church's life. The church is called into being and exists to reach out to those who have not experienced God's grace in Christ, and to nourish them with all the means of grace."
5:30, "In carrying out the apostolic commission, the covenant community has encounted and continues to encounter people who belong to religions which do not acknowledge Jesus Christ as Lord. While respecting persons who adhere to other religions, Christians are responsible to share with them the good news of salvation through Jesus Christ."

As Cumberland Presbyterians the "Who So Ever Will" doctrine is central to our faith, understanding, and practice as Cumberland Presbyterians. John 3:16-17 KJV states: "For God so loved the world, that He gave His only begotten Son, that whosoever believeth in Him should not perish, but have everlasting life. For God sent not His Son into the world to condemn the world; but that that the world through Him might be saved."

It is with a want for understanding of the Mission and Purpose of the Encounter Publication that Arkansas Presbytery petitions the 2018 General Assembly to take the following action.

Arkansas Presbytery petitions the 2018 General Assembly of the Cumberland Presbyterian Church to form a Committee to study the mission and purpose of the Encounter Publication in an effort to determine if this publication of the Cumberland Presbyterian is promoting a theology and understanding that supports and upholds our Confession of Faith. In an effort to gather this information the Committee will be asked to review the Adult Encounter Publications for the last 3 years. In this endeavor the Committee will also be instructed to study the subscription list of the Encounter Publication to determine how many of the Cumberland Presbyterian Churches listed in the Yearbook, subscribe to the Encounter. The Committee will also be instructed to inquire of at least 50% of the Cumberland Presbyterian Churches that do not scribe to the Encounter Material, as to why they do not.

RECOMMENDATION 3: That the 188th General Assembly request the committee consisting of 1 representative from each synod. This committee will work with the Discipleship Ministery Team develop and to conduct a census/survey of all congregations in regards to particular churches use of the Encounter Publication with the results of that census/survey disseminated through the stated clerks of each presbytery by the 190th General Assembly. The committee members are: Vicky Goodwin, Mission Synod; Lisa Scott, Synod of the Midwest; Grady Prevost, Synod of the Southeast; Ben Lindamood, Tennessee Synod; and Mike Reno, Synod of Great Rivers.

Respectfully submitted,
The Ministry Council Committee

REPORT OF THE COMMITTEE ON STEWARDSHIP/ELECTED OFFICERS

I. REFERRALS

Referrals to this committee are as follows: The Report of the Moderator; The Report of the Stated Clerk; The Report of the Board of Stewardship, Foundation and Benefits; The Report of the Our United Outreach Committee; The Report of the Place of Meeting Committee; and The Line Item Budgets Submitted by General Assembly Agencies.

II. PERSONS OF COUNSEL

Appearing before this committee were: Reverend Robert Heflin, Mr. Mark Duck, and Board Representative, Mr. Randy Davidson (Board of Stewardship); Reverend Cliff Hudson, and regional representatives: Colatta Edsell, Jeff McMichael and Bruce Hamilton (Our United Outreach Committee); Reverend Michael Sharpe, Stated Clerk; and Reverend Kevin Brantley, Board Representative, Memphis Theological Seminary.

III. CONSIDERATION OF REFERRALS

A. REPORT OF THE MODERATOR

Concurred in the moderator's report and expressed gratitude for Reverend Lancaster's service as moderator. We agree with his assessment that column 5 in the yearbook is the best sign of health and wellness in our churches.

B. THE REPORT OF THE STATED CLERK

The 187th General Assembly submitted to the presbyteries a Constitutional Amendment: Constitution changing 9.5 and inserting 9.6. The necessary number of presbyteries voted in the affirmative.

RECOMMENDATION 1: That Recommendation 1 of the Stated Clerk's report, "that the 188th General Assembly declare that the Constitutional Amendment has been approved," be adopted.

RECOMMENDATION 2: That Recommendation 2 of the Report of the Stated Clerk, "that the 188th General Assembly approve the following dates for the 2018-2019 Church Calendar:

CHURCH CALENDAR 2018-2019

July-2018
7	Program of Alternate Studies Graduation
7-21	PAS Summer Extension School, Bethel, McKenzie, Tennessee
14	Children's Fest
14	The Meet Up
21	Children's Fest East

August-2018
4   Bethel University Commencement
5-Sept 30 Christian Education Season
19   Seminary/PAS Sunday
20   Bethel University Fall Semester Begins
25   MTS Fall Semester Begins (tentative)
28   MTS Opening convocation (tentative)
28   Bethel University Fall Convocation

September-2018
9   Family Sunday
9   Senior Adult Sunday
16   Christian Service Recognition Sunday
16   International Day of Prayer and Action for Human Habitat

October-2018
     Clergy Appreciation Month
7   Worldwide Communion Sunday
7   Pastor Appreciation Sunday
21   Native American Sunday

November-2018
     Any Sunday Loaves and Fishes Program
1   All Saints Day
2   World Community Day (Church Women United)
4   Bethel University Sunday
4   Stewardship Sunday
11   Day of Prayer for People with Aids and Other Life-Threatening Illnesses
18   Bible Sunday
25   Christ the King Sunday

December-2018
     Any Sunday Gift to the King Offering
2-24   Advent in Church and Home
8   Bethel University Commencement
24   Christmas Eve
25   Christmas Day

January-2019
6   Epiphany
7   BU Spring Semester Begins
7-8   Stated Clerks' Conference
11   Human Trafficking Awareness Day
15   Deadline for receipt of 2018 Our United Outreach Contributions

February-2019
     Black History Month
1   Annual congregational reports due in General Assembly office
3   Denomination Day
3   Historical Foundation Offering
3   Souper Bowl Sunday
10   Our United Outreach Sunday
17   Youth Sunday

March-2019
     Women's History Month (USA)
6   Ash Wednesday, the beginning of Lent 6–April 21 Lent to Easter
17   Children's Home Sunday
24-31   National Farm Workers Awareness Week

April-2019
14   Palm/Passion Sunday
18   Maundy Thursday
19   Good Friday
21   Easter

May-2019
3   Friendship Day (Church Women United)
4   Bethel University Commencement
11   MTS Closing Convocation & Graduation
27   Memorial Day Offering for Military Chaplains & Personnel for USA churches

June-2019
9   Stott-Wallace Missionary Fund Offering/World penMission Sunday
9   Pentecost
9-14 General Assembly, Huntsville, Alabama
11-13 CPWM Convention, Huntsville, Alabama
16   CPC Ministries Sunday
23   Unification Sunday
23-28 Cumberland Presbyterian Youth Conference, Bethel University, McKenzie, Tennessee

July-2019
6   Children's Fest
6   The Meet Up
7   Outdoor Ministries Sunday
13   Program of Alternate Studies Graduation
13-27 PAS Summer Extension School, Bethel, McKenzie, Tennessee
16-20 Presbyterian Youth Triennium

August-2019
3   Bethel University Commencement
4-Sept 30 Christian Education Sunday & Season
18   MTS Fall Semester Begins (tentative)
18   Seminary/PAS Sunday
22   Bethel University Fall Semester Begins
25   MTS Fall Semester Begins (tentative)
27   Bethel University Fall Convocation

September-2019
4   MTS Opening convocation (tentative)
8   Family Sunday
8   Senior Adult Sunday
15   Christian Service Recognition Sunday
15   International Day of Prayer and Action for Human Habitat

October-2019
      Clergy Appreciation Month
6   Worldwide Communion Sunday
13   Pastor Appreciation Sunday
20   Native American Sunday

November-2019
Any Sunday Loaves and Fishes Program
1   All Saints Day
1   World Community Day (Church Women United)
3   Bethel University Sunday
3   Stewardship Sunday
10   Day of Prayer for People with Aids and Other Life-Threatening Illnesses
17   Bible Sunday
24   Christ the King Sunday

December-2019
Any Sunday Gift to the King Offering
2   PAS Advisory Council
2-24 Advent in Church and Home
7   Bethel University Commencement
24   Christmas Eve
25   Christmas Day," be adopted.

C. THE REPORT OF THE BOARD OF STEWARDSHIP, FOUNDATION, AND BENEFITS

We commend the work of the Board and appreciate their hard work on behalf of ministers, churches, and all others they serve.

RECOMMENDATION 3: That Recommendation 1 of the Report of the Board of Stewardship, Foundation, and Benefits, "that the General Assembly approve the amended plan and updates of the Cumberland Presbyterian Retirement Plan #2," be adopted.

Below is the amended portion:
"As a Participant, you may elect to defer a percentage of your compensation each year instead of receiving that amount in cash. There are two types of pre-tax contributions that you can make under the plan: basic contributions and elective contributions. You may defer up to 5% of your pay as a basic contribution. Once you have reached the contribution limit for the basic contribution, you may defer an additional percentage or dollar amount of your pay as an elective contribution. However, the total deferrals that you can elect to defer from your pay in any taxable year may not exceed certain dollar limit which is set by law. The limit for 2018 is $18,500."

D. THE REPORT OF THE OUR UNITED OUTREACH COMMITTEE

Although some ministries occasionally ask for additional offerings, the committee wishes to emphasize that OUO is the primary funding source for all denominational ministries.

Every member of the committee committed to support and promote OUO in our own congregations and presbyteries. We challenge every commissioner and attendee of the 188th General Assembly to do the same.

RECOMMENDATION 4: That Recommendation 1 of the Report of the Our United Outreach Committee, "that General Assembly adopt the following Our United Outreach allocations for 2019:

The allocation is to be as follows:	$2,600,000.00	
Development Coordinator Office and OUO Committee		92,044.00
Unification Task Force		35,000.00
		127,044.00
Sub-total	127,044.00	
(Amount to be allocated)	$2,472,956.00	
Ministry Council	$1,236,478.00	50%
Bethel University	123,648.00	5%
Children's Home	74,189.00	3%
Stewardship	148,377.00	6%
General Assembly Office	197,836.00	8%
Memphis Theological Seminary/ Program of Alternate Studies	173,107.00	7%
Historical Foundation	74,189.00	3%
Shared Services	408,038.00	16.5%
Contingency	12,365.00	.5%
(Next four items total 1%)		
Comm. on Chaplains	9,570.00	.387%
Judiciary Committee	9,026.00	.365%
Theology/Social Concerns	3,363.00	.136%
Nominating Committee	2,770.00	.112%
	2,472,956.00	

Our United Outreach Goal $2,600,000.00," be adopted.

RECOMMENDATION 5: That Recommendation 2 of the Report of the Our United Outreach Committee, "that the OUO committee meeting in an executive session requests General Assembly to direct the Unification Task Force and Development Coordinator Office of OUO to account for expenditures to this committee," be adopted.

Despite adequate promotion, the reality is that many Cumberland Presbyterians are unaware of the work and importance of OUO.

RECOMMENDATION 6: That Recommendation 3 of the Report of the Our United Outreach Committee, "that the OUO committee requests that the General Assembly challenge churches to invite an OUO Representative or member of the OUO Committee to speak in their congregations," be denied.

RECOMMENDATION 7: That the OUO committee requests that the presbyteries challenge churches to invite an OUO Representative or member of the OUO committee to speak in their congregations.

RECOMMENDATION 8: That General Assembly By-Law 11.06.01 The committee shall consist of five (5) persons elected by the corporation in such a manner that, immediately following any election, the committee shall have one person from each synod. Seven (7) additional members will include a member of the Ministry Council, a member of the Corporate Board, a member of the Board of Stewardship, Foundation and Benefits, a member of the Board of Trustees of the Historical Foundation, and a Cumberland Presbyterian member of the Boards of Trustees of Bethel University, the Cumberland Presbyterian Children's Home, and Memphis Theological Seminary. The executives of the above named denominational entities shall serve as non-voting, Resource/Advocacy members, be amended to read, *"The Committee shall consist of five (5) persons elected by the corporation in such a manner, that immediately following any election, the committee shall have one person from each synod. Seven (7) additional members will include a member of the Ministry Foundation and Benefits, a member of the Board of Trustees of the Historical Foundation, and a Cumberland Presbyterian member of the Boards of Trustees of Bethel University, the Cumberland Presbyterian Children's Home, and Memphis Theological Seminary. The executives of the above named denominational entities shall serve as non- voting, Resource/Advocacy members. In addition, the Corporation shall elect Three (3) Youth Advisory Members who shall be between the ages of 15-17 and be elected for one (1) year terms, with eligibility for re-election for one additional term."*

Recognizing that different generations receive information via distinct media, we are encouraged to hear that the OUO committee is developing a promotional DVD and challenge the committee to continue to innovate.

RECOMMENDATION 9: That the OUO utilize all forms of communication and technology in order to reach every generation.

E. THE REPORT OF THE PLACE OF MEETING COMMITTEE

The committee concurs in the Place of Meeting Committee Report.

F. LINE ITEM BUDGETS SUBMITTED BY GENERAL ASSEMBLY AGENCIES

The committee expresses appreciation for the hard work in preparing ministry budgets, and recognize the uncertainty involved in this task. We were quite concerned over the unbalanced budget of Memphis Theological Seminary but were encouraged by the assurance that there will be a balanced budget by 2021.

Respectfully submitted:
The Committee on Stewardship/
Elected Officers

REPORT OF THE COMMITTEE ON JUDICIARY

I. REFERRALS

Referrals to this committee are as follows: The Report of the Permanent Committee on Judiciary and The Report of the Joint Committee on Amendments.

II. PERSONS OF COUNSEL

Reverend Lynn Thomas, Director of Global Missions; Ms. Pamela Brown, representative of the Permanent Judiciary Committee; and Stated Clerk Reverend Mike Sharpe appeared before the committee. Elder Jamie Jordan, counsel for the Office of the General Assembly, consulted by telephone.

III. CONSIDERATION OF REFERRALS

A. REPORT OF THE PERMANENT JUDICIARY COMMITTEE

RECOMMENDATION 1: That Recommendation 1 of the Report of the Permanent Judiciary Committee, "that the Preamble to the Constitution be amended by inserting the following paragraph between the first and second existing paragraphs: "Cumberland Presbyterian congregations are found around the world. While the mission of the church is the same everywhere, the forms and structures of the *Constitution* do not always fit seamlessly with the cultures, traditions, and legal systems of some countries. In countries other than the United States the provisions of the *Constitution* should be applied so far as possible, but the *Constitution* is, at its heart, a document which exists to promote spiritual objectives. If there are instances in which the letter of the *Constitution* cannot be applied without compromising the mission of the church and the spiritual objectives identified in the *Confession of Faith*, it is the spirit of the law, rather than the letter, which must prevail," be denied.

Our *Confession of Faith* and *Rules of Discipline* are written specifically for U.S. laws, where churches do not pay taxes and pastors are exempted from many labor laws. This is not the case in other countries. Also, some provisions of our *Constitution* are incompatible with property laws of other countries. The Committee agrees with the intent of this change to the preamble. It must be noted that, although bound in the same printed publication, the *Rules of Discipline* and *Constitution* are, in fact, different documents. We therefore make the following recommendations to change the above wording to treat the *Rules of Discipline* appropriately as a separate publication.

RECOMMENDATION 2: That the Preamble to the *Constitution* be amended by inserting the following paragraph between the first and second existing paragraphs: "Cumberland Presbyterian congregations are found around the world. While the mission of the church is the same everywhere, the forms and structures of the *Constitution* and *Rules of Discipline* do not always fit seamlessly with the cultures, traditions, and legal systems of some countries. In countries other than the United States the provisions of the *Constitution* and *Rules of Discipline* should be applied so far as possible, but the *Constitution* and *Rules of Discipline* are, at heart, documents which exist to promote spiritual objectives. If there are instances in which the letter of the *Constitution* and/or *Rules of Discipline* cannot be applied without compromising the mission of the church and the spiritual objectives identified in the *Confession of Faith*, it is the spirit of the law, rather than the letter, which must prevail."

The Committee acknowledges that, more often than not, oversight of lower judicatories is in the form of review of minutes or appellate decision. As was stated in the Permanent Judiciary Committee Report, the higher judicatories exercise their "review and control" of lower judicatories through review and appellate authority.

RECOMMENDATION 3: That Recommendation 2 of the Report of the Permanent Judiciary Committee, "that Constitution 3.03 be amended from "The authority of each level of church government is limited by the stated provisions of the church's constitution. Although each judicatory

exercises exclusive original jurisdiction over all the matters specifically belonging to it, the lower judicatories are subject to the review and control of the higher judicatories in regular gradation." to read *"The authority of each level of church government is limited by the stated provisions of the Constitution. Although each judicatory exercises exclusive original jurisdiction over all the matters specifically belonging to it, the lower judicatories are subject to the review and appellate authority of the next higher judicatory,"* be adopted.

RECOMMENDATION 4: That Recommendation 3 of the Report of the Permanent Judiciary Committee, "that Constitution 3.35 be amended from "A particular church shall not sell, nor lease its real property used for purposes of worship, nurture or ministry, without the written permission of the presbytery in which the particular church is located, transmitted through the session of the particular church." to read *"A particular church shall not sell, convey, lease, pledge, mortgage, or encumber its real property used for purposes of worship, nurture, or ministry without the written permission of the presbytery in which the particular church is located, transmitted through the session of the particular church. In granting its permission, the presbytery does not become a party to the church's agreement, nor a guarantor of any indebtedness,"* be adopted.

This adds another layer of protection for a Presbytery in the event that a church defaults on a mortgage on its property.

RECOMMENDATION 5: That Recommendation 4 of the Report of the Permanent Judiciary Committee, "that Constitution 7.06, which refers to the relationships of pastor, assistant/associate pastor, stated supply, and interim pastor, be amended from "A person shall enter into one of these relationships with a particular church only with the approval of the presbytery in the bounds of which the particular church is located. The presbytery may authorize its board of missions to act on its behalf in examining the call and to give tentative approval to a relationship between a particular church and a minister, licentiate, or candidate, subject to formal approval at a meeting of the presbytery." to read *"A person shall enter into one of these relationships with a particular church only with the approval of the presbytery in the bounds of which the particular church is located. The church session shall bear responsibility for the selection of the person, and the presbytery's approval shall relate to the person's ministerial credentials, commitment to the theology and government of the Cumberland Presbyterian Church/Cumberland Presbyterian Church in America, and standing in his or her current presbytery, if any. The presbytery may authorize its board of missions to act on its behalf in examining the call and to give tentative approval to a relationship between a particular church and a minister, licentiate, or candidate, subject to formal approval at a meeting of the presbytery,"* be adopted.

This proposed change helps clarify the language regarding the differing roles of the session and presbytery in the calling of a pastor.

This Committee agrees with the Permanent Committee's Recommendations 5, 6, 7, and 8, which clarify the language related to the relationship between General Assembly and lower judicatories and denominational entities.

RECOMMENDATION 6: That Recommendation 5 of the Report of the Permanent Judiciary Committee, "that Constitution 8.5(f) be amended from "In general, to order with respect to the presbyteries, sessions, and churches under its care according to the government of the church, whatever may seem to edify the church;" to read *"In general, to order with respect to the presbyteries, sessions, and churches under its care according to the government of the church, whatever pertains to their spiritual welfare and the edification of the church,"* be adopted.

RECOMMENDATION 7: That Recommendation 6 of the Report of the Permanent Judiciary Committee, "that Constitution 9.4 (d) be amended from "Institute and oversee the agencies necessary in its work;" to read *"Institute and review the work of denominational entities,"* be adopted.

RECOMMENDATION 8: That Recommendation 7 of the Report of the Permanent Judiciary Committee, "that Constitution 9.4(g) be amended from "Take care that the lower judicatories observe the government of the church and redress what they may have done contrary to order," to read *"Take care that the lower judicatories observe the government of the church and exercise its review and appellate authority to redress what they may have done contrary to order,"* be adopted.

RECOMMENDATION 9: That Recommendation 8 of the Report of the Permanent Judiciary Committee, "that Constitution 9.4(m) be amended from "Oversee the affairs of the whole church," to read *"Keep watch over the affairs of the whole church,"* be adopted.

RECOMMENDATION 10: That Recommendation 9 of the Report of the Permanent Judiciary Committee, "that Bylaw 10.07 of the General Assembly Corporation be amended from "The corporation shall elect the twenty- four (24) directors of Memphis Theological Seminary as provided in its charter. The corporation shall elect the directors in such a manner that, immediately following any election, there shall be at least eleven (11) directors who are members of ecumenical partners of the Seminary." to read *"The corporation shall elect the twenty-four (24) directors of Memphis Theological Seminary as provided in its charter. The corporation shall elect the directors in such a manner that, immediately following any election, there shall be eleven (11) directors who are members of denominations other than the Cumberland Presbyterian Church,"* be denied.

The Committee found a typographical error in Recommendation 9 of the Permanent Judiciary Committee's report. The Bylaw being amended is actually 10.06.

RECOMMENDATION 11: That Bylaw 10.06 of the General Assembly Corporation be amended from "The corporation shall elect the twenty-four (24) directors of Memphis Theological Seminary as provided in its charter. The corporation shall elect the directors in such a manner that, immediately following any election, there shall be at least eleven (11) directors who are members of ecumenical partners of the Seminary." to read *"The corporation shall elect the twenty-four (24) directors of Memphis Theological Seminary as provided in its charter. The corporation shall elect the directors in such a manner that, immediately following any election, there shall be eleven (11) directors who are members of denominations other than the Cumberland Presbyterian Church."*

B. REPORT OF THE JOINT COMMITTEE ON AMENDMENTS

The Committee reviewed this report, which contains no recommendations. Pertaining to section II, we are supportive of the possibility of and look forward to the formation of union congregations between the Cumberland Presbyterian Church and the Cumberland Presbyterian Church in America.

Respectfully submitted, The Judiciary Committee

REPORT OF THE COMMITTEE ON CHILDREN'S HOME/HIGHER EDUCATION

I. REFERRALS

Referrals to this committee are as follows: The Report of the Board of Trustees of Memphis Theological Seminary, The Report of the Board of Trustees of Bethel University, and The Report of the Board of Trustees of the Cumberland Presbyterian Children's Home,

II. PERSONS OF COUNSEL

Appearing before this committee were: from Cumberland Presbyterian Children's Home: Reverend Duane Dougherty (Board of Trustees), Dr. Jennifer Livings (Interim President), and Mary Dickerman; from Bethel University: Dr. Walter Butler (President), Reverend Nancy McSpadden, Nancy Bean, Reverend Elton Hall Sr. (Board of Trustees); Dr. Anne Hames (Senior Chaplain) and Reverend Garrett Burns (Associate Chaplain); from Memphis Theological Seminary: Dr. Daniel Jay Earheart-Brown (President), Reverend Kevin Brantley, (Board of Trustees), and Dr. Michael Qualls (PAS).

III. CONSIDERATION OF REFERRALS

A. THE REPORT OF THE BOARD OF TRUSTEES OF THE CUMBERLAND PRESBYTERIAN CHILDREN'S HOME

The Cumberland Presbyterian Children's Home (CPCH) was established in 1904. The ministry has continually focused on service to children and families since its opening. We commend CPCH for their continued focus and the efforts they make to change their programs to meet the ever changing needs of children and families they serve. Currently CPCH has an interim President and a search is being conducted to fill the position of president.

Since CPCH bears the name of Cumberland Presbyterian the committee would like to know what percentage of the CPCH income comes directly from OUO, churches and individuals associated with the Cumberland Presbyterian Church.

Based on the conversations between the Committee and the representatives of the Children's Home the Committee suggested the Children's Home to provide a summary of contributions from Cumberland Presbyterian sources detailed into OUO, churches and individuals to General Assembly yearly in their annual report. This report may include what percentage of the overall income of the Children's Homes is from Cumberland Presbyterian sources.

Currently there are no Cumberland Presbyterian employees at the Children's Home. Advertising through the Communication Ministry Team will allow the entire church to know the job openings as well as other opportunities to assist this institution in meeting the needs of the children and families they serve.

RECOMMENDATION 1: That the Communication Ministry Team collaborate with the Children's Home to advertise open positions, volunteer opportunities, service trip opportunities or other areas of need of the Children's Home.

By increasing the Cumberland Presbyterian involvement in the activities of CPCH and providing opportunities for the children and families to be involved at Cumberland Presbyterian activities we will strengthen the ties to the Cumberland Presbyterian denomination.

The Committee feels that maintaining a Cumberland Presbyterian presence in the work of the Children's Home is important.

RECOMMENDATION 2: That all Presbyteries, and especially those close by, seek opportunities for support of and participation in the work of the Children's Home.

B. THE REPORT OF THE BOARD OF TRUSTEES OF BETHEL UNIVERSITY

Bethel University has served as the Flagship University of the Cumberland Presbyterian Church for 176 years. Its commitment to providing a quality private education at a reasonable cost is demonstrated by it being ranked in the top 10% of most affordable private colleges in Tennessee. Bethel has shown consistent growth. Its academic excellence has been demonstrated by the distinguished accomplishments of its alumni. For example, the Nursing Department achieved a pass rated of 100% 3 of the last five years, and a pass rate above 90% the other two years. Some of the most highly placed law enforcement officials in the state of Tennessee are graduates of the Criminal Justice program. Bethel students are not waiting until after graduation to achieve excellence as evidenced by their being recipients of the NAIA Champions of Character award, and just recently, their Bass Fishing team won the National Championship and finished the year ranked No. 1 of schools of all divisions and sizes. Bethel University has demonstrated a strong commitment to serving the Jesus Christ and the Cumberland Presbyterian Church.

RECOMMENDATION 3: That Recommendation 1 of the Report of the Board of Trustees of Bethel University, "that the General Assembly of the Cumberland Presbyterian Church encourage the churches and individuals to pray for Bethel University and send names of prospective students (both high schoolers and adults) to Bethel University," be denied.

RECOMMENDATION 4: That the General Assembly of the Cumberland Presbyterian Church urge the presbyteries to encourage the churches and individuals to pray for Bethel University and send names of prospective students (both high schoolers and adults) to Bethel University.

C. THE REPORT OF THE BOARD OF TRUSTEES OF MEMPHIS THEOLOGICAL SEMINARY

Since 1852 Memphis Theological Seminary has played a vital role in the education of the ministers and leaders of the Cumberland Presbyterian Church. The Seminary continues to minister in an ever changing world as it strives to meet the challenges and opportunities of ministry in the world today. We are grateful for the vital work of Memphis Theological Seminary and especially its trustees who have served with honor.

RECOMMENDATION 5: That Recommendation 1 of the Report of the Board of Trustees of Memphis Theological Seminary, "that the General Assembly express its gratitude to trustees Henson, Newell, White, Brantley, Maddox, and Shirai for their faithful service to Memphis Theological Seminary and the Cumberland Presbyterian Church," be adopted.

The Ministry for the Real World campaign is a vital strategy to insure that Memphis Theological Seminary continues to fulfill its calling.

RECOMMENDATION 6: That Recommendation 2 of the Report of the Board of Trustees of Memphis Theological Seminary, "that the General Assembly encourage individuals, churches, and groups across the Cumberland Presbyterian Church to consider investing in the development of future leaders through the "Ministry for the Real World" campaign," be denied.

RECOMMENDATION 7: That the General Assembly encourage Presbyteries to encourage churches, groups, and individuals across the Cumberland Presbyterian Church to consider investing in the development of future leaders through the "Ministry for the Real World" campaign.

It has been noted that the number of Cumberland Presbyterian Students graduating from Memphis Theological Seminary and PAS has been in decline.

RECOMMENDATION 8: That Recommendation 3 of the Report of the Board of Trustees of Memphis Theological Seminary, "that the General Assembly encourage all probationers to consider Memphis Theological Seminary and the Program of Alternate Studies as their first options for meeting educational requirements for ordained ministry," be denied.

RECOMMENDATION 9: That the General Assembly request all Presbyteries to encourage their probationers to consider Memphis Theological Seminary and the Program of Alternate Studies as their first options for meeting educational requirements for ordained ministry.

RECOMMENDATION 10: That the third Sunday in August, (August 19, 2018 and August 18, 2019) be included in the General Assembly Calendar as Seminary/PAS Sunday, and that the General Assembly instruct presbyteries to encourage all churches to share information about MTS and PAS and receive a special offering on that day, or on a more convenient day of the session's choosing.

This recommendation was referred to the Committee on Stewardship and Elected officials.
The Committee notes the recent resignation of Dr. Daniel Jay Earheart-Brown. Dr. Earheart-Brown has been a consistent advocate for the seminary, its students and the denomination. Therefore, we make the following recommendation:

RECOMMENDATION 11: That 188th General Assembly express its gratitude to Reverend Daniel Jay Earheart- Brown for his thirteeen (13) and one-half years of faithful service to Memphis Theological Seminary.

The Committee recognizes that while Memphis Theological Seminary is the Cumberland Presbyterian seminary, the actual presence of Cumberland Presbyterians in leadership and on the faculty has declined. Therefore it seems important that we seek out and recruit additional Cumberland Presbyterian leadership, faculty, and staff. With this in mind, the Committee makes the following recommendation:

RECOMMENDATION 12: That the 188th General Assembly encourage the MTS Board of Trustees to hire a qualified Cumberland Presbyterian to fill the office of interim and permanent president.

The Committee on Higher Education and the Children's Home makes the following recommendation based on the recommendation adopted by the 2013 General Assembly for the creation of periodic Evaluation Committees to assess the entities and programs overseen by the Cumberland Presbyterian Church. The Committee recognizes and appreciates the mission and work that the Memphis Theological Seminary in preparing the future ministers and leaders of the Cumberland Presbyterian Church. We commend them on their efforts for diversity and relevance in our modern and ever changing world. We express our concern over the financial deficits incurred by the Seminary over the last six years. We commend the Trustees for their decision to balance the budget within the next three years. We recognize that enrollment in the Seminary, and in Seminaries nationwide, is declining and endorse the measures taken by the Board of Trustee and the Faculty to increase the educational opportunities available to the student body of the Seminary. In recognition of General Assembly's responsibility to maintain oversight of the Memphis Theological Seminary, and in partnership with them, the Committee makes the following recommendation to ensure that General Assembly has the necessary information to effectively complete its oversight responsibilities.

RECOMMENDATION 13: Pursuant to the previously adopted recommendation of the 183rd General Assembly, that an Evaluation Committee be appointed to conduct an assessment of the Cumberland Presbyterian Historical Foundation and the Memphis Theological Seminary. This Committee recommends that an assessment of the Historical Foundation and the Memphis Theological Seminary be completed. This assessment shall of the Seminary shall be divided into two separate assessments: 1.) the Board of Trustees and 2.) the Seminary Faculty and Staff. The Evaluation Committee shall conduct, and complete their assessment for presentation to the 189th meeting of the General Assembly of the Cumberland Presbyterian Church.

The assessment of the Historical Foundation may include, but not be limited to:

1. An assessment of the stated mission of the Historical Foundation;
2. Assessment of the progress towards continuancy of their stated mission;
3. Assessment of the procedures, tools and equipment used and/or needed by the Historical Foundation to continue their stated mission;
4. Recommendations to the General Assembly related to the Historical Foundation; and
5. Any other relevant area of inquiry as determined by the Evaluation Committee.

The assessment of the Memphis Theological Seminary shall include, but not be limited to:

1. An assessment of the make-up of the Board of Trustees of the Memphis Theological Seminary;
2. Assessment of the short and long term goals of the Board of Trustees;
3. Assessment of the Board's fiduciary responsibilities and the governance of the Seminary;
4. Assessment of the financial solvency and stability of the Seminary;
5. Assessment of the recruitment and hiring procedures of the faculty and staff of the Seminary;
6. Recommendations to the General Assembly related to the Board of Trustees;
7. An assessment of the curriculum and theology taught at the Memphis Theological Seminary as it relates to the practices and beliefs of the Cumberland Presbyterian Church as set forth in the Confession of Faith;
8. Assessment of the make-up (theological/diversity) of the faculty (full-time and adjunct) and staff of the Seminary;
9. Assessment of the practical preparation and skill set training provided by the Seminary to equip and prepare seminary students to become and succeed as ministers of the Cumberland Presbyterian Church;
10. A statistical review of the placement of recent graduates of the Seminary in churches within the Cumberland Presbyterian Church;
11. Assessment of the relationship between the Seminary and the Presbyteries of the Cumberland Presbyterian Church;
12. Recommendations to the General Assembly for improvement of the faculty, staff, curriculum and programs provided by the Seminary based upon the above assessment.
13. Any other relevant topic as it relates to the Board of Trustees, the faculty or staff, curriculum and programs of the Memphis Theological Seminary as determined by the Evaluation Committee;

If the unification of the Cumberland Presbyterian Church and the Cumberland Presbyterian Church in America is not completed by the conclusion of the 189th General Assembly the Evaluation Committee shall continue their work and complete an evaluation of the current boards and agencies of the Cumberland Presbyterian Church for the 190th General Assembly. Any replacement members of the Evaluation

Committee, which shall be required, shall be made by the current General Assembly Moderator and the Stated Clerk of the General Assembly. Should the unification process occur the entities of the denomination to be evaluated may need to be re-defined and will be determined by the Evaluation Committee in consultation with the Stated Clerk and the General Assembly Moderator at the time.

The Evaluation Committee shall be comprised of a minimum of one member of the previous Evaluation Committee, one member from each of the five Synods, one "at large" member, and any other members with technical or professional experience deemed necessary for the Evaluation Committee to conduct and complete their evaluation in a timely and efficient manner. The Evaluation Committee members shall be appointed by the General Assembly Moderator and the Stated Clerk of the General Assembly. However, due to the position of the current Moderator of General Assembly, and pursuant to Rule 12.5 of the Rules of Order (See also: Robert's Rules of Order, Section 45), the appointment authority of the General Assembly Moderator shall be exercised, in this instance, by the Board of Directors of the General Assembly Corporation.

The Committee on the Children's Home/Higher Education makes the following recommendation based on the need to ensure that future General Assemblies have the required information to perform their oversight responsibilities of the entities and programs overseen by the Cumberland Presbyterian Church.

RECOMMENDATION 14: Contingent on the passage and adoption of Recommendation 13 by the General Assembly, it is recommended that the 188th General Assembly encourage future General Assemblies of the Cumberland Presbyterian Church to conduct an assessment of the Boards and Agencies of the Cumberland Presbyterian Church, the Historical Foundation, and the Memphis Theological Seminary. These assessments should be completed every five years beginning with the close of the 188th General Assembly, or as directed by the General Assembly Moderator. Specific questions, or areas of inquiries, may be added or removed by the Stated Clerk or the Moderator of the General Assembly at that time.

The Committee notes the strong leadership of Reverend Michael Qualls in the PAS program. The program has shown great initiative and creativity in identifying needs and solutions for ministerial candidates who need an alternative route to ordination. It is also noted that Reverend Qualls has implemented increased rigor in the curriculum. One area that that committee notes improvement might be made is in clarifying class expectations. Therefore, the Committee makes the following recommendation:

RECOMMENDATION 15: That the PAS use a standardized template for class syllabi.

(Note: August 20, 2017 and August 19, 2018 as the date of Seminary/PAS Sunday are included in the Stated Clerk's Report under Church Calendar 201-2019)

Respectfully submitted,
The Committee on Children's Home/Higher Education

CHURCH CALENDAR 2018-2019

JULY 2018

7	Program of Alternate Studies Graduation
7-21	PAS Summer Extension School, Bethel, McKenzie, Tennessee
14	Children's Fest, Bethel, McKenzie, TN
14	The Meet Up
21	Children's Fest East

AUGUST 2018

4	Bethel University Commencement
5-Sept 30	Christian Education Season
19	Seminary/PAS Sunday
20	Bethel University Fall Semester Begins
25	MTS Fall Semester Begins
28	MTS Opening convocation
28	Bethel University Fall Convocation

SEPTEMBER 2018

9	Family Sunday
9	Senior Adult Sunday
16	Christian Service Recognition Sunday
16	International Day of Prayer and Action for Human Habitat

OCTOBER 2018

	Clergy Appreciation Month
7	Worldwide Communion Sunday
7	Pastor Appreciation Sunday
21	Native American Sunday

NOVEMBER 2018

	Any Sunday Loaves and Fishes Program
1	All Saints Day
2	World Community Day (Church Women United)
4	Bethel University Sunday
4	Stewardship Sunday
11	Day of Prayer for People with Aids and Other Life-Threatening Illnesses
18	Bible Sunday
25	Christ the King Sunday

DECEMBER 2018

	Any Sunday Gift to the King Offering
2-24	Advent in Church and Home
8	Bethel University Commencement
24	Christmas Eve
25	Christmas Day

January-2019

6	Epiphany
7	BU Spring Semester Begins
7-8	Stated Clerks' Conference
11	Human Trafficking Awareness Day
15	Deadline for receipt of 2018 Our United Outreach Contributions

February-2019

	Black History Month
1	Annual congregational reports due in General Assembly office
3	Denomination Day
3	Historical Foundation Offering
3	Souper Bowl Sunday
10	Our United Outreach Sunday
17	Youth Sunday

March-2019

	Women's History Month (USA)
6	Ash Wednesday, the beginning of Lent
6-April 21	Lent to Easter
17	Children's Home Sunday
24-30	National Farm Workers Awareness Week

April-2019

14	Palm/Passion Sunday
18	Maundy Thursday
19	Good Friday
21	Easter

May-2019

3	Friendship Day (Church Women United)
5	Bethel University Commencement
12	MTS Closing Convocation & Graduation
27	Memorial Day Offering for Military Chaplains & Personnel for USA churches

June-2019

9	Stott-Wallace Missionary Fund Offering /World penMission Sunday
9	Pentecost
16	CPC Ministries Sunday
9-14	General Assembly, Huntsville, Alabama
11-13	CPWM Convention, Huntsville, Alabama
23	Unification Sunday
23-28	Cumberland Presbyterian Youth Conference, Bethel University, McKenzie, Tennessee

www.ingramcontent.com/pod-product-compliance
Lightning Source LLC
Chambersburg PA
CBHW082111230426

43671CB00015B/2664